JUSTICE
DEFILED

JUSTICE DEFILED

Alan N. Young

PERVERTS,
POTHEADS,
SERIAL KILLERS
AND LAWYERS

KEY PORTER BOOKS

National Library of Canada Cataloguing in Publication Data

Young, Alan N.
 Justice defiled : perverts, potheads, serial killers and lawyers / Alan Young.

Includes bibliographical references and index.
ISBN 1-55263-225-3

 1. Criminal justice, Administration of—Canada. 2. Sociological jurisprudence.
I. Title.

KE8813.Y69 2003   345.71'05   C2003-902832-1
KF9223.Y69 2003

The publisher gratefully acknowledges the support of the Canada Council for the Arts and the Ontario Arts Council for its publishing program. We acknowledge the support of the Government of Ontario through the Ontario Media Development Corporation's Ontario Book Initiative.

We acknowledge the financial support of the Government of Canada through the Book Publishing Industry Development Program (BPIDP) for our publishing activities.

Key Porter Books Limited
70 The Esplanade
Toronto, Ontario
Canada M5E 1R2

www.keyporter.com

Text design: Peter Maher
Electronic formatting: Heidy Lawrance Associates

Printed and bound in Canada

03 04 05 06 07 08 6 5 4 3 2 1

*I dedicate this book to the memory of
four great men who are no longer with us.
For nourishing my spirit of irreverence,
I tip my hat to Lenny Bruce,
Abbie Hoffman and Frank Zappa.
For teaching me the value of ethical conduct,
I thank my late father, Sam Young.
My father often told me that I was very fortunate
to have been given a voice in public affairs.
Chances are he would have found my voice
to be abrasive in many portions of
this book, but he would still have
respected it nonetheless.*

Contents

Preface

DROWNING IN CONFLICT. That's the human condition. The price of having a trickster brain. There's conflict between strangers, between neighbours, between business associates, between married couples, between lovers, between people and state entities and between people and animals. And what do we do when conflict gets out of hand? We call in the lawyers. Every time disharmony rears its ugly head, the legal professionals come running to get the lay of the battleground. Who are these people who have convinced us that any time we run into a conflict we have to recruit an army of lawyers to advise, counsel and represent? Are we really so stupid or lazy that we can't attend to the resolution of our own conflicts? Despite having a rather bleak view of humanity, I believe that most people are more than capable of taking care of their own problems, but the knowledge elites, including lawyers, have convinced us that the complexity of social problems requires expert assistance. We have been deluded.

Who the hell am I to cast a shadow on this noble profession? I have been active in the legal profession for twenty years, both as a criminal lawyer and a professor of law. I've done a few high-profile cases, and have stepped on the toes of quite a few self-proclaimed important people. A few publishers approached me, and asked me to write this book after a profile of my life aired on *Studio Two* (TVO). On the show I ranted about lawyers becoming a cancer on society, and I guess the message resonated with many viewers.

The suicidal folksinger Phil Ochs once said "in an ugly world the only true protest is beauty." I've seen an ugly world, but I regret that I have not been able to produce a work of beauty. This book is a celebration of the vulgar. Only the vernacular of the obscene can capture the tone and timbre of this sordid little aria. I use profane speech to distance myself from the knowledge elites who will dismiss this book as a poor excuse for academic scholarship. My language is my revolt. I renounce the formal trappings of academic discourse and take language into the gutter.

If the reader is looking for an homage to Hegel, Kant and other great thinkers who have pondered the question of justice, he or she should look elsewhere. Of course, most of my ideas come from other thinkers, but I have never been interested in scholarship as an intellectual fireworks display. Anyway, this book is not about the construction of a delicately crafted argument. It is an expression of disgust. Disgust transcends argument. It is a feeling. It defies rational discourse.

Having spent the past two decades exploring the legal profession, I have singled out this profession for ridicule. But my critique could apply to any other profession or knowledge elite claiming privileged access to a non-scientific truth. Because I have worked almost exclusively in the field of criminal law, it is the criminal lawyers who bear the brunt of my rant, but the corporate, commercial types are probably worse. I just don't know enough about what the fat cats of the legal world actually do.

I have to be fair. Many law students, lawyers and judges are committed to the pursuit of justice. There are many lawyers with integrity, and many who work hard to help disadvantaged or oppressed individuals. Regrettably, it is difficult to maintain this commitment and nourish this integrity within the framework of the criminal-justice industrial complex. I tip my hat to all the legal professionals I have known who have learned to balance self-interest and the public interest, and who continue to help those in need. I hope they do not think I am writing about them.

But I also know that in writing this book I adopted the aesthetic of a satirist and not that of a scholar, so I take some comfort in the words of Jonathan Swift, who said, "satire is a sort of glass wherein the beholders do generally discover everybody's face but their own." I do not write this book with the intention of humiliating anyone in my profession, and that is why I often do not identify the players by name, rank or serial number. If the case is reported and is a matter of public record, then names are used. And when I have something good to say about someone, I break the code.

I have divided the book into four distinct parts. Part I: Entering the Arena is a preliminary exploration of why I reached the conclusion that the legal profession is a social cancer. In Part II: Sex, Drugs and the Illegality of Paradise, I discuss how criminal justice wastes our time combating consensual but controversial lifestyle decisions. Legal professionals know that consensual crimes (sex, drugs, etc.) do not threaten the fabric of society, but they have duped the public into believing that their crusade is a worthy one. In Part III: Victims, Violence and the Beast, I turn to the world of serious, predatory crime, with a view to showing that pursuing trivialities and failed exercises in moral hygiene has left criminal-justice officials tired and ill-equipped to deal with serious issues of violence and exploitation. These officials parade around as if they understand the nature of crime and violence, but there has been a complete intellectual failure when it comes to understanding the psychology of evil. This has led to a system that processes violence but never controls it. Finally, in Part IV: Legal Professionals as Fallen Beasts, I examine the nature of adversarial legal culture to show that it breeds arrogance, elitism and a captious spirit. These qualities tend to close the mind and stunt intellectual growth. Despite the polished linguistic skills of the legal professional, the profession is governed more by the dead weight of precedent than it is by reflection and contemplation.

I have championed a lot of lost causes and fought some strange battles in the courts. At times this was a fun game, but as time went on, I grew weary. I saw too many bad decisions and too many people needlessly hurt. The institutional values of adversarial criminal justice are bad for the human spirit. Competition, arrogance and deceit are embraced within this adversarial legal culture, and it takes true strength of character for the legal professional to transcend these institutional values.

I've done my time in the criminal-justice industrial complex, and I should have just walked away from this dying beast. But I felt compelled to write this book, and acting on compulsion will have its costs. Exposing the idiocy of lawyers and judges does not bode well for maintaining a successful career in law. Neither law nor religion takes kindly to ridicule. Painting a picture of hypocrisy and stupidity within a sacred institution can only lead to my being shunned as a heretic.

So let the heresy begin.

PART I

Entering the Arena

Some random musings upon entering the arena of law. One can make sense of what has been seen along the path only by knowing the landmarks of other pathways already crossed. On the way to the arena, I paid a visit to Lenny Bruce and the Buddha. They cannot be blamed for my cynical perspective, but they are responsible. In the end, all I really know is that motivation affects perception, and people see what they want to see when they enter the arena. Scholarship that obscures the subjectivity of opinion is a sham. So for better or for worse, here I am. Sort of.

1

Killing All the Lawyers

Question: What do you call a hundred lawyers
chained together at the bottom of the ocean?
Answer: A good start.

Question: How do you know when a lawyer is lying?
Answer: His lips are moving.

L ET'S NOT MINCE WORDS. People hate lawyers. Surprisingly, many people also respect or fear lawyers and cling to the illusion that justice will prevail if a trial is conducted with competent prosecutors, defence lawyers and judges. But begrudging respect aside, people hate lawyers. I knew this when I entered the profession, and I know this now. Public opinion polls consistently show that only a small percentage of Canadians believe the legal profession is characterized by honesty and integrity.[1] The public's confidence in lawyers has steadily eroded in the past twenty to thirty years. If not for journalists, politicians, car dealers and telemarketers, lawyers would truly be the bottom feeders of our fragile social order.

Lawyer-bashing is endemic in popular culture. It is at times so vicious that it would constitute hate literature if directed against any other association or collective group. In an age in which ethnic jokes are taboo, jokes about lawyers flourish. As a lawyer, I have heard a thousand variations on the same themes. The problem with lawyer jokes is lawyers don't laugh and no one else thinks they're just jokes.

This type of character assassination predates modern adversarial justice. It seems to be present in any society with a formalized system of justice. In 423 BC, when Aristophanes wrote his comedy *The Clouds*, lawyers per se did not exist, but advocates and sophists roamed through ancient Greece looking to sell their oratory skills. These prototype lawyers were the subject of scorn and derision throughout the country. The playwright detested these people who took money to argue falsehoods and champion bad causes. In his play, he described such a person as "a shuffler complete, well worn in deceit/ A supple, unprincipled, troublesome cheat."

Two thousand years later, Shakespeare entered the arena and in Henry VI, Part II, had Dick the Butcher issue his famous proclamation: "The first thing we do, let's kill all the lawyers." This is not a psychopathic fantasy; it is a political statement. In the play, the rebel, Cade, promises Dick the Butcher a future paradise where "there shall be no money." All Dick the Butcher can think of is killing the lawyers. The butcher knows that lawyers have no place in paradise.

In contemporary times, Mojo Nixon's rock rant "Destroy all Lawyers" captures the same sentiment. To a heavy backbeat, Mojo starts by telling us "there's a plague on the planet—and they went to law school." He wants to kill all the lawyers because these people are a "bunch of evil weasel posers." Mojo recommends that we "spay and neuter them, so that they can't breed."[2]

Popular culture, whether high or low brow, simply detests this profession.

At the level of theoretical discourse, many explanations have been offered to explain the universal disdain for lawyers. In the academic community, critical literature abounds, and it might even be considered a sign of intellectual weakness to paint a rosy picture of the law and its menials. Law is about oppression. Law is about privileged classes taking care of their interests through the illusion of a fair and equitable legal system.

I have come to view law school as an exercise in irony: naive and eager law students are prepared for a career in law by professors who teach that the practice of law is base and corrupt. As professors we act as anti-cheerleaders. "Down with law" we chant, while our students dream of large retainers or conducting dramatic Perry Mason–like trials.

There is no shortage of critical literature exposing all manner of evil within the legal profession. We do not need another sophisticated polemic to argue the case against lawyers. The "law as oppression" rant is so well known I don't have the academic strength to recount it here. Furthermore, I am not interested in exposing the most obvious and trite reason for lawyer-bashing—the exorbitant cost of legal representation. But I do want to make one brief comment about the money problem. Even lawyers who never steal from trust funds look like thieves when they charge $500 an hour for their services. Who the hell is worth this amount of money? It's not like the lawyer is scaling Mount Everest for you. You're paying this large sum for their posh offices and fancy suits, and as payback for all those years they had to spend in law school listening to people like me rant and rave about the corrupt aspects of law. I do not need a control-group survey to know that most law students are in it for the money. I see it in their eyes. Even when they say "I want to seek social justice," they usually mean "I want a BMW." Law is a business. This also means, of course, that justice is open to the highest bidder on a free market.

In my privileged position as a law professor, I realized I had the time and tools to assist poor people in trouble with the law. Not having to worry about the business aspects of a legal practice, I have spent my time providing pro bono services for hookers, druggies, gamblers and an assortment of minor criminals. I have dealt with people who had been screwed over by cops and prosecutors. This does happen. What most of my clients had in common was their moral objection to being labelled "criminal." Most were factually guilty. In a technical sense they broke the law, but the "criminal act" did not represent the essence of who these people were. If they had actually caused any harm, they were usually prepared to apologize and make amends. But the law was simply unprepared to deal with them as anything other than accused criminals. The process was not set up for people to make amends and take responsibility for minor mistakes.

Of course, there are some moments of brilliance in the law, when bold lawyers combine with bold judges to break through the dead layers of irrelevant precedent, but this happens only sporadically. The rest of the time, law sails through the doldrums—floating aimlessly by virtue of no wind power, occasionally throwing horses and black slaves off the boat to lighten the load. I discovered very soon in my journey that the criminal-justice system has little to do with justice. I confronted the power-hungry cops, the abusive Crown attorneys and the uncaring judges. It always horrified me, but ultimately I could cope with this moral quagmire because I believed I was fighting the good fight.

I knew I could continue to swim upstream and be frustrated by a strange and uncaring legal system because, for me, it was a battle only at a theoretical level. It was my clients who would end up with criminal records or prison terms. It was my clients who were made to feel shame and humiliation. I experienced only frustration and dismay, and that alone is not enough to stop a person from fighting a battle he or she believes in. But in 1997 and 1998, the battle took on a personal dimension. In the course of one year, I was exposed to the machinations of an adulterous judge, an emotionally disturbed law student, a crooked lawyer and a backstabbing colleague. The irony was delicious. For years I had taught law students about the moral excesses of lawyers engaged in an adversarial process, and now a whole bunch of asshole lawyers came forward to prove me right. All in all I just ran into a long bout of bad luck, but this bad luck streak confirmed all my fears of how far institutionalized justice has strayed from the ideal.

As tempting as it is to weave a tale of my personal woe, an exploration of my personal hardship can explain only why I might have adopted Dick the Butcher as my role model. It cannot explain why millions of others entertain the same resentment towards the legal profession. But there is a connection. Take the adulterous judge. With four or five failed marriages under his belt, the judge continues to sit on matrimonial cases relating to support and custody. Knowing this, one might begin to wonder whether a judge is still able to make an informed and reasonable judgement about another person's marital dilemma without the judgement being skewed and distorted by emotional baggage carried from so many marital breakdowns. And the deeply troubled student? The crooked lawyer? The backstabbing colleague? With the exception of the crooked lawyer, who ended up in prison, they all remain members of this "honourable" profession. Other people will surely get hurt. We seem to care very little about the moral character of those who inhabit the legal profession.

Legal professionals are not doing the job we think they are doing. Beneath the thin illusion of an objective legal science resides an elitist profession that marches to a different beat than lay people, who are presumably too stupid or too lazy to try to understand the intricate workings of this so-called legal science. Realizing this during my year from hell made it impossible for me to continue helping people with their problems. I was spiritually drained. I received no support from a profession that should have encouraged my extensive pro bono services. When my personal life ended up colliding with other legal professionals, I truly realized that these professionals, whose lifeblood is judging others, have no capacity to truly distinguish between good and evil. Too many lawyers are making decisions based upon hidden agendas that are ill-suited to the pursuit of justice. The profession has gotten real good with witch hunts and show trials. But more and more often it is chasing the wrong people.

So killing all the lawyers started to make sense to me, and as a first step I knew I had to turn the gun on myself. My building resentment towards the profession forced me to examine my motivation for helping people. If I resented the lack of appreciation and respect for my work, then perhaps everything I did, I did to stroke my ego. The reward in helping others is the fact that selfless acts polish your spirit, not your ego. That is all you should expect. But expecting legal professionals to stand up and notice how I was advancing the aspirations of a so-called honourable profession may have been based solely on pride, arrogance and an inflated sense of self-importance. I had become what I had been condemning for years. I guess that is why I am writing this book. Maybe it's like a professional suicide note.

To advocate lawyercide is serious business, and the reasons for it are not always clear. Most people complain about the high price of lawyers. Others believe that lawyers are dishonest and predatory. Of course, both complaints are well founded, but they're hardly sufficient reason for justified homicide. If that were the case, we might as well kill all business executives at the same time (this, of course, is another book). In this book I will try to provide a whole new set of reasons for hating lawyers.

In a nutshell, I wish to show you that the legal profession is built upon intellectual dishonesty. Put aside the greed and the arrogance, the real sin of lawyering is that it is "full of sound and fury signifying nothing." It is full of empty Latin maxims. It is full of intellectual shortcuts to save the effete jurist from having to struggle with difficult moral issues. It speaks in a language cold and unfamiliar to those outside the profession, and it relies upon thought-terminating clichés and rigid categories dressed up as legal doctrine.

Lawyers are part of a knowledge elite (sanctioned by the state) that claims to have a monopoly on the effective and rational pursuit of justice. Nothing could be further from the truth. Unlike other professionals (engineers, architects, etc.), lawyers do not deal in concepts that are beyond the purview of lay people. Justice and fairness are matters of everyday living. Lawyers dress up the pursuit of justice as rocket science so they can exclude ordinary people from participating. This is intellectual dishonesty at its worst.

Before I can really get into the meat of this book, I need to talk a little about the Buddha and Lenny Bruce. Not in any great detail, but as a way of revealing my framework. I didn't even know I had a framework, or general conception of justice, until I started to work within the conventional justice bureaucracy, but there it was, all shaped and mapped out by the time I was fourteen and reading the *Lotus Sutra* and Bruce's *How to Talk Dirty and Influence People*.[3] One of the reasons I have grown to dislike traditional academic literature is that it is disembodied argument with no human face. As self-indulgent as it may be, I want to be transparent. I want to clearly identify the roots of my jaundiced perspective on the legal profession.

Some 2,500 years ago, Gautama Buddha reached enlightenment. Forty years ago Lenny Bruce was arrested in a San Francisco nightclub for saying "cocksucker" during his act. Seemingly unrelated events? I guess so. But these two events shaped the contours of my character and, eventually, my perspective on criminal justice. The sacred and the profane all wrapped up in one—the simple and noble truths of an Indian aristocrat who renounced worldly pleasures to taste of divine wisdom, and the Jewish comedian who made a career and life by shocking complacent and smug Americans who believed they had conquered both the civilized world and nature itself.

The Buddha was a spoiled brat. Beautiful women, rich furnishings and exotic cuisine were part of his childhood. But Prince Siddhartha renounced his wealth and privilege and spent seven years under a bodhi tree as an act of spiritual devotion. It worked. This spoiled brat unlocked some of the secrets of the universe by doing absolutely nothing. That in itself is an important lesson for all those type-A lawyers, bankers and power-brokers who see so much self-importance in their frenetic multi-tasking.

Buddhism has its complexities and its own cosmology, but the Buddha did not dictate dogma; he would say "all views are wrong views."[4] Enlightenment has little to do with reason providing perfect understanding. The Buddha simply provided a path to help us embrace affliction and suffering with courage and nobility. He provided a recipe for an authentic life free from the delusory constructs of a hyper-rational mind. This is the perfection of the human spirit.

Life as we know it is an illusion. This illusion is filled with pretty things and remarkable creations. But for most people, the beauty of this world is overshadowed by suffering born of desire and craving. Everyone suffers, whether rich or poor, because suffering is not an objective reality but a state of mind. The good news is, everyone can be liberated from suffering. Spiritual enlightenment is not some sort of explosion in understanding; it is simply the discovery of harmony, both microcosmically and macrocosmically. It is open to Lenny Bruce. It is open to Officer Friendly. And it is open to you. You see, the Buddha is in Lenny Bruce, and spiritual advancement is not necessarily incompatible with a life of urban decadence. Lenny may have abused drugs, and he may have deeply offended and disgusted many people in power, but ultimately he had as much spiritual potential as Mother Teresa or Pope John Paul II.

This might sound like a crock of shit to many people. It doesn't matter. What remains important is the realization that Eastern religion is about liberation. Western religion is about salvation. Eastern religion is an equal opportunity employer—everyone can achieve enlightenment. Western religion is an elitist and arrogant employer—salvation presupposes that there is someone out there who will save us and to whom we will be forever indebted. Talk about condescending and patronizing!

The hierarchical elitism of Western religion is reflected in the elitist structure of modern law. Remember, the legal profession more or less took over from the priests and bishops, who used holy scriptures as a form of social control. Now we have the Criminal Code and the legions of lawyers appointed to administer its prescriptions.

Eastern mystical thinking would have spawned a very different type of penal law. A perspective celebrating a path of liberation open to one and all would not give rise to rigid knowledge elites, like priests and lawyers, who claim to hold the keys to salvation. A perspective advocating non-attachment to material wealth and achievement would not give rise to a battering ram of laws designed to regulate our private lives. Temperance and sexual modesty may be necessary restrictions on the path to spiritual development, but no Buddhist is going to shove this down your throat with a bunch of paternalistic laws. The gentle wisdom of Eastern mysticism could help a much maligned profession. Lawyers are supposed to help people with their social problems. The cultural norms of an adversarial legal culture do not breed helpers animated by the spirit of helping. Buddhist norms do.

Most people fail to see the relevancy of the Buddha as head jurist. They think it's just New Age drivel. For most people, Buddha is about the path of renunciation. He's all about withdrawing from the world—turning within and without, but not "with it." It's easy to talk about the cessation of desire and suffering when you're some sedentary dude sitting under a bodhi tree with no Viagra, no super-models and no infernal racket from cathode tubes and transistors constantly trying to sell you a Top 10 list of dreams and desires. I know all that.

Can the teachings of the Buddha really have any relevance to Western secular law? As currently formulated, our legal system is like matter, and the Buddha is anti-matter. Not a good mix. But if he were around today, I doubt he would even be given a chance to show the practical relevance of his way of thought. I'm sure our legal system would have found some way to prevent the Buddha from squatting under a tree for so many years. I'm sure the bodhi tree was on land owned by the Crown. "Get that chubby trespasser off Crown land" would be the response of our legal system to the Buddha.

My point is this. Not everyone can follow a path of renunciation. I've tried a few times. But developing a gentle spirit in the Buddhist tra-dition is relevant to the practical realities of political/legal life. In the Western tradition, everyone sees political life as jumping on organized bandwagons. Carefully orchestrated political rituals, with great orators expressing opinions on all manner of topics. You are political only if you participate. If you vote. If you follow a political party or a political platform. This is nonsense. Often, the most important political state-ment you can make is in how you live your life. That is your true polit-ical voice. Living in accordance with simple, moral precepts is a more important political statement than voting liberal or conservative or democratic or green. The way you live affects everyone around you, and politics is about everyone around you.

There is a story of a feverish battle between American soldiers and the Viet Cong. In the midst of this battle, six Buddhist monks walked through the gunfire. One after another. Perfectly calm and at peace. As one American soldier recalls:

> They didn't look right. They didn't look left. They walked straight through. It was really strange, because nobody shot at 'em. And after they walked over the berm, suddenly all the fight was out of me. It just didn't feel like I wanted to do this anymore, at least not that day. It must have been that way for everybody, because everybody quit. We just stopped fighting.[5]

When was the last time the oratory skills of politicians, lawyers or preachers stopped a flurry of bullets? The spirit and strength of character cultivated by the monks, without words or deeds, had more impact on trained killers than anything that will ever be done in a contemporary criminal-justice system. So don't tell me the Buddha has nothing at all to do with justice.

If entering the stream of Buddhist thought made me suspicious of law and lawyers, reading and listening to Lenny Bruce when I was fourteen pushed me over the edge. Here was a guy who could make me laugh, make me think and make me want to fight the many injustices of modern, urban living. Yet, the legal system branded him a criminal in 1962 for doing a shtick on orgasm and for using a ten-letter word. In 1962 we still had trouble with four-letter words, so a ten-letter word was positively subversive.

The Buddha was in Lenny Bruce. Sure, he committed a few cons and took a few too many drugs and shocked a lot of conservative conformists, but this does not mean he was a moral degenerate deserving of state punishment. Maybe you don't like being called a cocksucker. Maybe you don't like someone making the pope look like a cheap whore. But are these reasons for locking up a comedian, especially a comedian whose obscene rant forced a lot of people to re-examine their values?

Lenny did not tell the world to "fuck off" for cheap shock value; his whole shtick was to force his listener to realize that it is senseless to be shocked by raw linguistic vulgarity. Shock and offence should be reserved for pictures of the Mai Lai massacre in Vietnam, or the lynching of black men in the deep south. In Lenny's words, "My concept? You can't do anything with anybody's body to make it dirty to me. Six people, eight people, one person—you can only do one thing to make it dirty to me: kill it. Hiroshima was dirty."[6] Lenny also knew that "the word's suppression gives it the power, the violence, the viciousness"[7]; in other words, using the big guns of the criminal law to prohibit the use of the word "cocksucker" in a public performance merely empowers the word and gives it new life and vigour. As sociologists like to say, it is a mistake to dramatize the evil.

You can probably see how my admiration of Lenny Bruce led me to become a civil rights lawyer. A foul-mouthed, drug-taking comic and social critic being persecuted for the manner in which he chose to express his thoughts—this would inspire any civil libertarian. I grew up in a world of social upheaval and revolution. I worshipped the Chicago Seven. I saw the Buddha in Abbie Hoffman, Jerry Rubin, Tom Hayden and Bobby Seales. And as a young, Jewish man I could relate to Bruce's glorious *chutzpah*. By being arrested for saying "cocksucker" in San Francisco, "schmuck" in Los Angeles, "tits" in Chicago and "fucking" in New York, Lenny became a free-speech martyr. As a teenager, I was puzzled. Here was this guy who could make me laugh and think, and for doing so he was being carted off to jail. Why did the law wish to protect me from something I embraced? This was the second time as a teenager that I found myself questioning the need for legal intervention into personal choice.

The first time took place when I was a science geek in my early years of high school. I understood biology and reproductive strategies, but I really had no idea what the rush of pleasure from sexual contact would feel like. I was fourteen or fifteen. Despite having hit puberty much earlier, I had not figured out what the actual act of masturbation would entail. I really could not understand how touching myself would get me off. I read in the newspaper about a book in England that had been banned because it counselled and instructed young people on matters relating to sex, drugs and beating the system. It was called *The Little Red School Book*.[8] I had to find a copy, and in 1971 I found one in an underground bookstore in Toronto that I frequented. I could not believe that legal authorities in England had banned this book; it was a gold mine of useful information that all kids seek out.

This subversive little book provided me with everything I needed to know as a young adolescent exploring the boundaries of pleasure. I still can't believe that this book was banned by the law. As a fourteen-year-old, I already had a reason to question the legitimacy of my legal elders. From the day of my first orgasmic rush and my introduction to the world of hedonism, I decided that when it comes to fundamental personal decisions I will (and I hope everyone will) decide for myself what is healthy or unhealthy for my mind, body and spirit.

Ultimately, Lenny Bruce and his shattering of conventional boundaries paved the way for the political force of the youth rebellion of the 1960s. "Question authority" was the only slogan worth living for. For better or worse, I became nourished by the spirit of irreverence. Of course, these shit-disturbers had nothing good to say about the institution of law. Lenny believed that "in the halls of justice the only justice is in the halls." What a prophetic statement, considering that, in contemporary times, justice is usually a product of plea-bargaining arrangements made in the hall. (Hoffman took the indictment one step further: "I learned something on that last bust. Lenny was wrong. There isn't even justice in the halls."[9])

What the Buddha and Lenny had in common was their knowledge that truth or wisdom can be acquired only by shattering illusion by vigorously questioning the conventional order. We so desperately search for meaning in this bleak existence that we often blind ourselves by settling on some half-baked truths that help us get through the day. We construct our identities and then hold on for dear life, all the while mistaking symbols for reality. We confuse wealth with money, wisdom with education and justice with law. The actualization of human potential comes only with the shattering of illusion. True wisdom comes from shedding our skin and seeing the world with new eyes. So Siddhartha renounced worldly pleasure, and Lenny struck out at language taboos. Both tried to make the world a better place, one by taking a path of renunciation and the other a path of action. Spiritual development can take place in a monastery or while protesting on the streets. There are many paths that can be taken and this is what gives me hope in a world full of cruelty and suffering.

These are some of the thoughts that shaped my character and led me to the following conclusion about criminal justice: Law is coercive and thus destructive, but it is a necessary evil. Even in a city of angels we would need to enact rules of the road. But once you recognize the law's destructive potential, keeping the law within narrow boundaries becomes a political imperative. It should extend only to target behaviour that is seriously harmful to others. It should never be used as a tool of moral hygiene. Constraining the growth of state social control leads to a civil libertarian perspective in which criminal justice gains legitimacy only if convictions are obtained in accordance with basic human rights and notions of due process.

The state has only one true mandate with respect to criminal justice: to protect citizens and provide the infrastructure for orderly relations. Beyond that the state should not stray. True democracy and freedom encompass the freedom to construct one's own heaven or hell. Orderly economic relations may fall within the mandate of the state, but the regulation of interpersonal relations is clearly beyond the pale. People pursue self-fulfilment in many and varied ways, and the state should never close available paths, no matter how perverse and mystifying. The state should have nothing to say about our choice of girl- or boyfriends or our choice of diet or our artistic proclivities or our choice of intoxicants. Some people will hump themselves to death or intoxicate themselves into oblivion, but that is no business of the state unless the excess decadence truly hurts an innocent third party.

The real problem in pursuing moral hygiene as a state objective is that it has distracted the state from effectively pursuing its one true objective—protecting citizens. Lawyers as messengers and apologists for the state are universally hated because they are members of a club that has failed miserably. Failure comes from the folly of manufacturing crime and moral panics instead of actually combatting real, predatory crime.

It has become clear that legal professionals simply do not have the stamina and focus to do justice in tough, morally complex cases; they are too busy demonizing people like Lenny Bruce. They are too busy applying stale precedents and deciphering legalistic rules to get their hands dirty unravelling the secrets of violence and exploitation. We hate criminal justice (and its messengers, the legal professionals) because it has demonstrated absolutely no interest in acquiring even a kernel of insight into serious predatory crime, and remains impotent to curb the tide of modern, senseless violence. If you don't believe this, take a look at the two cases I lay out in the next two chapters, one the response of the state to a man who wishes to pay for a hand job, and the second the response of the state when the rigid, bureaucratic machinery of criminal justice catches up with a notorious serial killer.

2

When the Honourable Profession Meets the Oldest Profession

THERE'S THIS GUY, let's call him Homer. He's basically a horny guy who is left feeling sexually unsatisfied within his otherwise good marriage. Every day after work he drives by at least six massage parlours along the Queensway in west-end Toronto. Every day he gets a little rise when he drives by, fantasizing about some voluptuous attendant in Victoria's Secret lace spreading oil over his body. More importantly, he's almost sure that these massage parlours will end the session with a vigorous and oily hand job. Should he take a chance? What if it's just an ordinary Swedish massage? To him, that would not be something worth paying for. Homer needs a more profound release.

One day he gives into temptation. He circles the industrial mall that houses the Blue Danube Massage Centre before mustering the courage to enter. Clean. Pleasant receptionist. No one staring or gawking. So far, so good. He's ushered into a little room, told to take a shower, put on a terry cloth robe and wait for Alexandra to arrive. When she arrives, it's like a cold shower. Far from the Cindy Crawford look-alike in his fantasy, Alexandra is a plump and slightly pimply Eastern European woman. Full of smiles, but not the Helen of Troy that Homer needed to launch his sails. "Thank god for eyelids," Homer thinks, as he tightly shuts his eyes and lets his mind drift from this disappointing scene while Alexandra oils down his back and starts to gently knead his flesh.

Homer actually enjoys the back massage, but with eyes wide shut he waits eagerly to be turned over for the fun to begin. It seems to take an eternity before Alexandra turns him over and oils down his stomach. Slowly she works her way down, and Homer grins as a wave of pleasure rolls over him. He starts to writhe on the massage table, and in no time at all he explodes. Alexandra giggles and Homer gasps for air.

His heart pounding away, he hears a commotion from the reception area. As Homer reaches for his robe, two police officers barge into the room. While Homer is wiping the sperm off his stomach, Officer Friendly begins the incantation: "You are being arrested for being a found-in in a common bawdy house. You have the right to retain and instruct a lawyer. You can also call a duty counsel lawyer at any time at 1-800, blah, blah, blah. Do you understand?" Homer looks up at the officer and nods his head. He understands he can call a lawyer. But for what? Because he paid a few bucks for a cheap orgasm? With the flush of humiliation spread over his face, Homer signs his Appearance Notice, commanding him to attend court in three weeks' time.

Now here's the deal. I feel I have to help Homer. He cried in my office. He has little money; hiring a lawyer would consume most of his meagre savings. The charge he faces is not very serious, but it is still a criminal charge. If convicted, Homer will have a criminal record. Some of the guys at work might think his situation is kind of funny, but Homer believes most people will think he's a sick pervert for going to one of these places. The worst thing is that his wife has no idea of the arrest. In some ways, I am bugged by his deceit, but I know one thing: charging someone as a criminal for trying to get his rocks off only serves to dramatize the evil. His wife might forgive and reconcile if it was a private transgression, but once you put the label "criminal" on the behaviour, it takes on sinister connotations. Not only will she feel betrayed (if she had greater expectations from Homer), but she will also feel shamed by her husband's official criminality.

Having a lot of experience with bawdy-house cases, I take Homer under my wing. He's basically a nice guy. Little education, makes little money, but manages to smile and maintain an intelligent conversation. I don't feel like Homer's lawyer, but more like his tag-team partner in the justice game. Here's how the game is played.

It's basically a waiting game. I tell Homer he just has to sit tight. Once the "keeper" (owner/manager) of the bawdy house pleads guilty, the prosecutor will cut loose all the "inmates" (attendants) and "found-ins" (the horny johns). I can't remember the last time I saw a prostitute or keeper challenge their charges. It's against the rules of the game.

No one really cares about hand jobs for hire except, perhaps, for some religious groups and parent associations. And despite their vocal claims of widespread support, they represent a minority. The cops truly don't care. But morality departments of the local police forces receive enormous budgetary allotments, with the rule "use the money or lose it." So every once in a while, the cops do sweeps of downtown streets and massage parlours, and make the occasional futile attempt to infiltrate the escort industry. Usually, the prostitutes show up in court, pay their fines and get back on the street all in one breath. What a monumental waste of criminal-justice resources! In 2000, Canadian law enforcement processed 5,036 prostitution offences, down more than half from the recent high of 10,721 charges in 1988. If the police enforced the law with vigour, the courts would burst at the seams. Millions of dollars are spent to enforce laws no one really cares about.

Bawdy-house keepers invariably plead guilty for a fine that is not really a punishment—more like a licence fee. But wait, if setting up a business of selling sexual favours for money is immoral, corrupt and evil, then what's this nonsense of the fine? Either the business is criminal and those involved are deserving of punishment, or it should be a regulated industry with real licence fees, not stupid fines.

People are getting murdered, beaten and robbed and I'm showing up in court ten times because Homer allowed his dick to make a decision. That's right—five or six remands, two pre-trial conferences, a couple of meetings with the keeper's lawyer and ten mornings off work for Homer. If he had to pay for a lawyer, his bill would easily be over $2,000. For what? To wait for the charge to be withdrawn. This is criminal justice? Forget about exciting and dramatic morality plays. Criminal justice is more like waiting in that never-ending line at the passport office; the only difference is that, in criminal justice, you hope your number is never called.

For Homer, the justice game is breaking down. You see, the keeper is indignant about being charged. He believes he runs a clean, sanitary operation. The female attendants are treated with dignity. He speaks to me privately, asking me to challenge the constitutionality of the bawdy-house laws. I remind him that he already has a lawyer and that, unfortunately, the challenge would probably be like pissing in the wind. But he really is reluctant to admit guilt when he believes he has done nothing wrong. I understand completely, but it's out of my hands.

However, the reluctance of the keeper to play the game is bringing out a whole Pandora's box of ugly state action. Although the cops know they have to speak to me and not to my client, they call Homer directly to ask him if he will testify against the keeper in exchange for having his charges dropped. Homer's wife now knows about Homer's indiscretion because she fielded the initial call. Now Homer's calling me about major marital discord, and there's nothing I can do about it. It's just a waiting game. Homer has to keep his world together while waiting for the oracle of law to set him free. The keeper will plead guilty. I know this in my heart. I tell Homer not to fight against the inevitable. Just let it happen. Of course, I also tell Homer not to speak to the police right now, and I call Officer Friendly and rant about interference with the solicitor-client relationship. I let off some steam, the cop insincerely apologizes, and then we wait some more.

Ten months pass before word comes down that the keeper will plead guilty. It's a purely economic decision. Even if you think the law is unjust, it will cost you at least $20,000 to $50,000 for a good lawyer to mount a complete defence and a constitutional challenge. Your chances are slim, and most people cannot afford to spend $50,000 on a good song and dance. You want results. So the keeper pleads guilty, and Homer is cut loose. No one is happy, and no one seems to have noticed that this unhappy resolution took more than ten months, involving hours of court time. However, the keeper's lawyer no doubt made a pretty penny for achieving a result that was preordained.

Now let's put this into perspective. The machinery of criminal justice was set into motion because Homer needed a little rub and tug. Let's look at this masturbation thing from first principles. Human beings, dolphins and some monkeys love to play with themselves. It seems that as a species acquires superior intelligence it starts to jerk off more and more. What a waste of a cerebral cortex. But it's an even bigger waste to use state funds and state power to curb masturbation for hire.

Almost everyone masturbates. In 1948 Alfred Kinsey shocked many repressed individuals with revelations of wide-scale premarital sexual practices and homosexual fantasies. His famous report revealed that 92% of men and 62% of women masturbate.[1] Even the Supreme Court of Canada has acknowledged that the majority of healthy Canadians masturbate in their spare time.[2] We're talking about basic human desire. Almost everyone is stricken by sexual desire. Some people have no outlets, some people have healthy outlets and others have unhealthy outlets. Bottom line: most people will engage in masturbation because it is the safest and healthiest outlet for unfulfilled sexual desire.

Now, people will say the law is reasonable. It doesn't prohibit masturbation (how could it?). It requires only that you don't masturbate in public (s. 173, indecent act), and that you don't pay for someone to jerk you off, whether in public or private (s. 215, prostitution or s. 202, bawdy house). Seems reasonable in some ways, but do you really think that Homer deserves the label of "criminal" because he wanted a little variety in his masturbatory practice?

If the law is trying to protect my moral values by preventing me from hiring a woman to masturbate me, it is wasting its time. No one has ever developed a moral conscience by acting in accordance with state demands. Moral development is a personal, subjective matter. It evolves internally. It is not mere unthinking obedience to stupid laws.

If the law is trying to protect the sexual integrity and safety of the female attendants, this is a pretty bizarre way to go about it: we will protect you by charging you with a criminal offence if you foolishly try to earn money making men come. No one is being protected by these laws.

What is the law afraid of? Even without subscribing to the neurotic theories of Freud, I think it is fair to say that the pursuit of orgasm is a fundamental component of daily living for our species. We don't go into estrous cycles. Many of us are horny all the time. But the law, infused with religious inspiration, does not want to admit any of this. It wants us to keep our sex at home, with our partners, without the type of sordid variety one would expect from a species that is perpetually horny.

Now if masturbation is so fundamental, it is obvious that the masturbator will seek out sources of arousal. Only those who dream in colour can sustain a lifetime of masturbation solely based upon their own internal, erotic thoughts. Hence the birth of pornography. Some pornography makes a pretence of literary ambition, but most is just jerk-off material. Since most masturbators do so thinking of another sexual being, it is inevitable that many will long for someone else to do their masturbating for them. It seems simple enough. Pay someone a few dollars to do something you would do for yourself anyway. It's the same as hiring someone to clean your house, walk your dog or polish your toenails.

Face it. People will pay for anything. Everything in our society has become commodified. Nothing is sacred. At a certain level, everything is a business. Where there is demand, there will be a supply, legal or illegal. We may wish to maintain a sacred and sombre air around some human functions and activities, but in a free society we are allowed to commodify and cheapen both the sacred and the profane. It may not be a pretty picture of humanity, but trying to use the law to preserve a distorted but prettier view of humanity is an insult to the truth and to my rights as a free thinker. Hiring a woman, or a man, to jerk you off may not be everyone's cup of tea. But that's not a reason to make it a crime.

Personally, I have little interest in hiring rub and tug attendants, or hookers for that matter. For me, most of my sexual arousal comes from having a partner who is equally interested in and aroused by me (my poor fragile ego!). Although I understand the concept of a "willing suspension of disbelief," I would never be fooled by the histrionics of a sex-trade worker trying to convince me that I truly am an exciting sexual being. That's good sex-trade business, but it sort of deflates the sexual experience for me. However, I see no moral or social problem in other men paying for sex. If that gets you off, so be it. So why has the honourable profession taken it upon itself to regulate and suffocate the oldest profession?

Beats me. But one thing is certain: the origin of the legal regulation of sexuality has a religious genesis. Its roots are found in a Christian ethic that managed to find a home in secular law. Religious types acknowledged sex only as a procreative necessity. Pleasure-seeking was generally taboo and was considered unseemly behaviour for one who wished to enter the kingdom of God. The Judeo–Christian God is not a fun-loving deity. Greek and Hindu gods got laid in a variety of sordid ways. The Sumerian god, Enki, masturbated into the Tigris River to fill it with flowing waters. But *our* God just couldn't get his head around *Deep Throat*. Starting with Sodom and Gomorrah and ending with papal bulls, the Judeo–Christian sexual ethic pushed secular law in a direction it had no business going.

In the Western world, the Church, and ecclesiastical law, started to lose its governing power in the late Middle Ages. As the law of the state grew in power, the Church tried to get the state to punish some of the illicit fornication it objected to. For the most part, the state was compliant because leaders still feared the threat of hell. But as populations grew more literate in the nineteenth century, fewer and fewer people feared hell. Perhaps religious influence on law should have diminished. This did not happen. The nineteenth century was a remarkable century: impressive developments along the road to industrialization were accompanied by a growing middle class that aspired to a mythical image of aristocratic moral purity. For centuries the aristocrats were sodomizing their daughters and humping their way to oblivion, but they always managed to maintain a mirage of pure Christian morality. So the middle class aspired to this illusion and this, in turn, triggered silly moral crusades like temperance and combating a nonexistent white slave trade. Combined with a sanctimonious Queen Victoria, all this paved the way for religion to sell a whole moral code to secular criminal-justice officials. The regulation, prohibition and condemnation of non-conventional sexual practices became an important criminal-justice priority.

Many of the Victorian moral hygiene measures have been abandoned since the late 1960s, but some still inform our law. Our friend, Homer, got caught up in a time warp by violating a law only Queen Victoria and her cronies felt passionate about.

Plain and simple, our contemporary law grew out of a climate where it was a capital offence to have anal intercourse, so we should expect some irrational and hysterical leftovers. But this does not explain why contemporary law and sophisticated legal professionals still think it is legitimate to criminalize sex for hire and other non-conventional sexual practices. Just when conservative moralists, fuelled by tired religious rhetoric, lost their influence during the cultural and sexual revolution of the 1960s, morality laws received a jump-start from an unlikely source. The birth of feminist scholarship provided conservative thinkers with a politically correct way to reformulate their opposition to "in-your-face" sexuality. Conservatives believe that excessive and unusual sexual behaviour is morally reprehensible, but in the 1960s and 1970s people were too busy getting laid to pay much attention to these conservative types. Besides, it was the conservative types, like Jim Swaggart and other fire-and-brimstone preachers, who were always being caught with their pants down in hooker heaven. Without so intending, the developing body of feminist thought ran to the aid of the conservative sexual ethic. On pornography and prostitution issues, many feminists became reluctant bedfellows with conservative thinkers.

Feminist thinkers have done a great deal to enlighten us on the history of discrimination against women. They have also achieved great success in removing some of the shackles that kept, and still keep, women in subordinate roles. However, many feminist thinkers created an inhospitable environment for men and women to explore nonconventional and commercial sex. Some have argued that sex for hire is a manifestation of an oppressive and patriarchal social structure; that commodifying a woman's sexuality is demeaning, degrading and dehumanizing; that women can never achieve complete equality when they are still being hired as sexual playthings. Some feminists believe that hookers and sex-trade workers operate under a false consciousness by not recognizing their state of oppression.

I have never been able to understand this line of thinking. "False consciousness" is just a fancy lie used when great thinkers cannot understand why more people do not subscribe to their point of view. In my mind, being a sex-trade worker can be empowering. Men are weak. Men will do almost anything to have their dicks and egos stroked. Exploiting this weakness as a sex-trade worker is a way of seizing power. It is not degrading unless you truly believe that sexual exploration is dirty. I respect the hookers and body-rub attendants I have represented. Many of them sell sex to pay for school or to provide for a young child.

The law treats sex-trade workers like little children who are incapable of taking care of their basic interests. How can some feminists support a law that treats women as if they are too stupid and victimized to be able to make sound decisions on how to express their sexuality, whether for commercial purposes or for pure recreational fantasy? Labelling a hooker a criminal cannot be empowering for women, yet some feminists have overlooked this paradox and have now provided a new rationale for maintaining laws that could no longer be supported by conservative moralism. The greatest paradox for feminist thinkers is how to reconcile championing a woman's right to do what she likes with her body when it comes to aborting a fetus, but not when it comes to selling her body for a man's erotic pleasure.

Of course, women who sell sex to buy crack or to avoid beatings by pimps or cruel johns are not being empowered. But these horror stories are largely a product of criminalizing sex for hire. Pushing sex for hire into a black market triggers a whole host of dangerous results. Hookers who are not part of an enlightened legal regulatory enterprise cannot rely upon state officials to protect them from evil johns. They are compelled to work with pimps in order to secure protection and territorial exclusivity. The pimp is a pure manifestation of the worst excess of patriarchy. But the pimp is also a creation of the law. Between 1991 and 1995, sixty-three prostitutes were murdered in Canada. Only three were murdered by pimps; they prefer to terrorize the living. Fifty were killed by clients.[3] Hookers are also the prime targets for serial killers. This is the legacy of prohibition.

In 1999–2000, the police in London, Ontario, made a concerted effort to close massage parlours offering "rub-and-tug" services. Over a dozen body-rub establishments were taken down in one evening. I represented a woman who owned and managed one of the establishments. She was an affable and intelligent woman who treated her employees with respect and dignity. In fact, she was a participant in a municipal committee that was examining the issue of violence against women in the sex trade. She wanted to challenge the law, but had few resources to mount this challenge, so when I was able to arrange for her incorporated company to plead guilty in her stead (thus avoiding a personal criminal record), she took the deal. In my last conversations with her, she told me that in the wake of all the recent police raids and the closing of establishments, bikers had moved in to take over the local body-rub industry. That is another legacy of prohibition. A sensitive and caring manager is forced out of business to be replaced by black market entrepreneurs who, in all likelihood, do not give a damn about the sex-trade workers, the johns or the moral integrity of their operation. Regulated prostitution would increase the security and safety of all participants.

Despite the so-called sexual revolution, we live in confused times. Instead of shining the light of day on prostitution through proper regulation, lawmakers continue to propose laws to drive the trade further into the dark recesses of the underworld. It is time for the honourable profession to show some respect for the oldest profession. I'm certain that quite a few lawyers and judges have had occasion to buy an orgasm, and it is time for the hypocrites to come clean. The honourable profession will lose what's left of its honour if it continues to waste time and money on social problems that are not truly criminal in nature. We respect a process that controls and punishes Charles Manson, but not one that spends the same resources protecting us from Heidi Fleiss. The honourable profession should never have met the oldest profession except to buy a trick. While we waste time investigating escort services and sweeping prostitutes out of residential areas, some psychotic demon is terrorizing an innocent victim, knowing the police are too busy completing their paperwork for another rub-and-tug sweep.

3

Is the Buddha in Paul Bernardo?

PAUL BERNARDO ASPIRED to be a rap artist. In his words, he yearned to be "larger than life." Too bad he lacked talent. While he failed miserably as a white rap star, he achieved fame as Canada's best-known serial killer. During his trial, I spent countless hours transcribing audio cassettes of Bernardo's megalomaniacal ramblings, looking for clues to explain his demonic fall from grace. Here's a taste of his recorded explanation to his half-asleep wife, Karla Homolka, of why he wanted to name his first rap album Deadly Innocence:

> ... what we are trying to do is coin the phrase "deadly innocence" ... This is a phrase that I want a lot of home-boys to start using because that's a great thing. They're fronting, they think they can take you on, man, but you're a deadly innocent guy. Like, hey man, you think I'm innocent, but behind this I'm packing a lot of deadliness. So come at me, come at me, I got a fucking nice face, I look like a pretty boy, why don't you come at me man, take your best shot. See what's happened to you pal, you're out of here man, you come out with your beer pot-belly, you think you're really rough and tough, man. I come back with my B-boy hat looking like I'm thirteen years old but I'll kick your ass and fucking blow your fucking head off, I'll kill your fucking parents, I'll come at and shoot your fucking girlfriend, and your fucking sister. I'll fuck your sister. I'll fuck your girlfriend and shoot the rest of you. We're tired of these people want to try to look ugly to look tough. You know, you want to come at me, I'll fucking kick your ass, man, and that's the whole image you want to get across. That's what deadly innocence is all about, that's the theme of the album ... that's where it be at, you know what I'm saying man. Anyways, this is now 12:34 on some night, some day, some time and Karla's not feeling so well. I'm going to fuck her, huh. I may ... not. You never know.

His words are pretty creepy, but this whole late-night rant is so pedestrian. Paul Bernardo was a Vanilla Ice wannabe. That in itself makes him a rather pathetic loser. He failed to make the charts, but he actualized the violence that defines a fair amount of contemporary rap and hip-hop music. "Gangsta" rappers appear to advocate violence and aggression, yet the vast majority never commit the acts they glorify. By the same token, the Marquis de Sade's personal life was tame in comparison with his barbaric writings.

What pushed Bernardo over the edge? Why do some people make their violent fantasies come to life? These are the questions I hoped to answer by attending the trial and studying everything I could about serial killers and their prey.

The Bernardo/Homolka trials were by no means Canada's first exposure to the brutality of serial rapists and killers, but for whatever reason, this dangerous duo attracted hordes of media attention. I attended the Bernardo trial on a daily basis because I had been hired by CTV to provide legal commentary on the nightly news. This was 1995. The year of O.J. Simpson. The year that criminal trials started to be televised, as if a new genre of soap opera had been discovered by the network geniuses. I knew the Bernardo trial would be a flop; it wasn't a real "who-done-it?" The trial was a slow guilty plea. It really didn't matter if it was Bernardo or Homolka who had pulled the ligature that caused the death of two young women. We knew it was one or the other. This charming couple had already kidnapped, raped and sodomized these women together, so did it really make a significant moral difference who was actually responsible for the final killing? Both would burn in hell, if hell exists, and the gatekeeper of hell would not give a rat's ass if it was Bernardo or Homolka who was technically responsible for the deaths.

Nonetheless, I was initially fascinated by the opportunity to intensely study these notorious crimes. The case provided an ideal opportunity to explore the development and manifestation of the antisocial criminal. Despite an extensive academic background in the area of serial and mass killing, I had never had the opportunity to meet or observe these killers. Now I would be able to watch a killer closely and listen to his words on the stand. I even tried to arrange, on a few occasions, to interview Bernardo. I have always believed that the Buddha is in everyone, no matter how inhuman; now I had the chance to see for myself whether the Buddha is in Bernardo. Was Bernardo beyond redemption, or did he have some moral worth buried deep in his soul? What made this man stray so far from his Buddha nature? Is there an irreducible core of evil in some people that strips them entirely of their humanity?

The only significant difference between cruelty and kindness is that kindness has its limits. Beyond that things get murky. Defining the essence of evil is elusive, yet I still thought my participation in the Bernardo trial experience would provide me with some practical insight. After four months of watching, studying and reflecting, there was nothing. Some interesting speculation and not much more. I kept thinking about how the despicable aspects of human character can grow with little nurturing, yet the admirable qualities of our species seem to require careful and constant cultivation. This was the sum total of the wisdom I acquired from the Paul Bernardo trial. Four months of anguish simply to confirm my already jaundiced view of the human race. Is the Buddha in Bernardo? Does Bernardo have a redeeming essence? Who the hell knows?

There are some cases in which the simple question of guilt or inno-cence is hotly contested, and a real mystery surrounds the crime. There are also cases that appear to forge new law. Controversial cases some-times trigger public debate, and many people become engaged and informed. This is exciting. It's what criminal lawyers really want to do. But these cases are few and far between. Most of the time we're just processing and warehousing bodies. Negotiating settlements. Under-standing little about the people we represent. Caring little about the people we prosecute and judge. When the legal system caught up with Bernardo, it had only one objective in mind—to make sure this bas-tard got life for first-degree murder. In a limited way, this objective is fine, but do we as a society really gain anything of value from the painful process?

Bernardo and Homolka brutalized, sodomized and killed two teenage girls. They also drugged and raped other young girls, including Karla's sister, who died from a bad reaction to the drugs Halcion and Halothane, which were administered to her as an aid to her sexual assault. Millions of dollars were spent on the investigation and prose-cution of these crimes. Four months of court time were taken to deter-mine whether this man was guilty, even though there was little doubt from the outset that Bernardo was a cruel, psychopathic man who was more than capable of murder. How could there be any doubt? Not only was he discovered to be the Scarborough rapist, but he also videotaped his murder victims' horrors so the whole world would be able to enter into his recorded fantasies. The tapes showed Bernardo and his enigmatic wife orchestrating an orgy of forced sex with his young victims. It's not a great leap from recorded rapes to proof of murder. The trial of the century in Canada did not live up to its advance billing. While listening to his victims' recorded pleas for mercy, I sat in court wondering what was being accomplished by this lengthy trial.

Bernardo was sentenced to life, and his wife to a paltry twelve years in prison. For many, justice had been done. The criminals had been caught and justly punished. But after months of testimony, and the publication of numerous books on this case, we are no closer to understanding how two charming and bright individuals could devote themselves to a life of such cruelty. Everyone has their theories, and intellectuals will engage in countless hours of mental masturbation. But we may never break the code that provides us with true insight into the workings of a soul dedicated to the subjugation and destruction of the human spirit. Bernardo's motivation remains grey and undetermined and Homolka remains a diagnostic mystery.

A criminal trial will never uncover the secrets of human behaviour. "Did she or he do what to whom and when?" is the refrain of the law. But when you're incontrovertibly dedicated to the infliction of pain, the precise details of the events become unimportant. What is clearly more important is trying desperately to understand the *why* of the event. With its focus on *mens rea* and *actus reus* (guilty mind and guilty act, the formal elements of an offence) and the admissibility of evidence, the criminal trial misses the mark. It asks all the wrong questions and, in the process, transforms reality into one recognizable only to lawyers and other reptiles. Finding the precise details of who did what to whom is the weather-report approach to criminal trials. What is clearly more important is trying desperately to understand the "why" of the event. Life, in all its worst perversions of human dignity, cannot be made to fit comfortably into the inflexible categories of legal thought, and so the "why" of an event is rarely addressed in any meaningful fashion in a court of law.

Is it too much to ask of the law and of lawyers that they uncover the mysteries of the dark side of human development? As the law and legal process is currently structured, this would be demanding the unattainable. Besides, who can truly claim expertise in the field of human behaviour? Outside of the world of pure science, we still float around in the dark. Theories come in and out of vogue like pop stars. Surely lawyers and judges cannot be asked to answer questions that have confounded and perplexed psychiatrists, psychologists and sociologists. However, we have been deluded into thinking that the traditional criminal-trial process is the only institutional mechanism for dealing with "deadly innocence." This is simply not true. A fundamental reformulation of the process could assist in making the criminal trial something other than an exercise in futility. But a complete overhaul of the system is needed, not just some tinkering here or there within the existing structure.

I know the criminal-trial process was not designed to be a forum for intellectual exploration. But why not? What are we afraid of? Understanding our criminals may require a lot more work and dedication than simply warehousing them, but coming to an understanding of tragedy makes it so much more bearable than simply sweeping it under the carpet.

An understanding of Paul Bernardo, Ted Bundy, John Wayne Gacy, Clifford Olson and Jeffrey Dahmer will not be achieved through legal argument, nor is it a topic that should be reserved for the ruminations of many-degreed experts. The knowledge elite can help us understand, but not within the current format of the adversarial, criminal trial. Just as the door to spiritual enlightenment is open to all, whether Oxford-trained or television-tamed, the fundamental question of why some people hurt others should be open to debate in classrooms, in courtrooms and in taverns. No one, no matter how educated, has a monopoly on truth when it comes to the human condition. Criminal justice should be a community ritual. It should be driven by public participation and not professional domination. We may not achieve profound insight through personal participation, but I do believe that a criminal trial should at least serve to heal the community.

Even the intellectual giants Freud and Einstein had no greater insight into the workings of the criminal mind than you or I. In the 1930s, the League of Nations encouraged an exchange of letters between leaders of thought, and to that end Einstein and Freud were recruited to write on the subject of war.[1] Einstein initiated the correspondence, and expressed the hope that Freud's insight would lead to "fruitful results" in "tackling the problem of world peace." Einstein himself seemed resigned to the impossibility of eradicating war-like behaviour; as he wrote to Freud, "man has in him the need to hate and destroy."

Freud's response was ambiguous. On the one hand, he said that the "killing of an enemy gratifies an instinctual drive"; yet he also optimistically noted that the building of "emotional ties between human beings must inevitably counteract war." Ultimately, Freud resigned himself to the fact that aggression is part and parcel of the human condition. He wrote to Einstein:

> We conclude for our immediate purposes that there is no prospect of getting rid of the aggressive instinct. It is said that in some fortunate areas of the globe where nature abundantly provides all that man needs, there are people whose existence passes in gentleness, among whom coercion and aggression are unknown. I can hardly believe in these happy people, and I would like to know more about them. The Communists too hope that they can eliminate human aggression by guaranteeing the gratification of human needs and by creating equality among their citizens. I consider this an illusion. For the time being they are most carefully armed, and they keep their adherents together at least in part by their hatred of outsides. Besides, as you yourself remark, there is no question of removing man's aggressive instinct completely but only of trying to divert it so far that it doesn't have to find expression in war.[2]

While these two great thinkers pondered organized violence, Hitler was planning the greatest holocaust in human history. Despite the sophistication of their thought, their insight is no greater than that which would be acquired from a study of high-school history.

It is easy to conclude that man is a beast, whether noble or brutal, whose instinctive drive to aggression fuels endless wars. There has never been, and there never will be, a utopia. There will always be conflict, and some conflicts will resolve themselves in violence. These are all trite observations. But it is far more difficult to explain and understand Bernardo's "deadly innocence." Einstein remarked that "it is easier to denature plutonium than to denature the evil spirit of man."[3] It is a daunting challenge to explain violence that lacks rational motivation and achieves nothing other than a perverse form of gratification for the aggressor. And that is the changing nature of violence in the twentieth and twenty-first centuries. Jack the Ripper, and the unsolved mystery of his gruesome mutilation killings of prostitutes in the 1880s, heralded in this new era of unspeakable violence. Thankfully, the incidence of this type of violence is pretty low, but since Jack did his ripping, there has been no turning back on the path of increasingly bizarre and disturbing crimes.

I have often asked myself how Freud and Einstein would explain the Zodiac Killer, who, in the 1960s and 1970s, killed at least six victims and possibly as many as fifty, and who has never been caught. He sent cryptic letters to newspapers that required experts in code-breaking to decipher his message. In one coded message he wrote: "This is the 'zodiac' speaking. I like killing people because it is so much fun. It is more fun than killing wild game in the forest because man is the most dangerous animal of all to kill."[4]

Simple aggression? I don't think so. The type of aggression Freud and Einstein believed to be at the foundation of war bears little resemblance to the words and deeds of the modern serial killer. And when we capture and convict these killers, we execute or incapacitate them, but we never really get to the heart of their passion.

Morally neutral aggression is inherent in all species that compete in the food chain, and war and other manifestations of violence can often be interpreted as a deadly competition for scarce resources. However, violence within many Western industrial nations has reached cancerous proportions far in excess of what may be expected from any beast. It is this cancer that begs for understanding and a cure, and it is this cancer that has baffled experts and perplexed legal professionals.

This cancerous evil is a never-ending source of fascination for people young and old. In the 1990s, as a law professor, I began to supplement my diet of cases, statutes and subsections by studying serial killing and mass murder. It is a gripping and frightening field of study, so when the CTV television network offered me the opportunity to provide legal commentary on the Bernardo trial I was genuinely thrilled. And no matter how pedestrian and banal the trial became, it still attracted media and public attention to a degree previously unknown in Canada. The whole world was watching. Journalists from places as far flung as Germany, England and Sri Lanka filed stories about this Canadian horror. On most days, when I arrived at the courthouse at 7:00 a.m. to conduct a television interview, hundreds of people were lined up to get a seat in the courtroom. Everyone seems fascinated by barbarity, but no one likes to admit that this fascination may tell of a strange form of identity between the fantasies of a Bernardo and the dreams of the average law-abiding citizen. Forget whether the Buddha is in Bernardo, perhaps the more important question is whether these crime voyeurs see Bernardo in themselves.

There are many different explanations for the insatiable appetite to consume stories like the Bernardo story. This modern voyeurism is not merely a product of conditioning by the media. This perverse fascination taps into an ancient, and uniquely human, response to stories of unimaginable cruelty. Just 150 years ago, those spectators at the Bernardo trial would have been the unruly bunch attending public executions in the great British tradition of eating greasy meat pies while reading broadsheets chronicling the life and times of the poor scoundrel who was dangling at the gallows before their eyes.

One thing is certain. It cannot be said that the Bernardo trial was a drawing card because this case represented the loss of Canadian innocence. Although serial killing is largely an American phenomenon (with England and Germany having their fair share of horror stories), we have had our share of psychopathic serial killers in Canada. Clifford Olson murdered eleven children in Western Canada in the 1980s; Russell Johnson killed between seven and seventeen women in the 1960s and 1970s in small-town southwestern Ontario; James Peter and Robert Brown raped and killed at least two young women (and perhaps as many as seven more) in the 1980s in Calgary; and Jimmy Odo committed numerous ritual sacrifices in Atlantic Canada in the 1980s. So much for a loss of Canadian innocence. Bernardo was not the first, and he won't be the last. The week I started this book, Michael McGray received his sixth life sentence for a series of murders in Atlantic Canada. By the time you read this book, Robert Pickton will be on trial in Vancouver for allegedly murdering a large number of prostitutes and burying them on his pig farm.

Nor can it be said that the Bernardo trial was a drawing card because the case exceeded other serial killings in barbarity. I watched the media and spectators gape in horror as testimony unfolded about Bernardo using a circular saw to dismember Leslie Mahaffy's dead body, but I sat unmoved. I had come across this type of cruelty all too often in the huge body of literature I had been reviewing. All I could think of was

Douglas Clark and Carol Bundy, who in the 1980s in California killed at least six women. Clark used to keep the heads of his victims in the refrigerator. On occasion, Bundy applied makeup to a decapitated head so that Clark could have sex with it in the shower. I realized at this time that I had better stop reading books on serial killers.

It seems to me that one of the reasons the world became so mesmerized by this trial was that Bernardo and Homolka were a charming and attractive couple. Bernardo's baby-faced good looks gave him the appearance of a sensitive man who would cry at the slightest provocation. Homolka had an unusual charm. At times she could even look angelic. How could such attractive people commit such ugly acts? Shouldn't a serial killer have a hunched back or a cold, pock-marked face? Shouldn't the malice possessed by the serial killer transfigure his face and render him grotesque and frightening? People find it incongruous that a pretty face can unleash such a hellish fury. That in itself is an indication that, in matters of behavioural deviance, we are often ignorant and self-deluded.

In 1996, John Martin Crawford was convicted for three murders committed in Saskatchewan. He had been on parole for a 1982 manslaughter conviction and was the prime suspect in three other murders. This guy killed at least twice as many people as Bernardo, but where was the national media at this trial? Nobody remembers this killer. Why? He was ugly, and his victims were poor aboriginal women.[5] This is really pathetic. It's kind of sad when people base their dating decisions solely upon considerations of appearance, but it is downright perverse that our interest in brutal crime peaks when the killers seem like beautiful Hollywood stars.

It is not surprising that people would draw a relationship between appearance and character. Our subconscious perspective on the human condition is formed more by aesthetic judgement than by logic and science. That which is pleasing to the senses is good, and that which is hideous is bad. And we will go to great lengths to delude ourselves to ensure that the belief in a connection between beauty and goodness is not challenged. Take Jesus Christ. Most portraits depict him with soulful eyes, gentle and pleasing features and soft, flowing hair. However, the most contemporaneous physical description we have of this saviour does not match modern reconstruction. A "wanted notice," probably signed by Pontius Pilate and later quoted by Jewish historian Josephus, described Christ as follows:

His nature and form were human; a man of simple appearance, mature age, dark skin, small stature, three cubits high (about five feet), hunchbacked, with a long face, long nose and meeting eyebrows, so that they who see him might be affrighted, with scant hair with a parting in the middle of the head, after the manner of the Nairites, and an undeveloped beard.[6]

We cannot stomach the idea that the Messiah and Saviour could have been as ugly as sin, so we have transformed him. If reality does not conform to our beliefs, then to hell with reality.

This form of self-deception is not restricted to the uneducated. In fact, the father of modern criminology, Cesare Lombroso, believed, after extensive study, that criminals were atavistic throwbacks who would have ape-like features. While examining skulls, Lombroso wrote of his discovery:

> This was not merely an idea, but a revelation. At the sight of that skull, I seemed to see all of a sudden, lighted up as a vast plain under a flaming sky, the problem of the nature of the criminal—an atavistic being who reproduced in his person the ferocious instincts of primitive humanity and the inferior animals. Thus were explained anatomically the enormous jaws, high cheek-bones, prominent supercilliary arches, solitary lines in the palms, extreme size of the orbits, handle-shaped or sessile ears found in criminals, savages and apes, insensibility to pain, extreme acute sight, tattooing, extreme idleness, love of orgies, and the irresistible craving for evil for its own sake, the desire not only to extinguish life in the victim, but to mutilate the corpse, tear its flesh and drink its blood.[7]

Lombroso's theories corresponded to the school of phrenology, which was all the rage in the nineteenth century. Phrenologists would try to detect criminals by the examination of physical characteristics, especially the shape of the skull. The nose of a thief would be twisted, upturned or flattened, whereas the nose of a murderer would be aquiline or beaklike. The phrenologists should have realized they were barking up the wrong tree. When the body of the Marquis de Sade was exhumed for examination by the world's leading phrenologist, Johann Gaspar Spurzheim, this expert concluded from the shape and contours of the cranium that de Sade had no indicia of excessive sexual desire, nor of belligerence or cruelty. In fact, Spurzheim noted that the skull was "similar in all respects to that of a Father of the Church."[8]

If only the understanding of criminality were as simple as the measurement and description of facial features. There are few people left in the world who would pledge allegiance to Lombroso and the phrenologists, so why were people so shocked and bewildered by the fact that a comely and vibrant man like Paul Bernardo could kidnap and kill young sex slaves? We yearn for simple and clean explanations. Attractive is good. Ugly is evil. Lombroso and the phrenologists may have been idiots, but we all have a basic impulse to confuse sound, moral judgement with a subjective assessment based upon what we find aesthetically pleasing.

The modern serial-killer profiler does little better. Many of our intellectual constructs and profiles that reduce human conduct to a set of recognizable patterns are absurd and naive. But there is no doubt that there are recurring patterns to human behaviour. That is why, despite my cynicism, I still believe in academic study and rumination. One day we might attain real insight. However, the social sciences will never replicate the astounding achievements of the natural sciences. Uncovering basic laws of natural science has not only allowed our species to walk on the moon, but has given us the power to crash fast-moving vehicles while making cell phone calls to faceless commodity brokers halfway around the globe. We will never be able to achieve the same type of control over people that we have over nature. If trains had to run based upon the laws of social science, there would be weekly train wrecks and even European trains would never be on time. No matter how much we think we know about people, the unexpected always breaks our frame of reference.

Sure, there are basic manifestations of instinct that drive behaviour—sometimes in a transparent way and sometimes in a mysterious way. Some behaviours can even be controlled by chemical intervention. A multi-billion-dollar industry is fuelled by the belief that better living can be achieved through chemistry. But beyond manipulating complex molecular structures to mental disorders, we know little about why people do what they do. Finding a few patterns does not constitute science. No matter how many multiple-regression analyses are performed by intellectually acrobatic social scientists, we will never uncover most of the secrets of human behaviour. And, therefore, the state will usually fail in trying to control the conduct of its subjects.

So do we simply throw up our hands in dismay and admit there is nothing we can do to understand and, hopefully, curb the disturbing trends in violent crime in the past century? Painful resignation in the face of violence is not the intended result of this book. A healthy dose of cynicism is prescribed, but not a total loss of faith and hope.

The Bernardo trial did not benefit anyone except the legal professionals. Crimes such as Bernardo's and Homolka's are too painful and socially disruptive to end up with a process "full of sound and fury, signifying nothing." Legal professionals act like they know what they are doing when they process criminals, but they never ask themselves the hard questions. I had a question: Is the Buddha in Paul Bernardo? You might formulate the question differently, but most of us want an informed and clear perspective on why people inflict harm on innocent others. That is all I am asking for. Why can't criminal justice be a vehicle for advancing understanding? The more we understand, the more we acquire some metaphysical solace in the face of enormous cruelty. Right now, criminal trials and media manipulation give birth only to fear and insecurity. This is ass-backwards. Criminal justice should repair damage

I am now ready to get to the heart of this book—explaining why contemporary criminal justice has become a failure and an institution held up to ridicule. Enough abstraction. Time for some meat on the bone. I feel kind of bad that legal professionals will emerge as the villains in most of the stories I will tell, but I guess they deserve it. But remember, they were only following orders. Many are innocent players in this horrible travesty of justice; some deserve to be shot.

PART II

Sex, Drugs and the Illegality of Paradise

Intoxication and orgasm are both constrained and regulated by Big Brother. Billions of dollars are wasted every year as law is used as a tool of moral hygiene. And in this we find one reason why legal professionals are held in contempt: they waste our time manufacturing criminals out of law-abiding people who simply get their rocks off in alternative ways.

4

As Nasty as I Wanna Be

I put my hand down and felt around. What
rapture to feel my machine buried! Nothing but
the balls to be touched, and her cunt hair wet-
ted with my sperm, mingling and clinging to
mine; in another minute nature urged a crisis,
and I spent in a virgin cunt, my prick virgin
also. Thus ended my first fuck.[1]

D ID YOU LIKE THAT? Are you turned on? You would never say.
Pornography is a multi-billion-dollar-a-year business, but no
one ever admits to watching porn. When's the last time someone showed up at work and told their co-workers that they must run out
and rent *The Cum-Suckers from Hell*? Pornography exists in a world of
denial. We indulge and we condemn, sometimes in the same breath.

The opening quotation is basic pornographic pulp written between
1888 and 1892. *My Secret Life* is an eleven-volume sexual autobiography of
Walter, a man obsessed with sex and penetrating young virgins. Published
anonymously in Amsterdam, this book represents the worst and best of
pornography. You can call it erotica, or call it smut—it doesn't matter. It is
always cocks and cunts thrusting and gyrating in a frenzy of orgasmic
pleasure. Whether the paintings in the caves at Lascaux or Larry Flynt's
Hustler, every era has its share of objectified sexual organs on parade.

Check this out:

Her breasts were jiggling on top of her chest. Her skin was so hot. I wrestled
with her a bit. She wouldn't lie still. She was still laughing. I used all the
strength I had to turn her on her stomach. She was half on the bed and half
off, her legs stretched wide in an upside-down V towards the floor. She was
thrusting her pelvis up in the air and reaching under herself. She was
spreading the front of her pussy with her hand. And she was mashing into
the sheets furiously, never stopping for a second, going: "fuck me fuck me

fuck me!" I never knew anyone could say it so much. I grabbed a hold of her ass cheeks and I spread them so wide. I could see her ass hole and her slit lining under. The two were so close. I watched my fingers knead hard into her flesh. I was thinking: I know I can make this girl come easy ... I let go of her for a second and she turned around to watch me. I got a condom and started to put it on. She was humping her pelvis up watching me. I knew she was drunk.[2]

This erotic novella, called *Lie with Me*, was published in 2000. Same words, same thoughts. Sex, and talk of sex, hasn't changed that much through the centuries. People do it. People write about it lewdly (I always had a fondness for that word). But there is one fundamental difference. Talking about sex has become mainstream. There are still taboos, but in the twenty-first century, everywhere you turn sex is staring you in the face, on billboards, on television commercials, on rock videos and in the papers. *My Secret Life* had to be published anonymously, circulating around genteel society in a secretive way. *Lie with Me* is available in many urban bookstores and is reviewed like any conventional literary effort.

What about the dirty pornographer who reduces women to tits and ass? What about the sleazy pornographer who has to force innocent women to perform degrading acts so everyone else can make a few bucks? There are people like that. I've met them. But these people are few and far between. *Lie with Me* was written by a youthful and beautiful woman, Tamara Faith Berger, who teaches yoga when she's not writing about cocks and pussy. She's the type of person I'm thinking of when I say that the Buddha is in Lenny Bruce. Some people would call her book "erotica" because it has distinctive, literary merit. It's pretty compelling reading. Nonetheless, I still call it pornography because a hundred years ago, hell, even twenty years ago, this book might have been the subject of an obscenity trial. The beautiful yoga teacher/pornographer would be dragged before Her Majesty's courts to defend herself for writing this provocative work. I guess it could still happen today. The same laws have been on the books since Victorian times. But now that sex has become mainstream, most cops can't be bothered enforcing the law unless there has been a series of complaints from the public. They may act proactively if mainstream sex drifts beyond the pale, even in these sleazy, Jerry Springer times, but for the most part, police have better things to do than monitor the latest literary sex romp.

When I talked to Tamara, she told me she was "mystified" by the law. She is aware of its existence and operation, but she does not feel constrained by it. She did not write the book to shock, but she does say, "I like the idea and actuality that arousal can happen from the word to the person. I know that this is counter to much of the acceptance of obscenity in art today; that is, it does not incite the audience to arousal —yet using a literary tool to potentially arouse the reader is not something I am afraid of doing." Tamara was just playing with the power of the word. But combine that with the mysterious power of sex, and suddenly society finds offence. Even though obscenity law is used less and less to regulate expressive activities, there still remains a sense of the taboo. Tamara told me she did have a "fear of people knowing"—that friends and family would shy away, thinking she was some misguided slut. We still have some residual problems with vulgarity, and that infects the law.

But remember Lenny Bruce: "the word's suppression gives it the power, the violence, the viciousness."[3] We always seem to fall for the forbidden fruit syndrome: an ordinary pleasure becomes magnified when doing it makes you a rebel against the big, bad state. So many language and cinematic taboos have been lifted (thank you, Lenny Bruce), that some may think there is nothing left to get offended by. But there is plenty. Many people reading this book will be offended, and they will dismiss me as an immature, intellectual lightweight because of my use of vulgarity. Nothing pleases me more. Now that I have these people's attention (because being offended does not necessarily mean repelled—it may actually attract), I want them to know that even in these so-called permissive times, the state still calls in the big guns when a performer, filmmaker, painter or writer takes vulgarity to a limit that supposedly violates the elusive "community standards of tolerance." In a free and democratic society, we still have censorship. This often goes unnoticed.

We need to maintain some element of taboo in language. Look at swearing. Every culture has its fair share of curses, insults and swear words. With a few exceptions, they concern sexual acts and excretory acts. I checked them out. *Suksi vittuun*—that's the Finnish variation of fuck off, literally meaning "ski into a cunt" (how Nordic). *Buwa ka ng ina mo*—that's a Filipino curse meaning "you're the *smegma* (or foul secretion) of your mother." Pretty basic stuff. There may be some forms of cursing that don't invoke your anal region, or the vaginal accessibility of your mother, but not many. For example, the Quebecois curse *tabernac* is a religious invocation. Now the picture becomes clear. Curse words and vulgarity have power only because they invoke things we avoid, or things we should avoid. There has to be some taboo element, whether it comes from the inherent offensiveness of an object or act ("shit") or because the object or act invokes something (God) or someone (mother) considered sacred. Vulgarity can partake of both the sacred and the profane, but only when these vulgar objects are also considered untouchable or beyond touch.

Without a sense of the taboo in language, telling someone to "fuck off" would be about as powerful as telling them to "please remove yourself from my sight." Resorting to language with some residual element of taboo tells the audience to pay attention. You are serious. You are mad. You want them to hear you loud and clear. Some social restrictions on vulgarity are needed to maintain its potential as a linguistic clue to our state of mind. But why has the criminal law continued to stick its nose into this form of expression? When the law decides to take on a movie, book or public performance, it always looks stupid. We know this obscenity stuff is somewhat taboo, but do we need the law stepping in like a sanctimonious father to remind us that we really shouldn't be painting a portrait of the pope with a dildo stuck up his ass?

Here's an example of the law looking foolish when it meets up with an expression it dislikes. In June 1980, this guy Stewart crossed the border into Sault Ste. Marie, Ontario, on a motorcycle, wearing a button on his jacket that said "Fuck Iran." This was around the time of the Iranian hostage crisis, and it is clear that Stewart was expressing his condemnation of the taking of 400 American hostages in Tehran. Nonetheless, Customs called the police, who laid a charge against Stewart for exhibiting a disgusting object (yes, there is such an offence). The judge expressed dismay over the charge being brought, but he intoned with that Nurembergian refrain "ours is not to question why." Of course, he acquitted Stewart—not all judges are fools—but in doing so he was compelled to give fatuous reasons like "the author did not intend to convey the notion that everyone should engage in sexual intercourse with Iran."[4] The judge concluded this was not a disgusting or lewd statement but rather a "forceful way of saying, 'Down with Iran.'" So justice was done, but justice came out looking like an ass for getting involved in the first place. I can't imagine many people would think that a "Fuck Iran" button warranted the activation of the machinery of criminal justice.

But what if Stewart really meant that he wanted to fuck Iran? Maybe be was some sort of fetishist who had developed an erotic fixation with geographical land masses. Should the criminal law then step in to punish this pervert for expressing a sexual thought in a muted public fashion? I'm not saying that people can go around erecting billboards declaring: "Call me. I need to get my cock sucked." I can already hear the Helen Lovejoy church-going types crying, "Think of the children. Think!" There should be time, place and manner restrictions on expression and actions that can cause offence. But this is a matter for by-laws and municipal regulation. It's not a criminal matter. The label "criminal" should not be put on people who are just crude pigs; it diminishes the solemnity and significance of the criminal record. A permanent record of shame should be reserved for those who have committed truly shameful acts.

Stewart was probably a motorcycle rounder who mouthed off at Customs officials and police. He probably told them to "fuck off" and that was the sole reason he was charged—to harass him with an abusive process. But that's a whole other issue. The point is that the law on the books will be invoked arbitrarily by state officials because nobody really knows what "disgusting," "indecent" or "obscene" really mean. It's a personal judgement call. I don't want our men and women in blue, the ones with the guns, to have the power and authority to threaten criminal sanction because someone's mode of expression may be offensive to them. It's a stupid waste of time. It's also dangerous. These types of laws on the books are not just reserved for the prosecution of crude pigs (who, of course I would set free), as some of these alleged crude pigs may actually be expressive geniuses playing whimsically with linguistic taboos.

We live in relatively permissive times. In the span of thirty short years, so many linguistic and visual taboos have been shattered that octogenarians, whose youthful pornography was restricted to watching women decked out in one-piece bathing suits, are now watching fucking and sucking on cable movie channels. How much farther can we go? Many people may feel we have liberalized expression to such a degree that I'm wasting my time ridiculing the state for punishing expressive pigs. I still see the obscenity law used as a tool of harassment. I feel fairly certain we will never return to the era when the works of Faulkner, Joyce and Lawrence were judged and banned by literary philistines parading around as judges, cops or Customs officials. So I worry less and less about the law suffocating artistic innovation. Even if we never again become ignorant censors of art, I still worry about obscenity laws and the fools, "ours is not to question why," who enforce them. Even if few charges are laid, and even if fewer trials are conducted, having the law in the policing arsenal can lead to low-visibility abuse. The police can simply go to a bookseller or art gallery and tell them that a certain product is obscene and they will be charged if they continue to sell this product. No charge. No trial. The product is removed. It happens all the time.

Leaving a law on the books also means it can be revitalized at the first scent of moral panic. I remember when Kimberly Rabot was brutally slain in the 1970s by a teenager who had an elaborate collection of bondage and torture pornography.[5] Following this, the third session of the 30th Parliament presented no fewer than ten bills recommending increased restrictions on obscene materials. Parliament can spring into action with ease when it comes to the preservation of our moral order. We see evil, and we look for a scapegoat: "The boy bought bondage mags; the boy listened to heavy metal; the boy was an addict"—we better toughen up the obscenity and drug laws if we want to fight crime effectively. Pure evil is laughing at these feeble legislative measures, and eventually some artistic genius will get swept away in the post-Rabot moral panic.

In this chapter I am not talking about pornography involving children—that's an entirely different problem. Child porn with kids under the age of consent (generally fourteen) is not just expressive activity, it is child sex abuse recorded for posterity. The making of the permanent record of abuse aggravates the initiating crime of abuse. So this type of material clearly warrants criminal intervention. Canada's child porn law may go a bit too far, in that it potentially captures work of imagination not involving real children, but that concern is for another day. This chapter relates solely to the stupidity of trying to regulate and prohibit expressive activity, made by and for people old enough in law to make autonomous, personal decisions regarding their sexual behaviour.

Obscenity is defined in s. 163 (8) of the Canadian Criminal Code as "any publication, a dominant characteristic of which is the undue exploitation of sex, or of sex and any one or more of the following subjects, namely, crime, horror, cruelty and violence." It is obvious that "dominant" and "undue" do not lend themselves to quantifiable analysis. Without the aid of some judicial algorithmic analysis, the court will be faced with making evaluations that are not guided by discernible standards.

The Supreme Court of Canada attempted to give the statutory definition content that was capable of judicial application. In *R. v. Brodie*, the *Lady Chatterley's Lover* case of 1962, the Court created the "internal necessities test" and the "community standards test."[6] The internal necessities test requires an examination of artistic purpose to determine if the treatment of sexual content is necessitated by the aesthetic design of the publication. Being uncomfortable with playing the role of literary or dramatic critic, the courts have decided few cases on the basis of this test.

The true flavour of the obscenity prohibition is found not in the evaluation of artistic design, but in the application of the community standards test. The Supreme Court of Canada has confirmed that the community standards test is the appropriate benchmark for all manner of obscene material (including recordings) and performances that are proscribed by the Criminal Code. The community standards test was designed to insulate the judiciary from the criticism that their application of the modern statutory definition is as subjective as their application of the earlier common-law Hicklin standard (a bizarre test that asked "whether the tendency of the matter charged as obscenity is to deprave and corrupt those whose minds are open to such immoral influence and into whose hands the publication may fall").

The community standards test requires the court to determine whether the community would tolerate dissemination of the material in question to others. The Supreme Court of Canada has clearly stated that "the cases all emphasize that it is a standard of tolerance, not taste, that is relevant. What matters is not what Canadians think is right for themselves to see. What matters is what Canadians would not abide other Canadians seeing because it would be beyond the contemporary Canadian standard of tolerance to allow them to see it."[7]

In determining whether material exceeds the community standards of tolerance, expert evidence is admissible, but not actually required for the Crown to prove its case. Further, the courts need not look to the circumstances of the material's distribution in order to evaluate it; that is to say, the current law would not accept as a defence the fact that viewers or listeners were not upset by the presentation or that the manner of distribution ensured that the material would not be thrust upon a captive audience. Moreover, obscenity prosecutions are rarely conducted before a jury as representatives of the community. So we end up with the ludicrous result that judges must attempt to place the judicial finger on the pulse of the community without any assistance whatsoever, and without the participation of the very community whose elusive tolerance is being measured.

Here's an example of the danger in having an obscenity law to do occasional moral-hygiene work. The year was 1990. *As Nasty as They Wanna Be* by 2 Live Crew was raising eyebrows across North America. A London, Ontario, bookseller announced that he was going to sell the controversial album despite warnings by local police that they would charge anyone who did. I called the bookseller, Marc Emery, and told him I would help him if he was charged.

Obscenity law had rarely been invoked for an audio recording. Obscenity was usually about dirty mags and hard-core video. That is not to say that popular music was not seen as pernicious evil by the moral minority. Remember, on September 9, 1956, Ed Sullivan televised a performance of Elvis Presley from the waist up to protect America from the potential offensiveness of Elvis' purportedly lewd, pelvic dance movements. Rock and roll, and related forms of popular music, poses a threat to its detractors because it celebrates a counterculture of drug use and unbridled sexual energy and trashes mainstream values. The threat posed by this music has always been more apparent than real because, eventually, the commercial packaging of the music destroys any supposed revolutionary potential; nevertheless, many people still find the lyrical content of the music offensive. Janis Joplin said rock and roll was about fucking, and many moral entrepreneurs hate this bold sexual enticement. But state intervention into the morality of popular music did not really happen until the 1980s. People may have burned Beatles records in America in the mid-sixties, but they did so without the assistance of the state.

In the eighties, moral entrepreneurs started to recruit the state to fight prurience in the recording industry. By the end of the decade, rap music, with its aggressive beats and its tendency to invoke misogynous and violent imagery, had become the scapegoat. Sometimes it was targeted because of its caustic political message. If freedom of speech and democracy mean anything, they have to protect political speech no matter how rabid and incendiary. But when it came to rap, freedom of speech took a back seat. The scaredy-cat white officials knew they had to attack rap where it was politically weakest—when protest turned prurient.

The *Nasty* album by 2 Live Crew has no overt political content. It is simply sexual boasting. The band released a sanitized version of the record, *As Clean as They Want to Be*, but this version sold a mere 400,000 copies, while the explicit version sold 1.3 million.[8] The record carried a label warning of explicit lyrics; nonetheless, it was the subject of a number of complaints eventually culminating in the declaration of legal obscenity in Florida in 1990. This declaration triggered the interest of Canadian law enforcement.

In the spring of 1991, the *Nasty* album went on trial in the conservative heartland of Ontario—London. The American virus had crossed the border. Manifest Destiny. This was only the second prosecution in Canada of a record: In 1990, Fringe Products Ltd. was tried for the distribution of the punk recording *Feed Us a Fetus* by the Day Glo Abortions. The company was acquitted by a jury.

I went to trial in London to defend this vulgar black rap recording before a white-haired white guy. As in most obscenity trials, we were denied a jury trial by decision of the Crown. Anyway, even if I could have had a jury, I'm not sure it would have helped. The entire time I was in London doing the trial, I don't remember seeing any black people in the city. This was not an auspicious sign.

What had 2 Live Crew done to offend Her Majesty? Two excerpts from the album seemed to disturb the prosecutor deeply at trial. He would intone in a deep voice the lyrics of the song. No rhythm. No smile. He'd just put these excerpts to my witnesses and ask: "Do you think that's funny witness? Do you?" The first excerpt comes from "My Seven Bizzos":

On Sunday there's Connie, who fucks with slick Ronny
She's a tricky dick bitch who's out for his money
She's always schemin' and hot like a demon
I thought I came in her mouth, but I was only peein'

MALE VOICE: Say what?
All these ho's belong to one player
My hard dick brother and a pussy surveyor
Now ya'll ain't heard, you better go ask your mother
That's your sister bein' dicked by Marquis, your brother
MALE VOICE: Say what?[9]

And the Crown's personal favourite—he loved to rely on this one—from "Reggae Joint":

Went to Strawberry's, got me a girlie
Made up and down and I bust the cherry
She threw a Heineken bottle at me, ah
I said, "Bitch ya better not try me, ah
I'll buck you down with this nine millimetre
But instead, I'll put you down with black peter"
Come sucky, sucky, bitch bend down, bo![10]

Pretty nasty stuff. I had heard the album way before the trial. I actually liked the song "Me So Horny," and the beat on a lot of the tracks was infectious. But in preparation for the trial I listened to the entire album, with the lyrics transcribed by the local police, from start to finish. All the songs devolved into juvenile pussy humour. The bits of garbage humour and the infectious beat got lost in an onslaught of aggressive sexual bravado. It tested my limits.

But I'm a basic free-speech guy. You cannot prohibit expression. It is politically unwise in the long run, and it can stunt the full development of character. Sure, the old "yelling fire in a crowded movie theatre" should still be against the law, but other than direct incitement to chaos and violence, I see no need to bring the government in to fight our battles when confronted with offensive expression. You don't like the recording? Don't buy it. Don't let your children buy it (but be real careful with this one). Complain to private enterprise. The retailers don't give a shit about artistic integrity; if they don't think they can sell a product, or if selling a product comes with the cost of inconvenient protests outside their store, they simply won't stock the product. The community never has to mobilize if it always thinks the state will do its dirty work.

The battle lines for trial were clearly drawn. The Crown said the recording was pernicious. We called it parody. The Crown said the album spoke for itself. We said there's more than meets the eye, calling expert evidence from a musicologist who traced the brash vulgarity of some rap music to the cultural traditions of black slaves. "Toasting" and "Doing the Dozens" were unique cultural holdovers from plantation days, involving an escalating series of insults delivered in a rhythmic flurry. The Crown said this type of material causes harm to women. We said that no one really knows that, and laws curtailing expression should not be created based on hunches and assumptions. The Crown said this type of trash was not protected by s. 2 (b) of the Charter (freedom of expression). We clamoured for a vibrant and expansive interpretation of the Charter. The Crown said white. We said black. And so on and so forth.

In this enlightened age, it is rare for the state to argue that a tape is disgusting or offensive to moral sensibilities. This is dinosaur talk. The current buzzwords are "degrading and dehumanizing." The stock argument is that the material before the court is "degrading" and "dehumanizing" to women who are cast in subordinate, commodified roles. There is some truth to this stock argument, but I believe there are better ways to combat degradation than reliance on the criminal law. The prosecutor claimed that the album sent a message that it is all right to abuse women and that recordings like this are partially responsible for the rise in violence against women. As he droned on, I couldn't help thinking that the trial was being conducted without the participation of a woman. This was a trial for white men. No persons of colour and no women were heard from. A white-haired judge, a goyishe male prosecutor, a troublemaking white accused and me, the typical Jewish civil libertarian defence counsel. My expert witness on musicology was another white male, and the courtroom was filled with freakish, white teenage males who saw the retailer as a free-speech crusader. What type of trial was this? A bunch of white guys telling the world how women and black people should feel about *As Nasty as They Wanna Be*. The community being protected and the community being judged were nowhere to be found.

Once the Crown played the misogynous gender card, I could only counter with the racist card. It was the only chance we had. A sexist recording vs. a racist prosecution. It was a heavyweight title fight for political correctness. I proposed to tender into evidence magazines purchased freely in London, and transcripts of tapes and records readily available in London. All of this material was as nasty or worse than that of 2 Live Crew. But they were all the creations of white people. I wanted the judge to have a basis for comparison. The presence of accepted white artists doing the same shtick as 2 Live Crew could mean one of two things, both favourable for the defence: either the community actually tolerated this type of material, or the prosecution was racist in targeting only black artists.

In 1991, Andrew Dice Clay was still regarded as a popular comedian. I wanted to introduce a tape of his live performance, in which he explains why women should not be comics:

> What are they tellin' jokes? There's a million things chicks can do. Ya ever go over to 42nd street, the little booths right? Ya got chicks shovin' bananas outta their asses, they're wiggling their asses, they're smokin' outta their pussies. That's a job; I'll go watch that for two hours. Don't tell jokes! If I was a chick, I'd be on a street corner suckin' dick till I had a mansion! There's so much more for them to do. You're a lady—don't you agree? You know what I'm sayin? I mean, how fucking funny would you be if you came up here? You wouldn't be! I go to a porno movie, there's a chick, dick in her mouth, couple stickin' between her tits, one in her vagina—to me that's entertaining. They're doing what women do. Don't try to break new ground, it's silly.[11]

Sam Kinison, another big-selling comic, gave this rant on breast reduction surgery:

> What kind of fuckin' bitch from hell would go to a doctor and go, "Could you make these smaller? Because I really want to piss my husband off. Take some meat out of these titties." That's sick, man, only a fuckin' cunt bitch would fuckin' do that. Just when you think that women have found out everything they can do to piss you off, they come up with something like breast reduction surgery. They go: "Oh my back hurts!" Then lie down, bitch, spread your legs, your fuckin' back hurts.[12]

If a listener cannot see any humour in this material, and takes the content at face value, it would be reasonable to assert that this type of material is degrading to women. But does it harm women either by leading to criminal acts of sexual aggression or to male attitudes of gender disrespect? For assholes who already harbour malicious thoughts about women, Clay, Kinison and 2 Live Crew must seem like prophets and not just comics. But for most of the population, these vulgar comics are just that—vulgar comics. They should be feared as much as Popeye should be feared for encouraging jealous rages and constant brawling.

I proposed introducing this comparative material (a practice supported by precedent), and the judge ran for cover. He ruled the material inadmissible. People have to realize that judges are the gatekeepers of legal truth. They make rulings on admissibility of evidence, and so filter a truth that has already been filtered by the lawyers presenting the evidence. As a judge you can simply avoid dealing with a difficult issue by deeming certain evidence inadmissible. Upon my application to introduce the comparative materials, the judge ruled: "I agree with the Crown, and with respect, disagree with Mr. Young. I'm not prepared to receive the comparative evidence, being of the view that it is not relevant to the narrow issue before me as framed in the Information, and that's my ruling accordingly."[13]

Notice that this ruling says nothing. "I rule it is not relevant." That was easy. But why? The judge must determine community standards. Is not the best evidence of what the community tolerates to look at what is freely and openly available in their market? The way I see it is this. If the judge admitted the tapes of other comics, this would expose the unspoken racist overtones of this trial. The accused on trial was Marc Emery, and he was an infamous local troublemaker, so he was able to get good media coverage for the trial. Remember Cardinal Rule #1 of Judging: Never let the trial become an occasion for challenging the legitimacy of the system—it's too dangerous. Plain and simple, you cannot morally justify prosecuting 2 Live Crew when Clay and others are allowed to frolic freely in the marketplace. So just make it legally disappear.

I also tried to lead evidence, through our expert musicologist, about female rappers who employ the sexually aggressive tone of 2 Live Crew. Application to admit evidence denied. I demanded that *As Nasty as They Wanna Be* be played in open court. The tape was never played. How can you not play the tape and still call this a public trial for the community's edification? Again, I see this as damage control. If the tape were played in court, many people, primarily the teenagers in the attendance, would giggle and laugh. It's really hard to think of an event as a criminal trial when the criminal is making some of the observers laugh. There is never a good laugh at a murder trial, at a sexual assault trial, at a robbery trial. The absence of laughter defines the event as a solemn trial of guilt or innocence. Laughter subverts the pretence of solemnity in an obscenity trial.

I think the judge understood what we were trying to say about this nasty recording. There wasn't a lot of redeeming value to speak of, but we had the evidence of parody and the historical tradition of "dissing" with a series of increasingly vulgar insults. The judge characterized our evidence as follows:

> The publication "Nasty" concentrates primarily on the braggadocio or sexual boasting theme. The witness, in his evidence, used different phrases to give his opinion of the lyrics on the "Nasty" tape, such phrases as: parody, comedic overtones, large-scale fantasies, identity assertions, caricature, exaggerated beyond belief, metaphoric and humorous. The witness stressed that the lyrics on the tape speak of the braggadocio or sexual boasting theme in such an exaggerated manner that no reasonable hearer would take them at face value. He said if you consider the lyrics as overstatement, and/or comedy, and, as well, look at the historical and cultural background of this particular type of rap music then, in effect, the alleged sexual exploitation in the cassette publication would not, overall, be undue.[14]

This was pretty much the message we tried to convey. So far, so good. But by putting blinders on, the judge was able to make this a simple task for himself. Forget about what the white comics are doing. Forget about what the community is doing. Just ask yourself, in the Ozzie and Harriet land of community standards, if this tape is just harmless parody and caricature. You'll have to answer no—it is too over the top, too virulent. Look at the judge's conclusion:

> My opinion, and finding, is that the "Nasty" publication exceeds the community standards of tolerance. I find the average reasonable Canadian, male or female, taken from any portion of the country's national mosaic would not abide other Canadians hearing this particular musical publication. When one analyses the overall lyrics of the "Nasty" cassette tape, one is struck by the very substantial use, throughout, of the "f" word, of the very substantial use of the explicit terms for male and female genitalia, of the substantial repetitive description of oral sex, of the substantial repetitive use of the word for female dog, all of which are intermingled repeatedly with

more commonplace vulgarities amidst a recurring theme of the denigration of women.[15]

This was an obscenity trial, and he was judging the language of an audio recording, yet he could not bring himself to write "fuck" or "bitch" in the reasons for judgement. If he was that bashful, how could we expect him to objectively determine whether this recording exceeded community standards? We have to stop fooling ourselves. I'm not sure if there is even such a thing as a community standard. And if there is, isn't this just a sugar-coated way of masking that it is the tyranny of the majority over the minority? And even if the standard does exist, and it is sensitive to the nuances of our national mosaic, I don't think there are many individuals, especially judges, who have any real sense of this standard.

When we were leading evidence on cultural tradition, on how black rappers can refer to themselves as niggers without running afoul of hate literature laws and on how female rappers can refer to women as bitches, the judge interjected: "But surely the test is not what may be thought or said in some offshore culture, but what the tolerance level is in Canada."[16] Offshore culture? I'm sure it was just a slip of the tongue, but it wasn't comforting to hear this comment from a judge in a town with no visible black population.

Failing to convince the judge at any level that *Nasty* would be tolerated within some mythical Canadian community, I had to rely upon the hackneyed "freedom of expression" argument. Free speech is a pornographer's wet dream. As much as I am a free-speech advocate, I was not thrilled to flog this dead horse in the context of obscenity. First, it has become apparent that courts worship free expression in the abstract, but as a practical matter they do little to protect this right. Second, I've always felt that free speech misses the mark when pornography or obscenity is under analysis. Porn is not about speech or expression, but rather is about stimulating the erotic centres of the brain and body. It expresses little, but it has a visceral impact.

Courts call freedom of expression a fundamental right, and many times the Supreme Court of Canada has said things like "the content of a statement cannot deprive it of the protection accorded by s. 2 (b) [freedom of expression], no matter how offensive it may be"[17] and free speech is "little less vital to man's mind and spirit than breathing is to his physical existence."[18] Yet, despite the passionate rhetoric, our courts routinely uphold legislative burdens on free speech on the basis that the burden is a "reasonable limit demonstrably justified in a free and democratic society" (this is the text of s. 1 of the Charter).

Raising the Charter in the 2 Live Crew case was a losing proposition. I knew going in that no court would take away the state's right to sanitize expression when it felt threatened. The judges know that "community standards of tolerance" is a vague benchmark, but they still uphold it. The judges know that the obscenity provision has the capacity to suppress valuable literary experiments that surface on the fringes of the commercial market. But this is neither here nor there, because most judges are not the type of culture consumers who care about William Burroughs, Kathy Acker, Robert Mapplethorpe or Eli Langer. I argued passionately and forcefully, knowing I was on a sinking ship. The judge expectantly announced that the law on obscenity was a reasonable limit on the exercise of the right to free expression.

In 1992, the very next year, the Supreme Court of Canada, in *R. v. Butler*, concluded that there were no constitutional problems with the obscenity provision.[19] For the Court, obscenity law had transformed itself from a moral-hygiene measure designed to maintain the moral fabric of society to a criminal prohibition designed to protect women and children from being degraded or dehumanized by a graphic, offensive depiction. With this new purpose, it was constitutionally sound. As for the evidence of a causal link between pornography and violence against women or the development of misogynous attitudes, the court admitted this was "subject to controversy" and "inconclusive." The court concluded that when social science evidence supporting the law is inconclusive, Parliament may still act if it has "a reasoned apprehension of harm resulting from the desensitization of individuals exposed to materials which depict violence, cruelty and dehumanization in sexual relations."[20] Pretty fancy language. In my terms, it means Parliament can criminalize expression when it has a hunch that the expression is pernicious. Liberty should never be restricted on assumptions, especially when the liberty concerns the "fundamental freedom of expression."

The only aspect of the *Butler* decision that is positive is the court's clear condemnation of violence. It's about time we started to focus on the violent aspects of expression instead of obsessing over vulgarity and graphic sexuality. The Court ruled that the violent depiction of sexuality will always be considered to exceed community standards of tolerance. In theory this sounds good, but upon reflection there is a major problem with this, too. A violent sexual depiction can be saved only if the court finds artistic merit in their work. Nothing is more stupid than turning a criminal court into a forum for discussion about competing visions of art. A criminal court is no place to judge art. Art is not a litigious issue. So in practice, this "bright line" *Butler* test will still fail in many cases. Courts may be relieved of the burden of ascertaining the elusive community standard in some cases of violent sexuality, but in many other cases they will still labour under the even sillier burden of having to play the role of art critic.

Further, many judges seem to characterize vigorous, lustful sex as violence. One judge deemed something obscene because it tried to "vilify sex and treat it as something less than beautiful."[21] Another condemned a movie because it portrayed people as "having animal characteristics."[22] For this judge, pornography was acceptable only when it portrayed "positive and affectionate human sexual interaction between consenting adults participating on a basis of equality." Even the judge in the 2 Live Crew case fell into this trap, noting that "there is nothing of love and tenderness on the 'Nasty' tape, but only a message of violent sex and denigration of women."[23] What's love got to do with this? In the world I know, there is lots of loveless fucking, and sometimes the participants get downright nasty while in the act. That is the human condition, and no amount of legal intervention can compel human beings to restrict their sexual expression to descriptions of making polite love to Mary Poppins.

Occasionally, a clever writer like Tamara Faith Berger will use the vernacular of porn to express sophisticated ideas, but for the most part porn is nothing more than jerk-off material. Porn is all about sexual arousal. Not free speech. This seems to bother people. It bothered the judge in the 2 Live Crew case, who noted that "the frequency and graphic descriptions of the sexual acts in the lyrics of many of the songs evinces an intention to arouse the hearer to sexual activity." I can't really imagine that *As Nasty as They Wanna Be* would be used by listeners as jerk-off material, but even if this was the intention, so what? Why are we so concerned with sexual arousal?

We can do a lot more sexual things these days—but don't talk about it publicly and don't paint a picture. People get worked up about anything that threatens to expose them as the sexual creatures they deny being. There are some strong feelings out there. But it is important to protect our right to speak freely, to offend, to provoke and to arouse. There's no need for the state to come running with its guns and prisons as censors.

Obscenity law is an embarrassment. Despite some fine-tuning in *Butler*, our obscenity law defies rational application. It is impossible to define the obscene, and the whole enterprise of suppressing some modes of expression is based upon a false premise: Expression does not have an immediate causal impact on action. What we say is not necessarily related to what we do. The expression of misogyny in the context of a sexual depiction is clearly reflective of some current reality, but it is not necessarily the creator of a future reality.

I do not embrace the "trigger" hypothesis, which says that obscenity causes antisocial behaviour. This hypothesis defies empirical verification. It is overly simplistic: "In a study of twenty serial rapists, we discovered that fifteen of the twenty each had a glass of milk every night before going to bed, leading us to conclude that there may be a causal connection between late-night consumption of milk and sexually aggressive behaviour." That's the kind of argument made by second-rate social scientists who have their own hidden agenda for seeing a connection between a breakdown in social order and obscene materials they find personally offensive. Sometimes we treat people like autonomous actors who can make independent choices, and at other times we treat people like children in need of protection from undue mass-media influence. Obscenity law is a law for children. It presupposes that when a man watches porn, he will mimic the attitudes and actions of the film, and will take on a one-dimensional perspective in which women are nothing more than tools for sex. Of course, there are some cretins who think this way, but their stunted attitudes developed independently of porn.

I've always believed in the "safety valve" hypothesis of obscene expression: By releasing aggressive, hyper-sexual, and vulgar thoughts in the expressive material we create and consume, we have no need to act upon them. They remain dormant. They exist only at the level of imagination. Of course, for a few lunatics, certain types of pornography may fuel an already developing passion for inflicting harm on women. But for the vast majority of people, obscene materials are not the trigger for violent behaviour or misogynistic attitudes.

As a law student, I remember reading this: "If pornography is a vile monster ... it belongs to a special breed of science-fiction monsters which are nourished by the explosives being shot at it. This kind of monster—assuming it is one—starves and withers through lack of attention. After all, a monster only remains ominous as long as it is able to scare."[24] The author, Bert Kutchinsky, had studied the impact of the liberalization of obscenity laws in Denmark in the 1960s. At first the market was flooded with sex mags of every variety, but soon the people grew saturated and the thrill of tasting forbidden fruit became less compelling. The free flow of obscene materials in Denmark did not lead to any meaningful rise in crime of a sexual nature.

There are lots of horny people out there and lots of crude pigs. That is the human condition, and no law can change that. It is embarrassing to see mature adults obsessing over sexual imagery, whether hideous or beautiful. Get over it. If you don't like what someone is saying, speak louder than your opponent. It is an act of cowardice to ask the government to banish from sight that which does not cohere with our vision of humanity. It's time to tackle some real social problems instead of fighting imaginary monsters.

5

Getting Laid

ON AUGUST 12, 1833, Captain Henry Nichols was hanged from the gallows in Southwark, England. The local broadsheet, a news summary sold to the local audience witnessing the execution, began with this passage: "Heinous, horribly frightful, and disgusting was the crime for which the above poor Wretched Culprit suffered the severe penalty of the law this morning."[1] And what was this horrible crime? Sodomy. Sodomy has never had a fixed meaning in law, but it usually applied to anal sex (buggery in some jurisdictions) and oral sex. It theoretically applied to both heterosexual and homosexual conduct, but in actuality was reserved for the gay men of the Commonwealth. Whatever its meaning, sodomy was a crime that attracted official disgust and revulsion. The indictments of past centuries were commonly drafted to accuse the sodomite of "wickedly, devilishly, feloniously, and against the order of nature [committing that] sodomitical, detestable, and abominable sin called buggery (not to be named among Christians) to the Great Displeasure of Almighty God and to the disgrace of mankind."[2]

Similarly, when the Earl of Castlehaven was executed in 1631 for sodomy, an account published in 1699 explained that "an abomination that shocks our Natures, and puts our Modesty to the Blush, to see it so commonly perpetrated, is the Devilish and Unnatural Sin of Buggery, a Crime that sinks a Man below the Basest Epithet, is so foul that it admits of no Aggravation, and cannot be expressed in its Horror, but by Doleful Shrieks and Groans of the Damned."[3]

Despite the fire-and-brimstone condemnation, and notwithstanding the hangman waiting at the gallows, people were not deterred from exploring their bodily orifices. Most men and women want to get laid on a regular basis, and some will even risk death in pursuit of the ultimate orgasm. I'm not even talking about freak accidents from autoerotic asphyxiation (cutting off the breath at the moment of climax in pursuit of a cosmic orgasm). I'm talking about people who have risked execution at the hands of the law for fornication, adultery, sodomy and other "crimes against nature."

Fellatio, cunnilingus and anal sex ("not to be named among Christians") were punishable by death, but this did not stop the curious in search of the perfect blowjob. Well, actually, most sodomites were probably engaged in anal sex, because oral sex was in all likelihood physically repulsive in an age before the advent of hot showers, bidets and toilet paper. Mouth to genital contact played a lesser role in the sexual practices of bygone times, but it was still demonized as "... a Man's putting his erected Penis into another Person's (Man or Woman's) Mouth, using Friction between the Lips, a way so very beastly and so much to be abhorred, as to cause at the mentioning, or but thinking of it, the utmost detestation and loathing."[4]

I agree that an inept and amateurish blowjob can attract the "utmost detestation and loathing," and maybe that should be a crime, but what manner of perverse thinking would demonize orgasmic experimentation as a crime on par with murder and kidnapping? The history of our sexuality shows a lustful species whose pursuit of orgasm is filled with imagination and adventure. It also shows that rulers and knowledge elites infused this adventure with guilt, neurosis and moral hysteria. And when religious guilt and shame could not deter the sexual adventurer, those who were not getting laid recruited the institution of law to punish those who were. Historically, getting laid was indeed a risky venture, but as with war and holy crusades, it was a venture worth dying for.

Imagine the shock of these moral crusaders if they could time travel to the 1990s. Barely 150 years after we were hanging sodomites, in the modern era there are clubs, such as Remingtons Men of Steel Tavern in Toronto, where sodomites congregate to watch dancers jerk themselves off on stage. The managers of the club were eventually charged in 1996 with keeping a common bawdy house, but these jerk-off performances went on for years before the police decided to intervene.

The trial judge used these words to describe some of the festivities at the club:

A typical evening at Remingtons for the purpose of these charges began with the masturbation/ejaculation performance on stage called "Sperm

Attack Mondays" followed by "Free Dances" where the performer/dancer had close physical contact with patrons and finally "Private Dances" where the performer/dancer invited patrons to private booths for "dances" in exchange for money. There was a continuum or logical sequence to the three activities described. Patrons were invited to participate in "viewing" these activities.[5]

Only a judge could find a "continuum or logical sequence" when scrutinizing the activities of some fun-loving gay men looking for arousal and big cocks. No one really knows what happened in the private booths, but we do have a pretty good idea of the stage shows because there were undercover cops in the tavern for over three months. The cops must have been having a gay old time because they kept coming back (of course, they always say that they never "came" whenever they did come). They noted in meticulous detail every gyration, thrust and stroke they witnessed. Ultimately, many of the patrons disputed whether there was ever any contact between a patron and a performer, but the cops always saw some. Surprise, surprise, the judge believed the undercover cops. Here's the judge's description of one performance as seen through the eyes of the police:

> On December 4, 1995, a dancer known as Eric was announced ... He removed all his clothing and began masturbating while walking around the stage in full view of approximately forty-five patrons. At one point, while standing at the edge of the stage, Eric used his penis to deliberately hit an unsuspecting patron on the head. The patron appeared surprised and displeased by the act and moved farther away from the stage. Eric ejaculated onto the stage near the end of the fourth song. He squeezed an amount of ejaculate from his penis onto the fingers of his right hand and held these fingers out towards three patrons standing at the edge of the stage. The first patron turned his head away to avoid Eric's fingers. Eric then touched a second patron on the forehead with the ejaculate, then thrust his fingers towards the face of a third patron, who licked it. The crowd groaned audibly in disbelief. Eric picked up his clothes and left the stage. No one was observed to clean up the ejaculate from the floor or on the stage after Eric's performance.[6]

Actually, I find it really distasteful that no one cleaned up after Eric's performance. That bugs me. Otherwise, I can see no criminal act being committed. Of course, the judge saw things differently. After reciting page after page of precedents, the judge asserted that the performances were "indecent" because they were "degrading and dehumanizing." To whom? The police were not acting upon any complaint, and most of the patrons seemed to be having a good time. There were no minors present. Who was degraded, and what exactly does it mean to say that a performance was dehumanizing? As my friend Professor Shannon Bell has written: "'Degrading, obscene and dehumanizing' are empty categories that get filled with such content as homophobia, whorephobia, ageism, sadomasophobia, transgenderphobia and fear of difference."[7]

We have come a long way from the era of hanging sodomites. The law is not as involved in our day-to-day sexual choices. The "criminals" at Remingtons were given conditional discharges (the lightest sentence possible), with the obligation to make charitable donations and perform community service. They were not incarcerated and executed. What liberal and understanding times we live in! I still wonder why contemporary law would spend three months in an undercover operation, and five years in countless court dates, to judge, stigmatize and punish a bunch of guys having a good time. Despite the monumental change in sexual attitudes and legal response, contemporary criminal justice still harbours some quaint Victorian attitudes.

Sexual attitudes started to change dramatically in the 1960s—the so-called sexual revolution. In the early 1960s, Lucy and Ricky slept in separate beds; by 2000, Samantha from *Sex and the City* was complaining about the taste of her lover's sperm. Popular culture has embraced lust, but the law still lingers in the shadows. Even as recently as the 1970s, the law was still debating whether cunnilingus was considered an act of "gross indecency" for the purposes of the criminal law. Even in modern times, it was still struggling with a question of profound importance: should eating pussy land you in prison? A 1971 indictment read: "The jurors for Our Lady the Queen present that on or about the 3rd day of September, AD. 1971, at the City of Sault Ste. Marie in the District of Algoma you did unlawfully commit an act of gross indecency with [the complainant], to wit; cunnilingus, contrary to the Criminal Code of Canada."[8]

The accused in this case was actually convicted by the jury, who were undoubtedly strongly influenced by this statement made by the trial judge in his charge to them:

It may be of some help to you if I were to read to you very briefly from a judgement of the Manitoba Court of Appeal, and this was not a case of cunnilingus, but one of fellatio, and that is the putting of a penis in someone's mouth. There the Court said: "An accused who engages in an act of fellatio with a female is guilty of the offence of gross indecency whether or not the female consents to such an act. The conduct as such is so repugnant to the ordinary standards of morality and decency that it cannot be called anything other than gross indecency ... The accused's behaviour was unnatural and depraved and violated the common standards of conduct accepted by the people of our land, and it is our view that Canadians are not prepared to condone such acts as falling within acceptable standards of behaviour."[9]

Ultimately, the Court of Appeal overturned the conviction, primarily on the basis that it was an error for the trial judge to have read to the jury portions of another court judgement. But the point remains: as recently as the 1970s, the law still felt it had a role to play in regulating and dictating sexual practices to people who couldn't give a rat's ass about what the law had to say on this matter. It's laughable that the law still believed that writhing in pleasure from the joys of oral sex was a criminal act. There must have been a pretty high recidivism rate for this offence.

The rigorous war on sexuality springs from the Judeo–Christian ethic, and in particular reflects early Christian perspectives on sex. Even though religion is no longer a dominant force in social and political affairs, it still manages to modestly inform and influence modern criminal law.

Early Christianity could not tolerate fucking unrelated to marital efforts at procreating. In Corinthians, Paul clearly tells Christians that the kingdom of heaven will not be open to fornicators, adulterers, the effeminate and the "abusers of themselves." He also tells us that "it is good for a man not to touch a woman," but knowing this is impossible counsel, he advises that "to avoid fornication, let every man have his own wife, and let every woman have her own husband." That's the extent of the early Church's tolerance of sex. This noble institution tried very hard to get the peasants to stop fucking with reckless abandon. The only good news is that this noble institution did not punish the transgressors with great zeal. Punishment for transgressors usually consisted of an act of penance with some form of public denunciation.

Often the libidinous criminal had to stand naked in public with a sign indicating he or she was a lecher or an adulterer.

By the sixteenth century, the state had taken over. Queen Elizabeth I empowered the secular courts to "punish all Incests, Adulteries, Fornication, Outrages, Misbehaviours and Disorders in Marriage."[10] The state started punishing sexual miscreants with unabated fervour. In 1650, adultery was made a crime punishable by death, and public officials started to take measures to close all the houses of ill repute that had flourished in London for centuries.

The active efforts to keep fucking in the home, between partners in marriage, was not only fuelled by religious fervour but also by the fear of women's mysterious sexual powers. In today's time we would label this fear misogyny. The classic medieval handbook on witchcraft, *Malleus Malificarum*, put it simply: "all witchcraft comes from carnal lust, which in women is insatiable."[11] Women were the property of men, and man's social, legal and political obligation was to control this volcanic, insatiable commodity and prevent women from causing another divine fall from grace.

In the latter half of the eighteenth century, the state seemed to give up on the quest to control sexual relations. But this ceasefire was short-lived. The Victorian age heralded a whole new era of mindless sexual regulation. Taking their inspiration from the anti-sex religious precepts of the Church, nineteenth-century moral entrepreneurs erected a detailed, legislative code of sexual conduct. Their justification was the fostering of family values. (I find our contemporary talk of "family values" is really creepy when you know that its roots are in the Victorian conception of woman as nothing more than mother, homemaker and husband-helper.) The idealized family was celebrated as the crowning achievement of a middle-class rising out of the frenzy of nineteenth-century industrialization. The family unit was seen as the very foundation of the Commonwealth; the home was a place where the husband could beat his wife, but not beat off with his wife.

With the birth of the notion of the "welfare state," nineteenth-century reformists saw nothing wrong with intruding into private lives to protect women and children from the harm of sexual activity. There were some good things about the emerging welfare state, like compulsory education and labour laws to protect children from factory exploitation, but the paternalistic efforts to use the law to control the sexual welfare of its citizens was one really stupid enterprise.

Ironically, the nineteenth-century woman was no longer feared as a mysterious sexual siren. Victorian culture reconstructed women as chaste and decorous. Women were constructed as a mixture of angel and idiot, and not as beings with latent sexual drives that could bring men to their destruction. As Dr. William Acton said in 1864: "I should say that the majority of women (happily for them) are not very much troubled with sexual feelings of any kind. ... The best mothers, wives, and managers of households, know very little or nothing of sexual indulgences. Love of home, children, and domestic duties are the only passions they feel."[12] These stupid Victorians did not even realize that constructing women as model wives and lifeless fucks was great promotion for a burgeoning prostitution trade.

Religion still had a significant role to play in this secular insanity, but now control of sexuality was primarily medicalized. When the law is unsure of its mission, it always brings in the experts to find phony cause and effect. Sexual decadence and debauchery could reasonably lead to insanity and a whole host of debilitating illnesses. Again, let's look to the Victorian wisdom of Dr. Acton. Here's his take on the medical risks of masturbation:

> The frame is stunted and weak, the muscles underdeveloped, the eye is sunken and heavy, the complexion is sallow, pasty or covered with spots of acne, the hands are damp and cold, and the skin moist. The boy shuns the society of others, creeps about alone, joins with repugnance in the amusements of his school fellows. He cannot look any one in the face, and becomes careless in dress and uncleanly in person. His intellect has become sluggish and enfeebled, and if his evil habits are persisted in, he may end in becoming a drivelling idiot or a peevish valetudinarian.[13]

Knowing that I have already become a drivelling idiot, I guess I can still look forward to a future as a "peevish valetudinarian."

Don't think that these bizarre medical claims are just the nonsense of an era remarkable for its stupidity. We still make outlandish claims about the risks of adventurous sexuality, but we are much more sophisticated and less apt to resort to hysterical claims about growing hair on your palms. For example, in the 1970 U.S. Presidential Commission on Obscenity and Pornography, the conservative members called for tighter restrictions because "sexual restraints promote cultural progress."[14]

They argued that the "creativity and excellence of our system and people" have largely been fostered by legal restraints on unbridled sexual energy. I can't believe they actually believe this nonsense, but it sounds a lot more credible than the risk of hairy palms. There will always be a small, but vocal and powerful group of conservative thinkers who will call for greater restrictions in order to save society. For whatever reason, there are some people who truly believe that the Roman Empire humped itself to death, and that modern civilizations will also decay and crumble if we don't impose greater legal limits on the "who, when, where, what and how" of getting laid.

Until the 1970s, the law relating to sexual conduct was still fairly intrusive. There were many remnants of old-fashioned ideology and practice within our justice system. We have largely abandoned the Victorian mission of social engineering, and in the new millennium there is a great deal of sexual liberty. The Supreme Court of Canada has given a positive judicial endorsement to getting laid by noting that "sexual intercourse, which is not in itself either criminal or unlawful ... can indeed be both desirable and pleasurable."[15] But only a true anarchist would believe that there should be *no* official, legal limits on the pursuit of sexual gratification. Some limits are necessary to protect the vulnerable from aggressive sexuality.

Some argue that the law has been too ambitious and has strayed beyond the task of protecting the vulnerable, and others argue that the law does not go far enough. All I wish to do here is provide the reader with a brief guide to the world of legal sex in Canada. The Criminal Code has its complications in this regard, and this guide does not capture all the nuances of the legal regulation of sex, but it does give you a pretty good idea of what you can legally do with your erogenous zones and bodily orifices.

The "What" of Legal Sex

Here's the best news of all. Current law does not tell people what type of sexual acts they can engage in. As long as the sex takes place in private, people can pursue all types of fetishes and paraphilia. For the most part, any couple, whether gay or straight, can, in a private setting, take a pound of Genoa Salami, shove it into any available bodily orifice, cover their bodies in Dijon mustard and consume the salami while stimulating their partner to orgasm (if they're lucky). I have no idea why anyone would want to do this, but being able to do these stupid things is what freedom entails.

The only current taboo on the *what* of legal sex relates to anal intercourse. Before 1985, the offence of "gross indecency" was broad enough to cover oral sex, anal sex and any other "indecent" sexual act. Historically, the offence was reserved for harassing gay men, and in 1985 Parliament decided to repeal a section whose ambit and operation was vague and disturbing. In its place, s. 159 was created to specifically prohibit anal intercourse unless: a) it was committed by married couples in private; or b) it was committed by two people over the age of eighteen in private. If more than two people are present, it will not be considered a private activity.

Why would Parliament single out one particular sexual act for criminal regulation? I'm not a fan of the idea of anal sex; the ass is an exit and not an entry point. But I know lots of people who enjoy this act, and I cannot see any reason for the law to intervene. I know that there was not a strong lobby by concerned proctologists to include this offence in the Code. The creation of the offence seems like a veiled attempt to deter gay sexual conduct among young people.

In 1995, the Ontario Court of Appeal ruled that the anal sex offence was unconstitutional—not because it was a stupid law, but because it discriminated on the basis of age.[16] One judge actually had the courage to recognize that it discriminated on the basis of sexual orientation. Of course, one of the quirks of our law is that this decision is technically only binding in Ontario. So as an officer of the court, I would have to advise young men in Alberta to watch where they are putting their penises. They may be committing a criminal act.

The "Who" of Legal Sex
The question of *who* you can fuck is subject to far more regulation than the question of "what" you can do with the "who" you are able to find. Let's see who we are able to play with.

- No animals: Section 160 prohibits bestiality. If you consider this a serious deprivation of freedom, then you are actually too sick for me to even defend.
- No immediate family members: Section 155 prohibits sexual intercourse with a parent, child, brother, sister, grandparent or grandchild. This applies to consenting adults. You can give your brother a

blowjob; you just can't fuck him. I'm not really sure this offence has a solid rationale, and much of the genetic hysteria is scientifically unsound, but the section has been upheld by the Courts of Appeal in Nova Scotia and British Columbia as constitutionally sound.[17] There may be a valid civil liberties claim here, but it is an issue I have not explored fully. I'm not that bothered by the fact that out of the millions of available sexual partners, the law has taken away a handful of potential fuck-buddies. I know this is not a valid argument, but I just don't see the important liberty issue in barring your mother from being your fuck-buddy. Get over it.

- No children: Children are unacceptable sexual partners because we can never know whether they truly understand and consent to the activity. People disagree about when a child becomes an adult for the purpose of sexual experimentation. I know lots of people who started playing around with sex at the age of twelve or thirteen. (I always hated these people because I was a late-bloomer.) I also know twelve- and thirteen-year-olds who are incapable of understanding the significance of sexual play. Who knows? The law arbitrarily sets age limits, and we can only hope that they reflect the reality of adolescent sex. Section 150.1 (1) stipulates that anyone under the age of fourteen is incapable of consenting to sexual activity.

  There are some nuances. Section 150.1 (2) allows children from twelve to fourteen to engage in sex as long as their partner is: a) under sixteen years of age; b) less than two years older; and c) not in a position of trust or authority. But s. 153 prohibits any sexual touching with people up to the age of eighteen if you are in a relationship of trust with or authority over the young person.

The "When and Where" of Legal Sex

Here's where criminal law starts to impact on sexual liberty. When can you have sex? Any time. This is not something the law has regulated. Sex is a 24/7 activity. But the "where" has severe restrictions. Section 173 (1) prohibits the doing of an "indecent act" in a public place in the presence of one or more persons. The vague allusion to "indecent act" encompasses all manner of sex acts, so the bottom line is that there is always a legal risk in getting laid in public.

Of course, I believe in "time, place and manner" restrictions on sex. I don't want people fucking in my backyard (well, I guess it depends a bit on who they are), and there must be rules governing when and where you can get your rocks off. But why criminal rules? Why not municipal regulation? If I were not such a voyeur, I would probably be offended if I stumbled on a heated sex session as I walked down a laneway. But being offended would not propel me to seek the protection of the criminal-justice system. There has to be a less drastic and less stigmatizing legal response to men and women who drop their pants in socially unacceptable situations.

In 1994, the Ontario Court of Appeal appeared to open the door for legal sex in a car.[18] In that case, a prostitute was giving some guy a blowjob in a parked car in the corner of an empty parking lot. As luck would have it, Officer Friendly came by and put an end to the fun. One judge reversed the conviction on the basis that the accused did not intend to commit the act in a public place; she thought she was in a private setting. One judge reversed the conviction on the basis that in the facts of the case the car was not a public place. One judge affirmed the conviction on the basis that the purpose of the law was to prevent public displays of sex and it did not really matter if you took precautions to avoid detection. The problem is that no one really knows what the case stands for and it is binding only in Ontario. So, fucking in cars is probably not a good idea (from a legal point of view).

For the most part, private sex is unencumbered by rules. However, sex in the privacy of your home can be a legal problem if children under eighteen are exposed to your activity. Section 172 criminalizes the participation in adultery, sexual immorality, habitual drunkenness and "other forms of vice" if children are exposed to it and it "endangers the morals of the child." Fortunately, there are few prosecutions for this offence as, despite its best intentions, it is one of the only remaining Victorian social hygiene measures. Any Criminal Code provision that employs the term "sexual immorality" as a defining element of crime is a dangerous restriction on liberty.

Sex in private settings will attract legal busybodies if the location is considered a bawdy house. Most people think of bawdy houses as brothels with hordes of resident women waiting to service horny men. In Canadian law, a bawdy house is any location that is used on a habitual and frequent basis for the purposes of prostitution or indecency (non-conventional activity of a vaguely sexual nature is included by this term). So any hotel that has been used by prostitutes two or three times in a week will be deemed a bawdy house. If you have hired a prostitute (this is not illegal, per se) and are then found in a bawdy house (which could be a Marriott or a Hilton Hotel) you will be charged as a found-in. The hooker will be an inmate and the owner/manager will be the keeper. One big, happy family.

The "How" of Legal Sex

Don't get excited! The law does not tell us how to get laid, but it does have something to say about the processes to be used to get laid in a legally proper manner. There are two basic rules. First, there must be mutual consent in order to be engaged in legal sex. This is obvious. But there are some real problems in maintaining a clear definition of consent, and I will return to this issue in a moment. The second rule is a bit harder to express. Some people are not getting laid and thus look to the private sector for sexual fulfilment. Big mistake. Although there is nothing illegal about paying for sex, it is illegal to "communicate for the purposes of prostitution." Therefore, the how of legal sex requires that, if you are paying for your orgasm, the sexual act cannot be preceded by discussion and negotiation. The illegalities are the conversation and discussions entered into for the purposes of prostitution. So in the commercial sex world, it is of great value to be able to communicate telepathically, to be able to read minds and to decipher body language; otherwise, trying to pay for an orgasm may lead to a criminal record. Although paying for sex is a consensual, and arguably harmless activity, this exchange of sex for money triggers the whole punitive arsenal of the state. "Bring out the big guns" and we naively believe that people will stop doing strange things for sexual gratification. We should put away the big guns and start to legalize and properly regulate commercial sex.

Drained of all initiative and creativity, lawmakers sit in cloistered towers trying to construct the perfect "get tough" measure that will remove prostitution from the streets of Canada. It's embarrassing to see grown-up men and women acting like their political power is any match for the power of orgasm. Some things in life cannot be changed. In 1994, the federal government proposed yet another series of tough new measures.[19] These measures were to include impoundment and forfeiture of the john's vehicle. This proposed measure never made it into law, as many politicians silently wondered how they would get to work if the law were passed.

The how of legal sex also mandates that mutual consent be secured. But in recent years the line between legal sex and illegal sex has become increasingly blurred by a highly politicized debate concerning the proper operation of consent. Consent is the demarcation line between "desirable and pleasurable" sex and criminal activity, and this line has been steadily moving in the past ten years.

The how of legal sex has become a political battleground. In the past, the law cared little about protecting the sexual autonomy and integrity of women; even the historical genesis of the crime of rape shows that much of the law's concern was with the proprietary rights of men—rape was a crime because it damaged the property of men. In recent times, we have recognized the injustice perpetrated upon women by the failure of the legal system to treat rape victims with respect and to effectively prosecute those responsible for the attack on the victims' sexual integrity. There have been significant legal reforms designed to facilitate reporting of sexual assaults and to ensure that the sexual assault victim is treated fairly in court.

But the pendulum may have swung too far in the other direction. Recent developments with respect to the substantive elements of the law of sexual assault have the potential to capture sexual activity that in past eras was considered obnoxious and disrespectful, but not criminal.

Playing with definitions changes the understanding of a problem. In the past, non-resistance or acquiescence to sexual activity was enough to constitute consent. Under current law, communicating opposition and resistance is no longer essential. Now the law looks at communicating agreement and desire.

I would never wish to minimize or trivialize the seriousness of the problem of sexual violence against women. However, I am always perplexed and suspicious when I read that one in four women—or three in four women—will be subjected to sexual violence in their lives. These are startling and upsetting claims that can be made only if sexual violence is defined in the broadest terms possible. Granted that patting someone's ass is offensive and can be disconcerting, but is this the behaviour we had in mind when in 1983 we changed the narrow rape offence (penetration) to sexual assault (any manner of sexual touching)? In 1982, the ass-patter was an asshole; today he is a criminal.

The current, broad definition of sexual assault widens the net of social control. An assault is an "intentional application of force" and it becomes a sexual assault if "viewed in light of all the circumstances ... the sexual or carnal context of the assault [is] visible to the reasonable observer." Here's what the reasonable observer must look to:

> The part of the body touched, the nature of the contact, the situation in which it occurred, the words and gestures accompanying the act, and all the other circumstances surrounding the conduct, including threats which may or may not be accompanied by force. ... The intent or purpose of the person committing the act, to the extent that this may appear from the evidence, may also be a factor in considering whether the conduct is sexual. If the motive of the accused is sexual gratification, to the extent that this may appear from the evidence it may be a factor in determining whether the conduct is sexual.[20]

So if some sleazy guy saunters up to a woman in a bar, touches her shoulder and whispers, "I can make the earth move for you, baby," this could constitute a sexual assault. It is clearly an assault on good taste and social grace, but a criminal assault?

You might say that surely the law would not be invoked in these circumstances, as public officials will exercise sound and reasonable discretion not to prosecute. So how about this case? A father was convicted of sexual assault for grabbing his three-year-old son's genitals as a disciplinary response to the child doing the same thing to others.[21] Clearly a misguided form of discipline, and it would constitute a common assault, but do we really want to say that the father sexually assaulted his son, with all the nasty connotations this raises? The father argued that he did not have an intent or motive of sexual gratification, but ultimately the Supreme Court of Canada focused more on the genital touching than on the motivation behind the touching. This case may have brought up some serious child welfare issues, but it should never have been resolved by convicting the father of sexual assault. That's a real family-building move for the state to make.

In 1995, an armed forces officer, Sergeant Chau, took personnel on a winter exercise. He was accused of committing two sexual assaults on a female soldier, Private C. During one march, Private C. complained of being cold. Sergeant Chau then:

> took the ends of her scarf and re-wrapped it around her head to protect her head and neck and crossed it in the front and unzipped the top of her out-

door jacket and tucked the scarf ends in under the jacket but on top of her combat shirt, then zipped the jacket shut again. Sergeant Chau's hand when it went inside her jacket came close to the top of her breasts but was never actually touched them except with the scarf and the whole motion was quick and not at all lingering. Private C. testified that she felt violated by such an action on the part of Sergeant Chau but that she did not say anything to him by way of complaint, because "she was scared to because he was her sergeant."[22]

The second assault occurred when she was crawling on her hands and knees to go into the tent. Sergeant Chau was behind her. She felt a "grab" on her buttocks. Chau admitted touching her, but he said it was just to speed her up. Chau was behind her with all his gear in both his hands waiting to get into the tent. The trial judge dismissed the charges. He could not find any sexual context to this touching. In addition, he noted the "overkill" in prosecuting the sergeant and applied the maxim *de minimus non curat lex* (the law does not deal with trifling matters).

Another judge might have convicted. Every coach who pats players on the butt and every tailor who is marking clothes for alteration should beware—they may be criminals in waiting.

With the shifting political tide, the Supreme Court of Canada has recognized that the courts must ensure the line between getting laid and sexual assault is clear. In a 1998 sexual assault case, *R. v. Cuerrier*, the Court stated: "The courts should not broaden the criminal law to catch conduct that society generally views as non-criminal. If that is to be done, Parliament must do it. Furthermore, the criminal law must be clear. I agree with the fundamental principle affirmed in English cases that it is imperative that there be a clear line between criminal and non-criminal conduct. Absent this, the criminal law loses its deterrent effect and becomes unjust."[23]

Maintaining a clear divide between fucking and felony may not always be possible when our criminal law can cover any form of touching, from kissing an earlobe to intercourse. But this is where the notion of "consent" comes to the rescue. By law, every form of touch must be preceded by some form of consent in order for the activity to be legal. The Criminal Code defines consent as "the voluntary agreement of the complainant to engage in the activity in question" (s. 273.1). But how is this agreement to be expressed? By a handshake, by a contract or simply by just doing it without expressing objection?

There is no conceptual problem with consent being defined as voluntary agreement, but as a practical matter people rarely approach sex as a business negotiation. Usually the less said, the more romantic. Couples who have been together for years may preface their groping by asking "Should we have sex now?" But strangers going through the dating/mating game often act on unspoken cues. If a cue is picked up to start kissing, then the kissing might escalate to a touching of body parts without the preface "Can I touch your breasts now?" You touch, and you see if your hand is left in place. If it is, you may start touching other parts of the body. But where is the "voluntary agreement"?

Getting laid is often a messy business, but the law reconstructs it as a formal business negotiation. If you don't play by the rules, your sexual advances may turn out to be criminal activity. Most people understand their partner's sexual cues and, without entering into frenzied negotiations, they engage in consensual groping. But others, usually strangers and casual acquaintances, run a greater risk of miscue. In past times, women bore the burden of the miscue; now men stand to lose by ignoring the possibility of a miscue. Where before the woman had to express resistance, now the man has to ascertain agreement. Politically and socially, this is good development, as men have exploited the ambiguity of sexual interaction for years, but is the legal requirement of ascertaining voluntary agreement a practical and realistic dividing line between getting laid and committing an assault?

The 1999 Supreme Court of Canada decision in *R. v. Ewanchuk* may represent the wave of the future.[24] A seventeen-year-old mother was being interviewed about employment opportunities in Ewanchuk's trailer. Ewanchuk was approximately thirty years of age. Upon entering the trailer, the complainant believed that Ewanchuk locked the door, and she became frightened. Eventually, the complainant was asked to provide a massage, and she did. Ewanchuk then offered her a massage, and she accepted. As the massage progressed, Ewanchuk's hands strayed to her breasts, but when the complainant protested the touching, he desisted. The problem was, he kept coming back. With every touching, the complainant protested and the accused desisted. He even managed to lie on top of her, grinding away. When he removed his penis from his pants, the complainant asked him to stop, and he did.

Throughout the incident, the complainant remained passive and non-responsive. The accused would see how far he could go with his touching, and upon being told "no," he always stopped.

Twenty years ago, Ewanchuk would have been characterized as a "male pig"—and there's no doubt that he is. However, chances are he would have never been convicted of a crime because of the absence of resistance from the complainant. Her passivity would have been taken as a sign of consent, and the court would have concluded that whenever the complainant told him to stop, he respected her wishes. But no longer will the horny men of this country escape the clutches of criminal justice on the basis that they were just testing the waters. With the decision to convict Ewanchuk, the Supreme Court of Canada constructed the law in a manner that effectively tells men they will be criminally liable for wandering fingers on a reconnaissance mission.

First, with respect to consent being implied from the fact that she was submissive and passive whenever the touching first started, the court said: "If the trier of fact accepts the complainant's testimony that she did not consent, no matter how strongly her conduct may contradict that claim, the absence of consent is established ... There is no defence of implied consent to sexual assault in Canada." Similarly, with respect to the complainant's assertion that she was afraid, the court said that "the complainant's fear need not be reasonable, nor must it be communicated to the accused in order for consent to be vitiated."

Bottom line: convictions will be obtained even if women do not express or manifest their fears, and even if women do not express or manifest a lack of consent. Criminality is established once the complainant testified that she subjectively and internally felt this way. Finally, with respect to the accused's perception of the events, the court held: "In order to cloak the accused's actions in moral innocence, the evidence must show that he believed that the complainant communicated consent to engage in the sexual activity in question. A belief by the accused that the complainant, in her own mind, wanted him to touch her, but did not express that desire, is not a defence. The accused's speculation as to what was going on in the complainant's mind provides no defence."[25]

Perhaps Ewanchuk's convictions was justified. Considering the age difference, that the teenager was in his trailer, and that he persisted despite her protests, Ewanchuk was reckless. He was indifferent to her protests. But I worry about what this case may mean for others who still move in a sexual world filled with ambiguity and impulse. If you think my perspective is skewed because of my testosterone, let me quote the words of a female lawyer who has significant concerns with the Ewanchuk formulation of consensual sex. Deborah Hatch wrote:

> The Ewanchuk decision will result in convictions where a woman says "no" but offers no physical resistance, and this is undoubtedly the right result. It will also, however, mean that criminal liability can attach where the complainant says "yes" and even actively participates in sexual activity with the accused but testifies that she did not in fact consent as a result of some factor entirely independent of the accused and is found credible by the trier of fact. Thus in such circumstances, the accused will be convicted notwithstanding that there were no indications of non-consent, and every indication was that consent had been obtained and freely given. Sexual assault has been re-conceptualized to reflect an ideology that elevates slogans above reality. The result is that in the absence of intention, the innocent will be convicted.[26]

Elevating "slogans above reality"—she is so right. "No means no" is a simple, evocative and powerful slogan that has fuelled many of the law-reform measures designed to improve the legal treatment of sexual assault victims. But it is only a slogan. In a 1988 survey at Texas A&M University, 39% of women indicated they sometimes said no even though "they had every intention to and were willing to engage in sexual intercourse." A 1994 survey of American university students showed that 38% of women sometimes said no when they meant yes.[27] For many, sex is a game, and the rules of the game are not necessarily the same as the rules of law.

But the "no means no" movement does not recognize that games are still played in pursuit of getting laid. It is a humourless movement. Just look at the caustic exchange between two judges in the Ewanchuk case. In his original trial, Ewanchuk was acquitted. His acquittal was upheld by the Alberta Court of Appeal. One judge from the appeal court, Mr. Justice McClung, may have spoken his mind too freely. With respect to the complainant, he said, "It must be pointed out that the complainant did not present herself to Ewanchuk or enter his trailer in a bonnet and crinolines." With respect to the accused's persistent groping, the judge said that this "would hardly raise Ewanchuk's stature in the pantheon of chivalric behaviour" and that Ewanchuk's advances "were far less criminal than hormonal." The judge noted: "in a less litigious age, going too far in the boyfriend's car was better dealt with on site; a well-chosen expletive, a slap in the face or, if necessary, a well-directed knee" and said "we must also remain aware that nothing can destroy a life so utterly as an extended term of imprisonment following a precipitately decided sexual assault conviction ... 'No Means No,' 'Zero Tolerance' and 'Take Back the Night' ... while they marshall desired social ideals, are no safe substitute for the orderly and objective judicial application of Canada's criminal statutes."[28]

Although Mr. Justice McClung picked the wrong forum to express his opinions, he is right in many ways. But it's dangerous to express dissent from the current political and legal vogue. In the Supreme Court of Canada, Madame Justice L'Heureux-Dubé put McClung on her lap for a judicial spanking. She said that his comments "help reinforce the myth that under such circumstances, either the complainant is less worthy of belief, she invited the sexual assault, or her sexual experience signals probable consent to further sexual activity," and "minimize the importance of the accused's conduct and the reality of sexual aggression against women." L'Heureux-Dubé claimed McClung's reasoning relied upon a stereotype in which "women should use physical force, not resort to the courts to deal with sexual assaults and it is not the perpetrator's responsibility to ascertain consent."[29]

Madame Justice L'Heureux-Dubé ended her judgement with a "well-directed knee" right into McClung's judicial balls:

This case has not dispelled any of the fears I expressed ... about the use of myths and stereotypes in dealing with sexual assault complaints.... Complainants should be able to rely on a system free from myths and stereotypes, and on a judiciary whose impartiality is not compromised by these biased assumptions. The Code was amended in 1983 and in 1992 to eradicate reliance on those assumptions: they should not be permitted to resurface through the stereotypes reflected in the reasons of the majority of the Court of Appeal. It is part of the role of this Court to denounce this kind of language, unfortunately used today, which not only perpetuates archaic myths and stereotypes about the nature of sexual assaults but also ignores the law.[30]

What started as a case about whether Ewanchuk's sexual advances constituted sexual assault became a political battleground for competing ideologies about getting laid. McClung sees horny men who mean no harm but try a bit too hard to get laid. L'Heureux-Dubé sees the horror of sexual violence reflected in every groping session that ends on a bad note. I wish these judges would fight their political battles on their own time. Their politics skews their judgement. McClung sees a temptress rather than a victim. Instead of seeing Ewanchuk, L'Heureux-Dubé sees every male who has used aggression and violence to extort sexual gratification in the past.

Will we ever be able to get laid without all this cultural baggage getting in the way? For centuries, religion played out its battles in secular courts, condemning adulterers and executing sodomites. Our criminal law still has a few remaining casualties from religion playing out its ambitions in courts of law. Now we have political battles being waged in sexual assault cases. There are fewer and fewer cases and more and more causes. Just when I thought sex was becoming less analytically complex, just when I thought our society could enjoy some lustful debauchery without priests and moral crusaders raising the spectre of hell, the knowledge elites just had to go and reconceptualize fucking as a political statement.

If you don't think that getting laid has become all mixed up with political battles and power struggles, I suggest you enrol in law school. You may find in the curriculum theoretical writings like this:

> Intercourse is commonly written about and comprehended as a form of possession or an act of possession which, because of which, a man inhabits a woman, physically covering her and overwhelming her and at the same time penetrating her; and this physical relation to her—over her and inside her— is his possession of her. He has her, or when he is done, he has had her. By thrusting into her, he takes her over. His thrusting into her is taken to be her capitulation to him as a conqueror; it is a physical surrender of herself to him; he occupies and rules her, expresses his elemental dominance over her, by his possession of her in the fuck. ... The normal fuck by a normal man is taken to be an act of invasion and ownership undertaken in a mode of predation; colonializing, forceful (manly) or nearly violent; the sexual act that by its nature makes her his.[31]

For feminist theorists like Andrea Dworkin (the author of the pre-ceding passage), it is hard to conceive of women ever validly consent-ing to sex because, in a patriarchal society, the consent is often just an unconscious submission to an existing political structure. For Dworkin, "violation is a synonym for intercourse."[32] In this world, fucking is pre-sumptively a crime. I read this stuff and I feel guilty about having a penis. I feel turned off by my usual prurient desires. But after five min-utes, the guilt subsides, and the desires return to form.

One day we may acquire a truly enlightened perspective on sex—one in which satisfaction is enhanced without sacrificing respect and autonomy. But this enlightenment will not emerge in a court of law. Of course, sexual violence must be fought with resolve, but otherwise the law should leave people alone. The less it does about sex, the better. If someone wants to pay for sex, so be it. If someone wants to go to a club where men jerk off on stage, let 'em go. All the law has to do is assess accusations of truly coercive sexual activity, without looking through a lens of political ideology. But the law wants to do so much more. It wants to protect us from things that are "degrading and dehumaniz-ing." To get laid, you should need only the permission of your partner. You should not need a note of permission from Officer Friendly, who works within a legal framework of slogans and stereotypes.

Here's another mindless slogan for you: "Just Do It."

6

Approaching
the Fringe

I HAVE A DREAM. Not as important as Martin Luther King's, but a dream nonetheless. I dream that one day thousands of Canadians will join together on the playing field at the SkyDome, sing the national anthem, and then engage in two days of orgiastic revelry, with every orgasmic minute being displayed on the Jumbotron. Much to my regret, I am not an orgy guy; I would probably be to shy too participate. Nonetheless, I wonder why we don't have any good Dionysian festivals any more. In modern times, a "day off" means a day off from work; in ancient times, it meant a day off from everything. We need a modern-day Saturnalia.

People can maintain the facade of social and legal propriety for only so long. Once in a while all hell has to break loose, and through ritual some degree of order can be maintained. The Roman festival Saturnalia was a time for the Lord of Misrule to take over. The conventions and rules of society were suspended. Slaves derided masters, employees mocked employers and holy men were profaned. Invariably, the festivals were crowned by drunken orgies. These "fuck you" festivals continued into pagan Europe—the Festival of the Fool, the Festival of Madmen, the Festival of the Ass—until the Church put an end to these ancient "raves." The Church really had no choice. These festivals were a complete inversion of the social order, and the Church was commonly the subject of the fiercest derision and satire in festival times. Today, instead of Saturnalia, we have Valentine's Day. Instead of mass fucking, people send cards.

A good, old-fashioned Dionysian festival to let off all that gritty, urban steam would be a good thing. We never invert values anymore. We never take a day off from the law. And public orgies are criminal. There are limits to the enormous sexual liberty granted in modern times, and having too many cooks in the kitchen is one of the ways that fantastic sex fantasies can become legal nightmares. Public exhibitions of sexual behaviour and orgies may not be considered "fringe" by a lot of people, but they still are beyond the legal pale.

In recent years, there have been two distinct phases in the legal response to alternative sexual lifestyles. The sexual revolution of the late 1960s led to the decadent, tight-panted, cocaine-laden, Looking for Goodbar 1970s. Sexual mores were shifting, but the law stood resilient. Even the play *Hair*, with its one nude scene, attracted the attention of Canadian criminal law. People were exploding sexually, and the law was there to ensure that they did not explode into public spaces. Experimental theatre, strip clubs and gay bars were monitored to ensure that Canadians would not be exposed to raw sexuality. Trudeau said that the state had no business in the bedrooms of Canadians, but he said nothing about bars, boardrooms and brothels. The law was now prepared to tolerate fellatio, cunnilingus and intercourse in private spaces, but it remained vigilant guarding against excursions into the public domain. The law has, for many years, allowed women to bump and grind on a catwalk for male audiences, but that was the extent of our tolerance; any physical contact in these public spaces would bring Officer Friendly to the rescue.

Through the seventies, there were periodic clashes between the law and sexuality that oozes into public spaces. The law could not keep up with the rapidly evolving sexual mores. It had to make do with intervening on occasion to remind Canadians that there were limits to their newfound sexual freedom. The rapid evolution of sexual mores ground to a halt in the eighties. The law was able to take a nap. This was the decade of "Just Say No." Pleasure-seeking was reconstructed as vice, and the advent of AIDS put a real damper on sexual freedom. Swingers' clubs, like Plato's Retreat in New York, went the way of disco and bell-bottoms. The eighties had about as much eroticism as Nancy Reagan. But there was no way that the sobriety of the eighties could kill the lascivious spirit of the sixties and seventies. Everything was just dormant. Slowly through the nineties, drug consumption and sexual experimentation started to increase again.

Hedonism is an irresistible force that, once unleashed, will never be completely subdued. And many people will never be satisfied by vanilla sex. Some people need to be straddling the public domain to gain private pleasure. Some gay men will want to go to bathhouses to have their cocks sucked by anonymous mouths in dimly lit back rooms. Some heterosexuals will want to get fucked while surrounded by a whole bunch of strangers doing the same thing. For some people, misery loves company, and for others, orgasm needs onlookers.

In 1998, L'Orage, a swingers' club in Montreal, was taken down by the police. More than 300 people were members of this club. For an annual fee of $200 and a cover charge of $30, members could attend evenings of group sex. Now that's value for your dollar! For the state, this was not seen as giving more bang for the buck, it was seen as a bawdy house. On raiding the club, the police found twenty-two nude people tangled in twosomes, foursomes and larger groups. The raid capped two years of cat-and-mouse games. Undercover police paid visits to the club no less than seven times. The club operators were charged with running a bawdy house. The judge who heard the case handed down a condemnatory verdict, calling the swinging lifestyle "degrading and dehumanizing for all participants and incompatible with the acceptance of human dignity."[1]

Is L'Orage the modern Sodom and Gomorrah? Hardly. In the biblical version, the cities of Sodom and Gomorrah were destroyed. L'Orage was sentenced to a $2500 fine.[2] In the biblical version, Lot visited Sodom and Gomorrah once before God decided to destroy these cities of sexual ill-repute. Officers had to visit L'Orage seven times before taking down this house of ill-repute. They were probably having the time of their lives. This was a way better undercover assignment than real work like infiltrating the inner circle of organized crime.

Once again the unconventional expression of sexuality was met in criminal court with the judicial maxim "degrading and dehumanizing." It is this mindless expression that establishes the boundary for acceptable fringe behaviour. The law patrols public expression of sexuality in three ways. All three ways target "indecency," thus all three are controlled by the notion of community standards and its handmaiden, the degrading and dehumanizing. First, s. 173 prohibits "indecent acts in a public place in the presence of one or more persons." This offence itself appears to criminalize Saturnalian orgies other than small-scale swapping among acquaintances in the privacy of someone's home. Second, the owner and managers of public places being used for sexual activity can be found guilty of keeping a common "bawdy house for the practice of acts of indecency" under s. 210. A bawdy house can also be a place resorted to for prostitution, but the "indecency" branch of the crime is broader. It monitors and regulates sexual practices short of, and different from, conventional heterosexual intercourse for hire. Finally, s. 167 criminalizes "immoral, indecent or obscene" theatrical performances. Once you take your sexuality out of your bedroom, you enter the world of the indecency patrol. The law has settled on indecency as the vague dividing line between what is tolerated and what is taboo, but nobody knows exactly when the public expression of sexuality becomes indecent.

In a modern twist, gay men and women are allowed to get away with a lot more public expressions of sexuality than are heterosexual people. Less than 200 years ago, we were publicly lynching the sodomites; now they are setting the standards for public displays of sexuality. From the point of view of both the law and popular culture, it is hard to see gay sex as fringe activity any more. Homosexuals have been persecuted in the past, and they still suffer discrimination in many facets of their day-to-day lives. Many homophobes are still breeding, and some of them are dangerous. But the law is no longer the feared nemesis of gay men. Gay magazines and videos have been disproportionately targeted in the enforcement of obscenity laws and customs regulation.[3] This is a problem. However, I am not talking here about literature and cinematic depiction of gay sexuality; I am talking about sexual conduct in public spaces. There is a greater element of Saturnalia in the gay community, and it can often spill into public spaces.

In 1999, the police arrested eighteen gay men for performing indecent acts in a public place. At the Bijou, known as "Canada's only hard-core porn bar," patrons could go to the "slurp ramp" to get an anonymous cocksucking through a hole in a plywood barrier.[4] After a brief media frenzy, all charges were dropped. The newspapers spoke of a secret deal between the police and the gay community, in which the police had agreed to turn a blind eye to sexual activity in gay clubs. The following year, a lesbian bathhouse, the Pussy Palace, was raided, but after another media frenzy, the only charges laid related to liquor licence violations.[5]

Gay men and women are painfully aware of their history of persecution and ridicule. For gay people, the "how, what, when and where" of sex is not only about orgasmic preferences, it is intimately related to the fundamental process of identity construction. As a result, the urban gay community has become politically savvy and is able to mobilize a community uproar if their sexual liberty is threatened by state action. The intrusive gay bathhouse raids of the 1970s may be a thing of the past because in current times the police are not prepared to deal with the political backlash that is triggered when they intrude into gay sex. Horny homosexuals have mobilized against the law to ensure greater sexual liberty in public spaces. The homophobic police are now afraid of taking on the gay community, either in the court of public opinion or in courts of law.

When the police raided L'Orage, there was no political backlash. There was no community uproar. There may have been some scathing editorials, but no one stood up for the rights of horny heterosexuals. Heterosexuals are submissive when it comes to legal intrusions upon their sexual liberty. They allow the law to dictate the acceptability of their sexual adventures. Many heterosexuals ignore the law and get their rocks off in an illegal manner, but they are content to live with the legal designation of criminality. They never stand up to protest the law. As a result, the police will intrude whenever they feel like it. Aided by the vague standard of indecency and a compliant heterosexual community, the police become the arbiters of acceptable public sex.

People can do whatever they like in public, as long as it is not indecent. That doesn't tell the horny heterosexual anything specific. A trilogy of cases from the Supreme Court of Canada in the 1990s sets out the current boundary for public sexuality, but this is a constantly shifting boundary that defies clarity and consistency.

The first case in the trilogy, *R. v. Tremblay*, concerned private dances at the Pussy Cat Club in Montreal. In the club were private rooms where patrons could observe a private dance—the novelty being that patrons could masturbate to the dancer's gyrations. The club's security could monitor the private rooms through a peephole to ensure that the activity did not escalate beyond jerking off. On occasion the dancer would use a vibrator on herself as part of the act.

In 1993, the Supreme Court of Canada ruled that this activity was not indecent and that the Pussy Cat club was therefore not a bawdy house.[6] I was shocked. I never thought any court would rule that private masturbation sessions in the company of an erotic dancer was within the community standards of tolerance. The court came to this decision based on a number of factors. First, the activity in question was masturbation, which the court recognized is healthy and safe.

Second, the club had a strict rule against physical contact between dancer and wanker. Third, the activities took place behind closed doors, out of the public's view. Fourth, the court concluded "there was no harm caused by the activities." (Is there ever any?) Finally, the court took into account the absence of any complaints about the club and the fact that the activities of the club were similar in nature to conventional strip or nude dancing available in other Montreal clubs.

For many, the Pussy Cat Club case was a harbinger of a revitalized judicial tolerance of sexual activity approaching the fringe, providing some hope that legal professionals were getting tired of dictating sexual morality. But here's the hidden secret behind all legal precedent: it doesn't mean very much. A case means only what the next case says about it. Lawyers stretch the precedent, manipulate the reasoning and put their legal "spin" on the decision.

We really know what the first case means only after a second case has finished dissecting it. Lots of people construed the Pussy Cat Club case as a green light for lap dancing. Lap dancing was a novelty at strip clubs, and the legality of the dance was unclear. Drawing upon the Pussy Cat Club case, bar owners concluded that offering lap dancing services was within the boundaries of the law.

In 1994, a trial judge acquitted tavern owners who offered lap dancing services in *R. v. Mara*. In this judge's view, lap dancing was not an indecent performance, because the Pussy Cat Club case suggested that far more public exhibitions of sexuality were permitted. Three years later, the Supreme Court of Canada told this judge he was wrong. The Supreme Court did not tolerate dancing that involved touching, grinding on the customer's lap, licking and fondling. The court concluded:

> ... a performance is indecent if the social harm engendered by the performance, having reference to the circumstances in which it took place, is such that a community would not tolerate it taking place. I agree with the Court of Appeal that the activities in the present case were such that the community would not tolerate them and thus were indecent.
>
> The relevant social harm to be considered pursuant to s. 167 [indecent performance] is the attitudinal harm on those watching the performance as perceived by the community as a whole. In the present case ... the patrons of Cheaters could, for a fee, fondle and touch women and be fondled in an intimately sexual manner, including mutual masturbation and apparent

cunnilingus, in a public tavern. In effect, men, along with drinks, could pay for a public sexual experience for their own gratification and those of others. In my view, such activities gave rise to a social harm that indicates that the performances were indecent. ...

It is unacceptably degrading to women to permit such uses of their bodies in the context of a public performance in a tavern.[7]

Here we go again with the "degrading" and "dehumanizing" buzzwords. But this time it is so transparent. Why can't these old men and women admit that they just don't like the idea of adults fondling each other in public spaces, whether for pay, for love or for momentary lust. Stop bringing the community into this. Courts have no real sense of a community standard. And stop hiding behind this bullshit about degrading and dehumanizing. How was it possible for the court to conclude that lap dancing is degrading (to whom?), when it had previously found that it is not degrading for a naked woman to be paid to gyrate erotically in front of a desperate man who is huffing and puffing, profusely sweating and making funny faces till he explodes in a messy delight?

Of course, the court has its answer; it's what lawyers call "distinguishing cases." The Pussy Cat was different. It did not involve any physical contact, and the conduct took place in a private room. Therefore the cases are distinguishable, and one does not govern the other. Is this not a distinction without a difference when it comes to the critical factor of "degrading and dehumanizing"? How does the incidental touching and the public nature of strip club lap dancing make it more degrading than the private jerk-off session?

If you don't believe me when I tell you that legal precedents often mean nothing, let me finish the trilogy. Two years later, in 1999, the Supreme Court released an incredibly brief judgement in *R. v. Blais-Pelletier*, a case in which patrons of a bar could pay for a cubicle dance. In small cubicles for two to four people, dancers would perform an erotic dance. The cubicles could be seen by some of the other patrons in the bar. During the dance, the men were allowed to touch the dancers' breasts and buttocks. This case is a perfect blending of the Pussy Cat Club case and the lap dancing case. Presumably, this should have posed problems for the court's determination of community standards in the context of degrading and dehumanizing behaviour. It did not. The entire judgement reads:

Arbour J. (McLachlin and Major J.J. concurring): Although he did not have the benefit of R. v. *Mara* ... and R. v. *Tremblay* ... the trial judge carefully considered all relevant factors in analyzing the standard of tolerance, which he properly assessed. More particularly, he was concerned with the nature and character of the touching that took place between the dancers and the police, and with the circumstances prevailing in the cubicle. In the present case it does not appear that the judge committed an error of law in his assessment of the standard of tolerance subsequently developed by the Supreme Court. In the circumstances the appeal is allowed and the acquittal is restored.

Iacobucci J. (Bastarache J.J. concurring, dissenting): On examining all the circumstances of this case in light of the tests in *R. v. Mara*, and *R. v. Tremblay*, we find the behaviour indecent and consequently contrary to s. 210(1) of the Criminal Code particularly on account of the sexual contact between dancer and patron and the fact that the acts were not private in nature. For these reasons this appeal as of right should be dismissed.[8]

What a vision of clarity! These are not reasons. They are pronouncements. They are no better than an adult answering a child with "just because." The court grew weary of the game. Is it more or less indecent if the man can touch the dancer but the dancer cannot touch the man? Is it more or less degrading to allow the touching in an open bar, or only in zoo-like cubicles within the sight of others at the bar? If it is not degrading to jerk off in front of a dancer, is it degrading to grab the dancer's breasts and ass while not touching yourself? These are the questions the court would have to address, and I think they just got tired of answering silly questions. Better to just issue a decree.

How are Canadians supposed to figure out what sexual conduct is permitted in public spaces? In the cubicle case, a trial judge found the conduct within community standards, three Court of Appeal judges and two Supreme Court of Canada judges found it indecent, and three Supreme Court of Canada judges found it not indecent. What a silly game, when so many legal professionals take a different position on the operation of the law. But it's a deadly game for any one who wants to explore sex with others in public spaces.

I have never had trouble defending public sexuality, but in 1998 the boundaries of my tolerance were stretched when I was retained to defend sado-masochistic fantasy. Despite some pockets of S/M mainstream chic, sado-masochistic fantasy is indisputably on the fringe of mainstream behaviour. I first heard the expression "vanilla sex" when I was preparing to defend the media-penned "Bondage Bungalow" dominatrix, Terry Jean Bedford. One of my expert witnesses kept talking about vanilla sex. After a while, I realized he was talking about my sex life: Ordinary. Conventional. Plain. Sex without the element of the spectacle. Preparing to defend sado-masochistic conduct in a court of law exposed me to an entirely different sexual world, a world in which fantasy and spectacle reign supreme—a world approaching the fringe.

I still don't completely understand the games of dominants and submissives, but I was never shaken in my conviction that the law has no business in the dungeons of the dominatrix. We are often scared of things we do not understand, but only a coward would run to the law for cover instead of trying to understand the passions that drive people to the fringes of sexuality.

Terry Jean Bedford, a.k.a. Madame de Sade, was arrested in 1994 for operating a S/M dungeon out of her home in Thornhill, Ontario. The first house I purchased at the outset of my career was in the endless subdivisions of Thornhill, and I was amused by Ms. Bedford's choice of location. Amidst young families raising children was a dominatrix meting out discipline and punishment to men and women who craved pain and humiliation. Amidst all the daycare centres and model homes, Bedford entertained scores of adults who paid hundreds of dollars to parade around in diapers, dresses, high-heels and leather. To cap off this delicious study in contrasts, the "Bondage Bungalow" was located right across the street from a church. Centuries ago, Christians would approach heaven by self-flagellation; today fallen Christians approach the sexual fringe on the tip of a whip.

I wanted to represent Bedford, but I could not find her. Four years later, as if by cosmic coincidence, I met Bedford while I was in court working out a deal to keep a pot grower out of jail. I introduced myself to Bedford and told her some professional bullshit about being an expert in the area. Next thing I knew, I was cast in the role of defender of S/M fantasy role play. In the four long years since her arrest, Bedford had hired a high-priced lawyer of some notoriety, and all her money had been spent on a tenuous, procedural, pretrial motion. The high-priced lawyer was now gone, but Bedford's will to fight on was strong. The moment I met this woman I liked her, so it did not bother me that I was being asked to wage a war without any resources.

The problem was, I wasn't sure if I liked the issue. Sure, I had been championing the cause of sexual liberty for years, but that was all about vanilla sex. Personally, I had never approached the fringe, and the little I knew about S/M from movies and books creeped me out. Images of men in rubber masks must have been in some movie I saw as a kid that scared the living daylights out of me; the whole time I worked on this case, I had to avert my gaze from pictures and movies of masked men breathing heavily through the small slit carved out for their impotent mouths.

I have always understood that there is an overlap between sensations of pain and pleasure; it's all about how the brain interprets a neuron firing in the area exposed to pain. So I can understand light spanking, mild whipping and nipple-clamps. But more often than not, the pain was mixed with humiliation and ridicule. I still cannot understand why people would seek out humiliation, let alone pay for it.

A couple of years before representing Bedford, I had seen a documentary on the New York club Pandora's Box, an upscale S/M club for banker and stock-broker types. I saw a Jewish man paying large sums of money to be treated like a concentration camp inmate. I saw a black man blindfolded and all fours, licking the toilet bowl while begging to be treated like a plantation slave. Talk about a baffling mind-fuck. I will never forget these images, and I will never understand the value and attraction of being treated like a concentration camp inmate or a plantation slave. Are S/M aficionados really just sexual deviants? When you approach the fringe, does your healthy lust become an obsessive, dysfunctional fetish or paraphilia? If there was truly something wrong with S/M, was I wrong in championing the liberty to be beaten, bound up and probed? This was the perspective I brought into the case, and I knew I had to get beyond these distracting aversions.

As time went on, much of the sinister associations I had fell away. Most of the S/M conduct pursued by aficionados was not very painful, and the humiliating aspects were so ritualized and scripted that the sting and degradation became muted. Sure, there were some fanatics— people who set themselves on fire, people who are flogged into a bloody pulp and people who endure the most excruciating piercings of body parts. Some of it is macabre. Some of it engages fantastic flights of imagination. In every aspect it is a spectacle.

Bedford was a quiet, demure, sensitive and moral person. She liked the spectacle aspects of S/M and avoided the fanatical and extreme aspects of ritualized violence. Bedford's dungeon was a museum of Victorian artifacts and antique clothing. The aesthetic was dark and heavy. From the school room to the boudoir, to the basement dungeon, every room was a work in progress.

When the police raided the dungeon, over a dozen officers stormed in like a SWAT team. There was evidence that the police pushed the women around. The police played with the whips and costumes. They ridiculed and insulted the women. They needlessly strip-searched the bondage bungalow dominatrix. They ransacked the dungeon. It took two trucks to cart away all the furniture and clothing, although there was no evidentiary need to take everything. The bungalow was padlocked, and Ms. Bedford was denied entry despite the fact that the dungeon was also her home and all the "evidence" had already been removed.

I asked the trial judge to issue a stay of proceedings because of irregularities and illegalities in the way the police raided the dungeon. The trial judge saw only a little "overkill," which gave him "a bit of bad taste." The cops' conduct was only seen as "rowdyism":

> ... if you want to get a reaction from a bunch of young bucks, present them with some imagery of the male anatomy, including images of penises plus equipment for cross-dressing and you might get a rather strange reaction. The reaction which flowed was almost predictable. You know, there was a lot of rowdyism downstairs and hooting and howling and ultimately the officer in charge had to tell them to put a lid on it. I do not know with what word you would describe it. Rude. I do not know. Something along those lines. So nothing, really.[9]

The law called this home a bawdy house, but it really was just a theatre of the absurd. In this home, "The Fly" paid big money to be allowed to buzz around the house all day looking for the mistresses to swat him with a fly-swatter once in a while. As Bedford testified:

> "The Fly" was a young man who was in law school and he needed some release, you know, I mean like it wasn't about sex. This is something physical. He wanted to sweat, he wanted to run, he wanted to have fun. So his scenario was that he wanted to—to pretend he was a fly. And he would buzz around the house. He had free reign to go wherever he wanted and pre-

tended he was sticking to the wall and I'd run around with a squirt gun trying to knock him off. And I threatened to dismember his wings and his little legs and things like that and I was the spider woman who was going to
suck all the mucous out of his body and stuff like that, you know. ... Or he
would hide behind curtains and I would have to—to try to find him and
that's how we would spend the afternoon. ... He would stay for quite a
while. And he ... he ... it was about $150 an hour.[10]

Bedford gave this testimony about "Mr. Floor Tile":

He stayed the whole day, eight hours, and he was hooded and he was—he
was placed on the floor and he was to act as a—as a floor tile. And the girls
would step over him and kick him and wash him and vacuum him and dust
our feet on him and drop food on him, just like a floor tile. And he—he
found that fascinating. And sometimes we'd lift the blindfold so he could
see us. ... That session would probably cost him about $500. There was
nothing involved, really. We didn't talk to him. He was a non-entity.[11]

Not all S/M role play is as non-sexual and whimsical as "The Fly"
and "The Floor Tile." Bedford's clients would provide her with written
fantasies prior to their sessions. The fantasies do not necessarily represent the services provided by Bedford, but they do shed some light on
how some people approach the fringe. A portion of one written fantasy
shows how blatantly sexual these fantasies can become:

At this time i wish to be abused by a male person, being forced to take him in
the ass and then be forced to clean off his membrane with my mouth. AT ANY
TIME THAT THE MISTRESS OR MALE PERSON MUST USE THE WASHROOM,
I WISH TO BE THE TOILET. All through my session i wish to be teased, but
never allowed to cum. At the end of the session i would like to be tied in a
manner that i have to suck my own cock and relieve myself and then made to
swollow my own cum. (i have heard that a person could be tied this way) (and
only if the MISTRESS thinks it safe for me.) If I cannot be tied this way i would
like to have my feet pulled over my head and then forced to relieve myself and
swollow my own cum.[12]

More frequently, though, fantasies did not involve overt sexual
aggression or even requests for sexual stimulation. The following
excerpt is a fairly characteristic fantasy received by Bedford. It suggests
little by way of conventional, orgasmic sexual activity:

Generous mistress, I propose the following science fiction/fantasy background scenario for our session together:

We are both powerful leaders of separate countries with wealth, power, armies to lead and slaves to command. Our countries are in natural conflict because yours is ruled by women and mine is ruled by men. Recently, I captured you, intending to make you a collared and branded slave girl. However, you escaped, and vowing revenge, have decided to capture me. You have several options.

1. You could kill me. But that would be too easy. There is no fun in that. You would like to see me degraded and humiliated and experience what I have done to others.
2. If you make me simply a slave and put me in prison I might escape, return me to my country, and then have revenge on you.
3. You have a device that could transform me into a female (or shemale). If I could be transformed into a female slave I will lose everything. Escape to where? I would just be a collared and branded slave girl, unrecognizable as my former self to anyone. All my power is gone. If I am trained for servitude and feminized then I will owe my existence to the generosity of my new mistress. In this way you have complete victory over your enemy.[13]

This is absurd theatre. Nothing more. Ionesco and Genet would be proud.

The whole idea that the dungeon is a bawdy house comes from an intangible sexual component that pervades it. Most dominatrices and mistresses work in provocative clothing of some sort, and most of the men get hard-ons when being beaten. Once this hard-on emerges, Officer Friendly is called to the rescue. In a true commercial S/M establishment, people are not engaged in conventional sexual activity, but men do get aroused. In Bedford's dungeon, the clients were allowed to relieve themselves after a bondage and beating session. But they still had to be dominated in the process. Bedford wasn't there for her clients' sexual pleasure. She was there to play with her clients' fears, emotions and unfulfilled fantasies. As leather-clad men with reddened buttocks furiously masturbated, the mistresses would ridicule, heckle and snap riding crops at them.

Bedford was charged with keeping a common bawdy house for the purposes of prostitution. In this way, the issue was cast in a weird light:

Is S/M role-play activity a sexual activity? A prostitute provides a sexual service, and the Crown would have to prove that Bedford was providing a service of a similar nature. It seems far more relevant to inquire into whether S/M role-play fantasy is within community standards of tolerance than to ask if S/M activity is an act of prostitution. But remember that the Pussy Cat Club case approved of masturbating in private to a stripper's gyrations. If this was not indecent, then perhaps the state would not be able to prove that Bedford's services were indecent. So the state chose to define this case as one of prostitution.

The cruel irony in framing the issue in this way was that Bedford had emerged from a sordid life of drug abuse and prostitution. She knew what it was like to be abused by men, and her transformation into a dominatrix was part of a conscious process to escape the role of the submissive prostitute. Calling her a prostitute made no sense. Prostitutes relinquish control of their bodies for the sexual gratification of men. A dominatrix controls a man's body for some elusive psychosexual arousal. A dominatrix would never stoop to directly providing sexual gratification for men. This would signal a loss of control, and the illusion of being in a dominant power relationship with the client would be lost. In theory, a dominatrix can never be a prostitute. I just had to figure out a way to convince legal professionals of this.

The plan was simple. I searched out experts from various disciplines and walks of life. Some were S/M practitioners, some were psychologists and psychiatrists, and some were academics with experience in the fetish world. Few empirical studies on S/M exist, and most of the available evidence is anecdotal, personal, literary and speculative. The experts were there for three purposes. First, as part of an overall press strategy, to give the public a better understanding of the issue. Even if we were to lose in a court of law, the case would still be a small first step on the road to law reform, as public demystification is a necessary first step in any law reform enterprise. Second, to indicate that the pleasures arising from commercial S/M activity were not entirely sexual in nature. The experts understood the sexually arousing nature of the activity, but they uniformly focused on the mysterious psychological gratification that accompanies games of domination and submission. Third, to create confusion. We really don't understand S/M fantasy role playing. This lack of understanding would allow me to argue that the Crown had failed to prove beyond a reasonable doubt that S/M activity is sexual activity. Confusion is the polar opposite of proof beyond a reasonable doubt.

The experts noted that 5% to 10% of people have tried S/M, and 2% do it on a regular basis. There are about a dozen commercial dungeons in Toronto, and another forty to fifty dominatrices working out of their homes. Clients tend to be educated, affluent and older. The practice is not necessarily considered a sexual dysfunction, but some 5% of clients do experience distress and confusion regarding their S/M adventures. The experts spoke to the primacy of psychological release as opposed to sexual release. They stressed that "a good scene does not end with orgasm—it ends with catharsis,"[14] and read passages like this from the small body of literature available:

> As theatre, S/M borrows its decor, props and costumery (bonds, chains, ropes, blindfolds) and its scenes (bedrooms, kitchens, dungeons, convents, prisons, empire) from the everyday cultures of power. At first glance, then, S/M seems a servant to orthodox power. Yet, on the contrary, with its exaggerated emphasis on costume and scene S/M performs social power as scripted, and hence as permanently subject to change. As a theatre of conversion, S/M reverses and transmutes the social meanings it borrows, yet also without finally stepping outside the enchantment of time's magic circle.[15]

All the evidence underscored the mystery and paradox of this fringe activity to convey that you cannot judge what you cannot understand. Some people, maybe most, become sexually aroused by S/M foreplay, but that does not mean the purpose of the S/M scenario is sexual gratification. The goal of the trial was to leave the impression that, with S/M, there is much more than meets the eye. The context is arguably sexual, but the experience is a blend of the cerebral and the visceral. For Bedford, S/M was spiritual and therapeutic.

But legal professionals could not see beyond the tip of an erect penis. Despite interesting testimony, provocative musings and an emerging consensus that dominatrices do not provide sexual services, legal professionals operated on a simple, mindless formula: hard-on = crime. The penis overwhelmed their field of vision and the thoughts and words of experts and practitioners fell on deaf ears. With the erect penis eclipsing the real point of this trial, the proceedings became downright ludicrous at times.

Shannon Bell is a professor of political science and specializes in the study of power relationships and sexuality. She had observed, and sometimes participated in, some 200 fetish nights and S/M scenarios. She is a colourful character, and her unique blend of theoretical study and personal experience made her a perfect witness for this trial. Her spin on S/M was that it was all about power inversions and "commodity fetishism in Marxism." Each expert's evidence spun out in a way consistent with his or her field of study, and it did not really matter what each was saying as long as the testimony served to desexualize S/M.

The Crown took the usual adversarial stance, trying to discredit her theories without offering any of their own. But with Shannon Bell, the Crown became more combative and angry. Maybe it was just the time of day, or maybe his time of the month, but the Crown seemed to be verbally attacking Professor Bell. The trial was becoming a S/M scenario. I think the genesis of the attack may be found in Bell's explanation for why some men would be erect during S/M scenarios:

Q. What about the primary objective? Is it one of sexual gratification?

A. The people I've talked to, no, because it's—it's much—it's much bigger, okay. It's much larger than ejaculating, having an orgasm. It's something that's happening with your head. I mean if—if S/M is working well, the body organ that's really going to be working is your head, it's not going to be your penis or your pussy. It's—it's about—I mean there's a level of—I don't know if I—if I want to call it arousal. There's a level of interest, energy and you can call it arousal if you call prayer arousal. If you watch people praying, intently praying, there's almost, in a sense, the same level of intellectual arousal. This may translate into a physical arousal. So I have seen some erections, but I think it's important to remember, you know, being a political philosopher, I think it's important to remember that Socrates died with an erection, most men die with erections. Men get erections when they are afraid. Women get wet when they are afraid. You know, we've seen this in a lot of rape cases, actually, as—as evidence that the woman was—was actually consenting. No. When one gets afraid or one is in pain, one has body responses. So, I don't think it's got—I don't think it's got to do with sex. I'm not talking about people that keep a couple of whips at home and are using them as part of their regular sex play or they keep a blindfold at home and are using it as part of their regular sex play. I'm talking about people who are out in a S/M scene either at a fetish night or in a commercial establishment. That doesn't involve sex.[16]

In my mind, I could see three things about Professor Bell that fuelled the Crown's aggressive approach to her in cross-examination. First, she was having fun testifying; prosecutors get really flustered with witnesses who are not demure or fearful. Second, she said "pussy." Happy women talking about pussy have no place in the courtroom. Third, she provided her thoughts on the meaning of a male erection. How can a woman tell a man what his erection may mean? This is male territory, baby, so keep out! Other (male) witnesses spoke to the nonsexual erection issue: the psychiatrist talked about men becoming erect from a bumpy ride over a country road; another expert spoke of nonsexual ejaculation with the aid of electrical devices. Yet the men were not vigorously cross-examined on this part of their testimony. Only Bell was.

The Crown would not allow Bell to blaspheme the erection. The erection is a sign of male sexual appetite and nothing more. How dare a woman suggest otherwise? It seemed to bother the Crown that this woman would not readily admit that S/M was about sex in light of these obvious erectile facts. So he hit her with the smoking gun of the case—the admission from one rogue mistress, Princess, that she would occasionally massage the testicles of men who chose to masturbate at the end of the session.

Q. What about men that masturbate to ejaculation?

A. Well, I don't believe that the female and male body is all that different. I mean women can ejaculate way more than men and way more often, but I—I don't think it's that different. I have seen men, and this is not in any S/M context, I have seen men that have been with ejaculate without having an orgasm. In fact, some training in tantric sex is being able to both ejaculate without having an orgasm and have an orgasm without ejaculating. They don't have to go together in either body. Take a look at Thomas Lacquer's—

Q. Hypothetically—

A. —work.

Q. —speaking, if you have a dominatrix involved with a submissive who is bound, who is masturbating and masturbates to—

A. Oh, sorry. How can he be masturbating if he's bound?

Q. Well, his arms are free.

A. Okay.

Q. Or his one hand is free.

A. So how is he restrained?

Q. He is on the bed, his legs are in the air, his anus has been shaved, he is masked. One of his arms is restrained, one of his arms is free. He masturbates to ejaculate while the mistress is either putting her fingers in his anus or massaging his testicles. Would you consider that a sexual act?

A. Well, it depends, I guess, is the mistress causing—putting her fingers in his anus to cause pain? Is she massaging his testicles or is she engaging in torture? That is, you know, what you see a lot of in S/M clubs if you want to call them fetish nights is guys being led around with a thing that's tied around their balls, led to a chain. You see mistresses going up, squeezing the balls, bouncing them, leading them around. Now to somebody who didn't know what was going on, they might think those are being massaged, but I'll tell you they're not being massaged.

Q. Do these men obtain erections?

A. Socrates, when he was dying, had an erection. When men get scared, they get hard.

Q. How do you know this?

A. I've been around.[17]

What a profound debate in a court of law! The true meaning of erections—the moral significance of spunk. Jurists rarely get to ponder such rarefied issues. This whole exchange between Bell and the Crown exposed the stupidity of this trial. The law always appears stupid when it needlessly intrudes into private domains. Bell ended the debate by claiming to have "been around," and the only message that should be taken away is that the law should stop getting in the way of people getting around.

The Crown was smug and complacent. It did not want to really engage in the issue of the true nature and function of S/M fantasy role play. The Crown had stumbled on what is called in the S/M world "cock and ball torture" and "ass play." The Crown thought this was the smoking gun. You touch someone's balls or stick something in their ass—it must be sex. Forget the context. Forget the costumes, the macabre setting and the scripted rituals. One person touched another person in a private area—it must be a crime.

Knowing that the law operates by decontextualizing events and filtering reality through a narrow lens, I realized that the Crown had good reason to be smug, with his evidence of hard-ons and incidental genital touching. So I concentrated much of my effort on the court of public opinion. The trial received massive media attention. I saw many articles in mainstream journals on S/M chic, so I knew that the press strategy had value. Sado-masochistic activity remains on the fringe, but the trial was one small step on the road to gaining some legitimacy. With legitimacy will come stronger cries for liberty. People cannot champion that which is alien and scary, so S/M had to be demystified in the eyes of the public.

Terri Jean Bedford was convicted. Focusing on the erection allowed the judge to avoid the question that precipitated the trial in the first place: Is commercial S/M beyond the legal fringe? The judge didn't want to tackle the issue of the proper legal response to alternative sexual practices. As the trial wore on, he became less and less amused. In his own words, "some of the evidence presented, although initially entertaining ... ultimately began to progress to the bizarre and ultimately disgusting."[18] Ultimately, the judge was relieved to be able to say: "A case against the accused has been made without the Court having to get into the broader question of whether every form of S and M for hire is sex for hire. The facts of this case were not difficult to interpret. Common sense allows no other interpretation for a scenario involving a naked man with a rope around his penis being attended to by a female, even more when she is wearing lingerie."[19]

If this incidental touching of erogenous zones is enough for the judge to conclude that the entire S/M session is sexual activity, then so be it. I always thought it was the wrong question to be asking anyway. But the judge still missed an important point of law: A bawdy house is a bawdy house only if it is used that way on a "frequent and habitual" basis. Princess's testimony was based on a few occasions scattered among hundreds of strange and bizarre sessions that had nothing to do with testicle-rubbing and anal insertions. Bedford was wrongfully convicted on the basis of the occasional lapse of a rogue mistress. The judge should have addressed the broader question of whether S/M activity constitutes prostitution. It was squarely before him. Despite the gains in the court of public opinion, we had wasted our time in a court of law.

Bedford was outraged. She had lost her business. She had been forced out of her home. All her possessions and collectibles had been seized. And it had all been for nothing. She wanted to appeal. I was reluctant because I was pretty sure the Court of Appeal would dismiss the appeal, but in a more sophisticated manner than did the trial judge. I was right except for the more sophisticated part. Once again Bedford's entire operation was decontextualized so that the judges could fixate on the erection as the linchpin of criminality. The Court of Appeal equated prostitution with "lewdness" (another term of imprecision) and concluded: "The phrase 'lewd', in my opinion, is broad enough to encompass acts that do not include genital touching but are intended to be sexually stimulating. Further, the appellant's submission in this regard is a bit of a red herring given that the trial judge accepted Princess's testimony about the kinds of services that were provided, particularly the 'erotica' sessions that appear to clearly have involved employees stimulating client's genitals in various ways."[20]

The Court of Appeal tried to send a message that S/M will not be well received in Her Majesty's courts, providing an unprecedented and bizarre interpretation of the term "prostitution." If prostitution is broad enough to "encompass acts that do not include genital touching but are intended to be sexually stimulating," then I guess S/M fantasy role-play is covered. But this definition of prostitution includes within its broad sweep strippers, disembodied phone-sex operators, and Pamela Anderson running down a *Baywatch* beach. The law should never be allowed to intervene simply because of an adult's intention to stimulate or desire to be stimulated. Criminal justice should not be wasting time debating the meaning of a hard-on.

Despite my championing of the S/M cause, I always had a bit of sadness when I thought about some of the characters inhabiting this subterranean world. It's somewhat pathetic that someone has to dress up as Louis XV or as an infant in a soiled diaper and yell *"Vive la France"* or whimper "Mommy, don't hurt me too bad" in order to get a sexual buzz. I find this sad because I still believe that vanilla sex is one of the most magnificent and oceanic experiences available in life's repertoire. Who needs the costumes and the humiliation? Well, I guess some people do. It will always be a bit of a mystery why people seek out pain and humiliation. Theories abound. The only one I gravitated to was the "escape from self" perspective.[21] People who exercise a great deal of control in their professional or personal lives seem to need to escape occasionally from the massive burden and responsibility of controlling others. Temporarily giving up control and placing yourself in the hands of a menacing dominatrix provides a psychic pleasure—a release from the burden of self. It's no coincidence that a large proportion of S/M clients are affluent, powerful people. They can live comfortably with the burden and moral guilt that comes from controlling others only by allowing themselves to be occasionally controlled and punished in ritualistic ways. Bedford always believed that her services were therapeutic in nature.

The notion of escaping the burden of self was probably the impulse behind the yearly Saturnalia of earlier cultures. Once in a while the social order had to be inverted. People had to be allowed to exercise enormous sexual licence at least one day a year. Saturnalia was a safety valve. Letting people approach the fringe every once in a while helps them cope with the burdens and responsibilities of everyday life. We have no modern-day Saturnalia. Sexual spectacles are prohibited by the Criminal Code, so people who need escape from self go underground. They create their own subculture in spite of the law. Here and there the law steps in just to show it hasn't gone to sleep, but it looks foolish in waking. We are *homo ludens*—a species that likes to play—and the law can never take that away.

Nothing good comes from trying to tell people how to have fun. The effort just makes the law look impotent, as perversions will flourish and the spirit of Saturnalia will live forever.

7

Getting Stoned

DRINKING TO STUPEFACTION is a good time. Getting stoned is a crime. When Dylan sang "everybody must get stoned," I was just a young boy. I really didn't like his voice, and I couldn't figure out why he would write a song about the ancient practice of stoning wrongdoers. I was going to a private, Jewish school at the time, and I knew all about death by stoning. I also knew all about scapegoats. The ancient Hebrews released a goat into the wilderness, carrying with it all the sins of the nation. Evil and social pollution were transferred to this poor animal; by casting it away, the accumulated bad karma of the Hebrews was also cast out. What I didn't know was that drug laws were a modern scapegoating ritual.

All ancient cultures had scapegoats to be periodically used to clean the moral stench of perpetually sinning people. To purify ancient Athens, two people, the *pharmakos*, were cast out of the city.[1] Whether they were ultimately put to death and sacrificed or just left to wander in the wilderness is unclear, but what is clear is that all societies had some form of ritual purification through scapegoating animals, people or inanimate objects. The human drive to find a scapegoat is so strong that the Ancient Greeks maintained at public expense freakishly ugly men and women who could immediately be converted into scapegoats in the event of a significant calamity. Famine or plague would strike, and the freaks would be cast out or sacrificed to purify the city.

The impulse to scapegoat is strong. People crave answers in the face of terror. Scapegoating an innocent victim allows scared people to regain an illusion of control over their lives. People believe that every horror has a cause. The universe must be ordered. Nothing is random. Everything is controlled by some cosmic law of cause and effect. Ancient societies confronted a famine by sacrificing a scapegoat to whatever petulant god was wreaking havoc with the environment. Practically useless, but psychologically effective in allaying fear and appeasing the need to take action. Until the Reformation, communities put rats, pigs and cows on trial for tragic events within the community. This impulse to transfer evil continued well into the nineteenth century with the law of deodand: in British law, the deodand, or the instrument of crime such as a knife or gun, had to be forfeited to Her Majesty and ultimately destroyed. The taint of crime infected even an inanimate object and the object had to be destroyed to prevent the taint from spreading like a virus. In the twentieth century, we witnessed the greatest spectacle of scapegoating imaginable—the Holocaust. And in the late twentieth century, the state singled out those who like to get stoned as scapegoats for urban decay.

It is a wonderful irony that the ancient Greek scapegoat was called a *pharmakos*. As renegade psychiatrist Thomas Szasz likes to point out, "the root of modern terms, such as pharmacology and pharmacopoeia is therefore not 'medicine,' 'drug' and 'poison,' as most dictionaries erroneously state, but 'scapegoat.'"[2] The men and women who partake in illicit pharmacopoeia are today's *pharmakos*. State officials want you to believe that our cities are in decay, crime is rampant and teenagers are educational failures because people are taking drugs. Billions of dollars are pumped into the war on drugs on the basis that casting out the druggies will lead to an urban renaissance. This amount of money is never spent on low-cost housing, employment opportunities or education. The state has converted the druggie into the *pharmakos* to cover up its inability to combat many social ills.

In the mid-1960s, American president Lyndon Johnson declared a war on poverty. The Americans quickly gave up on this war, and by the mid-1970s, Nixon had changed this to a war on drugs. Inner-city decay was a product of black men getting stoned. America's youth were too stoned to learn to read and write. Call in the military. Call in the holy ghost. North American society was on the verge of collapse because "everyone must get stoned." As this war unfolded, I was getting high, watching from the sidelines. It all seemed surreal and funny, until some of my friends got caught up in the scapegoating frenzy.

And this is big-time scapegoating. There were 87,945 drug charges in Canada in 2000.[3] In Ontario alone, over $100 million is spent annually on drug law enforcement.[4] And unlike hookers, who quickly plead out and get back on the street, druggies often have long, convoluted trials and end up occupying prison cells beside murderers and rapists.

Millions of people use illicit drugs. If we could arrest them all, we would have to convert dozens of schools and hospitals into jails. If we really wanted to rid society of drug users, we would have to create a gulag of unparalleled proportions. But that is not what we are really trying to do. We pick and choose our druggies at random. Some years we prosecute lots and lots; other years are quieter. Modern drug policy is satisfied as long as we arrest enough users and sellers to create the impression that our cities are safer, cleaner and healthier. Scapegoating and social hygiene are substituted for rational and effective criminal and social justice policy. Modern drug policy is the closest thing we have to an absolute religious taboo. All drugs other than state-approved pharmaceuticals are completely off-limits.

It should be noted that there is an extensive body of literature calling for decriminalization or legalization of illicit drug use. Even hard-line conservatives have begun to jump on the decriminalization bandwagon. You can comb through the literature, but you will be hard-pressed to find many commentators supporting the current prohibitory policy. Virtually everyone who takes the time to study and cut through state-sponsored propaganda ends up disheartened and disillusioned about contemporary drug policy. I cannot possibly do justice to this extensive body of literature, but I can provide some personal thoughts on why waging war on getting stoned is one of the most foolish enterprises ever entered into by an organized state. Much of my experience, both personally and professionally, has been with marijuana, and so most of my comments concern the "killer weed"; however, my comments equally apply to all other "harder" drugs.

Admittedly, when you move from pot to smack the risks are magnified, but instead of calling in Big Brother to scapegoat the smack user, the increased risks simply require greater prudence and responsible planning by the drug user. People will pave their own roads to heaven or hell. In a free society, the path taken in search of paradise is a personal decision. You may end up in a detour where paradise becomes hell, but that is the price we pay for freedom. Freedom does have costs, and some people will fuck up, but the vast majority of drug users, who exercise responsible choice, should not be demonized because a small percentage of their drug-taking colleagues are irresponsible.

Getting stoned is not a manifestation of sickness in modern society. Historically, drugs were an integral part of all pre-industrial religious experiences. Shamans could heal by entering into trance-like states induced by plant hallucinogenics. Tribes could achieve moments of great unity and communion by collectively getting stoned. People largely dismiss shamanism as superstition, and thus we dismiss the relevance of the drug-taking components of these ancient rituals. Nonetheless, the historical prevalence of getting stoned does suggest that the pursuit of intoxication is an integral component of the human condition. Maybe it is even an instinctual drive. Dr. Robert Siegel has made a compelling case that the use of drugs is a fourth drive after hunger, thirst and sex.[5] How else can one explain rats dancing around intoxicated after eating cannabis seeds, or boars digging up and eating the hallucinogenic Iboga plant, or cattle tripping out on locoweed, or snails getting stoned on coca leaves? Every species, from the smallest to the largest, looks for intoxication by ingesting plant products.

The law cannot curb the instinctive drive to get high. In previous centuries, rulers occasionally tried to prohibit mind-altering pursuits. When the Western world was first introduced to coffee and tobacco, rulers prohibited the use of these "vicious" substances, but the prohibitions were always short-lived and quickly forgotten. Why would we resurrect a prohibitory policy that always failed in past centuries? As a species we've done wonderful things with science and technology, but in terms of public policy we are often just groping in the dark.

Throughout the nineteenth century, there was a lot of drug experimentation going on, but as the century came to a close Victorian social engineering and a growing temperance movement combined to demonize recreational drug use. While the pharmaceutical industry started to grow rich developing therapeutic poisons, the law in Western societies started to wage war on recreational drug use. Of course, the temperance movement focused on the evils of alcohol, and for a short time this century we unsuccessfully tried to prohibit alcohol use. But this idealization of sobriety and temperance extended beyond control of the obnoxious drunk. All recreational drugs were cast in a sinister mould and between 1908 and 1940, the edifice of the Western drug prohibition was built. These temperance assholes not only worshipped sobriety, they were dangerous xenophobes. Opium was banned as a way of attacking Chinese immigrants. In the U.S., marijuana was banned as a way of attacking Mexican immigrants, and cocaine was banned partly on the basis that it was believed that black men high on cocaine could not be physically subdued by white law-enforcement officials. Sobriety and racism were indivisible.

Why do people get stoned? The temperance prohibitionist would like us to see this as moral weakness—people escaping reality because they are ill-equipped to deal with the "real" world. This is the demonized perspective. But look at the results of a 1990 California study of adolescent drug use and psychological health, which found that

> Adolescents who engaged in some drug experimentation (primarily with marijuana) were the best-adjusted in the sample. Adolescents who used drugs frequently were maladjusted, showing a distinct personality syndrome marked by interpersonal alienation, poor impulse control, and manifest emotional distress. Adolescents who, by age 18, had never experimented with any drug were relatively anxious, emotionally constricted and lacking in social skills.[6]

This is a critical finding, and it coheres with my personal understanding. Drug abstainers tend to be anal control freaks. This accounts for their anxiety and emotional constriction. Chronic drug users are completely messed up. No question. All drugs are governed by the law of diminishing returns. Whatever initial gains and benefits are produced from experimental drug use are lost over time. It is not surprising that the experimental drug users were the best adjusted in the sample. Altering consciousness is a valuable pursuit. Seeing the world through a different lens can lead to insight. The occasional trip to paradise provides the traveller with a more sophisticated perspective on life back in purgatory.

Admittedly, most young people try drugs solely to get "shit-faced." Beyond its availability, that's why alcohol remains the preferred drug for young people. However, for some, the attraction to illicit drugs relates to their capacity to alter ordinary consciousness. For centuries, people have taken drugs to commune with god. Like the ancient shamans, some people take drugs to enhance creativity or foster spirituality. Those who take drugs to get shit-faced, give terse descriptions of the experience: "I got real wasted last night, man." That's all they need to say because they were just looking for escape, not enlightenment. In contrast, we can look to the Club des Haschichins in mid-nineteenth century Paris. Here the literary intelligentsia of France met to eat a green paste made of hashish, cinnamon, cloves and butter to open their "doors of perception." The poet Baudelaire did not then write, "I got wasted, man." He wrote:

> At this stage of the intoxication, the drug sharpens the senses and the power of perception, of taste, sight, smell, hearing—all participate equally in this progression. The eyes pierce the infinite. The ears hear sounds that are almost imperceptible amid even the most tumultuous din. Then the hallucinations begin. By gradations, external objects assume unique appearances in the endless combining and transfiguring of forms. Ideas are distorted; perceptions are confused. Sounds are clothed in colors and colors in music. One might say that this is altogether natural and that every poetic intellect, in its healthy and normal state, could easily conceive of such analogies. But I have already informed the reader that there is nothing really supernatural in the hashish intoxication; only, through the growing faculties of the senses, these analogies assume an unusual purity and force. The mind is penetrated, invaded, and overpowered by their despotic character. Musical notes become numbers, and if you are gifted with any mathematical aptitude, the melody and the harmony, while retaining their sensuous and voluptuous qualities, are transformed into a vast arithmetical operation; numbers engender numbers, the phrases and generation of which you follow with inexplicable facility and an agility equal only to that of their execution.[7]

Baudelaire's high has much in common with spiritual advancement. If one takes powerful drugs or embarks upon a spiritual path of asceticism and meditation, more sensations and stimuli will be processed simultaneously, leading to an alteration of one's characteristic perceptions and understanding of these perceptions. "To see the world in a grain of sand" is the goal of the mystic traveller. When the mind has been opened, we see hidden connections between disparate objects, and this increased field of vision can lead to the beauty of art or the serenity of enlightenment.

Unlike a true spiritual path, drugs can give you only a taste of the divine; they cannot provide you with a permanent residence in nirvana. Baba Ram Dass told of giving LSD to his guru in India. (Ram Dass was formerly Richard Alpert, a Harvard professor who experimented with LSD along with his friend Timothy Leary.) Ram Dass gave the guru 300 micrograms of "white lightening" LSD. Even though "300 of pure acid is a very solid dose," the guru kept taking more until he had hit 915 micrograms. Ram Dass was poised for an interesting scientific observation, but "all day long I'm there, and every now and then he twinkles at me and nothing—nothing happens!"[8] Apparently, hallucinogenic drugs have no impact on people who have already tasted the divine through natural means. As Ram Dass learned, whether for artistic or spiritual objectives, drugs are just an *upaya* (Sanskrit for method or tool). Glimpses of the infinite can be found in intoxication, but they are only glimpses and they are fleeting. This is the law of diminishing returns: the more drugs you take, the less creative and spiritual you become. On a spiritual path, the objective is to *be* high; with drugs, you only *get* high, then you come down. With every crash, the artistic and spiritual potential of the drug is diminished.

I became interested in drugs because I liked the idea of transcendental hedonism. A spiritual quest seemed more interesting than the common shit-faced approach to drugs taken by my peers. I always liked the idea of an altered state of perception. As a kid, I would spin around madly to induce a dizzy spell. This is the first experience of an altered state of consciousness for most people. As a young teenager, I progressed to hyperventilation. My buddies and I would get together for penny poker, and then one by one we would hyperventilate until we passed out. Cheap thrills.

I remember reading in an Abbie Hoffman book about being able to get high from smoking the dried lining of a banana peel. So, as a fourteen-year-old drug virgin, I decided to lose my innocence by smoking the banana. No matter how much I tried to dry the banana scrapings in the stove, it still would not burn in the amateurish joint I rolled. I took so much time trying to dry the banana that my parents returned home before I could hide the bloated banana joint. Busted. I felt like such a loser. But even worse, I was too embarrassed to tell my mother that I was smoking a banana, so I let her believe I had entered the sinister world of marijuana. As any conscientious parent would, my mother then took every opportunity to show me newspaper articles about the supposed dangers of pot. Even at fourteen, I could see that many of the claims were hyperbolic and hysterical. Instead of succumbing to my mother's valiant efforts to make my body a drug-free zone, I decided to study and research these claims.

The more I studied, the more I discovered the state-sponsored lies and deceit. The more I learned about drugs, the more I wanted to experiment. For many of us, high school was not really a repository of knowledge; it was just a good place to score. My friends and I tried a cornucopia of illicit products. Admittedly, the quest lost much of its spiritual motivation as the hedonism overwhelmed the transcendence. Eventually I realized that the effect of synthetic mescaline seemed the same as the effect from Quaaludes and other downers. I then adopted a strict anti-synthetic position. I refused to ingest any substance that may have been made by a bunch of drunken bikers masquerading as chemists. But I admired the power of plant intoxicants. Ingesting plant intoxicants is about as close as I have ever been to being a vegetarian. I never saw god, so I gave up on hallucinogens too. But I have always remained a recreational pot smoker, sometimes smoking up a storm and sometimes avoiding it like the plague.

Like most drug experimenters, I would have probably forsaken the halcyon days of "high" school, had something in the world of law not forced me to continue pondering the drug question. Lots of lawyers drink. Some heavily. I don't. I couldn't care less if people drink, and I have had my share of drunken stupors in the past, but I couldn't make a graceful transition from court to the bar where my legal colleagues congregated. Sitting in a bar with lawyers seemed weird after spending a day cleaning up messes from alcohol-induced crimes. In court, virtually every case started off with the accused getting drunk. Drinking seemed to be the ticket to hell. My observation is borne out statistically: In Canada, 29% of spousal abuse cases cite alcohol as a precipitating factor, and only 1% involve other drugs. Sixty-six percent of murderers have been drinking before they kill.[9] Pretty scary.

Something did not seem right about a legal culture steeped in booze but so intolerant of other intoxicants. I got angry when I began to understand how the justice system was dealing with druggies. One trial in particular outraged me, and this thrust me back into the world of the potheads. But this time I was their spokesperson.

The source of my outrage was a large hashish conspiracy trial in the early 1980s. I was assigned to cover the preliminary hearing, and for three months I spent virtually every day in Provincial Court with approximately twelve to fifteen potheads who had been charged with conspiracy. With the exception of the ringleader, most of the conspirators were first offenders. These were people who, growing up in the 1960s, acquired a love for pot. This love blossomed into a major distribution ring, with tons of hashish being brought in from Lebanon. Despite the size of the operation, this was a pot case, pure and simple. No hard drugs, no weapons and no affiliation with organized crime. Immediately, I liked these people. They were no different than the goofs I got high with in high school. The difference was that my client and the ringleader were facing potential prison terms in excess of ten years.

A few years before this big bust, the ringleader, Rosie Rowbotham, had made a name for himself as one of Canada's premier hash dealers. Rowbotham gained notoriety at Rochdale College, the free alternative university in Toronto in the early seventies that became a haven for sex, drugs and rock and roll. In *Maclean's* Rowbotham was called "Johnny Reeferseed." Rowbotham's activities earned him a nine-year sentence in 1977. At his sentencing, he made an impassioned speech about the injustice of the law and his determination to continue bringing hash to Canadians. Because of this speech, the police began watching Johnny Reeferseed upon his release on parole. For eight months, the police conducted physical surveillance. For eight months, the police used wiretaps to listen to conversations in bedrooms, living rooms and warehouse spaces. Dozens of people were arrested, and Johnny Reeferseed found himself back in jail.

These hash conspirators were decent, law-abiding, productive citizens. Their only crime was a love of hash and a desire to make money doing something they loved. Even the police seemed to like the group they were bent on destroying. This was a fun-loving group, and the preliminary hearing was filled with laughter. One of my favourite days was when a one-pound brick of hashish was entered as a court exhibit. In law, the accused and their counsel are entitled to inspect any exhibit tendered in court, and, of course, all the accused insisted on examining the exhibit. The brick passed through dozens of hands until it arrived at the prisoner's dock, where Rowbotham stood alone. Everyone else had been released on bail. While the hashish was circulating, the Crown continued its examination of its witness. But in the middle of a question he came to an abrupt stop, pointed to the prisoner's box and exclaimed, "Your Honour, the accused is ingesting the exhibit." We all looked over to Rowbotham, who stood there with a Cheshire grin on his face. Kudos to a freedom fighter who had the balls to make a small feast out of the Crown's case!

Anyway, this was not really fun and games. Rowbotham and my client were both convicted. They received eighteen and fourteen years respectively.[10] The sentencing judge called these conspirators "social bloodsuckers ... they are criminal hoods, not Robin Hoods." (Funny, I thought they were nice.) Ultimately, they went through two year-long trials and two appeals before their convictions were final. Millions of dollars were spent investigating and prosecuting them. For me this was the final straw. I could no longer sit idly by and watch the state destroy people's lives for no reason other than fear of a plant and its derivatives. I was disgusted by an institution whose members could drink themselves senseless and at the same time condemn and severely punish those who smoked themselves silly. To prepare myself for battle, I resumed the drug studies I had commenced as a teenager.

Based upon my experience and research, I discovered five incontrovertible principles about the war on drugs. Here is a brief outline of my findings. This is only the tip of the iceberg.

First Principle: All Drug Law Is Born of and Maintained by Hysteria

The history of the cannabis prohibition is no different than the history of the prohibition of any substance. Hysterical claims are made to justify the appropriation of state funds for waging battle against a killer drug. If these claims were not made, the scapegoating nature of the enterprise would be too transparent. *Cannabis indica* was added to the schedule of prohibited drugs in 1923. There was no discussion or debate in the House of Commons about the inclusion of the drug other than the bald statement: "There is a new drug in the Schedule." Although there was no evidence of a problem relating to marijuana use in Canada in 1923, the unknown Department of Health official who added *Cannabis indica* to the draft of the 1923 legislation would have pointed to the writings of Emily Murphy, a crusading Edmonton magistrate. In 1920 she published a series of sensational and racist articles in *Maclean's* on the horrible effects of drug use and the deliberate debauching of the young by evil, often alien, traffickers. The articles were later expanded into a book, *The Black Candle*, published in 1922. Her views on marijuana were derived mainly from correspondence with U.S. enforcement officials. She quotes, for example, the chief of the Los Angeles Police Department:

> Persons using this narcotic [marihuana], smoke the dried leaves of the plant, which has the effect of driving them completely insane. The addict loses all sense of moral responsibility. Addicts to this drug, while under its influence, are immune to pain, and could be injured without having any realization of their condition. While in this condition they become raving

maniacs and are liable to kill or indulge in any form of violence to other persons, using the most savage methods of cruelty without, as said before, any sense of moral responsibility.[11]

The hysteria is always contained in some official file that no one is ever allowed to see. A 1938 *Toronto Star* report quotes an officer as saying: "Hideous crimes have been committed by smokers of these cigarettes, and we have had reports and investigations that show even school children have been smoking them. Our files also show that many victims are confined to institutions for the insane after smoking these cigarettes for a period of time."[12]

Do not think that hysteria is confined to earlier decades and centuries. Do not think we are too sophisticated to be duped by outlandish claims today. Sophisticated, critical analysis usually comes with hindsight when it is too late because the state has already passed another unjust drug law. Take LSD. Invented in 1943 during an experiment with rye fungus, this drug was praised by *Life* magazine in 1957 for its potential to curb aggression and to enhance vision and creativity. Timothy Leary introduced the drug to the counterculture in the 1960s, and suddenly the praise was replaced with fear of what the counterculture might do with an expanded vision. So in 1970 it was widely reported that LSD damages the chromosomes. A few years later, the supporting studies were entirely discredited. Apparently, LSD does not have a mutagenic effect.[13] This is a good thing. This never made headlines. It was a non-event. Hysteria is newsworthy. Bland accuracy is not.

Remember the 1987 Amtrak–Conrail collision outside Baltimore that killed sixteen people? The forensic toxicologist reported that traces of THC (the active ingredient in pot) were found in the blood of crew members. This made national headlines. The toxicologist subsequently pleaded guilty to charges of falsifying toxicology reports.[14] This was not reported. Hysteria caused the drug prohibition, and it remains the primary tool in maintaining an unjust law.

Second Principle: All Drugs Are Harmless If Used Responsibly

Drugs are harmless! Indeed they are. This is a variation on the argument that guns do not kill people, people kill people. But even though drugs are harmless, they contain the potential for harm. When you play with fire, you exercise caution; the same applies to drugs. People who are stupid about their drug consumption patterns invite disaster.

It may come as a surprise that even the use of heroin does not lead to any permanent physiological damage. The body produces its own opiates, so it is equipped to deal with the introduction of another. Of course, heroin can be addictive, and an addictive lifestyle will destroy your body and spirit. But that is about irresponsible use. Casual users will suffer no ill effects from taking heroin. Just don't share needles.

The statement that drugs are harmless is, of course, idealized. It assumes some degree of quality control in the production of psychoactive substances. However, we live in drug war zone. Drugs are available only on the black market, where there is no quality control. So people will die from taking E at a rave. People will die from heroin overdoses. These drugs may have been adulterated. They may not even be what the seller claims they are. A heroin user accustomed to buying heroin that is only 5% pure will overdose if heroin with a purity of 80% finds its way to the market. These deaths are casualties of the war on drugs; they do not speak to any inevitable and intrinsic risks of the drugs themselves.

The pharmacological properties of illicit drugs are not so powerful that human beings cannot tame them with responsible consumption patterns. The user should be aware of the effects of the substance and then tailor the "set and setting" of consumption to enhance the desired effect. For most drugs, set (one's mental and emotional disposition at the time) and setting (the when and where of consumption) are the most important determinants of the drug experience. Beyond that, the most important maxim in relation to drug use (and any other hedonistic pursuit) is *meden agan*—nothing in excess—the maxim carved in stone at the sanctuary of the Delphic Oracle in ancient Greece.

Third Principle: A Small Percentage of Drug Users Will Destroy Their Lives with Drugs

"I have seen the best minds of my generation destroyed by madness ..." Like Allen Ginsberg, I have seen some great people ruin their lives primarily because of out-of-control drug use. The official, state-approved image of the drug user is a dishevelled and dirty stick-figure, drowning in a pool of its own puke. These people exist. They are usually people who have taken the "shit-faced" approach to drug use. They are sad and pathetic. At times they can be dangerous. But they represent only a small proportion of those who have chosen to experiment with drugs.

There is a commonality to all "vice" activities, whether drug taking, gambling, prostitution or pornography: some of the participants will lose perspective. They will allow the pleasure of the vice to overwhelm their lives. Studies abound that state, for example, that 5% of gamblers are problem gamblers; 9% of cocaine users are addicts; 15% of drinkers are pathetic drunks. Different studies, different numbers. But I have yet to see any study indicating that more than 20% of users or participants in any vice activity lose control over their lives. At its highest, one in five hedonists ruins the party for everyone else.

You can bring in the experts, and they will spin out theories of addiction and dependency. I prefer to look at the problem as relating primarily to an obsessive, addictive personality, and so I focus on the user's strength of will and character, and not on some inherent pharmacological property of the drug itself. Of course, some drugs create physical dependency, which triggers physical withdrawal upon cessation of use. But even knowing this, I still focus on the will of the user, and not the drug. Even with physical withdrawal, the reality is that, for many "addicted" heroin users, going cold turkey is no worse than having a bad flu. For others, it is the media image of the convulsing, screaming lunatic in need of restraint and chemical maintenance. The fact that heroin withdrawal spans this wide spectrum of response underscores that addiction speaks more to the will and character of the user. By the way, I do recognize that withdrawal from alcohol can kill, but this drug has the state's seal of approval, and I am talking only about illicit substances.

Drugs can kill. But the use/abuse ratio is low. And spending billions of dollars on a criminal-justice war on drugs has done nothing to curb the incidence of abuse. If anything it has aggravated the risks.

Fourth Principle: "Just Say No" Is Stupid

In the 1980s, Nancy Reagan told a generation of young Americans to "Just Say No." A "just say no" approach to the drug "problem" is about as intelligent as saying "just cheer up" to someone who is clinically depressed. You can't tell people to just say no to pleasure. The pleasure just becomes that much more alluring. I assume that the Reagan administration came up with the slogan "just say no" because they were afraid that Nancy would screw up if she had to say something more meaning-ful with a few complete sentences.

This myopic approach to drug use demonstrates a failure to under-stand the use/abuse ratio. People learn how to live with freedom when they are given freedom. Telling people to just say no presupposes that people don't know how to handle freedom, that we are all weak-willed slobs who will get caught up in a spiralling web of drug abuse. The state's approach to drug use is horribly insulting to human autonomy.

The "just say no" approach conveys the callous attitude "You had a choice. You could have said no. Now look what you've done. You've fucked up your life. And we're not going to help you. Instead of help-ing, we are going to imprison you. And you know what? We're going to imprison everyone else who uses drugs, to stop them before they mess up just like you." That is the condescending and heartless foun-dation of modern drug policy.

But it gets even worse. Our state-sponsored perspective on drug use has unduly focused on the inherently dangerous psychopharmacolog-ical properties of the drug, without considering the will and character of the actor. It thus denies the significance of the "set." "Just say no" as a political slogan makes the same mistake, but this time it works to obliterate the importance of "setting." Removing consideration of "set-ting" is a sinister political ploy. Let me explain.

Conventional wisdom dictates that heroin is dangerously addictive. Try it once and chances are you will end up hopelessly addicted. So it is best to just say no. I wonder what Nancy Reagan would say when con-fronted with the reality that many hopelessly addicted Vietnam soldiers returned from combat and left their addiction in Vietnam. When they were taken out of hell on earth and returned to native comforts, heroin was no longer a significant recreational pursuit. Perhaps the following story would help Nancy understand:

> The most frequently cited evidence that exposure to opiate drugs causes addiction comes from animal research. Laboratory animals self-administer large quantities of opiates in some free-choice situations, both by drinking opiate-bearing solutions and by pressing levers that inject opiates through a needle that has been permanently implanted in a vein. ...
>
> My colleagues and I designed a laboratory environment for rats that was far more roomy and comfortable than the usual solitary, metal laboratory

cages that were in use. We called our creation Rat Park. Rat Park was amply provided with wood chips for digging, tin cans for general recreational purposes, and other rats of both sexes for social and cultural activities.

Rats in Rat Park and in individual cages were given free access to water and morphine hydrochloride solution. In a series of experiments, isolated rats consumed up to 16 times more morphine than did the animals in Rat Park. Under no circumstances did the Rat Park animals drink more.[15]

What's the moral of the Rat Park story? Setting is critical. When people live in shit, their drive to drown in the pleasure of drugs will be enhanced. People who live impoverished, dreary lives are more likely to drown in the pleasure of drugs. You are less likely to end up lying in a stupor in an abandoned warehouse after having scored another rock of crack if you live in the suburbs with a pool.

"Just say no" suggests that you are entirely responsible for your downfall and that the government bears no responsibility for the failure to address poverty and inner-city decay. For cheap political gain, the drug user is cast as the scapegoat. This pathetic sacrificial lamb is being used to mask the fact that wealthy societies still have countless hordes who live in poverty, with limited opportunities for advancement. This has nothing to do with drugs.

Fifth Principle: Drug Wars Are Moral Crusades

You cannot consider the criminal prohibition on drug use a rational policy. When was the last time, or even the first time, you heard a public official present a report on the successes of the war? We are not even close to living in a drug-free zone. Drug use ebbs and flows independent of any law-enforcement strategies. We spend billions and billions with no apparent results. If drug prohibition was designed to be the rational pursuit of public policy, we would expect to eventually see some positive and encouraging cost-benefit reports. None exist. Because this is not about public policy. It is a moral crusade. Public policy is designed to achieve a stated objective. Failure to achieve the objective leads to abandoning or redesigning the policy. A moral crusade is not evaluated by any measurable degree of success. It is evaluated by how the moral crusaders feel about themselves.

Every time the police make a big bust (they always seem to say it is the biggest ever), they strut their stuff in front of the cameras, showing off the contraband and proudly praising the courageous undercover officers who infiltrated the drug underworld. They are crusaders, but they haven't achieved anything. They throw one trafficker in jail, and three more take his place. Nonetheless, the cops have something tangible to show the public. With most arrests, all the public gets is the fleeting image of felons with their jackets pulled up over their heads. It's all so fleeting. The police show off a room full of drugs destined to wreak havoc on the streets. The police have clearly prevented a horrible tragedy. The proof is right there on the table in the police vault. It is tangible. Everyone should feel good. It doesn't matter if it all means diddly-squat; the crusaders are fighting the good battle.

After they show us the fruits of their battles, we then give them billions of dollars to waste on helicopters, wiretap operations, infrared detectors and lengthy undercover investigations that end in SWAT-team raids on our homes. They constantly violate constitutional rights in pursuit of the drug offenders, and some cops become corrupt in the process. If we were pursuing a rational policy, we would have to consider the impact of drug policy on police corruption, but we don't. Moral crusaders should be allowed to break the law once in a while. God is on their side.

These, then, were the conclusions I reached in my studies during the 1980s. However, it did not seem the time to launch an offensive. The "just say no" decade was not hospitable to cannabis law reform. The Cheech and Chong 1970s had given way to a mainstream culture that frowned on any drug talk that was not state-approved or produced by the Partnership for a Drug-Free America. But something started to change in the 1990s. Pot consumption was once again on the rise, and popular culture lightened up. After hearing many jokes on *The Simpsons* about bongs and the smell in Otto's jacket, I knew the time was ripe for subversive litigation.

The first order of business was to attack the drug literature prohibition enacted in 1988. This strange aberration of law criminalized any literature that was designed to "promote, encourage or advocate the production, preparation or consumption of illicit drugs." There had been no prosecutions under this new law, but it stood symbolically as a roadblock for the publication and distribution of pro-pot messages. Because this law was such a blatant infringement upon free speech, it seemed sensible to go after this vulnerable law before taking on the larger question of drug control. Section 462.2 of the Criminal Code had to be stripped out.

Marc Emery and I had just finished defending the rights of the vulgar in the 2 Live Crew case. Marc was looking for another free-speech fight, as he always felt the obscenity trial was a waste of time. I told Marc about s. 462.2. This was perfect, as Marc had already been selling "grow books" and back issues of *High Times* magazine. So Marc took steps to try to get arrested. He made public announcements about selling grow books and other material that clearly constituted drug literature in law. He invited the police to the store. The police would not take the bait. He arranged to sell the drug literature at a booth directly outside the police station. The police just watched from their building.

By a weird stroke of luck, while Marc was trying to get arrested for this offence in 1991, a friend of his was busted for distributing drug literature in London, Ontario. This friend had written a recipe for hash brownies that was included in a London restaurant guide. The recipe was supposed to be a parody of the recipe for Hashish Fudge in the famous 1954 *Alice B. Toklas Cookbook*. The first-ever drug literature prosecution in Canada was for a whimsical recipe. What idiots! It would have been far better for the police to arrest pushy Marc for selling "how-to books" on growing marijuana and producing other drugs than to arrest his quiet friend for a joke gone bad. Marc connected me with his friend, and I put together the materials to launch the constitutional challenge to this silly offence.

After I had spent hours completing the documentary materials needed for the challenge, the Crown withdrew the charge at the eleventh hour. I was pissed. They could have withdrawn the charge long before I had gone to the trouble to prepare all the materials. But prosecutors love to play this game: Don't make a decision until the very last minute. Why? Because I can.

I was left looking for a human face to put to my constitutional challenge. Marc grew tired of shit-disturbing and left for Asia. I started speaking with the director of the National Organization for the Reform of Marijuana Laws (NORML) Canada, Umberto Iorfida, about this law and other cannabis issues. Another stroke of luck. In 1992, the police in York region decided to raid Iorfida's home on a tip that he was selling drugs. Of course, they were barking up the wrong tree, and the raid started to look political when I discovered that the police had seized all the books and pamphlets in Umberto's home. He was charged with distributing drug literature, but the charges were withdrawn a few months later. Not wishing to lose a good opportunity, I figured out a way to sue the police for their actions, and thus indirectly get the law before the court for challenge.

In 1994, we convinced the court that the drug literature prohibition was nothing more than crass censorship. Beyond criminalizing how-to books, the law's majestic sweep would capture pro-drug messages, which are integral to many political arguments regarding legalization or decriminalization. We managed to kill this censor before it could do any real damage. Section 462.2 was declared of no force and effect.[16]

With this decision, the magazine *High Times* was once again available. Emery returned from Asia, settled in British Columbia, and started to publish *Cannabis Culture*. Pot consumption rates were still increasing, and there appeared to be a renaissance in stoner culture. The time seemed ripe for the second attack. Inspired by Emery, another London troublemaker, Chris Clay, decided to get himself arrested in order to challenge the constitutionality of the marijuana prohibition. Clay was a quiet and polite young man who had started to smoke marijuana only a few years earlier. He had studied the issue and was outraged when he realized that a benign drug was outlawed. He was also incensed that the law prevented sick people from obtaining this medicine and farmers from resurrecting the hemp industry that had existed in southwestern Ontario earlier in the century. Chris decided to sell "clones" (small plant cuttings from which to grow pot) in his store. The first day of the sale, an undercover officer bought some, and Chris managed to get himself busted with little effort.

The state had played right into our hands. We had our case: a committed activist selling clones as an act of civil disobedience. Of course, we had no money. Many of my cases had been done on less than nothing, but these earlier cases involved only my own work and my own time. For this case, we had to come up with some money for witnesses. Emery kicked in some money. Clay raised most of our funds by selling "victory bonds": buying one bond would entitle the buyer to one ounce of marijuana whenever marijuana was legalized. I recruited a former student, Paul Burstein, to act as co-counsel, and we lined up over a dozen expert witnesses to wreak havoc with the marijuana prohibition. Criminologists, sociologists, doctors, pharmacologists, sick people, pot smokers, and Clay and his parents all testified. We played the movie *Reefer Madness* in court. We kicked ass.

To counter our arsenal of experts from every discipline, the Crown relied upon one esteemed pharmacologist. Admittedly, he was a world expert on marijuana, and his integrity as a scientist could not be gainsaid. He had some cautionary words about the risks of marijuana for the small group of chronic users (approximately 1% of all users), but when asked about his political views in cross-examination he expressed support for decriminalization. We asked him on the stand how he felt about the 600,000 Canadians saddled with criminal records for marijuana possession. He said "regrettable."

The trial judge, an older, retired judge with little or no experience with pot, upheld the law primarily on the basis that decriminalizing pot was a decision for Parliament to make. But three extraordinary things happened. First, after the case had ended, the judge was on vacation in England, and he sent me two articles on marijuana from British newspapers. A very small gesture, but extraordinary because it showed that the judge actually became interested in the issue. Second, in a film documentary on the trial, the judge gave an interview in which he acknowledged that he learned a great deal of surprising information. Again, extraordinary, because judges never give interviews, let alone admit that there was a truth that was different than the official state position. Most significantly, we wanted this case to be a vehicle for public education. This was a success. The judge said in his judgement that marijuana is relatively harmless, and that Canada and the United States are "out of step" with the rest of the Western world. The press had a field day. The coverage convinced me that journalists are uniformly supportive of drug law reform.

On the day of the verdict, troublemaker Emery returned to London, Ontario. He gave out pot on the steps of the courthouse. The media people all seemed to be first in line for the celebratory gifts. In court, we had said that at least 2.5 million Canadians smoke pot; on that day everyone seemed to be smoking a big doob.

Despite the fact that the law was upheld, celebrations were held because we had won the battle in the court of public opinion. Newspaper headlines resoundingly declared that "Pot Is Harmless," and the information Paul Burstein and I presented in court started to seep into every nook and cranny of public debate. We asked the judge to make some specific findings based upon our evidence, and this is what he provided:

> I wish to turn now to some statistical evidence which was introduced by various of the witnesses and which I accept as valid. I heard from a most impressive number of experts, among whom there was a general consensus about effects of the consumption of marijuana. From an analysis of their evidence I am able to reach the following conclusions:
>
> 1. Consumption of marijuana is relatively harmless compared to the so-called hard drugs and including tobacco and alcohol;
> 2. There exists no hard evidence demonstrating any irreversible organic or mental damage from the consumption of marijuana;
> 3. That cannabis does cause alteration of mental functions and as such, it would not be prudent to drive a car while intoxicated;
> 4. There is no hard evidence that cannabis consumption induces psychoses;
> 5. Cannabis is not an addictive substance;
> 6. Marijuana is not criminogenic in that there is no evidence of a causal relationship between cannabis use and criminality;
> 7. That the consumption of marijuana probably does not lead to "hard drug" use for the vast majority of marijuana consumers, although there appears to be a statistical relationship between the use of marijuana and a variety of other psychoactive drugs;
> 8. Marijuana does not make people more aggressive or violent;
> 9. There have been no recorded deaths from the consumption of marijuana;
> 10. There is no evidence that marijuana causes amotivational syndrome;
> 11. Less than 1% of marijuana consumers are daily users;
> 12. Consumption in so-called "de-criminalized states" does not increase out of proportion to states where there is no de-criminalization.
> 13. Health-related costs of cannabis use are negligible when compared to the costs attributable to tobacco and alcohol consumption.[17]

In three weeks of court we had managed to debunk close to 100 years of state propaganda. The result of the case was unimportant. The prohibition was starting to crumble, despite being constitutionally upheld.

The case is currently sitting in the Supreme Court of Canada. The decision in the case will probably come out around the same time as this book. It is only a matter of time before Canada stops wasting billions to make cannabis criminals out of law-abiding, productive individuals. It does not really matter what the Supreme Court of Canada does, because the marijuana prohibition will fall like the Berlin Wall. But the fall of this prohibition is not just about marijuana. It is not just about getting stoned. This campaign relates to liberty and the control of information by state agents.

So far, the courts have upheld the constitutionality of the prohibition, based on the notion that smoking pot does not engage a "personal decision of fundamental importance." What would these judges do if Parliament were to outlaw alcohol or golf tomorrow? Suddenly you would see judges considering recreational preferences to be "personal decisions of fundamental importance." Recreation is not trivial. Many people work hard just to acquire the resources to pursue recreational activities. Recreation is an essential component of self-fulfilment and a part of the process of identity construction.

The problem cannot be that drug recreation is risky recreation. Deaths and injury (or their avoidance) are part of the thrill of recreational activities such as bungee-jumping and race-car driving. Risks are everywhere. The *Ottawa Citizen* reported in 1997 that 40,000 Americans are injured each year by their toilets.[18] No one is clamouring for a prohibition on flush toilets and the scapegoating of Sir Thomas Crapper as the anti-Christ. Lawmakers and legal professionals know that recreation is fundamental. They also know that recreational pursuits can sometimes be risky. So what is it that scares these mainstream power-brokers when it comes to illicit drugs? Why do they support recreation by alcohol intoxication and not by pot or opium? The state is not concerned about the health and welfare of its populace. If it was, it would outlaw French fries, chicken wings and spicy fried dumplings. These evil but delicious substances are rotting the gastrointestinal systems of our nation.

The primary fear that drives drug law relates to the close association of drug use with alternative lifestyles, especially those that question authority. Aldous Huxley believed that drugs can expand the reducing valve of the brain, so that familiar information and stimuli are processed within a new perspective. When the conventional can be viewed as surreal by taking drugs, many users will inevitably develop a more critical and questioning view.

In the late 1960s, drug use became associated with Leary's "Tune in, turn on and drop out." Middle-class drug users were moving to communes, talking about anarchism and fucking in a way that was contrary to state policy. As David Lenson, professor of comparative literature at the University of Massachusetts, has so aptly noted, "The real heterodoxy lies in the fact that cannabis's oneiric or aesthetically disinterested consciousness can momentarily detach the consumerist matrix on which the postmodern economy and its social order depend."[19] In plain English, getting stoned is inconsistent with the aspirations of the capitalist state. With alcohol, you may feel like hell the next day at work, but with illicit drugs you will actually question the value of continuing to work for a living.

Fostering alternative lifestyles and critical thought is the essence of true freedom in a democratic society. Indirectly controlling lifestyle and thought through the artifice of drug law scapegoating is just a more sophisticated and secular form of tyranny.

There are legitimate concerns about drug use. Not everyone merrily strolls down the drug path with visions of spiritual advancement. For some, use becomes abuse. Especially with hard drugs, there is a strong possibility that your pattern of use can completely overtake your life. Even pot has some land mines waiting to explode. Schizophrenics should avoid pot. People with heart conditions should avoid pot. Smoking pot may lead to chronic bronchial impairment. But this is all a matter of proper education. We don't need jails to deal with this. We don't need a criminal sanction to prevent Canada from becoming a nation of coughers and wheezers. We need stigma-free sanctuaries for withdrawal and treatment. Providing safety nets for the few people who go over the edge is the only true mandate of the state. Otherwise, the choice to partake in drug experimentation is personal, and part of the whole concept of individual autonomy that is protected by s. 7 of our Charter of Rights.

Even if you believe that a life of abstention is the best way to live, you should be alarmed by the war on drugs. The drug issue is not just about personal freedom. The war on drugs is a war on democratic ideals. The state still effectively controls information, despite constitutional protection for free speech and a free press. In preparing for *Clay*, I discovered that governments spend millions of dollars inducing disease in rats by overdosing them with cannabis. The findings of disease are never replicated in human population studies. We have millions upon millions of long-standing pot smokers in this country, but governments refuse to fund longitudinal, human population studies. In this way they control information and ensure that the orthodox, conventional perspective is never challenged.

Law reform seems inevitable, but it will be slow and circuitous because of one missing piece of the puzzle. What is missing are the voices of all the politicians, judges, police officers and doctors who spent much of their teenage years getting stoned. I wonder where all the stoners are from high school. I know many of them have good jobs, stable families and healthy lifestyles. I know many of them are now in positions of power. But they say nothing. They do nothing. Suddenly, they find themselves in positions of power and control and they don't want to give licence to other people to lose control. Many of these ex-stoner parents tell me they don't want their kids doing what they did when they were filled with the spirit of youthful adventure. Overcoming this hypocrisy is the missing piece of the puzzle. People will always get stoned. Maintaining an illusion of control and sobriety comes at a huge cost. Let's now take a look at the costs. The story now starts to get real ugly.

8

The Wages
of Hypocrisy

O N DECEMBER 1, 1999, the police burst into a home in Abbots-
ford, B.C., armed with weapons and a warrant, in search of pot
dealers. The surprise raid quickly turned into a nightmare. Over
a dozen children were attending a birthday party. The homeowner had a
pit bull. The dog jumped at an officer. The Emergency Response team
shot the dog dead. A young mother and her two-week-old baby were
splattered with the blood of the dead dog. One witness said: "It was gross.
There were chunks of meat from the dog and big globs of blood on the
infant car seat and the baby blanket."[1]

Another fruitless search for the killer weed, and a bunch of kids are
left emotionally scarred. Maybe for life. I know I wouldn't grow up feeling safe around cops if that had been my first childhood experience
with the police. The police are human, I guess. They make mistakes. But
when people carry guns, night-sticks and the power to suspend liberty,
the mistakes can be tragic and violent. These are the dangers we trigger
whenever we turn to criminal justice as a response to a perceived social
problem. This horrible mistake could happen with any intrusive police
activity. It could have happened while they were pursuing a fleeing murder suspect. It would still be tragic, but at least the shooting of a dog in
front of screaming children would have happened in pursuit of something important. But these violent intrusions into the security of our
homes often happen simply because people like to get stoned.

Criminal justice is about violence. It uses violence to fight violence.
Criminal-justice officials are vested with enormous powers. They are a
domestic military. This is often forgotten. A peaceful justice system
would still be an impossibility even in Mr. Roger's neighbourhood. The
institution of criminal justice has to be tough and aggressive because
there are a lot of vicious assholes out there who need to be dealt with
sternly and aggressively. But when the institution's violence is directed

at consensual pleasure-seeking activities, the whole enterprise becomes twisted and ugly.

With consensual crimes, there is no real villain. This is confusing for the average police officer who acts upon a simple good guy/bad guy world view. Policing pleasure-seeking throws cops into an identity crisis. There has to be a villain. So without even being aware of it, the cops turn into villains. Corruption runs rampant in the morality squads of civilized nations. Drug raids are conducted like military invasions. Cops shoot dogs in front of traumatized children. This has nothing to do with the price we have to pay in the battle to make our streets and homes safer. It is much more than just the price of policing—it is the wages of hypocrisy. Criminalizing consensual pleasure-seeking is an exercise in hypocrisy.

Take the example of pot use. Cannabis consumption is particularly high among professional groups. In *R. v. Clay*, we introduced a 1991 survey that showed that 54% of lawyers and 33% of physicians in Ontario have used cannabis. We also introduced a 1977 survey of graduating law students in Toronto, in which 85% admitted to getting high on pot and 70% professed an intention to continue doing so when they become officers of the court.[2] These stats are only the tip of the iceberg. I know plenty of cops, prosecutors and judges who smoke. How can these people feel good about themselves when they are persecuting their mirror images?

The same goes for illegal sex, gambling and obscenity. I already spoke of the demographic of S/M aficionados. Affluent people in positions of power. Sounds like some legal professionals are getting their bums spanked in their spare time. Let's get real. Do you not think that some lonely judges have called escort services for a night of precedent-setting sex? They're human. You don't have to be Saint Augustine to be a judge. You may be an insufferable drunk, but this would not necessarily prevent you from being a cop, a prosecutor or a judge. I am pretty sure that most cops and legal professionals are not murderers or thieves, but many of them are horny pleasure-seekers who are cast in the role of hypocrites. Their professional obligations require them to morally condemn activities they may actually desire and participate in. The prosecution of consensual pleasure-seeking is all about the "pleasure of indulgence and the dignity of disapproval." This dissonance is destroying the integrity of our criminal-justice system.

There is no room for hypocrisy in the world of justice. "Let he who is without sin cast the first stone" should be the aspiration for those who have dedicated their professional lives to judging and punishing others. Hypocrisy is a worm eating away at the core of the system. It takes careful planning for a hypocrite to operate without being detected. No one wants to be seen as a hypocrite. It is a particularly nasty vice. In the traditional Christian and Islamic conceptions of hell, hypocrisy was among the worst of sins. Hypocrites were always consigned to the lowest depths of hell. Pretty ironic, because, historically, many religious types have been the greatest hypocrites. They were clever enough to mask their hypocrisy by taking an extremely hard line against those who were not clever enough to hide the very vice that defined their persecutors. This is a mind-fuck of massive proportions.

The Inferno, Danté Alighieri's fourteenth-century masterpiece, takes us on a magical and frightening journey through the Christian conception of hell. As Danté descends through hell, he passes the lustful, the gluttonous, the avaricious, the wrathful, the heretics and the violent before he meets up with the hypocrites. Only traitors and sowers of discord are consigned to lower depths. In Danté's hell, punishments mirror the crime. They are metaphoric reflections on the suffering caused by sin and crime. For example, murderers lie submerged in a river of boiling blood. Sorcerers have their heads twisted backwards, so that their tears fall on their sorry asses to reflect their sin in having twisted nature with spells and potions. Hypocrites shuffle slowly in single file, weeping from the enormous weight of having to wear leaden capes that appear golden, light and diaphanous to all onlookers. In life, hypocrites hid their vice, so in hell they slowly and painfully collapse from the enormous weight of their deception. And they get no sympathy from the onlookers, as their pain is obscured by the deceiving beauty of their attire.

Hypocrisy is bad karma for criminal justice. In this chapter, I want to take a brief journey into the hell that is created when state officials turn to criminal law to monitor, regulate and prohibit consensual hedonistic pursuits. In previous chapters, I spoke of the pursuit of illegal hedonism as if it was the right of all residents of this country to get laid and get wasted in any manner they choose. Maybe you don't think that the pursuit of hedonism is a basic right. It doesn't really matter, because those of you who do not see the human-right dimension to gambling, prostitution, drug use and pornography will still have to consider the wages of hypocrisy. A simple utilitarian cost-benefit analysis will show that we pay a very high price for little return when we fight pleasure-seeking with legal threats. Whenever desired products or services are demonized by the state, a volatile and dangerous black market is created. If people want something badly enough, someone will find a way to provide it to them regardless of the law. All the law does is create a crime tariff. The product or service ends up a high-priced luxury item, as suppliers charge exorbitant prices to offset the risks of arrest and prosecution. An ounce of pot is sold for $300, when it should be sold for less than $50. Heroin is priced so high that its addicts become muggers, burglars and prostitutes to sustain their habit. There is nothing sadder than a fifteen-year-old crack addict turning tricks for a few rocks.

With inflated prices comes greed. With greed comes violence. The provider of the service wants to protect his investment. The police and the courts cannot help; they would just arrest his ass. So the black marketer resorts to guns and violence. People get ripped off, and people get whacked. That's the law of the jungle. This tape-loop of spiralling violence is most apparent within the drug trade. By embarking upon a drug prohibition, we have created a whole new class of violent criminal: the armed drug dealer. In 1999, Statistics Canada reported that one in every eight homicides is drug related.[3] Most of the time it is a trafficker being killed by a rival. The same report shows that since 1996 the number of gang-related homicides has doubled. Almost all of these deaths occur during turf wars for control of a lucrative drug market.

If we continue to wage war on drugs, we will continue to be plagued by escalating violence. The drug trade provides one of the greatest sources of funding for terrorist operations. North Americans spend billions on illicit drugs only to see the profits from this trade used to bring terror to this continent. Of course, the birth of terrorism has nothing to do with the war on drugs, but one of the products of this war is the perpetuation of terrorist activities. After 9/11, the United States attacked the financial assets of terrorist organizations. How about legalizing drugs? That would really bankrupt many terrorists.

The violence rampant in the drug market breeds violence within law enforcement itself. Here's a chilling example of senseless state violence during a fairly routine drug bust on the street. The cops saw two men exchange money, with one man appearing to take something out of his mouth. The following excerpt from the British Columbia Court of Appeal describes the violence that erupted:

> As the respondent passed by the two officers ran up to him from their place of seclusion in order to surprise him. They did surprise him. Detective Smith identified himself as a police officer. At once, he grabbed the respondent by the throat with both hands and yelled at him to open his mouth. The respondent refused to do so. There was a violent struggle. In an effect to force him to open his mouth Sergeant Warwick twice punched him in the stomach. Still the respondent kept his mouth tightly shut. In the struggle the respondent and Detective Smith fell to the ground. This resulted in the officer removing one hand from the back of the respondent's throat. He continued to apply force to the throat using his other hand. As well, Detective Smith continued to yell at the respondent to open his mouth. The respondent resisted. He continued to struggle, gritting his teeth together.
>
> Detective Smith conceded in cross-examination that he had no training in applying the choke hold which he employed nor did he recall having training with respect to any kind of choke hold. He said that he used the choke hold in this case not only to prevent the respondent from swallowing but also to prevent him from breathing.
>
> When the respondent continued to resist, Detective McKellar took out his handcuffs, knelt on top of the respondent, and yelled at him to open his mouth. Getting no results, Detective McKellar then "took the handcuffs, placed them between the lips and edge of the teeth and began to try to force the teeth apart, inserting the handcuffs and twisting them."
>
> The respondent began to bleed profusely from the mouth area. Detective Smith repeatedly yelled at him to open his mouth. He did not do so. This detective then using his free hand, pinched the respondent's nostrils and noticed blood coming from the nose. Detective McKellar continued his efforts to pry the mouth open. Detective Smith observed "a small, green bundle gurgle to the top of the blood, which was foaming in his mouth."
>
> This was a small green balloon in the respondent's mouth. Detectives Smith and McKellar continued their efforts to have him open his mouth. Eventually it was forced open wide enough for Detective Smith to "flick" the green balloon onto the ground. The detective then immediately released his grasp on the respondent's throat and recovered the balloon. Later analysis found it to contain approximately one-quarter gram of cocaine.[4]

This is not legitimate policing. Dozens of people were killed by police using choke holds in Los Angeles in the 1970s, yet Canadian police continue to choke suspects in search of a few grams of powder. When my dog finds a discarded piece of pizza on the street, I will pry his mouth open to retrieve the prohibited food product. Sometimes it's a struggle. But he's a dog. You can't do that to people, especially not in a futile effort to protect society from the one-quarter gram of cocaine this dangerous criminal was storing in his mouth. In granting to the police the right to use reasonable force, I'm sure we did not expect them to act like psychotic dentists probing for gold in the mouths of black marketers.

The police also like to turn their attention to the anus. Drug law is about monitoring lifestyle, and drug law enforcement is about monitoring bodily orifices. I cannot think of any offence in which it is necessary to monitor bodily orifices. People do not smuggle guns up their asses. People do not carry knives in their mouths. But in recent years, clever drug smugglers have started to use their alimentary canals to smuggle drugs across the border. Condoms filled with heroin or cocaine are ingested in the source country, to be excreted at the final destination. This is a horrible desecration of the body, but black markets never recognize any distinction between the sacred and the profane. With the crime tariff profits fuelling greed, drug traffickers will go to any extreme to get this valuable commodity to eager buyers.

To combat this new scourge, our border crusaders will perform a rectal cavity search based on suspicion alone. Officer Friendly becomes a proctologist. And the courts have no problem with this. In 1999, the Supreme Court of Canada approved of a nine-hour detention in a "drug loo facility" at Pearson International Airport in Toronto. The court called this a "bed pan vigil": the cop/proctologist patiently waited for the suspected alimentary canal smugglers to move their bowels. The shit was then collected and examined. Traditionally the criminal law does not even allow for a one-hour detention if it is based solely upon suspicion. Yet, the court did not see any significant liberty infringement here, stating: "Heroin pellets contained in expelled fecal matter cannot be considered as an 'outward manifestation' of the respondent's identity. An individual's privacy interest in the protection of bodily fluids does not extend to contraband which is intermingled with bodily waste and which is expelled from the body in the process of allowing nature to take its course."[5]

Thanks for the insight about feces and privacy, but what about the nine-hour detention upon suspicion alone? What about the degrading and dehumanizing nature of the investigation? I don't think courts would be so cavalier about the private nature of our excretory functions if someone convinced the state to begin urine-testing judges to ensure that they are not drunk when dispensing justice.

The Supreme Court of the United States has even less respect for bodily integrity. The war on drugs down there is completely out of control. In 1985, the Supreme Court approved of a sixteen-hour incommunicado detention leading to a rectal exam.[6] The dissenting judge noted that "indefinite involuntary incommunicado detentions 'for investigation' are the hallmark of a police state, not a free society." But this did not prevent the majority from giving their seal of approval. These judges, and most judges, operate on the belief that drug traffickers are sneaky bastards—the rules of engagement in this war need not be constitutionally sound. The Supreme Court concluded that the "respondent's detention was long, uncomfortable, indeed humiliating; but both its length and its discomfort resulted solely from the method by which she chose to smuggle illicit drugs into this country."[7] Blame the trafficker for turning police into anal probers. Maybe all those stories about alien abduction and probing are just people's twisted recollections of traumatic drug arrests.

During the heyday of the witch hunts (1450–1750 AD), there were specialists called "prickers" who would unveil witches by searching for the devil's mark, the *sigullum diaboli*, a mark on her body that would be impervious to pain. The prickers would take their needles and prick horribly sensitive spots, almost always on women, foolishly looking for a spot that would not react in pain. The war on drugs is the functional equivalent of the witch hunts, and drug-enforcement agents are the modern-day prickers, committing indignities on the body in search of indicia of criminality. Law-enforcement officials yearn for simple answers to combat the drug trade. Accordingly, both Canadian and American law-enforcement officials have constructed "drug courier profiles" to assist with detection of drug smugglers at the border. Here's a portion of the Canadian drug courier profile that was in use in the early 1990s. Law-enforcement officials are directed to stop and investigate travellers who have:

breaks in eye contact when being questioned, dilation of the pupils, rapid blinking or side to side movement of the eyes, tenseness in the lips or licking of the lips, loss of facial colour, arching of the eyebrows, yawning, lowering of the head and pulling in the chin, pulsing of the carotid artery in the neck, bobbing of the Adam's apple, visible perspiration, tilting the body forward, turning the body away from the officer, rigidity or stiffness of the body, pointing away from body with the hands, putting a hand near the mouth while speaking, touching or rubbing the nose while speaking, playing with their clothes or jewellery, closing of the hands, patting or ruffling the hair, pulling on an ear, scratching, shifting weight from one foot to the other, tapping the foot, shuffling the feet, flexing the knees, loss of coordination or lack of precision in movements.[8]

We have constructed criteria that could apply to all tired airport travellers, or to those demonstrating advanced symptoms of rabies. Yet, as much as the profile is a joke, it provides an easy and convenient answer. To hell with reality—let's just look for the sweaty and jittery traveller and subject him or her to a sigmoidoscopy to see what his or her ass may reveal. When Dickens wrote "the law is a ass," I don't think he ever imagined that the law would end up targeting the ass as a repository of evidence.

Studies in Canada and the United States show that the success rate of airport anal probes is poor—as low as 15% in some cases.[9] Most of the time the authorities decide to strip search the suspicious airport traveller they are barking up the wrong tree. Perhaps as many as four out of five of these travellers begin or end their vacations with an invigorating anal probe. You don't hear about these people. They're just happy to get the hell out of the airport.

Police corruption is another of the wages of hypocrisy. Enforcing an unjust law can never be good for the spirit. The prohibition of alcohol in the 1920s led to an epidemic of police bribery. With consensual pleasure-seeking, there is no ascertainable victim calling upon the police to take action, so it is easy for the cop on the beat to turn a blind eye for a fee. The cop can rest assured that the participants will never complain. The bribe is just a price to pay for an illegal pleasure-dealer to break the law under the watchful eye of a corrupt cop. The illegal speakeasy flourished in the 1920s, and its success was largely due to the fact that owners could pay police for protection from arrest and prosecution. Bribery is less of a problem in current times, but there is little question that the prohibitory drug policies of this century have tainted the integrity of modern policing.

From 1999 to 2001, 115 drug charges were stayed in Toronto because many of the investigating officers were under investigation for various charges of corruption and misconduct.[10] In 1999, I represented a young mother who was arrested for a very small quantity of marijuana found in her home. As is common in all drug raids, the police entered like a SWAT team. A male visitor was allegedly forced to the ground at gunpoint in front of my client's child. My client claimed that after the raid she discovered that $4000 in cash had gone missing from her home. The police file had no record of this money being taken. I spoke to the prosecutor about this problem, and he was very evasive. I did a little groundwork and discovered that some of the officers at this raid were currently being investigated for misconduct. I brought this up with the Crown, and the next thing I knew, the charges were stayed. Apparently, prosecutors want to avoid the embarrassment of prosecuting druggies who may actually be more moral than the cops who seek to condemn and punish. Of course, my client was happy, but she never saw her money again. The simple reality is that drug officers come in contact with large sums of black market money, and there will be some officers who live by Oscar Wilde's maxim "I can resist anything but temptation."

The pursuit of an amorphous enemy can lead certain cops to enforce the law in an overzealous and immoral way. Instead of giving up, these cops gets more and more determined the more they see that the drug war is failing. These crusaders believe that legal shortcuts must be taken to properly enforce the law. Perhaps these cops have seen too many Clint Eastwood movies, but their despair over a losing war leads them to break the law whenever they see fit. The end justifies the means. The best example of this comes not from drug law but from national security. As with drug law enforcement, the enemies to national security lurk in the shadows. The MacDonald Commission of the late 1970s discovered that the RCMP were engaged in all manner of wrongdoing in their zeal to protect national security. They opened mail, burned down a meeting place for political agitators, stole explosives, conducted surveillance on legitimate political actors and associations and stole files. They did lots short of murder.[11] The commission condemned this misguided zeal.

This same concern applies to the drug warrior. Cops break the law on a daily basis in the name of drug law enforcement, and legal professionals appear to tolerate illegalities and constitutional deviations when it comes to drug law enforcement. The trend was set early on. In 1949, the Ontario Court of Appeal wrote:

> Constables have a task of great difficulty in their efforts to check the illegal traffic in opium and other prohibited drugs. Those who carry on the traffic are cunning, crafty and unscrupulous almost beyond belief. While, therefore, it is important that constables should be instructed that there are limits upon their right to search ... they are not to be encumbered by technicalities in handling the situations with which they often have to deal in narcotics cases.[12]

This attitude still prevails. Law-enforcement officials paint a picture of drug traffickers as evil geniuses, so courts continue to give the seal of approval to morally suspect police practices.

In 1991, the police orchestrated a huge "reverse sting" operation in Toronto. At the time, a reverse sting was patently illegal. Playing by their own rules, the police moved one ton of hashish into a commercial storage locker with a view of trying to sell it to potential drug traffickers. The police began negotiating the sale. They took their prey to the locker to show off their hash power. Eventually, a deal was made, but only for 110 pounds. When the prey showed up with the $270,000 purchase price, their money was seized and they were arrested for conspiracy to traffic. Surprise. You are not on *Candid Camera*. This is real. The suckers of this reverse sting received sentences of six and nine years in prison. The way I see it, the only people who committed a crime in this case were the cops. The suckers had a criminal intent, but only the cops committed a crime.

The Supreme Court of Canada couldn't care less. It agreed that the reverse sting was clearly illegal in 1991, but ruled that this in itself did not taint the convictions of the suckers. The Court ended up ordering a new trial on the issue of abuse of process; however, in doing so, it noted:

> Even if it is established that the RCMP proceeded with the reverse sting contrary to the legal advice from the Department of Justice, the result would not automatically be a stay of proceedings ... it will be up to the trial judge

to determine whether or not a stay is warranted in light of the circumstances, including the countervailing consideration that police conduct did not lead to any serious infringement of the accused's rights, the RCMP was careful to keep control of the drugs and ensure that none went on the market, and the acknowledged difficulty in combatting drug rings using traditional police methods.[13]

Why bother with the new trial? There's little doubt that the Supreme Court of Canada is telling the trial judge to convict the bastards. Forget about the police illegality. Let the drug squad have their fun posing as big-time pushers.

Everything about policing consensual crime stinks. Cops have to be proactive in the absence of a complaint or a witness. Cops pose as johns to engage street hookers in negotiation over blowjobs. Cops pose as hookers, strutting their cop-like butts on the street looking for some poor john to bust. Undercover cops snort coke with suspects to gain trust and admission into the gang. Cops put junkies on payroll so they can infiltrate the drug trade. It's all smoke and mirrors. The line between law and crime becomes increasingly blurred.

Proactive policing sometimes leads police to entrap unwary victims, so that a criminal is not caught, but manufactured. In the late 1980s, "buy and bust" operations were in vogue in Vancouver. One day, at Granville Mall in Vancouver, an undercover female officer approached a young male and asked to buy some pot. She had a "hunch" he would be in possession: "I had a feeling. They fit my general criteria. I look for males hanging around, dressed scruffy and in jeans, wearing a jean jacket or leather jacket, runners or black boots, they tend to look at people a lot."[14] This cop would make Sherlock Holmes proud. The scruffy guy was not very interested in making a sale, but his friend took him aside and convinced him to sell a bit of his own hash. Maybe he could get laid if he helped the damsel in distress. So with hormones raging, the young man sold $15 worth of hash to the cop. He didn't got laid. He got busted.

No wonder youth culture has such a negative perspective of policing. Targeting "scruffy males wearing denim" can be only divisive of youth-police relations. This is sad. What is sadder is that the police transformed this horny young hash smoker into a trafficker. Trafficking is a serious charge. This guy was only trying to impress a woman. The state made him into a serious criminal, and the Supreme Court of Canada gave the seal of approval to this "buy and bust" operation.[15] In fairness to the Supreme Court, it has condemned the police for "random virtue testing" in some entrapment cases. But it takes a lot to shock these judges.

Overall, the war on illegal pleasure-seeking has spawned a culture in which civil liberties become diluted. Privacy is becoming an endangered species, largely as a result of proactive drug law investigations. The Charter of Rights provides constitutional protection for privacy, but the presence of constitutional safeguards has served only to curb the worst excesses of drug law enforcement. For less egregious violations, the courts rarely provide remedial relief for intrusions into privacy in search of killer drugs.

Let me tell you a quick story about the drug Ecstasy and its arrival on the criminal-justice scene. Ecstasy has become an integral part of youth culture. Some kids have died at raves, but the vast majority whirl away in a dervish heaven. Years before the raves, in 1976, the RCMP commenced an investigation into the activities of a chemist and his company. The police discovered that the chemist was manufacturing MMDA—now commonly known as Ecstasy. A related substance, MDA, was a prohibited substance, but the designer drug MMDA was unknown at that time, and therefore not banned by criminal law. On June 8, 1976, the RCMP advised Health Canada of its finding, and three days later the law was amended to include Ecstasy as a prohibited substance. No research. No study. No consultation. Just say no.

The RCMP busted the chemist a couple of months later. The chemist wanted to lead evidence in court to show the steps he had taken to ascertain the state of the law. He had no idea that MMDA had been criminalized overnight. The Supreme Court of Canada refused to allow this evidence to be called and convicted the chemist on the basis that "ignorance of the law is no defence."[16]

As a law student, I became curious about what the chemist had tried to do, and I went to the Court of Appeal for Ontario to obtain the original court file. I found out little about the chemist, but I discovered the *modus operandi* of the RCMP. They had made twenty-six surreptitious entries into the chemist's business premises. Initially, they picked the lock, but afterwards they entered at night with a key they had fabricated after the initial entry. The cops were serial burglars. They should have been charged and prosecuted; instead, the chemist was convicted, and the cops were probably praised for saving Canada from another drug nobody knew anything about.

Under the current Charter of Rights, it is unlikely that any court would turn a blind eye to twenty-six break-ins, and the police now have to be more subtle and sophisticated in designing constitutionally suspect investigative strategies. Maybe the break-ins have been curbed by the Charter, but that is about it. With respect to privacy in one's home, there is a widening gap between the rhetorical aspirations of the judiciary and the actuality of meaningful protection for the intangible and precarious privacy rights enshrined in the Charter. The courts have set the threshold for intrusion into a home with a search warrant so low that police can gain entry at whim. An anonymous CrimeStoppers tip, combined with a drive-by of the home identified, is becoming the standard for justifying an intrusion into the home.

This watering-down of privacy protection has taken place entirely in the area of drug law enforcement. Courts rarely exclude from evidence drugs that have been obtained through an illegal search. Perhaps with twenty-six break-ins the courts would exclude the evidence, but for more prosaic violations, the courts have developed a doctrine that serves to legitimate the illegal seizure of drugs. The doctrine draws a distinction between real evidence, like drugs, and conscripted evidence, like confessions, with the former rarely being the subject matter of an order excluding evidence. The scant evidence available shows that, even in the Charter era, the police show systemic disregard for legal and constitutional requirements for a valid search warrant.[17] They don't care. And the courts don't care, especially when it comes to drug law enforcement. Of course, when constitutional safeguards become watered down in the area of drug law enforcement, they become watered down in all other contexts.

The law itself contemplates a significant loss of privacy in pursuit of drug dealers. Canadians rarely think about electronic surveillance, but phone taps, room probes, tracking devices and video surveillance all have the potential to destroy privacy. Combining technology with a crusader mentality poses a great risk for privacy in modern society. Take wiretapping as an example. In 1974, Parliament gave the police this power. Wiretap is a giant vacuum cleaner that sucks up in everything in its path. It can start with one phone and one suspect, and by the end of sixty days it can expand to an entire subdivision and dozens of inno-cent pawns. It is basically an intelligence-gathering tool that operates on a 24/7 basis. It is highly effective, but highly invasive.

During one long drug conspiracy case I did in the 1980s, the probes and taps ran for eight months. The police knew more about the sus-pects than their best friends did. One day on the stand, the investigat-ing officer spoke of a pool conducted by the police in the monitoring room, in which officers were taking bets on when a suspect's marriage would end. The suspect's domestic strife became police recreation. I was appalled, and I have never quite felt the same about using the phone since.

Electronic surveillance was created as a tool to fight the sophistica-tion of organized crime. It never has accomplished much in this area, as the investigative tool is being used mainly for drug investigations. Sure, once in a while the police listen in to thwart a bomb plot, but most of the time they are just listening to druggies talking about mov-ing 10 kilos of "turnips" into some warehouse. There were 932 wiretaps in 1999: 613 were for drug offences (65%), 74 for Customs and Excise offences (7.9%), and 25 for Criminal Code offences (2.6%). A further 220 were for conspiracy offences (23.6%).[18] Conspiracy is a generic offence that, more often than not, involves conspiratorial drug activity. Therefore, it is possible that, with this grab-bag category of conspiracy, almost 90% of all wiretaps in this country are being used for drug inves-tigations. Out of thousands of wiretaps authorized between 1995 and 1999, only five were used for kidnapping, two for extortion, two for robbery and one for murder.[19]

Policing pleasure-seeking has exacted a heavy toll on legitimate law enforcement. After the O.J. Simpson trial, Alan Dershowitz spoke of police testimony as "testilying." Perhaps without awareness, officers exaggerate, confabulate and basically distort history to suit their pur-poses. I know this to be true. I'm not saying that police perjury is sys-temically encouraged. I am saying that police are prone to reconstruct reality through a lens of what is needed for a conviction. "Testilying" is particularly evident in the policing of the sex and drug trades because of the crusading element in this type of law enforcement. No one wants to believe that cops lie. They are the gatekeepers of the system. There is little doubt that legal professionals will be powerless to repair a crum-bling criminal-justice system if the police lack integrity.

Hypocrisy is built on a foundation of lies, so it is not surprising that, when criminal justice enters the world of the hypocrisy, lying becomes endemic in courts of law. We know this, but we really don't care. On September 14, 1996, two officers were sentenced to sixty days in jail for a conspiracy to plant cocaine on a suspect.[20] The suspect had been convicted and jailed for the cocaine, but the authorities eventually discovered the police illegality. Sixty days in jail? You have to be kidding. Sixty days is a kiss. Crack and coke dealers get penitentiary sentences. For example, in 1994, two men received sentences of thirty months and thirty-seven months, respectively, for selling $20 worth of crack cocaine.[21] So crooked officers can plant drugs on suspects, who will end up in prison for over two years, yet they only get a couple months' punishment. When the crack dealers were sentenced, the judge noted that Toronto's drug trade "grows inexorably, like a cancer." When the crooked cops were sentenced to sixty days, the judge noted that the two officers "lost promising careers ... suffering much humiliation and disgrace." Boo-fucking-hoo. The only cancer here is the act of lying in court and planting evidence. This has the potential to completely destroy the legitimacy of our system of justice. Yet, in the world of hypocrisy, the crooked cops are to be pitied and the illegal pleasure-seekers are to be crushed.

I truly resent what the criminalization of pleasure-seeking has done to the integrity of our criminal process. Within the general framework of the criminal law, police, lawyers and judges are all given enough discretionary power to enable them to temper the harsh stupidity of the law. Good people can make good decisions to mitigate the harshness of the law. But, sadly, legal professionals seem incapable of making good decisions in this regard, because being engaged in a process in which you must judge and condemn those who represent mirror images of your desires is not healthy for the spirit. You cannot maintain good judgement, compassion and clarity of thought when you are stuck within the "pleasure of indulgence and the dignity of disapproval."

Dickens had it right when he said the "law is a ass." The frenzied crusade to apprehend illegal pleasure-seekers not only fosters violence and corruption, but it takes away valuable resources needed to combat serious predatory crime. Modern media have painted a picture of the criminal process as an exciting, dramatic and entertaining morality play, and some murder trials fit this picture. But for the most part, criminal justice is a cumbersome bureaucratic maze overflowing with trivial cases of shoplifting, common assault, prostitution and minor drug possession. Thousands of law-abiding Canadians get dragged before criminal courts for pursuing alternative lifestyles, or for their involvement in interpersonal conflicts that lead to minor injury or property damage. These bullshit cases clog up the system, eat up valuable resources and diminish the majesty of the law.

Remember Danté, and the hypocrites weeping from the oppressive weight of their deceptively beautiful robes? Working within an institution plagued by hypocrisy places an enormous psychological burden on all those caught in this world. I know many legal professionals who struggle with nagging moral qualms about their institutional roles. I see lots of unhappiness and misery in the profession. But just like Danté's hypocrites, these lawyers in their fancy suits won't be getting any sympathy. They shuffle around carrying the oppressive weight of hypocrisy, but no one cares because they live in a world where ordinary people dream of killing all the lawyers. Everyone seems to know that something stinks real bad in the halls of justice, but the legal professionals are so caught up in their own psychological turmoil, they can't even smell it.

PART III

Victims, Violence and the Beast

Criminal-justice officials have never understood violence. They process violent cases but never achieve any degree of control over violent behaviour. The circle of victimization will never be broken by legal professionals, who have filtered the reality of both the accused and the victim into a form recognizable only to esteemed jurists. The knowledge elite flourishes, while victims of violent crime get lost in the shuffle. And in this we find another reason to hold legal professionals in contempt: they are so caught up in esoteric doctrine that they have forgotten how to respond in a meaningful way to the realities of flesh and blood.

9

Why We Punish

KICKED OUT OF THE GARDEN of Eden on our naked, vulnerable asses. That's apparently how it all started. Banishment was a real punishment. Not the milquetoast probation or house arrest of today. Banishment was easy and effective. Just cast out the tainted one, sometimes guilty, sometimes sacrificial lamb, and there's an end to the problem, once and for all. Too bad we can't employ banishment today. Our criminals are here to stay. For a short time—sometimes a long time—we lock them away in storage bins called prisons, but most of them come out. They're in our face. There is no modern banishment. At best, we tuck the criminals away for a while and then release them to a hostile world where the law-abiding bourgeois are either too busy to help or too scared to get involved. This is a beautiful system, self-perpetuating and cost-defective.

I always found it odd how we can conduct trials that can last weeks or months, yet when we come to sentence, the whole exercise is done in minutes or hours. Sentencing is treated as an afterthought, even though it is the raison d'être of the whole process. Criminal justice is a blaming, punishing machine. We bother to be meticulous at trial only to make sure we end up punishing the right person. We've more or less figured out how to blame someone, but the punishing part is underdeveloped. We rush through the sentencing hearing because we really don't know what we are doing, so the less time spent dwelling on it, the better chance our incompetence will not be exposed.

The Criminal Code doesn't tell us much about sentencing. It gives judges enormous discretion to choose from a limited array of sentencing options: absolute or conditional discharge, fine, restitution, probation, community service or imprisonment. Very little guidance is provided in the Code.

Whatever happened to that unique and perverse human ingenuity when it came to inflicting punishment? We're the same species that invented the bastinado, breaking on the cross, the ducking-stool, the garrotte, the guillotine, the stocks and the stake. We impaled, beheaded and disembowelled. As Nietzsche pointed out, "in great punishment there is so much that is festive."[1] But now everything is grey. Out of sight, out of mind. Punishment is administered by public officials, and there is no human face to it any more. In the civilizing process, we have become so over-socialized that we have forgotten how to punish. We're ashamed of our vindictive side, so we hide it away in rules and procedures. We have ingenuity when it comes to punishment, but we've become afraid to act upon it.

It doesn't surprise me that the impulse to punish has become a bit muted in modern society. And I don't think it has much to do with the spiritual development of forgiveness or with the civilizing process. We, as a species, still show a remarkable capacity for inflicting horror and suffering when we think we have the right reasons to do so. I think the impulse to punish has become muted because of the trivialization of criminal justice. It's hard to maintain an unforgiving punitive response when the majority of the riff-raff that shuffle through our courts are not criminals in any real sense of the word. We want to punish the cruel and the evil, but we keep coming face to face with the foolish and the reckless, and this kills the burning desire to mete out a stiff punitive sentence.

Contrary to the opinion of many in this country, I do consider a prison sentence to be a harsh punitive response to crime. You can conjure up as many country club metaphors as you like, you can moan and groan about prisoners having televisions and conjugal visits, but I have seen enough to know that prison is not a vacation. The fact that some prisoners have basic amenities should disturb you only when you know that many of them didn't have these amenities on the outside. For some, prison is an upgrade; that says a lot about the relationship between crime and socio-economic status.

The problem is we have no idea what we are doing when we send people to prison. We just pick a number of years, seemingly at random, and say goodbye. We mumble incantations about deterrence, rehabilitation or denunciation, as if this makes sense of the whole exercise. But ultimately, we don't have a clue how to apply theory to practice. Here's a little peek at the law in action, using two cases from the mid-1980s.

In 1981–82, Offender #1 was planning to import tons of Lebanese hash into Canada. He was a quiet, mild-mannered individual with a knack for entrepreneurial organization and a love of hash. He had hooked up with other hash lovers and a knowledgeable importer just released from prison. Offender #1 did not know it, but he and many others were under surveillance, both physically and electronically. The whole gang was followed for over six months.

In 1982, Offender #2 was having an entirely different experience. After a tumultuous one-year relationship, his girlfriend broke it off. Tired of being slapped around, she told Offender #2 to leave her house. Offender #2 was on probation at the time, but not under any surveillance or supervision. On two occasions, Offender #2 broke into his ex's apartment, terrorized her at knifepoint, tied her up, berated her and screamed at her. On the first occasion, she managed to bring him to his senses by offering to have sex with him. It was all she could do to end the terror. A report was filed, but Offender #2's probation officer asked the girlfriend not to press charges, as this would interfere with his ongoing probation. Offender #2 pulled the same stunt about a month later, and again the girlfriend feigned consent to have sex. This time, Offender #2 was charged with break and enter, forcible confinement and rape.

Meanwhile, the police grew weary of following Offender #1 and his confederates and rounded up dozens of conspirators. Most were first offenders. An army of lawyers was called in, but to no avail. After a year-long trial, Offender #1 was sentenced to fourteen years in prison. The sentencing judge called this gang of first offenders "social blood suckers." It took years to settle this mess. Drug conspiracy trials go on forever.

At some point during the unfolding of this conspiracy mess, Offender #2 was also tried. He was sentenced to five years in prison. He was probably out on parole by the time Offender #1 had started serving his fourteen years for being a social bloodsucker.

What type of justice system punishes a hash importer to almost triple the prison time of that given to a man who terrorized a woman? A woman received permanent scars from the assault on her physical and sexual integrity through the actions of Offender #2. This crime is a nightmare. Offender #1's crime, if a crime at all, is merely a nuisance. No one is really getting hurt, but someone is making loads of money from the folly of government creating a black market for this plant product. Yet we believe the hash dealer is deserving of greater punishment than the psycho. We are taking the war on drugs way too seriously, and we are not taking violence against women seriously enough. Only this double-barrelled stupidity could explain the perverse discrepancy between the five-year rape/break and enter sentence and the fourteen-year hash importing sentence. We really have lost our way completely.

I could provide countless examples in which courts were soft on violence and hard on drugs. I could provide countless examples in which similar offenders received disparate sentences, and ones in which very different offenders received the same sentence. I could provide countless examples in which dangerous men walk home from court on probation and harmless con men are hustled into holding cells. I'm not saying that judges never get it right. I'm saying there is nothing *to* get right—it is all arbitrary.

The conventional wisdom is that the public believes judges are soft on crime; however, studies have shown that when members of the public are given full and complete information about a case (as opposed to a newspaper clip such as "Father who brutally abused daughter for ten years gets two years"), most of them end up agreeing with the sentence reached by the judge.[2] With adequate information about the offence and the offender, people tend not to be as punitive as they are when they receive only spicy media tidbits. So does the five-year rape sentence versus the fourteen-year hash-importing sentence reflect the feeling of ordinary Canadians? Absolutely not.

Canadians might feel that Offender #2 received a fit and appropriate sentence, but only until they hear that Offender #1 received fourteen years. Knowing that a pot offender can receive fourteen years makes the five-year rape sentence appear weak and ineffective. If fourteen years is the sentence for large-scale hash importing, then wouldn't twenty years be an appropriate sentence for breaking into someone's home and terrorizing them for hours? Is protecting society from hash smokers more important than protecting our citizen's physical and sexual security? The folly of our sentencing practice becomes apparent only when you look at the whole package. Then you see that the pieces of the puzzle do not fit.

Let's try to put the best face on this picture. Beyond simple ad hominem attacks on legal professionals, Offender #1 committed a crime that required planning and consideration. It was an instrumental crime, in the sense that Offender #1 committed the crime for a distinct commercial motivation. In contrast, Offender #2 committed a crime of impulse, a crime more expressive of his being than instrumental in leading to desired results. Instrumental crimes can theoretically be deterred by law; expressive crimes cannot. It is doubtful that an expressive criminal would consider legal implications before acting; however, an instrumental criminal would consider the impact of the law in making plans to maximize the return on the effort.

An expressive crime, like Offender #2's offence, cannot be deterred, but at least the punishment should reflect society's denunciation of this conduct. Five years presumably expresses this disgust. For instrumental crimes, the law must inflict a harsh sentence to deter this offender and others from trying to commit the crime in the future. Two years might express the necessary disgust at this crime, but we end up tacking on another twelve years to send a message to all wannabe drug dealers.

That is the only conceivable rationale for this gross sentencing disparity. But most legal professionals don't think this way. In most cases, they unthinkingly adhere to past practice and the dead weight of precedent. Judges worship arbitrary benchmarks. When the Code gives judges the discretion to award sentences that range from probation to life imprisonment, they naturally yearn for some more determinate number to play with. Someone picks the number ten out of a lottery drum, and this becomes the new standard. What a relief. There is something to hang one's hat on. Then the sophisticated talk about specific and general deterrence comes to the rescue to provide justification for the ten-year figure that was randomly selected in the first place.

To my mind, five years does not adequately reflect society's disgust for a home invasion leading to a sexual assault. To my mind, fourteen years for hash importation is such gross overkill that it serves only to further trivialize the five-year denunciation of interpersonal violence. Do we have any idea what we are doing? Is our sentencing practice at all consistent with the purposes of punishment? And what exactly are we trying to achieve when we punish other human beings? This is probably the best place to start—the reasons why we punish other human beings. But we never start there. We never ask the hard questions. Instead of thoughtful deliberation, we make the punishment process an assembly line.

Most of the time, punishment is the product of a deal between Crown and defence. The judge doesn't have to ponder—it's all been arranged beforehand. We just plod along. Send people to jail. Make sure we're consistent with past practice without ever questioning whether past practice made any sense in the first place. We refuse to engage in any exercise that requires legal professionals to get their hands dirty by delving into the lives of those they punish. We need a coherent philosophical basis to justify punishing another human being, but legal professionals are loath to get back to basics. Try entering a plea-bargaining arrangement thinking about how Kant and Hegel would evaluate the legitimacy of your proposed sentence bargain. It just messes you up.

Many people think punishment doesn't need to be morally justified. It's just natural and inevitable. You commit a crime and punishment follows. Simple cause and effect. But putting someone in a cage for months or years is usually called forcible confinement, or even a crime against humanity. Punishment must have some justification, or else it is just crime. It is a moral absurdity to commit a crime to punish a crime. There must be some sound philosophical justification to lift punishment out of the arena of common crime.

Let's look at an easy case and try to explain, in words a child can understand, why the offender is being punished. If you cannot explain so that a child can understand, there is a good chance that your understanding of punishment is too muddled by overly sophisticated thought or emotional baggage.

Here's the case. Robert Harris and his brother were planning to rob a bank in California.[3] They spotted two teenage boys in a car and carjacked the boys. Robert Harris released the boys in a secluded spot, and when they turned to run he started shooting at them. Laughing and swinging a rifle and a pistol, he gunned down both boys. He then sat down and ate the lunches the slain youths had brought with them. Throughout the proceedings in court, Robert Harris continued to laugh at talk of his murders. In prison he alienated all his fellow prisoners with his obnoxious, confrontational style. He was sentenced to death, and many of his fellow prisoners were happy he was to be executed.

Robert Harris was the first person executed in California after a moratorium lasting a few decades. Sort of odd that Harris would be the first to fry in a state that spawned Charles Manson, the Hillside Strangler, and the Night Stalker. For what it is worth, I see no moral conundrum in executing criminals dedicated to the infliction of suffering. We kill during war because we feel justified in doing so, and I believe that raping, sodomizing and killing young teenage girls is sufficient justification for taking away a Bernardo's right to life. But, as a practical matter, I would oppose the reintroduction of capital punishment into Canada because we have proven insufficiently wise to competently carry it out. We have executed innocent people, and would continue to do so. Moreover, prejudice and bias taint the process. Studies in the United States show that black men who kill white men stand a four times greater chance of receiving a death sentence than white men who kill black men.[4] We are simply too human to take on a job usually reserved for God.

Putting capital punishment aside, the question is, why is the state justified in punishing Robert Harris? Here are the types of explanations usually given to children:

- He was a bad man.
- He was evil.
- He broke the law/rules.
- He killed another person.
- Punishing him will keep him from hurting others.
- Punishing him may stop other people from doing the same thing.
- Punishment may help him understand the horrible things he has done.

And so on and so on. These are simple explanations easily digested by a child. It is interesting because in simplifying the analysis you then begin to see that the seven explanations fall into two distinct categories of thought. There are really only two ways of thinking about punishment, and then our complex brains take the discussion into a myriad of obscure branches and tributaries. The first four explanations are what I call "just because" statements. He deserves to be punished because he is bad. Why? Just because. There is not much more to say about this. It is a categorical imperative. It is an absolute statement. This is what is called deontological argument. It presupposes that there is a right and a wrong, and that right and wrong are knowable by intuition, reason and emotion.

The other three explanations are based upon utilitarian thinking, which measures what is good or bad for society. It is a cost-benefit perspective, in which punishment is justified not because it is right but because it maximizes social good. Punishment is useful. It can deter the offender. It can deter others. It can be used to rehabilitate the offender. It can be used to protect society.

The past century has been an experiment in utilitarian approaches to punishment. With the rise of behavioural sciences, we started to assume that we understood behaviour, and thus could change behaviour. Punishment without a practical purpose was considered useless cruelty, so we started to invent fictions about the utility of punishment: punishment deters; punishment rehabilitates.

Recently, the shortcomings of the behavioural sciences have started to become exposed and we have realized we know shit about changing behaviour. So the pendulum has started to swing back to a deontological perspective called retribution, in which punishment is justified simply because the offender deserves to be punished. This is a good thing. Utilitarian ambition has led to a misplaced reliance on criminal justice to solve social problems. It has led to the false expectation that criminal justice can be useful. It is useless. As currently constituted it can do nothing to combat crime and make our streets safer. It can punish those who deserve punishment, but even this simple task has been clouded by utilitarian ambition. Offender #1's sentence is pure utilitarian thinking at its worst. I know Offender #1 very well. He is a gentle man who would not hurt a fly and his crime was not a serious, predatory crime, yet he received a sentence second only to murder in severity of punishment solely to deter some mythical others from considering hash importation as a career.

Nonetheless, utilitarian thinking still permeates criminal-justice policy. It is hard to shake, because cost-benefit analysis is the type of thinking we bring to bear on so many daily decisions. But it is an incomplete expression of justice. Let's say that two years into his sentence Robert Harris becomes a born-again Christian. Beyond his prayer and devotion, he starts to write newspaper articles on the evils of committing crimes. He becomes a model prisoner and is instrumental in defusing tension and fighting in the prison. Even so, I doubt many people would show up at his parole hearing to support early release. Sure, he is a changed man. Sure, he will never commit another crime, and is now a role model for crime-free living. Most people would still want him to remain in jail because he cruelly took two young lives. This desire to keep Harris in jail represents the non-utilitarian component of punishment. Even though the best-case scenario has already been realized, punishing Harris is necessary to reflect the enormity of his crime.

More importantly, utilitarian thinking, whether called deterrence, incapacitation or rehabilitation, claims to be a mode of thinking that can be measured and evaluated. Good and bad consequences are presumably measurable. Too bad that every study to date would call into question the utilitarian aspects of punishment. First off, forget rehabilitation. Maybe one day we will be able to modify behaviour, but our rehabilitation programs are currently limited and ineffective. I'll be the first to celebrate if someone discovers an effective mechanism for curbing pedophilia, but until we do we should stop talking about punishment as a rehabilitative tool.

What about deterrence? I'm sure criminal law has some mild impact upon instrumental crimes such as corporate fraud. But it has no impact on expressive crimes. I have yet to see a case in which a "get tough" crime policy has led to a reduction in crime.

Until the 1830s, there were over 200 capital offences in England. People could be executed for pickpocketing and stealing sheep as well as murder and rape. When people were executed, there was a huge public celebration. Loyal British subjects would wait for days to get a good spot close to the gallows. Meat-pie vendors would sell their greasy pies while the spectators watched some poor soul dangle from the gallows. Ironically the best place for pickpockets to ply their trade was at these bustling, public executions. The very sight of a fellow pickpocket having the life squeezed out of his body could not serve to deter, so why do we think some written laws no one reads would be a greater deterrent today? In many ways, the law is completely impotent. Good people will be good and bad people will continue to harm regardless of the law.

If anecdotes don't impress, how about Tennessee's concerted effort to crack down on serious crime? In the 1970s, Tennessee created a category of Class X offences (robbery, murder, rape, etc.), for which harsh procedures were invoked: trial within 150 days, no plea bargaining, no probation and no bail pending appeal. Sentences had to be served in maximum security facilities. A state-wide media campaign was launched to ensure that the people of Tennessee were aware of this law reform. Eight years later, social scientists studied one Class X crime— robbery—to determine if the reform had had any impact. Apparently not. In the Class X era, Tennessee experienced an increase in its robbery rate greater than any increase in any neighbouring state.[5] Getting tough with crime may buy votes, but it sure does not deter crime.

I cannot completely dismiss utility. Utilitarian perspectives on punishment cannot be falsified in any conclusive way. Total chaos very well might break out if criminal-justice policies were abandoned. When the police have gone on strike, there has always been rampant looting and lawless hooliganism. If there were no criminal justice, it is entirely possible that any law-abiding Joe might become a thief, a burglar or a murderer. I doubt it. But still, the institution of law does exercise some control over latent criminal behaviour. I, for one, am not interested in seeing what would happen if we disband our police force.

The institution of criminal justice may be a necessary component in forestalling total moral anarchy, but there is no reason to bring utilitarian thinking into the determination of a fit sentence. If an individual deserves to be punished, he or she should be punished regardless of whether society will benefit. But what does it mean to say that someone *deserves* to be punished? A child might be satisfied that Harris deserves to be punished because he is a bad man, but adults want a deeper explanation.

From the deontological perspective, there are two ways to justify this statement that punishment is the right thing to do. First, we can refer to some other universally accepted principle of justice that we believe to be true. This is a process of argument from logical implications. Or we can show that punishment best accounts for certain intuitive or emotional judgements that we believe to be true. This is a process of argument from an experiential base.

Logic is a fine tool, but the problem here is finding a bedrock principle from which to develop the argument for justifying punishment. So much is relative and variable, it becomes difficult to express a principle of justice that will be universally accepted. But there is something—something drilled into our heads from childhood: the golden rule. Do unto others as you would have them do unto you. Forget the religious underpinnings of the rule. It does express a universal principle of justice that only a nihilist could argue against. And we're not looking to justify punishment to the nihilists; they don't buy into the basic premise of governance.

The golden rule reflects a basic principle relating to the reciprocity of arrangements. Moralists may refer to the golden rule and political theorists may speak of social contract theory, but the underlying notion is the same. People come together to pick rules for the regulation of their mutual affairs. People will make rules to maximize their autonomy as far as it is consistent with other people's autonomy. So people will choose a rule prohibiting murder because they want to live in a society where other people are prohibited from killing. Even criminals believe in the social contract. Most criminals sitting in Canadian jails would be pissed if someone ripped off their possessions. Most criminals would also choose to live in a society governed by rational criminal laws, even though they may fail to always conform to these rules.

When a rule is broken, the social contract is broken. There is a breach in the social order. The state has a right, indeed an obligation, to punish the wrongdoer. We all take on the burden of living within the restrictions of the law, and the criminal has unjustly benefited from a release from this burden. The delicate balance of order that we have all tacitly agreed to live by is upset when someone shits on the rules. If the wrongdoing leads to a domino effect, the whole edifice of social order may collapse. We punish to restore the balance. We punish to denounce wrongdoing and symbolically bolster the importance of the governing law. This is not deterrence dressed up in retributive clothes. This is about a metaphysical balance and the intangible sense of order that this balance brings.

We punish the criminal for upsetting the intangible sense of order that is the whole point of making rules in the first place. Rules impose some order on the absolute chaos of human desire, and from order comes security. When I was a child in the early 1960s, children used to roam the streets in search of play. Today, parents put their children on short leashes. When I was seven, I used to go to the convenience store blocks away on a busy street to pick up stuff for my mom. Today, children are told never to talk to strangers. In the early 1990s, it was reported that 27% of Canadians were afraid to walk in their neighbourhood at night.[6] This is the pathetic price of crime: the reduction of our quality of life as we begin to adopt a fortress mentality, with security systems and perpetually locked doors. This is the upset moral balance that the state must repair through punishment. In fairness, fear of crime is often fuelled by media magnification. Media creates moral panics, but the trigger still is the commission of some heinous crime. The criminal bears some responsibility for the erosion of trust and security. Urban centres are breeding grounds for fear and insecurity. To combat this fear, the state is justified in becoming involved in our conflicts.

Punishment can also be justified by reference to fundamental emotional responses to wrongdoing. Punishment best accounts for the subjective feeling triggered when we are confronted with harmful conduct. If I were to spit into your face for no apparent reason, you would want to punch me in the face. You might not do it—we've all been socialized to different degrees and many of us do not react aggressively even in the face of a threat—but you would think of doing it. You would still have a gut reaction prompting you to retaliate. This is a basic reactive attitude to wrongdoing. We all expect some degree of goodwill and respect from others, and when injury is inflicted on us for no apparent reason, we experience resentment.

Punishment is simply resentment universalized. Empathy allows us to experience objective resentment when we see a crime unfold. We feel indignation when we know someone has been victimized. Punishment is a natural expression of the victim's personal resentment and the observer's moral indignation.

Criminal justice is institutionalized revenge. The institutional part is supposed to keep vengeance within bounds, but it is still about getting even. You can talk about upset moral balance or the breach in social order, but at heart we are getting even. If a virtuous emotion, like compassion, can ground distributive justice (the welfare state), then why can't a negative emotion, like vengeance, ground punitive justice?

Although this is rather simplistic, it does provide a justification for punishing people without having to worry about the fact that most of what we do in terms of punishment is useless. It does not achieve any concrete, good results, but that doesn't matter. It is right to punish simply to maintain the metaphysical balance governing social interaction. Nonetheless, this simple approach gains in complexity when human agency is taken into account. When our dogs piss on the carpet, we punish them immediately. When humans do something wrong, there is a pregnant pause to gauge responsibility for the harm before we launch into punishment. There is no swift justice for humans because of the pregnant pause. We don't punish for accidents. We punish for wrongdoing that is done intentionally or knowingly.

When I spit in your face, you want to retaliate. But if I quickly inform you that I have an exotic illness that manifests itself with involuntary spitting, you'll lose your will to punish. There is no upset moral balance when harm is *inadvertently* caused by another. Accidental harm may trigger a duty to compensate for the injury, but it does not challenge the existing legal order. Intentional harm shows a conscious disregard for the rules of the game. If you disregard rules, you lose your rights and the state acquires the right or obligation to punish you.

The state of mind of the offender is critical to the whole enterprise of blaming and punishing. People who knowingly cause harm manifest moral flaws such as cruelty or indifference to others. To feel good about punishing, we need to be able to conclude that the person being punished is morally flawed. Stupidity and carelessness are shortcomings, but they are not the type of moral flaws that trigger punishment. We may wish to avoid the company of the stupid and the careless, but we don't have the right to punish these people.

In criminal law, we carefully explore the mind of a person who has committed a harmful act. If we can conclude that he or she intentionally or knowingly caused the injury, we can draw an inference regarding his or her moral character. We want to know whether the crime was a reflection of the actor's character or wholly out of character. Although we may be foolish in drawing inferences from only one incident, this is what we do. Punishment is not justified unless the crime was committed with *mens rea* (a guilty state of mind). It is this elusive search for *mens rea* that makes the blaming/punishing game such a difficult exercise.

Once we recognize that the punishment game is really just an attempt to discern whether the accused person is evil or simply misguided, a host of other conceptual problems are raised. We judge the offence, but we punish the offender, so we are forced to at least pay lip service to discovering who the offender is before we lock him or her away from society. But we are often looking only at a snapshot of the offender—who they were at the time of the crime. What was the state of mind of the offender at the time of the crime? Just a snapshot. When we open up the inquiry and really start to look at the people we deem worthy of punishment, some moral ambiguity seeps into the equation.

Take another look at Robert Harris. Robert grew up in hell. His father was a raging alcoholic who abused Robert's sisters and brutally beat Robert. If he tried to seek affection from either parent, Robert would usually end up with a bloody nose. Robert was shunned at school. He had a learning disability, and the family was too poor to seek therapy.

By the age of fourteen, Robert was in a youth detention centre. The youngest inmate there, he was raped and twice tried to kill himself. His mother noted: "the sad thing is he was the most sensitive of all of us. When he was ten and we all saw *Bambi*, he cried and cried when Bambi's mother was shot. Everything was pretty to him as a child; he loved animals. But all that changed, it all changed so much."[7]

So many of the people we punish have already been punished just for being born. Harris should still be punished, but when we open the door to his life, we start to feel sorry for Harris. Ambiguity creeps in, and suddenly we're not so sure how we feel about punishment. The hardship and indignities that many criminals suffer at a young age do not justify or excuse the adult crimes, but they sure cut away at the foundation supporting the practice of punishment. Suddenly, reciprocity of arrangement, retribution and upset moral balance all seem like fairy-tale fluff. When some people derive no benefit from the social contract, when they are outcast, beaten and maligned, it does not make much sense to condemn them for breaking the rules. They aren't receiving the benefits of the rules, so why should they respect the burdens? To truly make sense, retributive justice must be accompanied by distributive justice; we can blame people for disregarding the burden of living by the rules only if they share somewhat equally in the benefits of having rules in the first place.

In my mind, everything starts to get muddy. What about resenting the criminal? You spit in my face, and I want to retaliate. I pause. I determine you are a competent individual who acted knowingly. I work backwards quickly. If you are the type of person who knowingly spit in my face, I can safely infer you are a bastard deserving of retaliation. Your moral character is flawed. But what if you were Robert Harris? What if you had just come from a session of two-by-four justice with a raging, alcoholic father? You're still a bastard, but becoming a bastard may not have been a real choice for you. You have a despicable character, but it's not necessarily a character of your choosing. You're a product of your environment—a product of your genetic predispositions—a product of every shitty thing you have ever been exposed to. Debates about free will and determinism haunt the process of punishment, and when you think long and hard about many of the criminals we sentence, you do realize that not everyone has truly chosen the character they project as their own creation.

The Pharisees were enraged when they confronted a prostitute. As they stood poised to stone her for the crime of adultery, Jesus arrived on the scene to tell the Pharisees, "he that is without sin among you, let him cast the first stone" (John 8:7). Everyone dropped their stones and quietly shuffled away. Taken literally, this famous turn of phrase seems rather silly. Being without sin cannot be a moral prerequisite to punishing. We all sin in some way or another. No true innocence, just degrees of guilt. So why did the Pharisees shuffle away? Well, the story cried out for a happy ending, but more importantly, Jesus exposed the Pharisees to the paradox and ambiguity of punishment. We all have the potential to sin. Some of us grow up in environments that activate this potential in a big way. Some of us suffer immeasurable pain growing up, while others can complain only about not getting enough candy floss at the amusement park. Perhaps the prostitute begging for mercy from the angry mob was one of those people living in poverty and pain. Jesus was telling the angry mob to sober up to this reality. The Pharisees may have been virtuous men, but they did not necessarily grow up in a hellish environment. Their virtue may have been more a product of moral luck than moral choice. And maybe Robert Harris's vice was also a product of moral luck and not a true, unencumbered, informed and free choice to be evil.

How can punishment mean anything when it is based solely on admissible evidence pertaining to the offence charged? True punishment requires a far-reaching exploration into the character of the offender. But who has the time? Do you really think legal professionals even care about this? It would drag them down into the pit where most criminals live. Instead of pondering the paradox of punishment, we do the exact opposite. We make the punishment process an assembly line. It is fast, knee-jerk, uncreative and meaningless. We have no idea how to use punishment so that it reflects denunciation of the crime and is proportionate and responsive to the true character of the offender.

Every criminal before the courts faces the chance of being imprisoned for his or her crime. It doesn't matter whether you are a thief or a murderer. You appear in the same court and await the same fate. The stakes are higher with a murder charge, but it is basically the same type of trial and the same type of punitive response. Prison is not inhabited only by aggressive, psychopathic types; we send the thieves, burglars, drug dealers, brawlers, reckless drivers and con men to the same place.

This is unimaginative. We build these huge fortresses to incapacitate the dangerous. Although prisons are a dismal failure from most perspectives, they do work as incapacitation devices. Few people actually escape from prison. So it makes sense to send the murderer or the rapist there, because some of these people may be dangerous. We should punish these aggressive psychopaths who upset our sense of security by sending them to prison. We get punishment and incapacitation. Not a bad deal. This part makes sense. But what about the thief and the con man?

In a society that values property, it is important to use the criminal law to protect basic property entitlements, but why punish with prison? Prison just breeds crime. Prison manufactures criminals. We should use it only when we have to consider incapacitation. Sure, con men can hurt people financially, and not everything is insured, but they do not pose an immediate risk to our daily security. These criminals are motivated by very different concerns and experiences than a rapist or murderer. The con man doesn't give a damn about the future plight of his victims. Not a picture of moral virtue, but not necessarily a character who will breed fear if left to roam in the community. So why not punish the con man in a manner reflective of the crime?

With a property crime, there is a measurable loss, one that can be redeemed through good deeds. So instead of three years in prison, give con men three years of community service, working for the victim and other unfortunate souls. Instil responsibility in the offenders and balance their previous acts of taking advantage with current acts of taking care. It's not that difficult to fathom, but we never do things like this. It would require labour-intensive supervision, and we do not want to get entangled in the lives of offenders. We prefer three years with the luxury of out of sight, out of mind. So we punish thoughtlessly, arbitrarily and aimlessly based upon a stereotypical image of the offender before the court. We are not sentencing real people. We are not punishing real people. We are sentencing abstractions. We are punishing a concept of wrongdoing, but not the actual wrongdoer before the court.

Sentencing will always be an imprecise art, but there are some simple steps that can be taken to make sense of this solemn act of punishing. First, the Criminal Code must be reformulated. Lawmakers should make decisions about which crimes are presumptively going to be punished by prison and which crimes should be dealt with through creative community sanctions. Let the vandal fix the windows, and let the thief deliver food to the poor. Reserve prison for the truly serious predatory criminal. That is the first step. Second, get rid of these far-ranging maximum sentences that bear no relation to sentencing practice. It makes no sense for the Criminal Code to stipulate a life sentence for robbery when almost all sentences come in at less than ten years. Narrow the range, take away sentencing discretion and make the prison term fit the crime. Having the mythical maximum sentence simply breeds uncertainty. Uncertainty breeds plea bargaining. And justice is subverted because no one wants to plead not guilty for fear that a maximum sentence may result. In this system, it is better to deal the case away.

In theory this is so simple. Identify the serious crimes. Stipulate specific prison terms to cover these serious crimes. Create a range of creative, community sanctions for all other criminals. Scale down the system. Get non-professionals involved in the supervision of offenders being punished in the community. Get rid of all the rubbish congesting our courts, so that judges have time to agonize over sentencing decisions. Punishment will never mean anything in modern criminal justice until we have freed up enough time and resources to treat sentencing as the solemn morality play it is designed to be. Five-minute sentencing hearings to rubber stamp a deal made by lawyers is not my idea of a meaningful process of punishment. It is processing indeed, but not punishment.

Yet even the modest proposal of trimming the fat off the Criminal Code and setting up a narrow list of serious offences deserving of prison is easier said than done. A recent survey of public attitudes towards criminal justice showed that men are more likely than women to prefer a prison sentence for a repeat break and enter, while women are more likely than men to prefer a prison sentence for a minor assault.[8] We all have different priorities in terms of what we consider important for our security, priorities based upon past experience, gender and socio-economic status.

We will never be able to satisfy everyone in developing criminal-justice policy. But I am talking about a fairly modest goal: making sure that we punish with courage and conviction, but only those criminals who pose a risk to our security and order. The way we sentence just leaves the public wanting more. The public clamours. They wring their hands in disbelief. So sentence terms are increased in response, yet the public still looks for more. If we had a more coherent and consistent sentencing practice in the first place, we could curb this appetite for striking back harder and harder at the criminals who haunt our nightly news. As it stands, the charade of punishment does not set the balance right. It's like oily junk food: you get a taste and you want more, even though the more you eat the worse you feel. Fast food, fast punishment—unhealthy consumers of insecurity. That's where criminal justice currently stands.

10

Our Criminal Code

CREATED IN 1955, the Criminal Code is the legal professional's bible. In many ways it is everyone's bible, telling us what's right and wrong, and what horrible fate awaits us if we don't play by the rules. The Criminal Code is a patchwork quilt of ancient common-law offences, procedural rules, trivial infractions and contemporary offences created in response to a perceived social crisis. Is it "our" Criminal Code? Not really. No one really knows how some repugnant behaviour ends up becoming a new rule of law. Some mornings we just wake up to hear there is a new criminal offence in existence. It has been said that there are two things people do not want to see being made: sausages and legislation. So most people just go along for the ride when politicians tell them they are creating a new crime or a new rule of conduct.

In 1976, the Law Reform Commission of Canada published *Our Criminal Law*, and in 1982, the Government of Canada published *The Criminal Law in Canadian Society*. Both texts sing the same song:

> The basic theme, however, is important, in stressing that the criminal law ought to be reserved for reacting to conduct that is seriously harmful. The harm may be caused or threatened to the physical safety or integrity of individuals, or through interference with their property. It may be caused or threatened to the collective safety or integrity of society through the infliction of direct damage or the undermining of what the Law Reform Commission terms fundamental or essential values—those values or interests necessary for social life to be carried on, or for the maintenance of the kind of society cherished by Canadians. Since many acts may be "harmful," and since society has many other means for controlling or responding to conduct, criminal law should be used only when the harm caused or threatened is serious, and when the other, less coercive or less intrusive means do not work or are inappropriate.[1]

I couldn't agree more. If this were actually true, I would not be writing this book. But in reality, we're wasting time and limited justice resources with trivialities, and the truly threatening stuff is slipping through our fingers. And it all starts with our Criminal Code. It's a mess. It was created to impose order on the chaos of the common law, but it has itself become a form of order unrecognizable to the common people. It is not "our criminal law"—it belongs to the legal professionals.

Let's get down to basics. Criminal law serves to transmit norms of conduct and to punish those who violate these norms. Simple but true. There can't be any other point. We've become so sophisticated in theorizing about the law that we have forgotten that criminal law is a no-brainer; it tells us what we can and can't do, and then sends in state agents to punish us if we transgress the boundaries of permitted behaviour. The purpose is clear, but implementation is a nightmare.

The rules must be clear, certain and coherent. Only then can they truly serve to guide conduct. Whether we are transmitting norms or punishing wrongdoers, the system makes sense only if accused people are able to ascertain beforehand what their obligations are under the law. Otherwise it is a cruel joke—a trap. Putting aside the content of the law and the type of conduct that should be captured, to give it legitimacy the criminal law must contain one minimum requirement: it must be capable of guiding the people.

Anglo–American–Canadian legal institutions draw their nourishment from the British common law. The British legal tradition allowed royal judges to create common-law offences through the development of precedent. Legislation was secondary in the original British scheme. The predominance of judicially made rules characterized British law and gave the Anglo–American–Canadian legal tradition its distinctive edge. In the common-law world, judges were not mere civil servants— they were power brokers. They still have a unique constitutional status. In the old common-law world, judges did not just interpret law; they created law under the guise of the evolution of precedent.

In 1727, Sir Charles Sedley was completely shit-faced from alcohol. He took to a balcony in Covent Garden and disrobed. Ranting and raving, he pissed in a few bottles and threw them down at the passers-by. No one was hurt, but Sedley had gone too far. Today, Sedley would be officially processed after being charged with common nuisance, or assault or a whole host of other overlapping offences found in the Criminal Code. In 1727, he was dragged before the Court of King's Bench and, by judicial fiat, declared guilty of an offence they were creating at common law. Not a violation of an existing rule, but a violation of the sensibilities of the presiding judge. The court said "that the Court of King's Bench was the *custos morum* [guardian of morality] of all the king's subjects; and that it was high time to punish such profane actions, committed against all modesty, which were as frequent as if not only Christianity, but morality also has been neglected."[2]

This is our heritage: people being dragged into court to be told that their behaviour could no longer be tolerated. No warning beforehand. No clear rule contained in a code. Just a bunch of old men telling you that you messed up big time and now would pay the price. And what happened to this drunken aristocrat in 1727? The court noted that "he was a gentleman of a very ancient family [in Kent] and his estate encumbered," so they gave him a kiss—a fine and a week in jail. *Plus ça change, plus c'est la même chose.*

Things started to change in the nineteenth century. More and more laws were created in the form of legislation, and England started to dream of consolidating all its criminal laws into one compendious penal code. Just like the Europeans. No matter how much the Brits tried, they did not succeed; to this day the Brits do not have a criminal code. But using their efforts, Canada enacted its first criminal code in 1892. This old code was a mess. The purpose of consolidating all laws into one code is to make the law accessible to the common people, but our original criminal code still allowed the creation of common-law offences by judges. Someone could study the Code night and day and still be hauled into court to be told they had violated some offence at common law they were unaware of.

In 1955, the Criminal Code was amended to prohibit judge-made criminal law. A simple incident transformed our legal heritage, making the Criminal Code the sole repository of all norms of conduct. In 1947, some goof named Frey tried to sneak a peek through a window at a woman who was standing in her bedroom in her nightgown. Her son, Fedoruk, was justifiably upset. Armed with a knife, he chased and apprehended Frey. Frey was detained until the police arrived. In a surprise twist, Frey sued Fedoruk for false arrest and imprisonment. In 1947, there was no offence of peeping-Tom voyeurism in the Criminal Code, so in theory Frey's arrest was illegal. But the lower courts exonerated Fedoruk, concluding that at common law it is a crime to do anything that provokes others to reprisal. Frey's conduct came within that principle, thus he committed a crime at common law.[3] What a principle! Common-law offences could cover anything. Insults could end up being crimes. You could never know in advance whether your conduct was provocative and, hence, criminal.

The Supreme Court of Canada put an end to this. In 1950, it allowed Frey's appeal and declared that criminal courts could no longer convict someone of an offence unless that offence was contained in the Criminal Code or was clearly established at common law in years past. No new judicially crafted crime was allowed.

All normative standards that prohibit injurious conduct must now be contained in our Criminal Code. These standards have been put in one large code so that people will be able to read them and govern their conduct accordingly. At least, that's the dream. But most people do not consult the Criminal Code and, even if they did, they would not find the answers to their questions. The Code has a chaotic structure, vague prohibitions and numerous gaps. Judges still wield enormous power under the guise of interpretation. At best, people may be able to find relevant offences, but then they'll need a lawyer to tell them what type of argument should be advanced in court to convince the judge that the law says something favourable for the client. This ambiguity fuels the legal profession and its fetish-like obsession with argument, debate and plea negotiation.

In fairness, there will always be some degree of ambiguity—there are limits to language. Language cannot clearly capture every nuance of wrongful behaviour. There will be gaps. There will be a need for lawyers and judges to fill in the gaps on occasion, but this should not be a frequent occurrence. But our Criminal Code makes no effort to reduce gaps and ambiguity. It just keeps growing and growing, often without rhyme or reason.

Even where the Code is relatively clear, judges find ways to modify Parliament's will under the guise of interpretation. In 1986, Jules Jobidon and Rodney Haggart agreed to fight outside the bar where they had been drinking. Haggart was not up to the match. Jobidon pummelled him with his fists. Haggart was taken away in a coma and later died from the blows Jobidon delivered to his head. Is this manslaughter? It sure isn't murder—there was no intent to kill. This was just another foolish barroom brawl; some territorial pissing by a couple of shit-faced idiots. To have committed the crime of manslaughter, Jobidon had to have been committing an illegal act when the killing occurred. It looks like he committed the offence of assault, but the Criminal Code, in no uncertain terms, states that an assault does not occur if the parties consent to the fight. Let the idiots suffer the consequences of their stupid decision to fight; this is what the Code clearly prescribes. If no assault occurred, Jobidon could not be convicted of manslaughter. The death would be a tragedy, but not a crime. In light of the Code, the court had no real choice but to acquit Jobidon. But there was a dead body in the parking lot. And there wasn't a good reason for the death; it was a product of behaviour most people would condemn. So the Supreme Court of Canada simply ignored the part of the Criminal Code that allows people to consent to fight. They fashioned a new rule: consent cannot operate as a defence to assault if bodily harm was intended and caused.[4] Seems reasonable. I'm not a big fan of the barroom consent fight. Most people aren't. But that is not the issue. The Criminal Code clearly allowed this behaviour, and it is for Parliament, as the elected officials of the people, to decide if consent fighting is to be outlawed. The court should not do Parliament's dirty work. Besides, more uncertainty is introduced into the law when judges try to make law. The Jobidon decision brings into question the legality of hockey fights, surgery, sado-masochistic spanking and daredevil stunts. No problem. The court says the new rule does not apply if the assaultive activity has social utility. Thanks a lot. Every time a consent touching case comes before the court, the court will have to explore the nebulous concept of social utility. How can anyone ascertain the law in advance? And besides, I'm not sure I want Judge Grumpy making decisions about what type of conduct has social utility.

We aspire to achieve the certainty demanded by the principle of legality, but often our criminal prohibitions are drafted at a level of generality that simply invites the judge to apply his or her moral predilections. Isn't the determination of whether S/M spanking or hockey violence has social utility just an example of judges making law in accordance with their subjective perspectives on sound, popular feeling?

Even the Criminal Code offence of fraud engages vague notions of popular feeling. It punishes those who "by deceit, falsehood or other fraudulent means, defrauds the public or any person ... of any property, money of valuable security or any service" (s. 380). "Deceit, falsehood or other fraudulent means"—this phrase has no self-evident interpretation; it requires the judges to assess community standards in relation to popular conceptions of dishonesty. I know it is hard to enact a law with an exhaustive listing of fraudulent behaviours, and maybe this is the best we can do. But people have to realize that the criminal law is not a science with determinate answers and incontrovertible conclusions. Everything is up for argument. Bad for the people, good for the lawyers.

Let's look at the content of our Criminal Code. (Note: our draconian drug prohibitions are actually contained in the Controlled Drugs and Substances Act.) The Code has 840 sections, with another 95 in our drug legislation. Most of these sections deal with procedural concerns, but there are still more than 300 crimes you can commit in Canada (and thousands upon thousands of non-criminal, regulatory offences). Are there really that many ways to hurt people? Is our species so ingenious when it comes to inflicting injury that we need hundreds of criminal offences to keep us in line? I don't think so. There are only five or six basic ways in which you can injure someone; the rest are variations on a theme. Stabbing, shooting, punching, kicking and clobbering with a baseball bat are all variations on the theme of inflicting bodily injury; it is still just one crime.

It seems that law is a beast with an insatiable appetite. It just keeps growing and growing. Sounds like a cancer. I remember seeing a comment in the *Atlanta Journal*: "The Ten Commandments contain 297 words. The Bill of Rights, 463 words. Lincoln's 'Gettysburg Address' has 266 words. A recent federal directive to regulate the price of cabbage contains 26,911 words."[5] We all know that legal professionals have linguistic diarrhea, but this exponential increase in the amount of words necessary to regulate society is ridiculous.

Considering that our law is grounded in a Judeo–Christian ethic, let's take a look at the Ten Commandments to see whether our laws have changed substantially in the past two thousand years:

1. **You shall have no other gods beside me.** All right, that's a little egotistical and smothering, but we have similar laws today. Treason and sedition are still in the Code. You shall not have any other form of government other than ours. Same thing.
2. **You shall not make for yourself a sculptured image, or any likeness of what is in the heaven above, or on the earth below, or in the waters under the earth. You shall not bow down to them or serve them.** This is

not very cool. This whole graven image prohibition clearly violates free expression; it would not survive in contemporary times. Curiously, legal professionals have borrowed the religious solemnity of bowing when entering the court.

3. **You shall not swear falsely by the name of the Lord your God.** This is just archaic superstition. But wait a second, most witnesses in court swear to tell the truth by placing their hand on the Bible. I've never really known what to make of this.

4. **Remember the Sabbath day and keep it holy.** Until recently, most Canadian jurisdictions had quasi-criminal law prohibiting Sunday shopping. Now the malls are packed every Sunday, and this fourth commandment is history.

5. **Honour your father and mother.** Biblical types took this very seriously. Stoning sons and daughters for disobeying the father was their idea of just law. I guess the ancients probably did not have a problem with young offenders and juvenile crime rates, but look at the social cost. Families were little dictatorships. And brutal ones at that.

6. **You shall not murder.** Sounds familiar.

7. **You shall not commit adultery.** We gave up on this one a long time ago, but we have blinded ourselves into believing the law still has a role to play in governing other consensual sexual activities.

8. **You shall not steal.** Proudhon might have believed that "property is theft," but for the same reasons that we now have Sunday shopping, we will always have laws relating to property rights.

9. **You shall not bear false witness against your neighbour.** In modern terms this covers all crimes against the administration of justice including perjury, obstructing justice, and so on.

10. **You shall not covet your neighbour's house; you shall not covet your neighbour's wife, or his male or female slave, or his ox or his ass, or anything that is your neighbour's.** Now this is just getting weird. Coveting has become the basis of the entire capitalist society. Marketers tell you how much better your life would be if you just had what Fred has. Fred is happy. You are not. So of course we do not have criminal laws prohibiting coveting; we have a culture built on coveting.

The Ten Commandments form much of the foundation of modern Western law. In fact, Commandments 1, 3, 6, 8 and 9 still have application. Add the modern offences of assault on bodily integrity, assault on sexual integrity, assault on psychological integrity, dangerous driving and invasion of privacy, and we are back up to ten. In fairness, we probably need around fifty or sixty offences to capture all the modern variations on causing harm or injury. But how did we get to over 300? Is this such a nasty society? We've invested billions and hired countless hordes of legal professionals to administer a convoluted and bloated statute that covers much of the same territory succinctly covered by the Ten Commandments.

Much of our Code is made up of archaic laws with no modern application. Section 49, for example, prohibits conduct that "alarms her Majesty." It is punishable by fourteen years. What does this even mean? Is belching at Queen Elizabeth's afternoon tea a crime? And why do we have an offence protecting the Queen of England? I thought we were an independent nation.

Section 68 pertains to the dispersal of riots. We still have riots, but they are pretty meek, with the employment of tear gas and water cannons. This provision is based on a reality that no longer exists. Section 68 directs the mayor (or another public official) to

> go to that place, and after approaching as near as is safe, if the person is satisfied that a riot is in progress ... command silence and thereupon make our cause to be made in a loud voice a proclamation in the following words or to like effect: "Her Majesty the Queen charges and commands all persons being assembled immediately to disperse and peaceably to depart to their habitations or to their lawful business on the pain of being guilty of an offence for which, on conviction, they may be sentenced to imprisonment for life. GOD SAVE THE QUEEN."

This is absolutely hilarious. Some mayor should try this. The rioters would be on the ground helpless with laughter. It's much safer than tear gas.

The Code is also wordy and redundant. We all have a pretty good idea of what theft is. Even when it is cunning and sophisticated, we know that the dishonest deprivation of property is theft, whether a bag lady steals groceries or an executive diverts millions of dollars through a corporate maze of offshore bank accounts. But in the Criminal Code, theft includes:

- s. 322: theft in general
- s. 323: theft from oyster beds
- s. 324: theft by bailee of things under seizure
- s. 326: theft of telecommunication service
- s. 330: theft by person required to account
- s. 331: theft by person holding power of attorney
- s. 332: misappropriation of money held under direction
- s. 335: taking motor vehicle without consent
- s. 336: criminal breach of trust
- s. 337: public servant refusing to deliver property
- s. 338: fraudulently taking cattle or defacing brand
- s. 339: taking possession of drift timber

The list carries on to s. 380, touching on credit card fraud, false pretences and eventually fraud; sixty sections of the bible to capture variations on one simple theme. And unlike "Variations on a Theme" by Paganini, these variations are dull and colourless. Sure, some of the redundancy was occasioned by the need to clarify a point of law—even the self-executing theft provision (the generic "dishonest deprivations of property") becomes unclear when it meets up with changing and complex definitions of property. But most of the time, the redundancy is a product of political scheming. Newspapers report on the occurrence of a rash of new crimes, let's say, in Nova Scotia at the turn of the twentieth century. Too many thefts from oyster beds. Member of Parliament, I.C. Opportunity, beseeches Parliament to address the problem. The Criminal Code is amended, and I.C. Opportunity goes does in history as the politician who saved the oyster beds of Nova Scotia. It probably went down something like that. And the crime of theft from an oyster bed still clutters up our bible.

Here's a modern example. You've probably heard of the anti-biker law—a creation of the 1990s. It covers extortion, pimping, drug running and murder, but only when committed by a criminal organization. Holy redundancy, Batman. We already have these crimes and many, many more. Committing these crimes as part of a gang activity is clearly relevant when talking about the severity of sentence or punishment, but it is not a new crime. So why is it now in our Code? Because the police in Montreal wanted the feds to respond to the increasing wave of biker violence. Even if it is useless, even if the law will not make the streets safer for a day, the feds will have made the police happy, which translates into votes in the next election.

The Criminal Code has become so diluted that it is no big deal to say you committed a crime. It should be big deal. If criminal offences were restricted to what is truly harmful, it would be a badge of shame to admit participation in a "crime." But in modern Canada, saying you are a criminal may simply mean you go water skiing at night. No joke. Section 250 criminalizes water skiing at night. Sure, it's a pretty stupid thing to do—and probably dangerous in most circumstances—but *criminal?* Not if you want the label to truly mean something. So forget norm transmission as a function of the Code. Who would take seriously a bible that views murder and water skiing at night in the same light?

This trivialization of our bible is not the fault of the legal professionals. It's the fault of our lawmakers. But when was the last time you heard of any legal professional spearheading reform of the Code? Even though the Charter of Rights provides constitutional protection against laws that are vague and overly broad, legal professionals appear to enjoy playing in an atmosphere of ambiguity and uncertainty.

The courts don't even really care about vague laws; they always seem to make some sense out of the nonsense. In the Lofthouse case of 1988, the Ontario Court of Appeal had to assess whether the offence of "gross indecency" was unconstitutionally vague.[6] This case involved gay men having sex in public bathroom stalls. The court concluded that it was understood by all that "gross indecency" meant "a marked departure from decent conduct expected of average Canadians in the circumstances." The court can't possibly be serious. I had not seen or heard the word "decent" in a sentence since high school. How does this judicial turn of phrase add any clarity to the term "gross indecency"? It's just another layer of bullshit. I guess the court is hoping the average Canadian doesn't actually read these judgements.

The joint effort of judges and the Code to guide conduct is an abysmal failure because legal professionals do not really care if ordinary people understand the rules; they care only that there are rules they can play with. Take the case of stripper Arlene Campbell.[7] In Edmonton in 1972, Campbell took off her G-string because a trial court decision in Alberta had decided it was not an "immoral, indecent or obscene performance" to strip to the buff. So she was doing her bottomless dancing, and meanwhile the decision she based her actions upon was appealed successfully by the Crown. Suddenly, bottomless stripping was once again beyond the pale. Charged with immoral performance, she raised the defence of a reasonable mistake of law: she thought she was following the dictates of a court ruling. How can she be faulted? She made a decision based upon the ruling of a court. Isn't this the whole point of the law? Nonetheless, the court hearing her case dismissed her defence because "ignorance of the law is no defence." The judge went on to say:

> There is no question that there is somewhat of an anomaly here. Reliance upon a specific order, of a specific judge, granted at a specific time and place, seems, at first sight, not to be ignorance of the law, but knowledge of the law. If it turns out that that judge is mistaken, then, of course, the reliance on that judge's judgement is mistaken. The irony is this: people in society are expected to have a more profound knowledge of the law than are the judges. I am not the first person to have made that comment about the law, and while it is all very amusing, it is really of no point.[8]

It is not very amusing at all. The entire fiasco is an embarrassment. And guess what? The decision that Campbell had relied on was subsequently appealed to the Supreme Court of Canada, who affirmed the original trial decision. Campbell was right all along. But she was arrested, charged and prosecuted, while the legal professionals played games debating whether G-strings are a necessary safeguard to preserve a performance from being branded a criminal performance.

Criminal law should not be debating the meaning of "gross indecency" or "immoral performance." Maybe public sexuality, whether gay or straight, is a bad thing. It doesn't matter. It certainly isn't bad enough to have a place in the Code with manslaughter or rape. And then to put it in the Code in such a vague, all-encompassing way—it's just going to occasion a whole lot of silly debate over things that mean nothing to anybody.

Let me finish with a brief tale of the trivial. I spent five years in the mid-1990s representing a lot of "hemp stores" in Canada. In an attempt to gain legitimacy, they went from being "head" shops in the seventies and eighties to being "hemp" shops in the nineties. But they carried the same old merchandise: beautiful bongs, large wooden pipes carved to resemble Jerry Garcia, and so forth. In 1988, the Criminal Code was amended to include a specific prohibition on drug literature (literature designed to promote, encourage or activate illicit drug use) and drug paraphernalia (instruments primarily designed for or intended to facilitate illicit drug use). Putting aside that the law was passed when head shops were already dying because drug use was at an all-time low (thank you, Nancy Reagan), this law was simply stupid and ineffective. You don't ban matches to prohibit cigarette smoking. You can use anything to ingest drugs. Just ask any drug user. Even if you find merit in the war on drugs, you still have to question resorting to the criminal law to ban drug paraphernalia. Where are our priorities?

But I could not question the merits of the law directly in court; I could not just waltz in and give fifty reasons why this law was stupid. This would not be the type of constitutional discourse accepted in a court of law. If I thought the law to be stupid, I should address this with Parliament. Like I have access to Parliament. Like the hemp store owners have powerful political clout. Every institution has its rules, and the rules of the game required me to argue the constitutional doctrines of vagueness and overbreadth. My clients really didn't know what I was arguing about, not because it was complex, but because they imagined a passionate rant about liberty and freedom until the big, bad state realized the errors of its way and returned all the seized inventory. They were pissed off. They felt their rights had been violated. And one thing I did know with certainty was that these counterculture retailers were not the type of people I thought of as criminals when I was starting to learn as a child that there were bad people in the world. As an adult, the term "criminal" has become meaningless to me.

Anyway, I could never really say in court what my clients wanted me to say. I could only try to wax poetic on the vagueness argument, cite the leading cases and make some snide innuendoes about the sanity of the lawmakers who enacted this law. All I was allowed to say was that the law affected my client's liberty in a vague, uncertain way; that the law failed to provide sufficient criteria to guide retailers who may sell items that have drug application by ingenious drug users. Pretty lame, when I wanted to say that this law was a needless intrusion into private choice and a scandalous waste of tax dollars that should be used to battle some of the real, evil bastards out there.

The "ban the bong" trials took up weeks of court time in different cities in Canada. I had no chance with the "gross indecency" mentality of the courts. The court hears the argument, recites the same case law, plays with the usual standards and tests developed in other cases to evaluate vagueness (as if it could be measured) and the result is always the same. The law is upheld. Everything is crystal clear from the judicial perspective.

Nothing was gained in this court exercise. Think of the time and effort invested by our protectors to raid these stores, haul away the vicious paraphernalia and process the criminals. Surely, the police must have better things to do. The police actually seemed pretty curious about aspects of drug culture. They thought a lot of the ornamental pipes were funny. Who could not adore a bong in the image of Homer Simpson?

In fact, the trials were quite civil as trials go. Everyone seemed to like each other. There was never any great threat of the hemp store dudes going to jail. Of course not. There wasn't a criminal in the courtroom. We should not have been there in the first place. This was not a real criminal trial. A pipe was on trial. We were all wasting our time. Thanks to our Criminal Code.

11

The True Nature of Crime in Canada

WHEN I STARTED WRITING this book, I remembered a murder case from 1983. I think it was the first murder case I worked on. In our office, I was the new kid on the block, so I was the lawyer who had to go to bail court on Saturday morning to meet the client after she was arrested. No one charged with murder is released at the first court appearance, and all the judge can do is remand the accused back into custody. Attending first appearance for an alleged murderer is just a courtesy call. I was told to attend to introduce myself to the accused.

My client was a little old lady charged with killing her husband. Half-asleep, I arrived at bail court at 9:00 a.m. My client, no taller than five feet, was gyrating and gesticulating from the prisoner's box. I went over to the box to introduce myself. When I told her I was her lawyer, she grabbed me tight and sobbed into my suit. "I am innocent," she kept repeating, with a thick accent. The guard pried us apart, and I tried to explain to her what the procedures would be in the next few days. She just kept crying.

The case was a bit weird. The autopsy showed the deceased had died from seventy-two stab wounds. When the little old lady hung on to my suit for dear life, I could not imagine that this tiny, weak body was capable of mutilating anyone. But here's how the case was built. This was the old lady's third marriage. She had three insurance policies taken out on her husband, and she stood to gain over $20,000 (at the time, not chump change). There was evidence of marital discord. In her husband's body, there were massive amounts of sedatives, and one of the sedatives, flurazepam, had been prescribed to the accused. Apparently, the husband's car had been vandalized recently, and he had taken to sleeping in the car to catch the vandals. He was found stabbed in his car in the early morning, and one obvious theory was that the vandals had confronted the deceased and killed him. But the Crown's theory was more exciting: the little old lady had doped up her husband that night so that he would be helpless and she would be able to stab him. Seemed far-fetched to me, but this was the case that went to trial.

Months later, I left the office and had no further dealings with the old lady. A year later, I read that she had been convicted of attempted murder but acquitted of murder. Weird. It seems the jury concluded that she had tried to kill her husband by an overdose, but the vandals got to him first, and before the overdose could work its magic, he was stabbed seventy-two times by an unknown assailant. Quite a story. What are the odds that he would be lying in a car dying from one murder plot only to be murdered spontaneously by car vandals? It seems to me the jury couldn't figure out what had happened. We can't unravel every mystery. So they compromised. Maybe she stabbed him, maybe she didn't, but there was evidence of massive sedative poisoning, which could be linked to her. So at least she should be taken down for ineffectively trying to kill her husband. The judge gave her three years for attempted murder (a really low sentence), and the case was closed.

But, of course, the case was not closed. The whole thing was too strange. So it went up on appeal and the appeal court entered an acquittal.[1] Why? First, the judge should have excluded an inculpatory statement she had made to the police, as it was obtained in violation of her right to counsel. Second, the judge had erred in allowing the Crown to call expert evidence relating to why the first blood work done on the victim did not show massive amounts of sedatives. The Crown's first expert had testified that the first blood test did not show these massive amounts because the lab had to use pig's blood as a standard in the absence of available human blood. The second test, which showed the presence of these drugs, was properly done with human blood. In rebuttal, the defence expert testified that it would make absolutely no difference if pig's blood or human blood was used. This evidence cast grave doubts on the accuracy of all the testing and the Crown's case was going down the toilet. So, at the end of the trial, the Crown called a further expert in reply to testify that the problem with the first test was not the use of pig's blood as a standard, but the fact that the pig's blood was not properly aged. Just like a fine wine. The Court of Appeal was not impressed by a prosecutor changing theories and experts at the eleventh hour, and the reply evidence was ruled inadmissible on appeal.

Finally, the court could not endorse the compromise verdict of attempted murder because no evidence was called that the massive amount of flurazepam could actually kill. The Crown's theory was that the little old lady sedated her husband to facilitate the stabbing and not with the intent to kill him with the drugs. As a result, nobody ever asked the experts whether the flurazepam given to the husband could have led to an overdose. Based on this record, the appeal court had no alternative but to enter an acquittal.

The little old lady went free. Notice why the verdict was overturned: games and more games. The cops not taking a statement in accordance with basic rules of the Constitution, and the prosecutor shifting theories midstream when the rules of evidence do not permit this last-minute adjustment. But who the hell killed her husband? I don't know. I never heard anything about the case again. This was just one of those interesting who-done-it cases that make for good television drama and exciting lawyering.

But we have to put aside good stories if we want to understand the true nature of crime in Canada. We have to erase from our consciousness every melodramatic docudrama we have seen on television, and then we have to stop watching television entirely (at least crime stories and law shows, but not *The Simpsons* or *Hockey Night in Canada*). In 2000, there were 2,476,520 recorded crimes in Canada: 0.01% (484) were murders and 0.03% (766) were attempted murders.[2] And over 75% of murder cases are solved by the police.[3] The little old lady's case doesn't fit the statistics and is not representative of crime in Canada. But it's good copy.

We live in an era of decreasing violence. By all historical accounts, previous centuries witnessed much greater interpersonal violence than we have had in the past few decades. Despite the conservative nostalgia for crime-free eras of the past, the reality is that prior to the twentieth century, violence was tolerated to a much greater degree than it is today.[4] Before the nineteenth century, there was no organized police force in the Commonwealth, and much of the response to crime was self-help. People resorted to violence to address interpersonal conflict, without the same social stigma attached to assaultive behaviour today.

Look at it this way. Until 1972, whipping, or corporal punishment, still remained in the Criminal Code. We may not have been beating many accused people in the twentieth century, but violence as a response to crime was an accepted mode of punishment for most of it. The state's power to legitimately inflict violence as an institutionalized response to crime says a lot about attitudes towards violence. Violence was tolerated to a much larger degree. Today, many people oppose the use of force even to discipline children or pets. In previous centuries, families were ruled by violence, and no one thought the state had a right to intervene. With the modern zero-tolerance approach to violence, we have entered an era in which violence is not part of every person's daily life. Some people's lives are still plagued by violence, but many people today are never attacked, assaulted or abused in their lifetimes.

Statistics have been compiled for over a century; however, uniform reporting did not really occur until 1962, so early statistics have to be taken with a grain of salt. But it appears that in most Western countries crime rates, and violent crime rates, declined through the latter half of the nineteenth century. This decline continued until the Second World War. Crime rates then steadily increased until 1990. From 1962 to 1990 violent crime rates tripled, and it was this phenomena that fuelled much of the despair over crime running out of control.

Many informed criminologists argue that the massive crime wave was largely an increase in the reporting of crime. More and more people started turning to state officials, when in the past they may have simply walked away from the crime and the conflict. Also, a decreasing tolerance for violence led to many more minor incidents being reported to police. So the fear of rampant crime was probably not warranted. But joy over the recent decreases may not be warranted either. Criminologists point out that our population is aging and, with most crimes committed by people under twenty-five, it is not surprising that crime is on the wane. Who knows what the next few decades will bring?

But a closer look at current figures—which I have summarized at the end of this chapter for those who care to wade through them—does not support the contemporary fear of a crime-ridden society. Any way you slice or dice the figures, you are still left with the impression that the modern rise in crime is just an increase in nuisance and annoyance. First off, the figures clearly show that criminal courts spend most of their time dealing with minor crimes. Petty interpersonal conflicts drive the system. "Theft under" and "common assault" are the lifeblood of criminal court activity. In addition, for both youths and adults, many offences concern failure to appear in court or to comply with court orders. These latter offences reflect massive disrespect for the majesty and authority of criminal justice. They may also mirror the triviality of the crimes. I have known some accused persons who told me they didn't show up because the incident was so trivial they didn't think the complainant would show up.

Impaired driving accounts for 13% of all cases before the courts. I don't think of impaired driving as trivial, but neither do I lump this offence in with intentional and vicious infliction of harm. It is stupid behaviour. It is the height of that mindless lack of judgement brought on by our favourite drug, alcohol. I have no patience for this behaviour, and it is not a hysterical perspective to view impaired driving as a prelude to homicide. But most impaired drivers do not cause fatal accidents, and many people can drive properly at our 80 milligram cut-off point.

We cannot continue to employ a monolithic concept of "crime" and employ one system of justice for processing all forms of criminality. Yes, impaired driving is a crime. Yes, impaired driving can lead to horrible tragedies. But why process the impaired driver in the same way as the murderer? Their motivations are dissimilar, and the circumstances of their crimes are worlds apart. Impaired drivers have shown that they cannot act responsibly when drinking. Driving is not a right. So why don't we construct a process where we explore the driver's reasons for acting irresponsibly, and where we supervise and monitor him and take away his license, and maybe even his car, until he has demonstrated a more responsible attitude towards drinking? A formal trial with the presumption of innocence is simply an impediment to dealing with this serious social problem. Drinking and driving is a serious social problem, but I don't like it being labelled a "crime," if this means that the deprivation of liberty will be considered the only appropriate societal measure. Impaired driving is not a minor offence, but it cries out for a more nuanced approach than the zero-sum game of a criminal trial.

Similarly, in evaluating criminal-justice policy, we have to begin to recognize the interpersonal nature of most crime, whether serious or minor. Most assaults and most murders take place between family members and acquaintances. Even break and enter, the paradigm invasion of the stranger, has this component. In 1999, where the relationship between burglar and victim was known (and this is just the tip of the iceberg, because break and enter has an extremely low solve rate), 24% of burglars were casual acquaintances of the victim.[5] Interpersonal conflict is never adequately resolved in a formal criminal court. Sometimes the conflict escalates to such a degree that the seriousness of the crime demands a formal, criminal court response. But when the level of harm remains low, why do we not recognize the interpersonal nature of the event and let the victim and offender explore this breach of order in a less formal setting than Her Majesty's criminal court? I'm not saying that domestic assault should not be seen as a crime. I'm saying that when we classify it as a crime, and process it as we process all criminal cases, we lose the ability to do something innovative, and perhaps constructive, with the problem.

We will never understand the nature of crime in Canada until we develop a more nuanced and realistic approach to the classification of crime. Crime rates will always appear high when we keep classifying every interpersonal conflict as a crime. Many of these conflicts are serious social problems, but they need a response that is less bureaucratized, less hierarchical and less alien to the common person. Criminal-justice policies fuelled by the so-called massive crime wave of the 1960s and 1970s should be laid to rest.

There is no way to determine whether there really is a crime problem. To say that over two million crimes were committed in 2000 is meaningless. To say that violent crime increased threefold from 1962 to 1990 is also meaningless, as there are so many disparate explanations for the increase. There is no crime-free utopia. Conflict is here to stay. People will resort to violence to resolve conflicts. People with limited economic opportunity will still on occasion take what is not theirs. The real question is, when does crime rise above an acceptable limit? It is easy to say that even one murder is one too many, but this is just rhetoric. A society of lobotomized people wearing tracking devices around their necks might be a murder-free society. But that is not our society. So when do we know that crime has risen to the level of a cancer?

Without a standard of acceptable and expected levels of deviance to work with, we can never make this determination. All we can do is compare ourselves with other countries and locate our crime rates along the spectrum of what is taking place abroad. Japan, Switzerland and Saudi Arabia have low crime rates compared to Canada,[6] but these countries cannot necessarily serve as standards of acceptability because various social, cultural and political factors serve to explain why they are blessed by low crime rates. We cannot compare Canada's crime rate with that of a country where alcohol is prohibited, or where religious precepts govern secular law. We also cannot compare Canada's crime rate with that of a country that has a history of tightly knit social groups and where workers sing anthems to their companies before starting their work day. When we look at countries that more or less share our cultural and social structure, we end up observing that Canada's homicide rate in 1999 (1.76/100,000) is less than the United States' (5.80/100,000) and Hungary's (2.48/100,000) but more than Germany's (1.24/100,000) and England's (1.25/100,000).[7] So what? We're not as bad as the American killing fields, but worse than most European countries. The numbers game is not very helpful. Just because Alex Mogilny scores more goals than Mats Sundin, it does not mean Mogilny is a better hockey player. Quantitative analysis does not always lead to a meaningful qualitative assessment.

One of the barometers in determining whether there is a crime problem is an examination of public perceptions of fear and insecurity. True crime is conduct that can erode the security and order people want to feel in organized society. The public interest in crime rises when crime has an unsettling affect on the community. Victimization surveys have been conducted that explore victims' perceptions of crime and the impact crime has had on their daily lives. In measuring the level of fear of victimization found in a given country, it may be possible to determine whether a real crime problem exists. A society riddled by fear of crime has a crime problem notwithstanding the actual level of crime in existence. Crime is a problem not only when large numbers of people are victimized, but also when lower levels of crime cause sufficient fear to compel people to adopt a fortress mentality to urban living.

Victimization surveys conducted in Canada in 1989 and 1992 measured the percentage of people who felt "a bit or very unsafe when walking in their own area after dark." These surveys revealed that 20% of the population feels this insecurity and fear. This sounds bad, especially when surveys show that other countries have lower percentages: 13.5% for Sweden, 17.9% for Finland. However, the 20% fear factor in Canada does not seem that outrageous when you consider that most Western countries have higher percentages: the Netherlands (21.1%), Australia (31.1%), England (33%), Italy (35%), the United States (41%) and Poland (45.4%).[8] The fear factor looms large even in countries that have lower reported crime rates than Canada. But does this really mean anything?

Fear is a subjective phenomena not easily subject to quantitative analysis, and even a slight change in the methodology employed in victimization surveys from year to year, and from country to country, will skew any meaningful tracking of trends.

The fear factor, if properly measured, could be a suitable barometer for measuring whether crime is a cancer or a cold, but measuring the fear factor is a joke in a society that is bombarded by media magnification and distortion. Mass communication and modern media have actually increased ignorance about crime, despite our naive hope that instantaneous communication of information 24/7 would make us a more astute, informed species.

Media distortion is the price we pay for a profit-driven communications network that caters to the lowest common denominator. Sex and violence sell. Everyone knows that. And this has infiltrated the news gathering profession. Despite falling crime rates in the 1990s, most people believed the crime problem was getting worse. Sheer stupidity in the face of contrary facts? I don't think so. Most of us live in narrowly constrained universes. We have our routines; we have our settled expectations. Constantly bombarded by cinematic and television celebrations of violence, it is no wonder we think the world outside our narrow bubble is inhabited by all sorts of dangerous villains. And I'm not just talking about movies and cop shows. It's the news that does it to us. In 1993 and 1994, the murder rate in Canada dropped by 8%, yet television reporting of murder cases on Canada's two major networks nearly doubled.[9] People who sell news all over the world discovered long ago the simple fact that sordid tales of terror sell papers and magazines.

Fear of the stranger is a popular theme. Although most crimes are committed by family members, acquaintances or business associates, we are intrigued by stories of random violence. A 1998 study showed that 22% of murder stories on CBC and 27% of murder stories on CTV involved random stranger killing, notwithstanding that stranger killing usually comprises 10% to 18% of all murders. The study also showed that 87.5% of stranger murder stories on CBC and 61% of those on CTV involved female victims, despite the fact that men are three times more likely to be killed by a stranger than women.[10]

This media magnification is linked to what sociologists call "moral panic." Moral panic theory shows how a kernel of truth can be magnified by the media, who are pawns in the games being played by interest groups that have a vested interest in the crime problem. Hysteria can be generated over a minor social problem by the nature in which the media dissect the incident. The media creates a panic that has been orchestrated by police associations, religious groups or educational institutions.

Sometimes, it is just the nature of competitive investigative reporting that is responsible for the panic. Whenever a sordid story breaks, journalists hunt high and low for similar stories. If you see one story of a dog being brutally dragged behind a car in the papers, you will notice similar stories published throughout the week, even if the story comes from some obscure hamlet in Bavaria. Moral panics predate modern media. We butchered hundreds of thousands of women from 1450 to 1750 in our panic to rid our towns and villages of witches. There seems to be something in our collective unconscious that yearns for scapegoats and villains to battle and humiliate, and the nature of modern media plays right into this.

I don't know what the true nature of crime in Canada is—it would be inconsistent with the premise of my book to claim such privileged knowledge. But there are some important points to underscore. We must remember Mark Twain's maxim "there are lies, damn lies, and then statistics," but the numbers collected to date do establish some basic trends. At a minimum, the numbers provide enough substance to remind us that our "crime problem" is not the problem set out in television law shows, nor is it accurately reflected by literary giants like Capote or Dostoyevsky. Over 2 million reported crimes a year sounds huge. But, as I've been saying throughout this book, much of our so-called crime problem relates to trivialities and useless social hygiene measures. The numbers bear little relation to the level of danger out there. It is the number crunching that has led Canadians to believe that serious crime is constantly on the rise. It is the number crunching that has led parents to keep their children on short leashes so they can't wander away into a dangerous neighbourhood.

Nonetheless, here's a selection of statistics, taken directly from numerous Statistics Canada reports. This is only the tip of the iceberg, but these figures provide a crude picture of the true nature of crime in Canada:

A. Crime Rate
- From 1962 to 1990, the total number of Criminal Code offences reported to police increased fourfold. Violent offence rates increased

three and a half times during this period and property crimes doubled. During the 1980s, violent crime increased 52%, whereas property crimes remained virtually unchanged. In the 1990s, the overall crime rate decreased consistently year to year.[11]

- In 2000, the crime rate fell for the ninth consecutive year. There was a 5% decrease in property crimes, a 3% increase in violent crime and a 9% increase in drug crimes. Prior to 2000, there had been seven successive years of decreases in the violent crime rate. 2001 saw the first increase in close to a decade in crime for adults, with the increase being a modest 1%. For young offenders, it was a second year of small increases after eight years of decline.[12]

- Of the 2.4 million offences charged in 2001, 13% were for violent crime, 52% for property crimes and 35% for other offences, such as mischief, disturbing the peace, prostitution and arson. This is essentially the distribution in most years.[13]

- By 2000, the crime rate had dropped to its lowest level since 1978. However, the rate is still 47% higher than it was in 1970.[14]

- The only categories of crime that showed major increases in the 1990s were disturbing the peace (up 31% between 1995 and 1999), drug offences (up 32% between 1995 and 1999), criminal harassment (up 32% between 1995 and 1999) and motor vehicle theft (79% increase between 1988 and 1996).[15]

- In 1995, it was reported that 34% of victims of violent crime do not report the incident to police. A 1999 victimization survey indicated that reporting to the police fell from 42% of incidents in 1993 to 37% of incidents in 1999.[16] A 1993 victimization survey indicates a much higher rate of non-reporting of crime: 90% of sexual assaults and 68% of non-sexual assaults are never brought to the attention of the police.[17]

- Crime rates for young offenders have been steadily dropping since 1992–93. Although the rate of violent youth crime also continues to drop, it remains 77% higher than the rate one decade ago. Fifty-eight percent of crime committed by young offenders involves theft under (15%), failure to comply with Youth Court order (12%), failure to appear (11%), break and enter (9%) and minor assault (10%). Six in ten violent incidents committed by young offenders involve acquaintances, and 52% of the victims were young people themselves.[18]

B. Violent Crime

- Minor assaults accounted for 62.6% of violent crimes in 2001, 60% of all violent crimes in 1996 and 59.8% of all violent crimes in 1994. Any modest increase in the violent crime rate in various cities in the 1990s was attributable to increased reporting of minor assaults.[19]
- Sexual offences represent 10% of all violent crime. From 1983 to 1993 the rate of reported sex offences rose. Since 1993 it has fallen, yet the rate remains 74% higher than in 1983. Sixty-two percent of sex offence victims are under the age of eighteen, whereas only 24% of other violent crimes are committed upon persons under the age of eighteen. Eighty-two percent of sex offence victims are female; however, when the victim is under the age of twelve, only 69% of victims are female.[20]
- Women and men are subjected to roughly similar rates of violent victimization. Men are most likely to be victimized by strangers outside the home; women are more likely to be victimized in their home by someone they know.[21]
- The national homicide rate in 1999 was the lowest in three decades. After increases in the late 1960s and early 1970s, the homicide rate has been steadily decreasing. The highest number of homicides in the last three decades was recorded in 1991 with 754. In 1999, the number had declined to 536, and in 2001 it stood at 554.[22]
- In 1999, consistent with previous years, 90% of murderers and 66% of victims were male. However, four out of five spousal homicide victims were female. Spousal homicides have been decreasing since 1991 and as of 1999 accounted for one out of every six solved homicide cases.[23]
- Homicide continues to be committed by people known to the victim. In 1999, 49% of victims were killed by an acquaintance and 35% were killed by a family member. In 1% of the cases, the relationship between victim and killer was unknown. Only 15% of homicides were committed by strangers, and of these stranger killings over half were committed during the commission of another crime (such as during a robbery). Fifty-one percent of female victims were killed by a person with whom they have had an intimate relationship, versus 6% of males.[24]
- Fifty-seven percent of all homicides in 1999 were motivated by an argument, a quarrel or an incident triggering a vengeful or jealous

reaction. Another 20% of homicides were motivated by financial gain or settling of accounts. In 13% of cases, the motive was unknown. There were no killings motivated by racial hatred in 1999; however, between 1991 and 1999 there were thirteen homicides motivated by hate or bigotry. One racial killing and three random murders occurred in 2001, with 58% of killings still being motivated by arguments, jealousy and vengeance.[25]

- In 2001, 75% of persons accused of murder and 56% of murder victims had been consuming alcohol at the time of the offence.[26]

C. The Official Processing of Crime

- A study of sentencing in provincial courts in 1993–94 revealed that the most frequent offence found before the courts was impaired driving (13.3% of all cases). The combination of impaired driving, failure to appear, common assault, failure to comply, theft under and other federal statutes accounted for 50% of all charges before the provincial courts. Crimes of violence accounted for only 17% of all cases sentenced. Property crimes accounted for 28%, traffic offences accounted for 23% and offences against the administration of justice accounted for 15%.[27]
- In 2001–02, 27% of all cases tried in courts were for violent crimes, 23% were for property crimes, 14% were for traffic offences, 4% were for drug-related offences and 32% were for other Criminal Code offences (with administration of justice offences accounting for 17%). The two most frequently heard offences in criminal courts were impaired driving and common assault, each accounting for 12% of all cases.[28]
- The overall conviction rate stood at 60% in 2001–02 and has been stable since 1994–95.[29]
- In 1996–97, justice spending totalled almost $10 billion. Fifty-nine percent was spent on policing, 20% on adult corrections, 9% on courts, 5% on legal aid, 5% on youth corrections and 3% on criminal prosecutions. In 2000–01, justice spending totalled $11 billion, with policing receiving the greatest proportion of the increase.[30]
- Of every dollar spent by governments in 1996–97, 3 cents was spent on the justice system. This was more or less equivalent to what was being spent on resource conservation and industrial development, national defence, recreation and culture and the environment. The

largest portion of government spending was directed to social services (31 cents), debt charges (15 cents), education (14 cents) and health (14 cents). These figures remained essentially the same in 2000–01.[31]

- Almost 120,000 people were employed full-time in the justice system in 1996–97. Over half (62%) worked for the police. In 2001, 127,000 people were employed full-time in the justice system, representing a 5% increase from the previous year.[32]

D. Prison and Prisoners

- In 2000–01, the average count of adults imprisoned in Canada was 31,500. An average of 151,500 adults were under the supervision of correctional agencies, 80% being under some form of community supervision and 20% being incarcerated.[33]
- In the early 1990s, Canada had the fourth highest rate of incarceration (130/100,000) behind Russia (558/100,000), the United States (529/100,000) and South Africa (368/100,000). The number of admissions to federal institutions has been dropping since 1994–95 (in 1997–98 there was a 6% drop from the previous year, the largest drop in decades), and Canada now ranks fifth, with New Zealand taking over fourth. The rate in 2001 (133/100,000) represented a 13% decrease since the peak.[34]
- In 1998–99, the average cost per year of incarcerating an inmate in a federal institution was $59,661 for men and $113,610 for women. The average cost of supervising an offender on parole or statutory release was approximately $13,000.[35]
- In 1995–96, 31% of prisoners in provincial institutions were admitted for property crimes, 19% for crimes of violence and 13% for impaired driving. (In 1997–98, 22% of admissions into provincial institutions were for failure to pay a fine.) In 1995–96, 24% of prisoners in federal institutions were admitted for robbery, 14% for sexual assaults, 12% for major assaults, 8% for homicide and 4% for drug trafficking. In 2000, 25% of the admissions into federal institutions were for homicide, 34% for robbery, 22% for drugs and 19% for sex offences. In 2001, federal admission comprised 53% violent crime, 18% property crime and 17% drug crime.[36]
- Over-representation of aboriginal persons in federal institutions continues to worsen. Aboriginal persons constitute 2% of the adult

population, but they constituted 11% of federal admissions in 1991 and 17% of federal admissions in both 1997 and 2001.[37]

- In 1996, 83% of inmates admitted to correctional institutions had had at least one previous conviction as adults, and 72% had already served prior prison terms. In 2000, 86% of federal inmates had served time in the youth and/or provincial systems.[38]
- In 2000, it was reported that 70% of federal inmates abused alcohol or other drugs. About half of federal inmates had a grade 8 education or lower.[39]
- In 1997–98, it was reported that most offenders serving their sentence on parole supervision complete the term without major breaches of supervision. In fact, only 10% of federal parolees are returned to prison as a result of new charges being laid, and only 1% are returned to prison because the new charge concerned a crime of violence.[40]

E. Public Perception of Criminal Justice
- Canadians have a much more negative view of the courts than they do of the police. In 1999, only 21% believed that the courts were doing a good job determining the guilt of the accused, only 15% believed they were doing a good job helping the victim and only 13% believed the court was providing justice quickly. However, 41% believed that the courts do a good job to ensure a fair trial for the accused. In contrast, 66% believed the police were doing a good job at being approachable, 62% believed they were doing a good job ensuring safety and 60% believed they were doing a good job enforcing laws.[41]
- Despite the overall decline in crime rates in the 1990s, public opinion surveys indicated that 75% of Canadians thought crime was getting worse. However, by 1999, most Canadians believed that crime levels had stabilized.[42]

12

A Taste of Cruelty

I SUSPECT THAT KILLING another human must be easy. I killed a rat once. I felt awful about crushing the life out of another creature, but I also caught a glimpse of blood lust—the thrill of total annihilation, the pride of the gladiator with a defeated foe lying lifeless at his feet. You just have to have a reason to kill. The good news is that people usually do not attack or kill others for no reason at all. The bad news is that, often, in the heat of passion, we delude ourselves into believing we have good reason to kill. People have to realize that, other than self-defence, there is no reason that can justify the taking of a life.

There are some sadists in the world who feed on blood lust without a reason, but I don't really worry about countless hordes of sadists walking the streets. A true sadist is a rare creature. Despite our fascination with serial killers and stranger homicides, there are still, thankfully, only a small handful of these raging psychopaths. There are lots of budding psychopaths. I know many lawyers and stockbrokers who fit within the diagnostic criteria for psychopathology, but the vast majority of these people keep their personality disorder to themselves. Hidden within the ordinary person is the potential for cruelty, and we are fortunate that this seed of cruelty remains dormant for most people.

The war on crime should focus on achieving two objectives: learning how to distinguish between the misguided and the walking time bombs and incapacitating the incorrigible. We need to better understand the process by which a petty criminal becomes incorrigibly cruel. We have to start examining the personalities of the criminals dragged before our courts. We've gone to the trouble of arresting and charging these people. They're standing before the court waiting to be judged. Why not take the time to examine whether they are psychopaths or misguided criminals who made a mistake? I would bet my life savings that almost every mass murderer, who has butchered dozens in a one-time explosion of violence (almost always ending in suicide), has previously appeared before criminal courts, on some charge or another, and the courts have simply processed these walking time bombs like common thieves or prostitutes. "Here's your five-year prison sentence, now get out of my court and out of my sight."

Over many years, I have begun to see four categories of criminal, progressing from nuisance to sinister: formally labelled, morally indifferent, state-raised, and sadistically cruel. The further along the criminal is in the sequence, the greater the level and virulence of the individual's alienation. Alienation is the key.

Alienation does not mean moral breakdown. We still live in relatively moral times. This is not *A Clockwork Orange*; at least, not yet. Alien-ation is simply an increased sense of distance between an individual and society. It is a gnawing sense of impotence, born of the feeling that individuals are powerless to change anything about themselves or their surroundings. It is the loss of the feeling of personal responsibility. It is the diffusion of conscience brought about by creating layers and layers of specialized bureaucracies and professional groups who make decisions for us.

I call the first category of criminal the formally labelled. These are the pleasure seekers: the pot smokers, the johns, the hookers and all the other hedonists. They also include those who indulge in youth crimes such as throwing rocks through windows for a giggle. The latter may hurt people, but these offenders are thinking only about the pursuit of a good time and not about the hurt. They are not malevolent. They are not evil. And they may not even be alienated to any significant degree. They are criminals only because they are formally labelled. For their descent into selfish pleasure, whether responsibly or recklessly, we bestow upon them the CRIMINAL RECORD. This first group of criminals, and it is a huge constituency, should never be caught up in the justice system. They don't necessarily see any wrong in their actions, and being condemned as criminals by public officials just serves to distance them from authority. Distance breeds alienation.

Most formally labelled criminals do consider whether their actions have hurt others, but they simply forget about the consequences to others when they pursue their fun and games. The second group, the morally indifferent, take things one step further. They are pleasure seekers who don't care how their actions affect others. They are not vicious people, although some may be in court for violent crime. But they are alienated to a small degree, and this alienation prevents them from truly caring about others. They do not want to hurt anyone, but in trying to over-come alienation by pursuing surrogate goals, the morally indifferent will never take into consideration the impact of their actions on others. After the fact, morally indifferent people will express regret, but this type of criminal can be dangerous in a reckless, negligent way. Fortunately, most of the time they are more of a potential threat than a day-to-day risk. Morally indifferent people are not committed to the infliction of harm, so they are dangerous only when the pursuit of their activities comes into conflict with other people's goals. The morally indifferent are modestly alienated, and when alienation is combined with a sense of material or emotional deprivation, all hell can break loose.

Category three is the state-raised criminal. Here is an individual whose indifference has turned malevolent because of overexposure to a loss of dignity, privacy and liberty. Incarcerated at an early age, state-raised criminals spend too much time in environments of insti-tutionalized violence. They have a sense of moral grievance that fuels anger and resentment. These criminals cannot function in a free soci-ety, as they have been nurtured in a prison ethos. They are caught in a revolving door of recidivism. This category of criminal is responsi-ble for the largest bulk of criminal activity in the country; they are career criminals, and they are often products of our own creation. Not all become sadistically cruel, but state-raised criminals rarely leave their world of crime.

Finally, the sadistically cruel bastards. Their motives are a complicated cluster of psychological and physiological factors that we do not yet, and may not ever, understand. Often there is some cruelty in their past, like child abuse, and they are almost always state-raised. The distinguishing element for the sadistically cruel criminal is an intense desire to injure. State-raised criminals do not necessarily *want* to hurt but, having learned life and social skills within the institutionalized setting of a prison or juvenile detention home, they know no better. The cruel bastard enjoys inflicting pain. Hurting others nourishes a cruel soul.

The morally indifferent criminal will eventually evolve into the sadis-tically cruel bastard if punished in the conventional manner. Thoughtless punishment fosters further alienation. Criminal intervention should be a last resort. In our world it is a knee-jerk response. At the level of the cruel bastard, all is lost. Forget rehabilitation. This should have been tried at the morally indifferent stage, but we were too busy wasting time processing the harmless formally labelled criminals.

Despite media magnification, there are not many cruel bastards. Lots of budding psychopaths roam the urban landscape, but most never blossom into cruel bastards. We are lucky. If cruel bastards were more plentiful, we might as well hand out guns and let everyone fend for themselves.

Surprisingly, when you look closely, these alienated misanthropes often still have a kernel of humanity buried inside. Is the Buddha in Paul Bernardo? Many serial killers appear to have the remnants of a conscience. On December 10, 1945, when William George Heirens finished butchering Frances Brown, he scrawled on the wall in lipstick: "For heaven's sake catch me. Before I kill more. I cannot control myself."[1] And he didn't control himself. One month later, he kidnapped a seven-year-old and demanded $20,000 in ransom. Later that day, the child's head was discovered in a manhole, and severed limbs were found in various sewers in Chicago. Chilling. Abhorrent. But somehow this monster's conscience managed to surface in a plea for help. Not the type of baiting game played by some killers, but a plea to catch him as soon as possible. History shows that many of the most proficient serial killers are caught because this little kernel of conscience forces them to bungle a killing so that police will have the information they need to solve the killing spree.

If you want to study the cruel bastard, you will most likely set up your fieldwork in the United States of America. Canada has produced some pretty deranged killers, but we are rank amateurs compared to the Americans. Of all the quasi-celebrity American killers, Carl Panzram stands out as the prototypical cruel bastard. At the age of eleven, Panzram was sent to reform school for breaking into a neighbour's home. Rebellious by nature, he was beaten senseless in reform school. When released, young Panzram travelled the States by freight trains, and on one occasion was raped by four hoboes. This experience gave him an idea of how he could inflict harm on a world he detested. Sodomizing men at gunpoint became his hobby until his execution in 1930.

When in prison, as he often was, he was incorrigible. He was able to wreck jails by burning furniture. He frequently escaped, and after one escape he decided to start killing. Luring sailors onto a stolen yacht, he would rob them, sodomize them and throw them into the sea. Panzram's initial body count was ten. When he went to West Africa to work for an oil company, the trip quickly transformed into a killing spree. His description tells all:

> While I was sitting there, a little nigger boy about eleven or twelve years came bumming around. He was looking for something. He found it too. I took him out to a gravel pit a quarter of a mile from the main camp. ... I left him there, but first I committed sodomy on him and then killed him. His brains were coming out of his ears when I left him and he will never be any deader. ... Then I went to town, bought a ticket on the Belgian steamer to Lobito Bay down the coast. There I hired a canoe and six niggers and went out hunting in the bay and backwaters. I was looking for crocodiles. I found them, plenty. They were all hungry. I fed them. I shot all six of those niggers and dumped 'em in. The crocs done the rest. I stole their canoe and went back to town, tied the canoe to a dock, and that night someone stole the canoe from me.[2]

Upon his return to the United States, he raped and killed three boys, bringing his body count to twenty. Eventually, he was sentenced to death for killing a foreman on a prison labour gang.

Panzram knew what he was doing and had no regrets. It was his life mission to hurt. He was also a thoughtful man, and we can catch glimpses of his cleverness in an autobiography he wrote in 1928 (which was suppressed for forty years, as it was believed to be too horrifying to publish).[3] He wrote the book because a guard, who had seen him beaten to a pulp by other guards, had shown him some fleeting compassion. The guard implored Panzram to tell his tale in a book. When this guard asked Panzram, "What's your racket?" Panzram replied, "What I do is reform people." When asked what this meant, Panzram replied that "the only way to reform people is to kill them." He described himself as "the man who goes around doing good."[4] For Panzram, life was hell, so killing someone was doing them a favour.

There's a fine line between madness and evil. Madness may excuse, but it requires a derangement of the senses and cognitive capacities. Panzram was deliberate, resentful and completely coherent and aware. He understood the world with a shocking clarity, and he knew exactly what he was doing. His words paint a clear picture of the cruel bastard:

> If any man was a habitual criminal, I am one. In my life I have broken every law that was ever made by both God and man. If either had made any more,

I should very cheerfully have broken them also. The mere fact that I have done these things is quite sufficient for the average person. Very few people even consider it worthwhile to wonder why I am what I am and do what I do. All that they think is necessary to do is catch me, try me, convict me and send me to prison for a few years, make my life miserable for me while in prison and turn me loose again. ... If someone had a young tiger cub in a cage and then mistreated it until it got savage and bloodthirsty and then turned it loose to prey on the rest of the world ... there would be a hell of a roar. ... But if some people do the same thing to other people, then the world is surprised, shocked and offended because they get robbed, raped and killed. They done it to me and then don't like it when I give them the same dose they gave me.[5]

When he was executed on September 11, 1930, it is reported he told the hangman, "Hurry it up, you hoosier bastard. I could hang a dozen men while you're fooling around." Another report claims his last dying words were, "I wish the human race had one neck and I had my hands around it."[6] He was vicious to the last breath.

Some fifty years after Panzram's death, Jack Henry Abbott dedicated his book *In the Belly of the Beast* to Carl Panzram (and others).[7] Who the hell would dedicate a book to such a despicable character? Abbott was another literate convict. Like Panzram, he could write. Like Panzram, he spent most of his life in prison. I borrowed the term "state-raised" criminal from Abbott. I hope he doesn't mind.

Following the classic pattern of broken home to foster home to reform school to penitentiary, by the age of thirty-seven Abbott had already spent twenty-five years in institutionalized settings. From age twelve to age eighteen, he was at reform school in Utah for "failing to adjust." As an adult, he was incarcerated for bum cheques. While in prison, he stabbed another inmate to death. Other than a brief six-week period of freedom when he escaped, he remained in prison until something remarkable happened in 1980: he was released.

One significant reason for his release was the publication of a series of letters/essays he had written for Norman Mailer. Mailer was working on *The Executioner's Song*, a book about Gary Gilmore, the first man executed in the States in the 1970s after a long moratorium. Abbott had been in a Utah prison with Gilmore, and he started to send Mailer his thoughts on violence and prison, hoping to educate the great American writer. The essays were so impressive that Mailer supported their publication and Abbott's release.

Panzram and Abbott were both state-raised criminals, as I'm sure most of the scary criminals who wreak havoc on the streets and in the homes are. Abbott's book has many powerful passages describing the evolution of the state-raised convict, but it is the following one that, for me, captures the resentment, anger and alienation that accompany a life of institutionalized living:

> The animal learns that any pain inflicted upon it by the being that nourishes and sustains it is pain it inflicts upon itself for disobedience. If it does not assimilate this "lesson" of self-inflicted pain, there is no recourse but the application of violence in order to destroy the animal. To kill it. It will defend itself with violence; it will become maddened and sullen. It will stand and fight or it will flee. It will do all this if it does not "learn" its pain is self-inflicted.
>
> Do not ask me what all this has to do with American justice; it is of the essence to the American system of justice.
>
> A prisoner begins his "training" in an American courtroom. He is told to shut his mouth unless spoken to. He is told he is a fool if he tries to be his own lawyer. He is told his motivations are not the subject matter of his indictment for crime.
>
> His court-appointed lawyer tells him what law he violated and how many years in prison the punishment carries. He is told that if he informs on and betrays his friends, he will receive leniency. If he is the only one charged with the crime, he is told that if he helps to solve other crimes, he could get leniency. He is told that because he knows the hours of the day and the day of the year and he is in jail, he cannot claim to be insane. It does not matter that he cannot either read or write or understand the vocabulary or the rules of the court. It does not matter why he robbed a store—just that he robbed it.
>
> If no violence was committed and he has a degree of wealth which places him above the need to rob a store, he will receive leniency in some form if this is his first indictment for crime. He will not be sent to prison.
>
> Yet he will go to prison if he does not have the degree of wealth which places him above the commission of such a crime. He is sent to prison if he is poor. That is, if he is poor and refuses to (or cannot) act as an agent of the police to betray his friends and solve whatever crimes they committed.

If his lawyer likes him, he will dicker with the prosecutor and the judge to obtain as short a sentence to prison as he can. If his lawyer does not like him, he will not make that effort. In America today over eighty-five percent of all defendants who go to prison have pled guilty.

In all this the prisoner never learns a single social value; never learns the definition of law or the customs of his society that the judicial system claims to be based upon.[8] [emphasis added]

This passage perfectly captures much of what is wrong with criminal justice, whether in the United States or Canada, and it gives the ivory-tower jurists a taste of what state-raised convicts think of their justice system. It is laughable that legal professionals would ever believe their justice system could have any impact on the state-raised convict. In this system, the petty burglar evolves into Carl Panzram before our very eyes.

Abbott became a self-fulfilling prophecy. Upon his release in 1980, he was invited to the best parties among the intelligentsia in New York City. He was a sensation—a spectacle. A few weeks into his freedom, he got into an argument with a waiter at 5:00 a.m. in the Bowery over whether he could use a restaurant lavatory. They agreed to take the argument outside. Abbott stabbed the waiter to death. The state-raised convict thought he saw aggression in the waiter's eyes. When the waiter looked around the street, Abbott believed he was checking to see if there were any witnesses around. Abbott thought the waiter was going to stab him, so he took a pre-emptive strike. Abbott's logic and actions make sense in a prison setting. But the waiter only wanted to take the argument outside the restaurant. He was not planning to plant a blade in Abbott's belly. Abbott was nurtured in the belly of the beast, and his state-sponsored fear and paranoia made him incapable of functioning in conventional society.

When does the state-raised convict become a cruel bastard? If we knew that, we might be able to avoid some tragic disasters. But there are no easy answers. Panzram and Abbott had miserable childhoods. The Boston Strangler and Charles Manson were brutalized as children. There's a kind of karmic symmetry to thinking that what goes around, comes around. It becomes easy to blame random violence on broken homes and domestic violence. Believing this, criminal justice should closely monitor homes filled with sexual or physical violence. And in some ways that has been the direction taken over the past few decades.

I used to think this way, but in 1995 one small statistic made me reconsider. When I was covering the Bernardo trial for CTV, and my mind was focused on the question of evil and malice, some lawyers at the trial gave me a copy of a 1990 study by Park Dietz and Robert Hazelwood, two prominent FBI serial-killer profilers. In a study of thirty sexual sadists, it was noted that 23.3% were physically abused as children and 20% were sexually abused as children.[9] These numbers are rather underwhelming. They do not support the karmic symmetry of abuse breeding abuse. If most sexual sadists were not physically or sexually abused as children, what is the trigger for the cruel bastard? Not all state-raised convicts become Panzrams. The debate will continue, and perhaps answers will be found in the future. For now, we have serious problems detecting and identifying walking time bombs.

In 1994, I started to correspond with Abbott. I was researching victims' rights, and I thought it would be interesting to hear what the state-raised convict would have to say about victims. How did he feel about his victims and his crimes? I sent Abbott books and articles he wanted to read, and in return he would answer my questions. He never talked directly about his sense of responsibility for his crimes, but he resented my suggestion that he was like Panzram. He understood that society was compelled to punish the criminal, and I guess he included himself in that category, but he was somewhat unclear. He felt that punishment may be a justifiable response to wrongdoing, but he detested the utilitarian notion that punishment can solve the crime problem. On November 25, 1994, he wrote:

> ... in the present, the problem of crime is pressing (I see it as the problem of policemen, but won't bother you with that). I am certain, however, that we cannot stop crime by blaming the criminal for it. We can stop <u>criminals</u> and contribute to the rehabilitation of <u>society</u>, however, only by facing unflinchingly the responsibilities a criminal has for his crime. <u>His</u> actions, <u>his</u> crime. This would be a big step forward in dealing with what we have no control over today (i.e. the condition of crime).

Deal with the criminal. Not an abstract symbol who represents crime at large. Punish the criminal for what they have done, not to send a message to other criminals. You deny convicts humanity when they are treated as a means to an end.

I think Abbott is right. But our justice system will never be able to deal with criminals as whole beings. This takes too much time. It's too much work.

We will not accomplish anything until we stop labelling pleasure seekers and alternative lifestyle freaks criminals. Once we free up resources and time by liberating the pot smokers, the prostitutes and the gamblers, we must invest these resources in working with the morally indifferent. With more time, we could stop instinctively throwing the book at the morally indifferent, only to watch them turn into state-raised convicts as we herd them off to prison. When we are faced with the kid who trashed his high school, or the first-time impaired driver, or the impoverished thief, or the crack-addicted burglar, we can spend time monitoring and supervising these wayward souls. The statistics show that prison costs almost three times more than supervision, so if we spent more money on supervision in the community, perhaps we could keep tabs on the morally indifferent and ensure that their feelings of alienation and anger do not become more virulent. But this is not even close to what we do. We incarcerate and ask questions later at the parole hearing. We place some people in community supervision, but this entails only much supervision as feeding goldfish once a week.

On November 25, 1994, Abbott also wrote:

America refuses to recognize the existence of social classes, and this is the root of the insolubility of crime. It abrogates all solutions. Prison industries help society with employment and local economies. The illicit drug market helps the poor as well as the economy and the justice system. The massive number of law enforcement organizations are now almost self-sufficient and confiscating the money and property of criminals. Taking all this into account, it becomes obvious that there is no real need to stop crime, indeed, from that point of view there is always the need for more and more crime. When you ponder these things about crime and victims open your mind to the idea that the system needs crime to continue functioning today. It's even entertaining! All this crying about crime in the media has more to do with budgets and politics than with enlightening anyone.

This is the hidden secret of criminal justice. It defies change. It needs to generate and manufacture 2 million crimes a year to maintain a privileged position among the pantheon of public services. Too many legal professionals, correctional officers and police officers have a vested interest in maintaining the status quo. We may or may not have a crime problem. We'll never really know, because the rulers will always want to make sure the ruled *think* there is a crime problem. It's good business.

While it may be good business to process 2 million crimes a year, this leaves little time for acquiring insight into predatory criminal behaviour. But the lawyers, judges, psychologists, shrinks and profilers act like they know what they are doing—as though they understand why people do bad things and what to do with these bad people. They don't understand. Developing a coherent psychology of evil is a painstaking endeavour. It has proven easier to land a man on the moon than to decipher the code for cruelty on earth. We will never break the code while we are distracted by millions of cases of no particular significance to the social order.

Yet, even if criminal justice stuck to what really matters, the legal professionals would still be unable to advance our understanding of predation and cruelty. As we shall now see, criminal justice often asks the wrong questions and usually answers the questions by speaking in tongues.

13

The Legal Construction of Crime

GAIL JONES ENTERS the law office of Peter Maxwell. This dishevelled lawyer, in his messy office, has been asked to help Gail, whose husband has been wrongfully convicted and is rotting in prison. The following exchange takes place:

Maxwell: The law is vulgar. Just like religion. Vulgar things, both of them. Institutions corrupted by their own self-importance. I'm immune to their seductive power. I've actually been around too long. Seen a lot of so-called illegal activity. Seen too much of it to believe it's just deviant behaviour. Anyway, more times than not, these days I come down in favour of the deviants. I'm not talking about the violent now. Especially not about the sexually violent. Violent sexual deviants I've got no time for. I don't want them executed or anything, but I think we have to construct a system of mutual protection. Us from them. And them from themselves. I'm in favour of increased government spending in the area of prison reform, medical facilities for the criminally dysfunctional. That sort of thing. You follow me so far?
Gail: No.
Maxwell: I'm talking about your situation vis-à-vis my situation.
Gail: Nothing you said in the last half hour has anything to do with my situation. I just want my husband out of prison.
Maxwell: I was talking about the law. Trying to let you know that even though I'm constrained by it, I'm not impressed by it. The law is vulgar in its rigidity. Insensitive to the nuance of human existence. Derived and constructed from knowledge within a narrow historical corridor. In short, it's in love with itself. You're marginal. Your cause is marginal. Outside the corridor, so to speak.[1]

This is the opening dialogue from George Walker's 1989 play *Love and Anger*, one of many brilliant Walker plays dealing with the underbelly of East End Toronto. I was stunned by this opening. How did Walker know? Who told him the hidden secret of criminal justice? Most people know that criminal justice has its failings, but very few people know that it is "vulgar in its rigidity. Insensitive to the nuance of human existence. Derived and constructed from knowledge within a narrow historical corridor." Wow! This is why we will never know whether the Buddha is in Paul Bernardo—because criminal justice sets it own agenda and then filters reality through procedural and evidentiary rules to make it manageable for the legal professionals.

After a few years of practice in the early 1980s, I returned to school in order to obtain a master's degree in law. Although practice was at times exciting and provocative, I found the whole experience spiritually draining. I couldn't quite put my finger on it, but something about criminal justice seemed like a black hole, sucking life energy into its vortex without any return. So I decided to pursue a teaching career in law, and this required that I obtain a master's degree. While back at school, I was exposed to the writings of the critical legal studies movement, the left-wing collective of intellectuals whose analysis was shaped by the perspective that law was a tool of oppression. I had seen this before in one shape or another, but I still was attracted to the dadaist sensibility of some of these intellectuals.

Surprisingly, critical legal scholars rarely turned their attention to criminal-justice issues, even though this legal institution is the most closely identified with oppressive and authoritarian tendencies, but one article on criminal justice caught my attention: Professor Mark Kelman's *Interpretive Construction in the Substantive Criminal Law*.[2] This scholar spoke of the "processes by which concrete situations are reduced to substantive legal controversies ... both to the way we construe a factual situation and to the way we frame the possible rules to handle the situation."[3] This was the black hole I had encountered in practice. In a highly sophisticated analysis, Kelman led me to the realization that criminal justice was spiritually draining for me because it required that I reduce my client's reality to a set of manageable legal doctrines. It forced me to deal with people as abstractions, and this was contrary to my natural spirit.

The legal process operates upon certain basic premises that are not in the interests of the general public—premises that seem to be immutable and often unconscious in nature. Intellectuals call this a paradigm. I call it a reality filter. We all filter reality. We could not survive if our brains had to constantly deal with the overload of stimuli present in our environment, so the brain ignores some stimuli and processes other stimuli in feedback loops that are preordained. Social institutions do the same thing. They filter the reality of their clients in order to achieve some degree of bureaucratic efficiency. There are times when the real claims of people will be subordinated to the bureaucratic necessities of the institution. At a rudimentary level, we know this: we have all felt the cold and alien touch of an impersonal bureaucracy, and criminal justice is no exception.

Bureaucracies need rules. Criminal justice needs rules. Rules are a good thing at a certain level; the rule of law does reduce arbitrary power and control. But rules deal in generalities, and human reality defies reduction to the abstract. An abstract rule cannot cover all the conceivable manifestations of human conduct. It is impossible. So the law creates its own reality, in which we act as if every criminal trial has resolved, beyond a reasonable doubt, the issue of the accused's guilt. There are no ties in the game of criminal justice. The institution demands a determinate answer. It will not tolerate an honest but equivocating judge who says, "I'm not really sure. This case is messy, ambiguous and confusing." The institution demands what I call moral shortcuts and "thought-terminating clichés,"[4] and what the profession calls legal doctrine, to ensure that the fallible and human judge can reach a conclusion.

Here's a classic example of a thought-terminating cliché: "Motive is irrelevant." According to the law, an accused person's motive may be relevant in determining punishment, but it is not relevant to the issue of guilt or innocence. So if the Crown proves the elements of the crime set out in the Criminal Code, it does not matter if you acted upon a noble motive. And if you are lucky enough that your conduct does not fit squarely within the elements, it does not matter if your motivation was sinister.

If motive is irrelevant, this claim as a defence to theft in a supermarket will never be accepted: "I was laid off last year. My six-year-old, Tommy, had only eaten hotdog buns for the last two days. He was hungry. He needed something healthy." At a moral level, this thief might be able to challenge the established economic order if we allowed motivation to be a claim in defence. Acquitting the hungry thief sends a message that the unfair distribution of wealth in this country, and all others, may excuse a person for breaking the rules. Remember Cardinal Rule #1 of judging: never let the trial become an occasion for challenging the legitimacy of the system—it's too dangerous. Deeming motive irrelevant is one way of ensuring that the criminal trial will not become an occasion for calling into question larger questions of social justice.

Moral reasoning can be messy and indeterminate, and resolute decisions may not come that easily. The law is afraid of unrestrained moral reasoning. It is afraid of the battle of warring creeds, borne out so dramatically in the abortion debate. So rules are enacted and legal doctrines constructed that serve to ensure that the criminal trial does not devolve into a battle of warring creeds. Sometimes the rules and doctrine are at odds with ordinary moral assessment, but legal professionals rarely admit that legal resolutions are often at odds with moral conclusions. I believe that a legal conclusion not consistent with a sound moral conclusion is worthless.

If I shoot you in the head and leave you for dead, yet somehow you are rescued and survive, I will be convicted of attempted murder. This offence carries a maximum sentence of life, and the characteristic sentence is between five and ten years. If you die, I will be guilty of murder with a minimum life sentence. From a moral perspective, there is absolutely no difference between these two cases. My moral culpability is identical. Yet in law, we fixate on the consequence. Death. Even though death may be a complete fortuity beyond our control, it is factored into the determination of personal blameworthiness. In a moral universe, people should be punished and blamed only for things within their control. Both the murderer and attempted murderer intend to kill their victim; it should make no difference if the victim dies or miraculously survives. But in the legal universe, it makes a huge difference.

To mask the divergence of law and morality, jurists construct legal doctrines that appear to be morally sound but that, in actuality, are just convenient moral shortcuts. Look at the 1977 case of *R. v. Smithers*.[5] During a rough hockey game, Smithers was subjected to racial insults from a player named Cobby on the other team. After the game, Smithers caught up with the racist and challenged him to a fight. Cobby declined, but Smithers still threw some punches at his head. Teammates intervened, but Smithers broke loose and managed to deliver one hard and fast kick to Cobby's gut. Simple case? Sure. Smithers assaulted Cobby. End of story. What about the racial provocation? No problem. The law says that provocation is a defence only to murder, not to other crimes. So the racial context of the event just disappears from sight. Out of sight, out of mind, and the judge can easily conclude that Smithers is guilty of manslaughter. But things get a bit more complicated. Most people who are kicked in the gut double over, and may vomit or get winded. Cobby was a special racist. He had a malfunctioning epiglottis. When he started to vomit from the kick, that small muscle failed to prevent the regurgitated material from entering his windpipe and lungs. Cobby died from aspirating foreign material into his lungs. Aspiration usually occurs with drug overdoses, alcohol intoxication and car accidents. It is a "rare and unusual" occurrence, and one not commonly associated with a kick to the stomach.

Is Smithers a murderer? Of course not—he had no intent to kill. Is he guilty of manslaughter? An assault that causes death technically constitutes the crime of "unlawful act" manslaughter. But did his actions cause death? This is not so easy. I say the death was caused by an internal cause—a malfunctioning epiglottis. It was a freak accident that the racist died. This was an assault, plain and simple, and that is all Smithers should be held accountable for. But most of my students say, "If Smithers had not kicked him, none of this would have happened. So he caused the death." I always respond, "If Cobby did not make racial insults, none of this would have happened." So who is to blame for the death? Smithers? Cobby? Nobody? Or maybe the tiny muscle that did not do its job. But there's no prison for malfunctioning epiglottises, and there was a dead body outside the hockey rink. Someone had to pay.

Determining whether Smithers should be held criminally accountable for the death is a difficult moral question. I have always felt that the manslaughter conviction given in this case was a major injustice, but many of my students seemed to agree with the verdict. The case went all the way to the Supreme Court of Canada, and no judge ever really tried to tackle the difficult moral issue head-on. In convicting Smithers, the courts discounted the importance of the epiglottis issue, stating "you take your victim as you find him," as if that was a self-evident truth. They even gave this vacuous assertion a name—the "thin-skull doctrine"—because if it has a name it must be worthy of belief. If you strike someone in the head and he or she suffers injuries far in excess of what would be expected because they have a thin skull, you will be civilly liable for the full extent of the damage. This makes sense. You caused the injury, you should compensate the victim. But there is a world of difference between an obligation to compensate in civil law and condemnation, conviction and incarceration in the criminal law. In the Smithers case, the court took a doctrine from civil law and transplanted it into the criminal law as a moral shortcut for determining whether to criminally blame Smithers for the death.

Criminal blameworthiness depends upon your intent, your character and your actions. It is your moral culpability that determines whether the state is justified in punishing and stigmatizing you. Criminal liability does not turn upon the state of repair of the victim's body. It does not turn upon freak occurrences that can transform an ordinary fight into a serious tragedy. But instead of struggling with difficult moral issues, the courts take a shortcut by dismissing the racist context of the incident with the rule that provocation is not a defence to assault, and skirting the difficult causation question with the catchy phrase "you take your victim as you find him."

George Walker was right when he said that law is "insensitive to the nuance of human existence" and has been "corrupted by its own self-importance." To show that Walker was right, I need to look at the types of arguments and issues that are being raised in court in the few criminal cases that actually end up in a trial. In most trials the defence simply challenges whether the Crown has evidence to prove the case beyond a reasonable doubt. These trials are contests of facts. What I will be looking at here are cases that raise issues of law—the types of cases in which judges are called upon to make rulings of law. I want to show you the type of issues that excite our legal professionals, and that leave the public confounded and cold. To do this, I will have to get knee-deep in legal doctrine. Sorry to have to take you into this pit.

Actus non facit reum nisi mens sit rea: "An act is not guilty unless accompanied by a guilty state of mind." There may be few lawyers who actually speak Latin, but every lawyer is familiar with this Latin maxim. Even law students who fail criminal law know that a crime consists of the *actus reus* (guilty act) and the *mens rea* (guilty mind). Beyond that, they may know very little, but this maxim is drilled into law students' heads from the first day they enter the hallowed halls of a law school. The *actus reus*, or guilty act, is the objective element of the crime as defined in the

Criminal Code. The Code sets out the details of the criminal act, the relevant circumstances of the crime and the harmful consequences of the act. All the Crown has to do is establish that each element of the *actus reus* is proved beyond a reasonable doubt. There may be some interpretive problems, such as what the word "solicit" means, or what constitutes "bodily harm," but for the most part, the analysis of the *actus reus* does not trigger philosophical controversies. It is the requirement of the guilty mind, or *mens rea*, that poses conceptual difficulties.

Acting with a guilty mind is the defining essence of a crime. If you hurt someone accidentally or inadvertently, you may be civilly responsible to compensate for the loss; you become a criminal only when you intentionally or knowingly cause this harm. The presence of a guilty mind is what justifies punishing a culprit. A guilty state of mind shows that the accused fully understood that he was hurting someone and violating their rights. With *mens rea* present, the accused can be seen as acting in disregard of and disrespect for the rules of civilized society. Therefore, punishment is needed to set the moral balance straight. *Mens rea* separates the foolish from the evil. Foolish people can cause enormous harm, but the criminal law was not designed to stigmatize and incarcerate people who act out of ignorance or folly. The foolish may be obligated to compensate injured parties, and we may choose to shun and avoid them. But criminal law is designed to combat and control evil, and *mens rea* is the law's barometer of evil.

Although it appears we punish people for specific acts of harm, in reality we are trying to judge overall moral character. On the biblical judgement day, God will not punish you because on October 1, 1972, you robbed a bank. God would also notice that you saved a drowning child on September 22, 1984, or that you helped a blind man cross the street on March 15, 1987. True judgement and true punishment require an assessment of the person's lifetime moral credits and debits. It is a fine balancing act, and God would never be so anal and hysterical as to punish someone for a bad mistake. Religious judgement understands the relevance of redemption and character. Criminal justice does not. So *mens rea* serves as an important reality filter. Instead of having to engage in a true moral appraisal of the accused's character, criminal law simply asks if the accused acted with some mental awareness of the risk of death at 3:00 a.m., on October 25, 2001, when he stabbed that bouncer. Reducing an accused's personal blameworthiness to a brief snapshot of mental awareness makes reality a lot easier for legal professionals to deal with. Of course, nobody's brain works this way. You can assess what an accused person was thinking only by examining his or her actions, words and characteristic behaviour before, during and after the crime. Yet, for better or worse, we stick to an assessment of whether the accused's brain was full of *mens rea* at the precise moment the crime was committed.

Criminal law compartmentalizes reality. This is why it took so long for courts to recognize the relevance of the battered woman syndrome. The traditional doctrine of self-defence requires an assessment of whether the accused reasonably believed they were in danger at the precise moment they repelled an attack with deadly force. Battered women were killing their spouses when the spouses were asleep, or in circumstances when danger was not present. In the compartmentalized legal world, these women were murderers. It took a groundbreaking decision in the 1990s before the law could take into account the repetitive history of abuse in determining whether the woman had a reasonable belief that her life was in danger, even though at the moment of killing she may have been in a perfectly safe situation.[6] It seems so obvious and trite that self-defence must be interpreted within the unique context of the attacker–victim relationship, yet this was a revolutionary concept for the law.

A biblical judgement day analysis is beyond the abilities of most judges. Last I looked, there were no deities on the bench. So having *mens rea* to act as a reality filter is not all bad. At least our system takes seriously the issue of "no punishment without fault," and efforts are truly made to distinguish the cruel from the careless. *Mens rea* may be only a snapshot of mental awareness at the precise moment the crime is committed; nonetheless, acting with intention or knowledge is still a crude approximation of character. Acting with intention or knowledge usually means that your action was "in character" and not an aberrant "out of character" mistake. But this process of filtering reality is often just another game for lawyers to play.

What exactly is *mens rea*? At a minimum, it requires that your actions be voluntary and deliberate and that you know or have awareness of the circumstances defining the crime. For sexual assault, this would mean that your touching was done deliberately, and that you knew or had awareness of the absence of consent (this being the circumstance defining the crime). If the *actus reus* requires proof of a consequence (such as causing harm or causing death), the *mens rea* may also include intending this consequence, being reckless thereto or negligently causing this harm. In turn, intent may be defined as desiring the consequence (direct intent) or simply being certain that your actions will lead to this consequence without desiring it, or striving towards it (oblique intent). Intent must be distinguished from recklessness, which is defined as having some foresight of probability or possibility that your action may lead to the harmful consequence. And this has to be distinguished from negligence, which is defined as causing the harm without knowing the risk, even though any other reasonable person would have been aware of the risk. This is only the tip of the iceberg. These various states of mind all have different implications for the assessment of moral responsibility.

Mens rea is a fundamental and essential component of fault. *Mens rea* is the defining feature of crime. Yet Parliament often does not indicate in the Criminal Code what type of *mens rea* is required for which offence. And when it does specify a state of mind requirement in the Code, there is no consistency in definition. The word "wilfully" is often used in the Code to signify *mens rea*, yet the courts have concluded that the word can have three different meanings depending upon the context. So the most fundamental aspect of criminal fault is left to debate among lawyers and judges. Lawyers love the ambiguity, as a lack of clarity will always provide the lawyer with work, but the ambiguity is like the worm in the apple for the ordinary person. Imagine sitting in court listening to the debate over what type of *mens rea* is required for the crime charged. It borders on the surreal to have a trial where the first order of business is figuring out what mental element the Crown has to prove. How could the Crown charge this person if no one knows the precise *mens rea* elements of the crime? This type of process is a bit too much like a last-minute improvisation to satisfy me that the *mens rea* inquiry is a reasonable and effective proxy into character.

It is very dangerous for the law not to fully and coherently define the elements of *mens rea*. It is a mistake to leave the development of this reality filter to judges and lawyers. Criminal justice is based upon an adversarial conception of truth-finding. Both sides present arguments on how best to interpret and apply the law, and from the clash of opposites the judge is supposed to discern the truth. This is a completely fucked-up epistemology, made even worse by the fact that our system allows accused people to remain in silence throughout their trial. The accused—one of the best sources of information—can exercise silence, not participating in the very ritual designed to figure out exactly what he or she was thinking. With these procedural components of our process taken into account, the reality filter starts to drift far away from anything understandable and recognizable to the ordinary person.

Leaving the elusive *mens rea* determination in the hands of lawyers easily leads the law into sophistry of the worst kind. Remember the bedrock principle of fault: there must be a concurrence of *actus reus* and *mens rea*. They must be contemporaneous; at the time of acting, there must be a flash of awareness or intention to convert the harmful act into a crime. Take this principle and put it in the hands of lawyers working within an adversarial framework, and you get interpretations and applications of the law that are senseless to the ordinary person.

Here's an example. A guy named Meli brutally beat his victim senseless and then threw him over a cliff to dispose of the evidence. He thought the victim was dead when he threw him off the cliff, but the autopsy revealed that the cause of death was exposure. So Meli's lawyer came up with this clever argument: Meli had the requisite *mens rea* (intent to kill) when he beat his victim, but the beating did not cause death. When Meli threw the victim off the cliff, he no longer possessed the *mens rea*, as he could not intend to kill a person he believed to already be dead. Therefore, the lawyer argued that Meli could not be convicted of murder. Perhaps attempted murder for the beating, or manslaughter for the cliff-throw, but not murder.[7] A pretty slick argument that has logical appeal, but really makes sense only in Wonderland.

The 1993 Supreme Court of Canada decision in *R. v. Cooper* demonstrates a similar departure from reality.[8] Cooper and his ex-lover had been drinking. The court outlined the events:

> At the parking-lot the respondent testified that he and the deceased engaged in some form of consensual sexual activity. He said that they began to argue at one point and that the deceased struck him. At this he became angry. He hit the deceased and grabbed her by the throat with both hands and shook her. He stated that this occurred in the front seat of the Jeep. He then said that he could recall nothing else until he woke in the back seat and found

the body of the deceased beside him. He had no recollection of causing her death. He pushed her body out of the Jeep and drove away. Later during the drive to his home he found one of her shoes in the vehicle and threw it out the window into the snow.[9]

Seems like an obvious murder case. The experts indicated that death by strangulation can occur in as little time as thirty seconds, but in this case it could have taken as long as two minutes. Just enough time for a lawyer to devise a clever argument. Cooper asserted that he did intend to cause bodily harm when he started to strangle the victim, and he passed out before he realized that his actions were likely to cause death. Therefore, *mens rea* did not exist at the precise moment the *actus reus* was committed (the moment when death was caused), and Cooper's lawyer argued that a murder conviction could not be sustained.

As with the Meli case, the court did not fall for this sophistry. Courts can act upon simple good sense. It concluded:

> This argument should not be accepted. It would require the Crown to provide expert evidence as to the moment at which death physiologically became a likelihood. It would be impossible to fix the time of the "'likelihood'" of death and difficult to provide evidence as to the duration of the requisite intent of the accused. That cannot be the meaning of this section. Neither the plain wording of this section nor any concept of fairness require the Crown to demonstrate such a complex chronological sequence. In order to obtain a conviction under s. 212 (a) (ii), the Crown must prove that the accused caused and intended to cause bodily harm that he knew was likely to cause the death of the victim. If death results from a series of wrongful acts that are part of a single transaction then it must be established that the requisite intent coincided at some point with the wrongful acts.[10]

We will never know what Cooper was thinking, and one has to be suspicious of the "blackout" claim. It has been said that the blackout is the last refuge of the scoundrel. But does it really matter what he was thinking at the moment of strangulation? This seems trivial. The evidence was clear that an argument broke out that led to an act of strangling. Does it really matter whether Cooper was thinking about the strangling or the Superbowl when his hands were on the victim's neck? I think not. He could have been singing Beethoven's *Ode to Joy* in his head the whole time, and I still would call this an act of murder.

In neither of the Meli and Cooper cases did the courts fall for the specious logic of the accused. But both cases made their way to the highest court, and along the way much time and effort and many justice resources were spent arguing about meaningless issues. The families of Meli's and Cooper's victims would have been shocked to hear Meli and Cooper try to escape justice by dividing up the circumstances into small units, only some of which are accompanied by a guilty state of mind. This is insulting gibberish for a grieving family, but it is these types of arguments that excite and stimulate legal professionals. No wonder only 34% of violent crimes are reported; once reported, your trauma becomes a messy collage of fleeting guilty thoughts superimposed on the *actus reus*. This is not, and never will be, the victim's vernacular or reality.

"You'll get no true satisfaction from the law." People will never be satisfied when thrust into someone else's reality. And the law, being in love with itself, is too self-absorbed to notice that it is drifting further and further away from ordinary reality. Jurists are proud of the development of *mens rea* as a legal doctrine; it is considered a crowning achievement in the shift from a barbaric system, which reflexively punished those who caused harm, to a humanist perspective, which punishes only if the bringer of harm intended the injury. Being proud of this doctrine, chances are slim that the law will abandon it. But as a reality filter, *mens rea* will eventually come into direct conflict with conventional reality. There will be fallout when an institution's reality strays too far from conventional perspectives.

Criminal justice took a real beating in the 1980s, when it struggled with the question of the *mens rea* for the offence of rape. As an offence, rape was restricted to forced sexual intercourse. The law required proof of "penetration." This archaic offence was replaced in 1983 with the offence of sexual assault, which includes all manner of non-consensual sexual touching. But on the question of the guilty state of mind requirement for forced penetration and unwanted touching, the courts' blind adherence to the reality filter of contemporaneous awareness brought feminist condemnation—and for good reason.

In 1974 a guy named Morgan invited his drinking buddies back to his home to engage in a sexual fantasy. He told them that his wife fantasized about being raped, and that they should come to his home to enact the scene. He told them to ignore her protests and screams, as they were part of the staging. Morgan was engaged in some cruel, psychopathic game he did not disclose. His wife was gang-raped, and at trial the drinking buddies asserted that they truly and honestly believed the wife was consenting. They took Morgan's story at face value.[11]

The defining element of the crime of rape is the absence of consent. In accordance with traditional doctrine, the *mens rea* would be knowledge of the absence of consent. At the moment of penetration, the accused would have to have that mental flash of awareness. So if you believe the story told by the drinking buddies, you would have to acquit because they subjectively believed the woman was consenting. That was the legal conclusion drawn by American, Canadian and British courts in the 1980s, and it drew fierce condemnation.

Who cares what Morgan's buddies subjectively believed? The story is bizarre, offensive and improbable. It borders on delusional. Feminist scholars immediately branded the court decisions as creating a "rapist's charter." Men could delude themselves that no means yes or that submission is the same as true consent. Subjective beliefs are often misguided and self-interested, so isn't it more important to examine whether the beliefs are objectively reasonable? When a man claims he believes his partner is consenting, he may be truly ignorant. But the question isn't whether he was ignorant, but why he was ignorant. Not "what was the accused thinking?" but "what was the accused capable of thinking?"

Feminists had discovered that the "subjective orthodoxy of *mens rea*" (that fault is measured by a subjective flash of mental awareness) is a bad reality filter. It does not provide even a crude approximation of the true character of the accused. Let's say you believe Morgan's buddies. They were probably drunk and liked the intrigue of the story. But who cares if they lacked *mens rea*? They're complete assholes. At a minimum, they should have made complete and frank inquiries of the wife before even considering Morgan's offer. This failure alone establishes culpability. So the pursuit of the traditional legal question, what Morgan's buddies were thinking at the time of intercourse, misses the mark. Even if the accused did not possess *mens rea*, it is more important to explore why they mistakenly believed they had consent. Most explanations turn out to be bullshit.

Here's the interesting twist. The doctrine of mistaken belief did not actually help these men. Morgan and his buddies were convicted. In fact, almost all accused who raise as a defence an honestly held, mistaken belief in consent are convicted. In fact, in every case I have examined so far, the accused were convicted. Law will always create its own vernacular and its own manner of framing issues, and sometimes the result achieved is the correct result. But the process of reaching the result is often so alien to those most interested in understanding the controversy that criminal justice leaves most people feeling unsatisfied. People don't want reality filters; they want the law to speak their language.

Another reality filter has the potential not just to distort the route taken, but also to skew the final result: a conviction will be entered only if a just and fair process has been used to reach the conclusion. Procedural rules and constitutional rights inform our vision of legal guilt. Every game has its rules; there is nothing sinister about legal guilt being dependent upon compliance with the rules of the game. In earlier times, many of the rules of the game were mere technicalities and conviction could be lost because the state did not draft the indictment properly. The era of technical acquittals has come and gone, and it is rare that a criminal will walk away from a serious accusation simply because the state made a picayune technical mistake.

In modern times, fair process is about conformity with various constitutional rights. In 1982, the Charter of Rights and Freedoms came into effect, and had the potential to dramatically alter the legal landscape. The Charter prescribes a set of legal rights that represent the supreme law of the land. Violation of these rights can lead to evidence being excluded or to the court entering a stay of proceedings to put an end to a constitutionally flawed prosecution. This new era introduced the American phenomenon of having a criminal go free because the "constable blundered." In effect, criminal trials transformed into a process that simultaneously judges both the criminal and the state officials seeking conviction.

For better or worse, the elevation of some procedural rights to constitutional prerequisites for conviction has created another reality filter. Determining legal responsibility, even with the filter of *mens rea*, was already a difficult exercise. Now it is made more difficult by the introduction of another set of concerns not directly related to the exercise of determining responsibility. Legal guilt means proof beyond a reasonable doubt on the basis of admissible evidence and proper procedure. The evidentiary and procedural concerns that animate our current system add to the bewilderment of ordinary people. Not many people understand, or accept, that a guilty person can escape justice because at the time of arrest the police did not allow the accused to call a lawyer. People understand why there is a right to "retain and instruct counsel" upon arrest, but they can't understand why an apparently guilty person is set free because this right was infringed upon.

Constitutional legal rights are the key ingredient in ensuring that criminal prosecutions do not become persecutions. Police, prosecutors and judges are given enormous power, and enormous discretion to exercise this power. Power corrupts even the most saintly person, and it is essential that there are legal constraints placed upon public officials. For these officials, engaged in the "competitive exercise of ferreting out crime,"[12] the end usually justifies the means. They believe no amount of trickery or treachery is wrong when the goal is public safety. Without a moral brake placed upon the pursuit of criminals, everyone could be exposed to needless and unjustifiable state intrusions.

Only constitutional rights prevent law enforcement from becoming an ever-expanding dragnet of epic proportions. Sure, the criminal is sometimes the lucky beneficiary of these rights, but the intended beneficiaries are you and me. Give state officials unconstrained power, and maybe we will lock up a few more dangerous criminals, but we will also end up imprisoning a lot of innocent people, and the marginal decrease in criminal victimization will be offset by the increase in victimization at the hands of state officials.

But here's the million-dollar question: why has the law established a connection between legal guilt and procedural rights? Why has another reality filter been introduced into a process already fraught with complexity and surreal doctrine? At least the filter of *mens rea* was a crude approximation of responsibility. Procedural and evidentiary rules are filters of the worst kind, because they bear no relationship to the ultimate question of guilt or innocence.

Rules that prevent the jury from being informed of the accused's bad character or criminal record may seem fair, but they distort reality. We exclude bad character evidence not because it is irrelevant to the blame game, but because we are telling the jury: "You can't handle the truth." If the jury convicts a murderer without having been told he has murdered in the past, we feel more confident in this verdict than in one delivered by a jury that has taken his history into account. A fully informed jury might convict on the basis that a "tiger never changes its stripes," when the accused may be one of those rare tigers who has. We filter reality so we can feel better about the ultimate result.

The exclusion of important evidence because of a violation of the right to counsel or the right to be free from unreasonable search is not just a filter, it is a negation of reality. A murderer confesses without being advised of his or her right to counsel, and we exclude this evidence at trial. Go home, murderer, even though we know there is no reality to your clean bill of innocence. For an assessment of guilt or innocence to include consideration of how the accused has been treated by state officials is weird and surreal. The introduction of procedural rules that impair the truth-seeking function of a criminal trial is an absurd achievement.

Don't get me wrong. I would not want to live in a country where public officials cannot be made accountable for rights violation. But why have we squeezed the process of vindicating rights into an already overloaded and inefficient criminal-justice system? It is no longer *Her Majesty* v. *The Criminal*, but *Her Majesty* v. *Her Majesty and The Criminal*. I have seen, and participated in, trials in which the examination of state misconduct takes weeks or months, while the determination of guilt or innocence is completed in a matter of hours. This is a sign of an institution in need of therapy.

Procedural and evidentiary filters are unusual in their operation. A filter usually serves to narrow the field. The *mens rea* filter operates to reduce the scope of the guilt determination by substituting a mental flash for a more far-reaching assessment of moral character. Surprisingly, most of the procedural filters emanating from the Constitution actually expand the horizons of a criminal trial by introducing issues entirely extraneous to the guilt-innocence determination. With these filters, trials become bloated. With these filters, a simple one-day trial can end up being a month-long exploration of every detail relating to how the police obtained a confession. Why would we introduce a filter that makes reality more messy? The purpose of legal fictions is to streamline the process and enhance efficiency of bureaucratic operation.

A filter that serves to expand the scope of controversy is the best evidence of a profession "in love with itself." The decision to expand the scope of inquiry into state conduct reflects an interesting set of priorities.

Legal professionals do not want to become embroiled in the sordid details of the lives of the accused and their victims. This would be emotionally laden and spiritually complex, and professionals avoid emotional involvement like the plague. But expanding the inquiry to look at the actions of lawyers, judges and police is a comfortable journey on familiar terrain for legal professionals. It is easier to clean the house you live in than to have to deal with all the shit found in other people's homes. But the public is far more interested in questions relating to the *accused* than in questions relating to the people who apprehended and prosecuted this individual.

It is truly stupid to set a criminal free because of a failure to respect constitutional rights. These issues should never have become intertwined. But in the absence of any other effective legal mechanism for inducing compliance with constitutional norms, we may have no choice but to be stupid. Take police misconduct. Policing is a difficult job. We should be paying our officers much more money, and they should have the prestige and status awarded to doctors and lawyers. As a quid pro quo for elevating pigs into lions, I would subject these respected preservers of peace and security to rigorous and effective disciplinary sanctions for violating the constitutional norms that animate our process. If officers entered a home without a warrant, I would fire their sorry asses. What we do with a bad cop should have nothing to do with the ultimate guilt or innocence of the accused. But in our society no one has the courage to effectively punish our public servants. Lawsuits against the police usually fail. Officers who violate rights usually get a kiss instead of a kick. While we live in a world that refuses to hold public officials accountable for misdeeds, we are forced to use the criminal trial as the forum for exploring issues relating to state compliance within the Constitution. It is unfortunate, but this is the cost of being cowards when it comes to sanctioning public officials.

One celebrated legal right that totally skews the truth-finding function of the trial is deeply cherished by legal professionals. Despite our obsession with *mens rea*, the accused has a right to keep his thoughts to himself. The right to avoid self-incrimination works at cross-purposes with the imperative of drawing a conclusion about the accused's state of mind. With the exception of cases involving mistaken identification, the accused is in the best position to explain the events that constitute the crime, yet our system gives the accused the option of remaining mute throughout the process. We have to draw inferences about the accused's state of mind without the benefit of hearing from him. This is a true handicap for the decision-making process.

We have the most ass-backwards system you can imagine. Prior to trial, police officers cajole, intimidate, manipulate and plead with accused people to provide a statement. Of course, they still have the option to remain silent, but this is not so easy when they're on enemy turf and they have to ask permission to leave the interrogation room to take a piss. So much time and effort is put into obtaining a confession, and this effort is exercised in a coercive police environment designed to break the will of the accused: a dingy interview room deep in the bowels of a police station, without counsel present and without a neutral judge to oversee. I cannot imagine a worse environment for obtaining reliable information. Because of the spectre of unreliable confessions, criminal trials require a detailed and lengthy examination of all the circumstances surrounding the confession in order to determine if it was voluntary and admissible. Knowing that the accused has the right to remain mute at trial, the cops try extra hard to extort a statement at the pre-trial stage.

Once we reach the trial stage, and the accused is in a safe setting with the support of counsel, we give the accused the option of sitting there silently. Now it is safe to talk, but you still have the right to refuse to speak. Pretty weird.

Yet we expect the jury to be able to make a finding, beyond a reasonable doubt, about the accused's mental state. Reasonable doubt exists because of the simple fact that we haven't heard the accused's story! However, that's not the way it works. It has been demonstrated that juries are more likely to convict an accused who exercises the right of silence.[13] Silence may be a right, but it is not a strength; it is usually interpreted by the jury as a sign of having something to hide. So not only have we given the accused a right that can completely skew the verdict, but the right is often a liability when exercised. Now that is something to celebrate as a crowning achievement of criminal justice.

Legal professionals do celebrate this right. The Supreme Court of Canada has referred to it as the "unifying principle of criminal justice."[14] This is misleading. The right emerged in the seventeenth-century common law, triggered by a specific concern. People were being dragged into royal courts upon an ex officio oath, meaning that they were compelled to testify under oath with respect to charges and allegations that had not yet been disclosed. So the accused started to assert the right against self-incrimination. For them, it was not about standing mute. It was about the right to remain silent until the state had provided a proper and clear accusation. The right was created and asserted to combat fishing expeditions designed to trap religious heretics and political renegades.[15]

No one really knows how this right expanded from its modest beginnings to a general right of non-participation in one's own trial. Once the precedent was established it took on a life of its own. The record may be sparse, but it's kind of obvious how the right became reconfigured so that it has application even when the state has provided a proper accusation and complete disclosure. Criminal lawyers didn't appear until the mid-nineteenth century. Before that, the system was one of private prosecution and personal representation. The accused spoke directly to the judge, to the jury and to the victim. It was unheard of not to say a few words at the social event thrown for your benefit or demise. When lawyers hit the scene, the process became encumbered with complex evidentiary rules. In constructing this new reality, the criminal lawyer seized upon the right asserted in seventeenth-century precedents as a divine revelation: "Think about it, Mr. Defence Lawyer. They've let you in their little club, and how better to secure your role than to assert a right of silence for your client. With a mute client, the process needs your voice. In the future, your clients will affectionately refer to you as their mouthpiece. This is a valuable right."

And so the criminal-justice system became a stylized debate between legal professionals, with the best source of information sitting quietly on the sidelines. This is not justice. This is a game. Lawyers will say that the right against self-incrimination is critical. If accused people are compelled to testify, we may end up with a system where the articulate accused is acquitted and the stuttering accused is convicted. Do we have so little confidence in our judges and juries that we are willing to skew the entire process out of fear that judges and juries will be overly impressed by the slick talker and inclined to convict for a poor performance in the box? This is bullshit. The way an accused person delivers testimony is part and parcel of the process of evaluation. It provides some insight into the character of the accused, and every day we are required to make decisions about whether a smooth talker is lying or not.

I am opposed to a process in which the police manipulate a vulnerable accused to collect information. I am opposed to a process in which a decision is made by a judge or jury about an accusation of criminal wrongdoing without hearing from the accused. The right against self-incrimination is not, and has never been, a "unifying principle in criminal justice." It is just another legal reality filter that serves the needs of the players and not the subjects.

The reality is simple. Once an allegation stands on solid ground, we expect the suspect to respond. The failure to respond is almost always taken as a sign of guilt.[16] A proper interpretation of the right would ensure that accused people can exercise silence when the accusation is weakly grounded, but once the accusation is solidly grounded, they should be compelled to participate. After a preliminary hearing that finds sufficient evidence to order the accused to stand trial, the cloak of silence should be lifted.

But lifting the cloak of silence ruins the game. Armed with reality filters that make the process incomprehensible to ordinary people, the defence lawyer speaks for the accused and the Crown prosecutor speaks for the victim. They have to. The accused and the victim cannot talk about the principle of contemporaneity between the *mens rea* and *actus reus*, and this is the type of speech the judge is accustomed to hearing. No legal professional wants John and Jane to tell their life stories unadorned by legal language and sophistry. If this were to happen, not only would the professionals lose control, but they would have to deal with a reality that is nuanced, emotional and messy. Some people take drugs to escape reality. Others become legal professionals.

14

The Circle of
Victimization

IMAGINE ARRIVING HOME to discover your daughter has been killed in your home while you were out for the evening. It's hard to imagine. Unrelenting grief follows in the path of the death of any loved one, but when the death is at the hands of another human being, it is unfathomable. A hurricane blows through, a car skids out of control on an icy highway—these are tragedies. We still grieve. We might even wonder why it had to happen to this friend, lover or family member. But somehow with tragic acts of god we are able to move on, despite the holes in our heart. But when another person shoots, stabs, bludgeons or strangles the life out of a loved one, it fuels a flame that never really dies out. The embers haunt you the rest of your life.

It is this feeling of vulnerability at the hands of another member of our supposedly moral community that converts tragedy into crime. Tragedies we accept at a certain level, but crime demands a response. And, in modern times, crime victims clamour that the response to serious crime is weak and insulting. "The criminals have all the rights" is the common refrain. Victims, too, want rights. The endless parade of unhappy crime victims, claiming the criminal process has re-victimized them, is a pretty good barometer of a failing criminal-justice system. And it is the failure of the criminal-justice system to adequately respond to the needs of crime victims that makes this institution one of the most maligned in our social and political landscape.

With the illusion of security shattered, crime victims bear an intangible burden that far exceeds any material loss. Being hurt by another human being diminishes our sense of worth. It painfully exposes our vulnerability. The criminal strips away our innocent belief of living in a civil society. Crime can strike either the rich or the homeless, and at the moment of harm both are equally vulnerable. Whether lawyers like it or not, the criminal-justice system has to address this feeling of vulnerability and low self-worth. It can be crippling. The punishment is supposed to set the moral balance straight; when a victim believes the criminal has been fairly, but sternly, punished, it goes a long way towards restoring the moral balance.

I have worked with the victims' rights movement for close to eleven years, and there have been only a few occasions when I heard victims speak in glowing terms about the prosecution of their offender. For most, their fragile self-worth has taken another blow at the hands of legal professionals. Made to feel like shit by the offender, many victims are then made to feel like children by agents of the law, who are more concerned with the victim's worth as a witness than as a complete, vibrant human being. The criminal has aggressively dominated the victim contrary to the law, and then legal professionals perpetuate this feeling of domination by claiming to be acting in accordance with the law. And so the beat goes on. Ultimately, the victim is left believing that the law is of no value. It did not constrain the offender, and it then gave permission to some agent of the law to push the victim around some more.

So begins the circle of victimization. Mistreatment at the hands of criminal-justice officials can foster only disrespect and contempt for legal institutions. The justice system cannot afford any more disrespect. Serious crime will remain unreported as people lose faith in the system, and it will become harder and harder to get people to assist police and prosecutors. The system will become even more impotent in its quest to reduce criminal victimization. Criminal justice will remain a joke until this circle is broken. The public will continue to see the institution of justice as "full of sound and fury, signifying nothing."

As long as victims are considered pawns in the games played by legal professionals, the circle will never be breached. It can be broken only when the justice system can operate without leaving an indelible mark of Cain on both the criminal and the victim. We shame the criminal, with no real concern for future reintegration into society, and we keep the victim perpetually feeling like a victim by failing to give the victim any real control or input concerning the prosecution of the offender. We say that a crime against the state has been committed, and therefore the state has to call all the shots. This is what Plato called a "noble lie," and it has been used to justify treating the victim like a child for the past two centuries. "Speak when spoken to" is how the justice system approaches victims, and in many ways this approach is not much different than the criminal's "don't move or I'll kill you." Both are nourished by the spirit of domination; the difference is more a matter of degree than a matter of kind.

In a country deeply involved in the circle of victimization, heroes will be made from vigilantes. Hollywood has for years worshipped vigilantes, churning out film after film in which fed-up and frustrated victims take the law into their hands. More often than not, the films end in a bloodbath of epic proportions, as it is only the bloodbath of epic proportions that can set the moral balance right. The legal professionals fuck up their chance to set the balance straight, so in steps the vigilante as a modern hero. Many people who have a sense of the impotence of criminal justice to respond effectively to predatory crime react positively to these images.

In 1984, the New York subway shooter, Bernard Goetz, became an urban hero to many Americans. If he had done his vigilante shooting in Toronto, he would have been an urban hero to many Canadians. Goetz was approached by four young black men on a New York subway. He quickly interpreted their approach as menacing in nature (he was right), and responded with four rapid gun shots. All four muggers were shot. Goetz paused, then fired a fifth bullet. This last bullet paralyzed one of the young men. Goetz disappeared into the night. While the police searched for him, the public began its debate. Was he a hero? Was he a racist? Was he a lunatic? The city was badly divided. As is often the case in the land of the free, the division seemed to be on racial lines.

Ultimately, Goetz as hero was the most powerful image. Standing trial before a jury on charges of attempted murder, he was convicted only of minor weapons offences, and his sentence was a kiss. How could the jury judge a man for repelling the attack of muggers (although preemptively and rather disproportionately), when they themselves were afraid of the New York subways? In the 1980s, the New York subways were the scene of thousands of daily crimes. The police seemed powerless. People were scared. Goetz achieved what the law was incapable of doing—sending a message, loudly, clearly and confidently, that if you choose to fuck with an innocent person you may suffer dire consequences. Goetz was given a kiss by the people because he did what people secretly want the law to do: barge in like Charles Bronson and shoot the hell out of the bad guys. Goetz was the Equalizer, a modern hero who knows that people secretly want epic bloodbaths to restore moral order. People are far more satisfied by Hollywood endings than by bland, delayed and confusing legal resolutions.

Years before the subway shooting, Goetz had been mugged on the street. He had suffered serious damage to his knee and sustained various other injuries. No wonder he started illegally carrying a gun. Once faith in the law is lost, the only real recourse is the gun. A gun can restore a victim's sense of power, something the criminal-justice system has no interest in doing. The circle of victimization turns the dissatisfied victim into a reluctant criminal. At some basic level, it seems to be true that "what goes around, comes around." If the justice system is not responsive to the needs of crime victims, how can it expect these same people to respect legal professionals as public servants devoted to the pursuit of justice? This is the legitimacy crisis facing contemporary criminal justice.

Trained as a defence lawyer, I was taught to see the victim as an adversary who wished harm upon my client. In many cases, my job was to discredit the victim, as is the job of all defence lawyers. At times, this felt like dishonest work, but institutionally this was the role to be played. It seemed natural and inevitable that the accused and their lawyers would be in an adversarial relationship with victims and the prosecutors. We believed that out of the clash of opposites the truth would emerge. When I became an academic, and had the luxury of reflection, my perspective started to change. I became unsure that the "he said/she said" game was really an effective path for discovering the truth. More important, I learned that the way we carry out justice is not the only natural way to do so.

History shows that victims were the paramount players in the process until the nineteenth century. Professionalization of the process was a nineteenth-century phenomenon, consistent with rapid industrialization and specialization. Contemporary European systems demonstrate that victim participation is still possible in a modern, highly professionalized system of justice. In most European countries, victims can attach their civil claims to existing criminal cases, and are then entitled to full participation with counsel. Once the victim is involved, the prosecutor cannot simply withdraw the case or bargain it away.

Victims were once the lifeblood of our system, and in some modern systems they maintain some degree of effective control over their cases. So why do we treat victims so poorly in our justice system?

Nobody really noticed the plight of the crime victim until the 1960s. They were seen as mere evidentiary fodder; give your evidence and get lost. With violent crime rates rising, researchers began to pay attention to the extremely low reporting of the crime of rape. Rape victims preferred to hide their injury from the state than to suffer the indignity of a criminal trial. This disturbing fact led researchers to study the impact of the criminal process on the victim, which gave birth to the concept of secondary victimization; that is, that the process adds insult to injury and further victimizes the vulnerable. "Cross-examination is the greatest legal engine ever invented for the discovery of truth" was the motto of the lawyer, and rape victims were grilled aggressively about their sexual preferences, their sexual practices and a whole host of irrelevant, mud-raking topics. The victim was on trial, instead of the accused. Everyone forgot that this witness was also, in most cases, a person still reeling from the trauma of being victimized. Instead of helping her regain some dignity, the state put her up on the stand like a lamb to slaughter.

The exposure of this injustice set in motion a rapid law-reform enterprise dedicated to addressing the needs of victims. First came state compensation in the late 1960s, then came victim services, like counselling and victim/witness assistance programs in the 1970s, and then came the revolution in evidence and procedure, allowing some victims to testify behind screens, or on closed-circuit screens, or with the assistance of a support person. Despite the reforms, though, the victim was still treated like a child in need of charitable assistance. The victim's welfare needs were being addressed modestly, but the victim was still barred from having any meaningful role in the process. Victims were eventually given a modest voice in the late 1980s, when victim-impact statements were introduced at sentencing hearings and parole hearings.

The changes were fast and furious. When politicians discovered that a law-and-order agenda was a political bestseller, victim-related law reform became the flavour of the month. Politicians assumed (and still do) that victims were clamouring for harsh punishment and a diminution of the rights of the accused. Victims have been sucked in by law-and-order promises made in virtually every election since the 1960s. The "get tough" policies of politicians have never adequately addressed the true needs of crime victims.

Admittedly, some victims are vindictive. But these are natural feelings that do not dominate, or in most cases even infiltrate, the criminal process. We know victims are mad as hell. We would be, too, if we were in their shoes. But the deal is simple: the victim gives up the hope of vigilante revenge, and in exchange, the state takes care of the messy business of prosecution. No one ever contemplated that sublimating the revenge impulse would mean victims would be completely silenced. This is where politicians have strayed. Sure, some victims buy into the "get tough with criminals" political rhetoric, but most victims turn to politics simply to find their voice.

The law will shield the victim from confrontation and aggressive cross-examination, but legal professionals cannot give the victim meaningful input. Even with compensation, counselling and victim impact statements, crime victims still feel overwhelmed by the indifferent and patronizing attitudes within the process. A conviction may be obtained and a jail term imposed, but for most victims the process is not a healing one, nor does it bring any closure. Victims enter the arena to gain empowerment, to gain mastery over a criminal who stripped them of dignity and control, and they often leave the arena carrying further scars of psychological domination. From the victim's perspective, no one in the profession really cares about their plight.

Victims do not want much; they simply want to play a role in the theatre of the absurd we call criminal justice. In 1999, I initiated a lawsuit against Her Majesty the Queen (in right of Ontario) on behalf of two crime victims.[1] The experience of these two women perfectly reflects the current relationship of victims and criminal justice. The concerns raised in this case are the very concerns that have served to reduce the legitimacy of the process in the eyes of many Canadians, whether victims or fortunate observers from a distance. I asked you at the beginning of the chapter to imagine arriving home to discover your daughter had been killed in your home while you were out. K.V. did not have to imagine. She arrived home to this very nightmare. Now imagine being intruded upon at home by an ex-boyfriend who decides to maim and wound you with a pair of scissors. L.E. will always carry the scars of being stabbed repeatedly. Let's take a closer look at what happened to K.V. and L.E. when they turned to the Canadian criminal process in search of justice.

On September 24, 1996, a young offender shot and killed K.V.'s fourteen-year-old daughter with a 45 mm semi-automatic weapon. The seventeen-year-old shooter was charged with second-degree murder. From the outset, K.V. had to track down the police and prosecutor to find out information concerning the case. She finally found the Crown attorney assigned to the case, and he explained the law as it relates to murder and manslaughter. A few days later, the Crown indicated that plea negotiations had commenced with the young offender's lawyer, but no further details were provided. Within a week, K.V. was notified that a deal had been made and approved by a judge in a pretrial conference.

The deal was shocking to K.V. The young man would not be charged with murder, nor would he be tried in adult court. The Crown and defence agreed to keep the young man in youth court to face a charge of manslaughter and a sentence of two years. In a matter of a few months, this murder case was settled. Justice may have been swift in this case, but something doesn't sit right when a fourteen-year-old girl's life can be bargained away for two years. K.V. expressed her dissatisfaction and anger, but no one seemed to care. Only when she took her complaint to the media did the Crown order a senior official to review the deal. Again, K.V. was not given an opportunity to provide input and, as would be expected from a private, internal review, the plea bargain was upheld.

The Crown did not believe it could prove the "intent" requirement for murder. So what? That is why we have juries. Let the jury decide, and in the worst-case scenario they will acquit on murder and convict on manslaughter. There was no reason to give this young man a manslaughter conviction on a silver platter, and it remains a mystery to me how the Crown and defence (ironically, some of the same lawyers involved in the notorious Karla Homolka plea bargain) arrived at this position. The Crown stated that the young man had said he brought the gun just to fool around, and it discharged accidentally. K.V. indicated that there was evidence that her daughter was afraid of the young man, and there was no evidence that the gun had a hair trigger. She also claimed that a number of young people in the house had played with the gun before the shooting, and there was no accidental discharge from this horseplay. In addition, a developmentally handicapped boy claimed to have witnessed the shooting, but the Crown asserted that his handicap would prevent him from testifying in a court of law. This is not completely true, of course, but it is a lot easier to take a quick and cheap guilty plea than have to struggle with eliciting evidence from a boy with significant verbal disabilities.

So the deal went through, and K.V.'s participation was reduced to the giving of a victim-impact statement. In her statement, she was critical of the public officials who had carriage of her case, but in reading the statement in court, the Crown was careful to edit out these portions. As K.V. said in her affidavit: "I felt that I was on trial, victimized and violated, and unable to defend myself." K.V. is an intelligent, courageous, assertive woman. I have a great deal of respect and admiration for her. If this strong woman could be manipulated by the process, it does not bode well for the vast majority of victims who enter the process in fear of, and with complete deference to, public officials.

L.E. had a similar story to tell, only she was the direct victim of a vicious attack. On November 5, 1996, P.M, L.E.'s ex-boyfriend arrived at her home and was let in by their daughter. P.M. asked his daughter to go upstairs, and she did. He then approached L.E. to talk with her. She asked him to leave. He put on a pair of gloves, stood over her and said, "there's one thing I gotta do before I go—I gotta kill ya." P.M. had brought a pair of scissors with him into the house; he began stabbing L.E. with the scissors. She shielded herself with a quilt and yelled to her daughter for help. The girl fled to a neighbour's house and contacted the police, while the neighbour pulled P.M. off L.E. and shoved him away. The neighbour saw that L.E. was bleeding and that P.M. was armed. The neighbour left the house and ran back to his own residence to get a baseball bat and to lock his doors. P.M. got up and renewed his assault on L.E., stabbing her several more times. Then he fled. P.M. was later apprehended by police and charged with attempted murder and possession of a dangerous weapon.

As a result of the attack, L.E's dominant hand is permanently crippled; she cannot close it completely. The range of motion in her hand has been significantly reduced, and after five operations to attempt to repair tendon and nerve damage, no further improvements are expected. She also sustained wounds to her temple, the top of her head, the back of her head, her right leg, both arms, her other hand and the back of her shoulder. She suffers from chronic pain and depression. Her daughter now suffers from paranoia, anxiety and sleeplessness, and has received counselling from Family and Children Services.

It was almost six weeks after the attack before L.E. finally met the Crown attorney who had carriage of the case. The Crown said he had a good case of attempted murder, and would be seeking eight years in prison. Three weeks later, a deal had been struck. The accused would be allowed to plead guilty to aggravated assault, and the lawyers would jointly submit that a three- to five-year sentence was appropriate. L.E. learned of the deal the day she attended court for the preliminary hearing. She should have suspected some monkey business when the investigating officer advised her not to bring any family or friends to court for the preliminary hearing. She brought them, nonetheless, only to be berated for bringing her supporters. In court, she was bewildered by the proceedings. After the charge of attempted murder was read out, she heard that the preliminary hearing was being waived and the accused would be allowed to plead to a lesser charge. Even the judge questioned whether this procedure was proper. The Crown did apologize for omitting to advise L.E. of the charge reduction, but the deal went through nonetheless.

On behalf of a victims' rights group, I was asked to review these two cases to determine if any legal recourse might be available. I set up a meeting between K.V., the Ontario attorney general and some senior officials. K.V. wanted some assurances that no other victim would ever be kept in the dark about decisions made by public officials concerning his or her case. The meeting was filled with good wishes. It was a perfect display of the politics of sympathy. However, K.V. was astute enough to recognize a snow-job when she saw one. Upon leaving the meeting, she decided to sue the government for failing to live up to its promise to treat victims with dignity and respect. L.E. was only too happy to jump on board, as was another mother whose daughter had recently been shot. Regrettably, a third victim backed off because her case was still before the courts, and she was concerned that if she took the public officials to court she would be treated even worse than she had been already.

You cannot sue the government for disingenuous political promises. They would have to build a hundred new courthouses in Canada if you could. However, in the frenzy of victim-related law reform introduced in the eighties and nineties, the Province of Ontario passed a piece of legislation, the Victims' Bill of Rights, which appeared to make the promise of fair treatment a legal obligation.[2] Every province has similar legislation, as does every American state. The legislation guarantees that victims will be kept apprised of the progress of their cases, will be advised of victim social services and compensation and will be told of any major decision pertaining to the case. Almost all of these pieces of legislation contain an oddity: they give victims no legal recourse if and when their rights have been violated.

For both K.V. and L.E., the guarantees provided by the legislation were honoured more in the breach than in compliance. Like most victims, they were never given much information about their rights and their role before the court. We all decided that a lawsuit should be initiated, not a lawsuit for money—no one was interested in that—but a civil action seeking a declaration that the rights of K.V. and L.E. had been violated and that the legislation was unconstitutional because it arbitrarily prevented aggrieved victims from seeking legal recourse in the courts if their rights had been violated by public officials.

We asserted that the Victims' Bill of Rights was just fancy window-dressing with no substance. After the passage of the Bill in 1995, there had been no training sessions and no changes in office procedures to ensure that victims were kept abreast of developments in their cases. The legislation had absolutely no impact on how public officials treated victims. Promising to treat victims with dignity is good politics, but it fits awkwardly with the elitist attitudes of legal professionals. But the government went to the trouble to enshrine their political promises in law, and we were going to make them accountable for failing to live up to their promises.

Our argument was simple and sound: it was a principle of "fundamental justice" under s. 7 of the Charter of Rights that all rights should have a remedy (*ubi jus ibi remedium*). The maxim had first been articulated by Lord Holt in 1703, and has been relied upon, or approved of by judges, in dozens of cases since then. Accordingly, we sought a declaration that the provision in the Victims' Bill of Rights that barred any legal remedy for violations was unconstitutional and of no force and effect. If Crowns could be made accountable for violations of victims' rights, then perhaps the prosecutors would start changing their routine practice to take into account the rights and needs of victims.

Our court hearing was not much different from the meeting with the attorney general—full of good wishes but short on practical significance. Nothing that happened that day would convince victims that the justice system truly cares about their plight. The judge showed up one hour late. He had been assigned the case only the day before, and court officials had provided him with the wrong case materials to review. We had filed volumes of evidentiary material, and as soon as the judge arrived, he asked for some time to review our "voluptuous" material. (He meant "voluminous," but he was so flustered upon arrival that he made this rather curious slip of the tongue.) As much as I felt sorry for him, I could not believe the court had assigned a judge with little experience in constitutional law, and that he had been assigned the case the night before. This was the first ever lawsuit brought by a victim in Canada, and it engaged novel issues of constitutional law. Yet we were assigned a judge who had to ask counsel, "Where can I find this section 7?" (of the Charter), which was being referred to in argument. Section 7 of our constitution is not some obscure statute like the Artificial Insemination of Cattle Act. You would expect most judges to know the "Supreme Law of the Land," off by heart. Yet I guess some judges have not even bothered to read its provisions.

The case was doomed to failure. The maxim "no right without a remedy" presupposes the existence of a right, and the judge determined that "the legislature did not intend to provide rights to the victims of crime. The Act is a statement of principle, beguilingly clothed in the language of legislation. It does not establish any statutory rights for the victims of crime … It is nothing more than a statement of governmental policy wrapped in the language of legislation. While the Applicants may be disappointed by the legislature's efforts, they have no claim before the courts because of it."[3]

Perhaps the judge was right; however, statutory interpretation is not a precise science, and we provided numerous cogent arguments to support the contrary interpretation. However, the judge chose to conclude that no rights were actually provided, as this made his job easier. Without rights, there is no relevance to the "no right without a remedy" maxim. With this conclusion, the judge did not have to make a ruling that would result in prosecutors being held liable for violations of victims' rights in the future. Instead, he blamed the legislature for "beguiling" the public. He was right. The Victims' Bill of Rights is an obscene distortion of rights legislation. It was enacted to placate victims, with no real intent to provide them with greater rights of participation in the process. The Court could have called the legislature's bluff, but chose not to. That would have taken courage and a desire to shake up the system, two qualities in short supply in Canadian courts.

Legal professionals are averse to the creation of a legal universe in which victims have an enforceable right to be provided critical information. For legal professionals, the victim is an intruder, an interloper. For judges and lawyers, victims simply get in the way. The victim's discourse is too emotional for these pragmatic deal-makers, and the victim's needs too compelling to simply ignore. By silencing these people, legal professionals can avoid dealing with their needs. The judge in this case discounted the importance and significance of victim input and participation because "the Crown knows best":

> When all is said and done, however, it seems what was truly at issue in this case was the Applicants' dissatisfaction with how the respective Crowns plea-bargained their cases. That being the case, it should be made clear that the Crown has complete discretion on these matters. The Supreme Court of Canada has held that the existence of prosecutorial discretion does not offend the principles of fundamental justice, but is "an essential feature of the criminal justice system" ... What may seem cut and dried to an untrained person, especially one who is a victim of crime, may in fact be a morass of evidentiary and procedural problems for the Crown Attorney. The decision to plead down from murder to manslaughter or attempted murder to aggravated assault may seem absurd to the lay-person, but it can be a decision of profound tactical and moral import for a Crown who is responsible for the final decision.[4]

With all due respect (this is what lawyers say before launching into a disrespectful and captious tirade), the judge is wrong. Granted, there are some legal issues of great complexity that would be daunting for any victim to understand. But these issues are few and far between, despite the self-serving claims of lawyers. Lawyers want you to believe that the issues in all criminal trials are complex; why else would you hire someone at $200 or $400 an hour? Why else would you leave all prosecutorial decisions to a legally trained advocate? But for K.V., the only issue was whether the young man shot the gun with an intent to kill. For L.E., the only issue was whether the ex-boyfriend stabbed with an intent to kill. These were the only real issues in the case, and they were simple factual questions, unaccompanied by a "morass of evidentiary or procedural problems."

It is better for everyone if twelve members of the community assess simple issues like these, rather than one Crown attorney sitting in an office with one defence counsel. In both cases, the decision to plead down was not "a decision of profound tactical and moral import for a

Crown." It was pure expedience. It was a way of clearing court dockets. The Crowns in both cases sensed that, even upon conviction, the accused would receive prison sentences close in range to what was agreed upon in negotiation. Why waste court time if the result will be virtually the same?

The plea bargain may make sense to lawyers who are looking solely at the bottom line and when they will be able to free up some time for golf. But for the victim it is "of profound tactical and moral import" whether the offender is convicted of murder or manslaughter. Even if you accept that it is a waste of time to conduct a trial when the sentence will be more or less the same either way, at a minimum, prosecutors should have to explain this rationale to the victim. Yet attempts to explain are rarely made. Legal professionals make decisions in secret, avoid the victim and then, when the shit hits the fan, say, "Sorry, we resolved your case without you present. Have a good day. Come again."

The paradox of the victims' rights movement is that, although rapid and substantial law-reform measures have been enacted, the level of dissatisfaction remains high. This conundrum has not gone unnoticed by critics: "for all the new initiatives, victims have gotten far less than promised. Rights have been unenforced or unenforceable, participation sporadic or ill-advised, services precarious and underfunded, victims' needs unsatisfied if not further jeopardized, and victimization increased, if not in court, then certainly in the streets. Given the outpouring of victim attention in recent years, how could this happen?"[5]

I think I know the answer to this question. Most of the reforms have only tinkered with the criminal process, and the reintegration of the victim requires deep, structural change. Structural reform of the process is not on the horizon, because lawyers and judges dread significant changes in the way they do business. Of course, I blame the legal professionals, but by now you probably think that my jaundiced view of the profession leads me to believe that the profession is responsible for all social evil from wrongful conviction to the introduction of the West Nile virus into North America. I'm not sure about the virus, but I can assure you that my suspicions that legal professionals have thwarted any meaningful possibility of victim participation in the process is borne out in the academic literature. Social scientists have shown that legal professionals employ various strategies to neutralize the impact of victim-related law reform, and that they are resistant to increased vic-

tim participation due to current institutional demands and the reluctance to consider institutional change.[6]

The legal professionals feign sympathy, but deep down they just want
the victims to go away. They claim to have principled objections to
increased victim participation. They cry that victims' rights will serve to
impair the accused's constitutional rights. They argue that victims seek
only vengeance and, as such, their involvement will distort the valid, retributive objectives of sentencing. This is utter nonsense. The rights of victims and accused persons can co-exist. The victims' rights movement
does not demand that the accused be deprived of the right to be free
from unreasonable search and seizure, or that the accused be deprived of
the right to counsel.

The only real clash of interests arises on rare occasion in the trial context. In certain situations, the accused's right to make full answer and
defence will clash with the victims' right to privacy. Recent years have
brought major battles in sexual assault cases in which defence lawyers
have sought disclosure of private and confidential records of the victim.
This is the only scenario in which the victims' rights and the constitutional rights of the defendant come into direct conflict. The lawyers are
simply wrong. Victims' rights can flourish without impairing the rights
of the accused.

As for vengeance, empirical studies reveal that victims are not unduly
punitive and that they are more interested in fair process than a punitive outcome.[7] As noted in Chapter 9, when they are fully apprised of all
the facts of a case, most Canadians believe our sentencing practices are
sufficiently harsh.[8] So I am left with the distinct impression that legal professionals simply do not wish to deal with victims and their emotional
baggage. Practising criminal law is just so much easier when the reality of
the crime is obscured by legal doctrine and the conventions of practice.
Victims represent the reality of crime, and their presence can ruin the
game of justice.

As things stand, the circle of victimization will never be broken, and
the breeding of state-raised convicts will never end. This is the perverse
beauty of our criminal-justice system: it is doomed to fail but not to
die. Without fundamental change, we will never adequately deal with
violent crime. We must become willing to invest time and effort in
dealing with people as *people* and not as legal categories like "accused"
and "victim." Our justice system never wants to spend time exploring

the victim/offender relationship or fashioning unique and responsive sentencing practices that fit the crime. The natural inclination within criminal practice is to find shortcuts: plea-bargaining, "zero tolerance" policies, the exclusion of evidence. We manage to create the illusion of care and concern when we speak about random violence and domestic abuse, but our deeds fall short when it comes to addressing the problems in a constructive manner.

Look at domestic violence. Women and children (and some men) suffer enormously when imprisoned in a domestic nightmare. Most jurisdictions worship the rhetoric of zero tolerance. Forget early intervention, counselling and the facilitation of dialogue between partners. Zero tolerance means you are a criminal, no matter how trivial the incident. With a true consideration of the needs of the parties, we could perhaps prevent the trivial from escalating into extreme violence. But instead, we lay the charge and proceed to trial and conviction, even when the complaining spouse has changed her mind about the criminal case. This should be a signal that we need to sit down and talk with these people. There is hope, and the system should be exploring this hope. Perhaps we will find out that the change of heart was coerced and delusional, and if so the prosecution will proceed, but we can know only if we take the time and effort to explore the issue. Instead, we assume that a beaten spouse is incapable of acting in her best interest, so we take away her authority to make autonomous decisions regarding the prosecution of her partner. How patronizing! We assist the victim by silencing and disempowering her. The process must run its course, even if it destroys any possibility of reconciliation or personal growth. Legal professionals refuse to take the time or make the effort to understand the people before the court.

Even the courts have begun to recognize that the criminal-justice system is becoming a bloated and effete beast of burden. In 1992, the Manitoba Court of Appeal had this to say:

> The crime rate in Winnipeg has been rising dramatically. The situation has got so bad that many women are afraid to walk the streets at night without being accompanied. Houses are broken into with great regularity. There are street muggings and sexual assaults. An overburdened police force is having trouble coping with all the complaints of violence and crime.

The case now before us is an example of why the state authorities are unable to cope with burgeoning crime. Instead of going after real criminals, men and women who wantonly attack innocent neighbours, the whole engine of the state has been concentrated in this case on the prosecution of a citizen who has been accused of using excessive force in disciplining his children.[9]

With less vulgarity and bit more hysteria, the court is saying the very same thing I have been saying throughout this book. What prompted this unexpected burst of judicial honesty? The case was before the court because of zero-tolerance policies. A man had been informed by his wife that she had been squandering the mortgage money, and the house was under power of sale unbeknownst to him. While he was receiving this upsetting news, his two-year-old son started choking on sunflower seeds left on the carpet by his eight-year-old son. The eight-year-old had been warned not to drop the seeds, and the irate father disciplined him physically, including kicking him with his stockinged foot. The mother ran away to a shelter with the two children. The police were called, charges were laid and a prosecution commenced, even though the wife wished to reconcile and had sent a written letter of apology to her husband about the mortgage fiasco. This is zero tolerance. This is a monumental waste of valuable judicial resources.

In 1995, I wrote an editorial in the *Toronto Star* to respond to an uproar over a murder committed by an offender on parole.[10] It is a myth that parolees often commit horrific crimes while on supervision in the community. It does happen, but rarely. In my editorial, I pointed out that any human enterprise is subject to error and mistake, and that the risk of mistake increases if the enterprise is too ambitious and large. I wrote that "parole tragedies are a sign of an overloaded criminal-justice system bursting at the seams." To underscore my point, I had obtained copies of the Metropolitan Toronto Police Force Operating Budget for the years 1992 to 1994. Seeing how the police allocate their funding gives one a pretty good picture of criminal-justice priorities. I noted that, in 1992, Metro police spent $5,388,000 for the mounted and dog services, and only $1,206,000 was allocated to the sexual assault squad. How can we efficiently combat unacceptable levels of violence against woman when the policing fiscal pie is being consumed by the appetite for pageantry, riot control and narcotic sniffing? It is fucking outrageous!

More justice resources being spent on dogs and horses than on the safety of women? I wrote this editorial deliberately to stir a public outcry, but not one letter, one comment or one statement was ever made. Where were all the feminists? Justice spending is a critical issue, yet when an absolute gem was delivered to all the critics out there, everyone was asleep.

By the way, it gets worse. The morality division (drugs, sex and gambling, etc.) had a 1992 budgetary allotment of $7,378,000—six times more than the money spent on protecting women. With these screwed-up justice priorities, we will never begin to straighten out the circle of victimization. This saddens me. The institution of criminal justice has been exposed for what it truly is—a beast being fattened on an unhealthy diet of pornographers, prostitutes and pot smokers.

Deep, structural reform will never happen until the beast of criminal justice loses some weight. It is too heavy and lethargic to respond to anything novel or emotionally taxing. It is time for a criminal-justice diet. Criminal justice will never be able to adequately respond to violent, predatory conduct if it continues to pursue trivialities and crimes of moral offence. There is no time to deal with real tragedies when the court docket requires legal professionals to address a whole host of relatively harmless crimes. I know I have made this point ad nauseam, but as Andre Gide once wrote, "everything that needs to be said has already been said. But since no one was listening, everything must be said again."[11] It really does seem like no one has been listening to the victims.

PART IV

Legal Professionals as Fallen Priests

Legal professionals expect to be respected. Instead, the profession is held up to universal ridicule. Forget that they are wasting their time with trivial moral peccadilloes. Forget that they have failed miserably at curbing serious crime. People hate legal professionals because their institutional personalities border on the despicable. Legal professionals may occupy the temple, but they are there only by force of habit. They still act like high priests in sacrificing clients at the altar, but no one really believes they have the moral authority to act the way they do. People continue to dream of killing all the lawyers.

15

No More
Mr. Nice Guy

IN SEPTEMBER 2000, I withdrew from a case that had been causing me a great deal of grief. One of Canada's premier lawyers, Eddie Greenspan, took over to clean up the mess. As printed in *The Globe and Mail*, my client said, "Alan is an amiable and intelligent fellow who has done a spectacular job, but we no longer have any intention of pulling our punches ... Mr. Nice Guy just got off the case. What Eddie Greenspan does is win criminal cases, and he wins a lot of them."[1]

I like being known as "Mr. Nice Guy," but the title was not given to me as a compliment. I was too nice to achieve the best results for my client. Being nice is being weak in the legal culture. Mr. Nice Guy does not make for a good lawyer. According to the conventional perspective, Mr. Bastard is a much better choice. Mr. Bastard can get the job done. Mr. Greenspan may not be Mr. Bastard, but he would never be professionally cursed with the moniker "Mr. Nice Guy." He would not be considered one of Canada's best lawyers if people thought of him as just a decent person.

One of the reasons Dick the Butcher wanted to kill all the lawyers is that lawyers can be rude and antagonistic bastards. You cannot charge anywhere between $200 and $500 an hour, act like an asshole and expect people to like you. Legal professionals are the gatekeepers to an exclusive club, and they have never learned how to be good hosts. No one really wants to visit this club, but sometimes you have no choice. Once you arrive at the club, you will never be allowed to forget that it is not *your* club. You are there only at the indulgence of the legal professional, and you had better be prepared to be pushed around, cajoled, insulted and patronized. Sounds like a great S/M scenario, but it's a lot more expensive. You have to pay big bucks for the privilege of being insulted by an elite member of the bar.

Is being nice a character defect for legal professionals? Yes! Nice = Weak. Like a dog playing in the park, as a legal professional you must always appear dominating and strong or some stronger dog will come over and piss on your leg. The institutional role of the lawyer is well defined: the bulldog, the shark, the champion of the weak and disadvantaged, the gilded mouthpiece, the sarcastic and intemperate advocate. These are the institutional expectations. Lawyers can be nice guys in their spare time, but when the robes are donned, you better come out fighting. I know lots of lawyers who are great people, but who buy into the asshole institutional role when in practice. As time wears on, it becomes harder and harder for a lawyer to maintain the boundary between the institutional and the personal. One of the occupational hazards of lawyering is that you may not be able to shake the asshole adversary posturing, even in your personal life. The institutional ethos of lawyering can tarnish the spirit.

We know people hate lawyers. A lot of this contempt is mixed with disdain for the system itself, and I have already addressed some of the systemic failures that tarnish the image of criminal justice in the eyes of ordinary Canadians. But the legal professional is not just an innocent messenger for a bad system. There is something about the culture of the lawyer that is ugly and contemptible. The system sucks, and the legal professionals do virtually nothing to counter this. Legal culture magnifies the alienation and distance already in place within a body of jurisprudence that means nothing to ordinary people. Legal culture is a culture of arrogance and condescension. It is a culture of argument and confrontation. For the right fee, lawyers will argue that black is white and white is black, and they will argue with vigour and passion.

Many lawyers are hurt by lawyer bashing. That's because many asshole lawyers are basically "nice guys" in their personal lives. They have feelings in their spare time. It's only in lawyerland that these creatures act with complete emotional disengagement. I had to laugh when I read the following statement from an American lawyer with hurt feelings:

> "I listened to one lawyer joke after another," said Fenton Wiley, in-house counsel for a Fort Wayne, Ind., manufacturing company. "All day, every day, I suffered relentless abuse and harassment. I heard jokes about sharks showing professional courtesy to lawyers, skid marks in front of the skunks and not road-killed lawyers, lawyers lying because their lips are moving.

Finally, I just couldn't take the hostile environment any more. I was constructively discharged and then lost consortium with my wife because of chronic emotional distress." Fenton is now seeking $752 million in lost-opportunity costs and for pain and suffering caused by the psychic wounds inflicted upon him."[2]

This is pathetic. I now have to add "whiny" to the list of character defects bred by contemporary adversarial justice. The lawyer could not take the insults, and became so distraught that he could not get it up for his wife, so he sued for $752 million. Basic maxim of everyday living: don't dish it out if you can't take it. The insults will continue to fly until someone takes a look at the impact an adversarial system of justice has on character development. It's not a pretty picture.

The profession knows it is breeding little monsters. In October 2001, I saw this report in the *Toronto Star*:

> They know the meaning of "unconstitutional" and "unjust." Now is it time to look up "unmannerly"? Lawyers and judges who gathered in Toronto yesterday to address a growing problem with rudeness in their profession would seem to think so. The collection of top-notch legal talent assembled for a one-day policy forum titled Civility in the Legal Profession. But it could have easily been subtitled "Hey Dumbo."[3]

"Hey Dumbo" refers to a well-known case in legal circles. Here's a brief look at the "unmannerly" conduct of a veteran lawyer named Balaban, which drew the attention of the Law Society. In the early 1990s, during the examination of a witness named Baker before a special examiner, the following exchanges took place between Balaban and the opposing lawyer, Berman:

> Mr. Balaban: Okay, Dumbo, you can start.
> Mr. Berman: Excuse me?
> Mr. Balaban: You heard me. Start, Dumbo.
> Mr. Berman: I'm sorry, are you addressing me, Mr. Balaban?
> Mr. Balaban: I'm glad you recognize my name. It's Mr. Balaban, Dumbo.
> Mr. Berman: I don't think that conduct requires that, Mr. Balaban.
> Mr. Balaban: I've already seen you in action, Mr. Dumbo.
> Mr. Berman: I won't be put in a position of antagonism, Mr.—
> Mr. Balaban: Why don't you? You're always doing it to other people. You wouldn't know the word "antagonism" if you saw it in English. You haven't

started yet. What's the matter with you?

Mr. Berman:

Q. Mr. Baker, I take it that you are a solicitor licensed to practice in Ontario?

Mr. Balaban: You mean to say you're able to read, Mr. Berman?

* * *

Mr. Berman: (To Mr. Rosenberger, the Special Examiner) Mr. Balaban has just leaned over and poured a cup of coffee over my notes.

Mr. Balaban: That's tough luck for you, Mr. Berman. It goes to show the enthusiasm with which you're acting.

Mr. Berman: I've never seen this happen before in my twenty-four years of practice.

Mr. Balaban: I didn't know you'd been practising for twenty-four years, the way you treat other counsel.

Mr. Berman: Do you have any reason why you poured coffee on my notes, sir?

Mr. Balaban: It's none of your business, Mr. Berman.

Mr. Berman: You purposely leaned over the table ...

Mr. Balaban: Take it up with the judge.

Mr. Berman: ... took your cup of coffee and poured it on my notes.

Mr. Balaban: Take it up with the judge, Mr. Berman. Is there any reason why you would insult a counsel in his office in front of his clients?

Mr. Berman: I don't want to be intimidated by the gentleman, Mr. Examiner.

* * *

Mr. Berman: Mr. Balaban, you're going to have to stop acting irresponsibly.

Mr. Balaban: I'm just acting in the manner in which you continue to act, Mr. Berman.

Mr. Berman: Mr. Balaban, this is not what I consider the way solicitors conduct themselves.

Mr. Balaban: You should know. It's the way you're always conducting yourself.

Mr. Berman: I must tell you, sir, this is taking a lot of control on my part.

Mr. Balaban: I beg your pardon?

Mr. Berman: This is taking a lot of control on my part, Mr. Balaban.

Mr. Balaban: I don't think you've got any. I've seen you in action, Mr. Berman.

> Mr. Berman: You have half a cup of coffee left. Do you intend to follow through the same way with this?
>
> Mr. Balaban: Mr. Berman, I'm not under examination. Don't ask me any questions.
>
> Mr. Berman: Mr. Balaban, I would like you to put the cup of coffee somewhere else. I don't want you leaning over any more. I will consider it a ...
>
> Mr. Balaban: Why don't you get down on your hands and knees?
>
> Mr. Berman: When are you going to apologize for insulting me?[4]

Lawyers can be such a bunch of obnoxious children! Petty squabbling, usually to the detriment of the clients. Clients seem to want to hire pit bulls as lawyers, but pit bulls inflict needless damage. Many social conflicts that end up in court need a sensitive, nuanced approach, and unleashing two pit bulls in an adversarial setting does not bode well for harmony, resolution and justice. How did we end up with an institutionalized justice system predicated on justice emerging from the competitive squabbling of opposing lawyers? Legal professionals celebrate adversarial justice as if it is the only natural and inevitable way of dispensing justice. Nonsense. Adversarial justice is a historical accident. Nothing more. The whole notion of lawyer as Mr. Bastard need not have happened.

As one scholar has noted, "No one set out to build the adversary system. It was neither part of a grand governmental design nor the scheme of an ingenious legal philosopher."[5] That's a relief. It would be a grand embarrassment for our highly evolved species to have consciously chosen a legal process that has more in common with sports entertainment than an epistemologically sound mechanism for discovering truth. In 1906, the famous jurist Roscoe Pound condemned the "sporting theory" of justice, concluding that "the idea that procedure must of necessity be wholly contentious disfigures our judicial administration at every turn."[6] Justice is rarely achieved by the clash of adversaries; fortunately, justice occasionally does happen despite the clash of adversaries.

The historical narrative is pretty complicated, but here's the *Reader's Digest* version. The year 1215 was an apocalyptic year for the institution of criminal justice. Until then, conflicts were solved by trial by battle, trial by compurgation (ritualized oath swearing) and trial by ordeal. By 1215, Pope Innocent III had outlawed most superstitious trial procedures, and Europe was left with one giant legal black hole.

Continental Europe turned to a highly bureaucratized, centralized inquisitorial system. The European system was judge-driven; the judge/inquisitor was responsible for investigation, the calling of evidence and issuing a verdict. As time went on, the tyrannical aspects of the inquisitorial became muted, but the contemporary system still remains dominated by the judge. England, by contrast, adopted a developing jury system that was already being used to resolve property disputes between landowners.

The British jury system did not start out adversarial in nature. In the original jury system, the jury actively investigated the case and then delivered a verdict. The parties had no control. But as the jury evolved, it became more passive in nature, and with the loss of an official investigating body, the parties to the legal controversy were required to take over primary responsibility for the case. A passive judge/jury now served as umpire between opposing parties who had responsibility for presenting their claims.

England had privatized justice, and this was the system we inherited in North America. The original adversarial form did not include lawyers. People participated in their own trials. Imagine that! There were some real problems relating to corruption and inefficiency in the early days, but not because of lawyers. Lawyers were historical upstarts in modern criminal justice. For centuries, people battled it out alone in front of juries, and the jurors would ask questions and offer comments. It was a bit of a free-for-all. Many accused were railroaded, and many victims were unable to articulate their stories. But at least this was a real process. Maybe too real. By the eighteenth century, lawyers started to pop up more and more—both as prosecutors and defenders. Over time, we got used to professionals speaking for us, and by the early twentieth century, lawyers were the norm and not the exception.

Professional lawyers were responsible for giving law its social conscience. Without lawyers, no one would have started to raise issues relating to the abolition of slavery, the adequacy of political representation and freedom of speech in courts of law. The lawyers infused political content into criminal law, but an insatiable beast was released in the process. Not content with being allowed to participate in criminal trials, lawyers began to flex their scrawny muscles to gain more and more power. They sought to reconstruct the system to their liking. They silenced the accused, thus making themselves indispensable.

They pushed the jury into the background. Juries could no longer ask questions and were required to leave the courtroom when lawyers needed to argue points of evidence. Judges receded into the woodwork to play passive and neutral umpires.

Lawyers were responsible for constructing the complex evidentiary maze currently used to filter reality. By creating a new legal reality that was unfamiliar to the ordinary person, the lawyers became permanent squatters in an institution originally designed for lay participation. Lawyers were granted the statutory right to participate fully in all criminal trials in 1836, and it took them only 100 years to reshape the criminal process and make it their game entirely.

During this process of territorial expansion, lawyers also adopted an aggressive, confrontational style that celebrated the insult, the snide putdown and the condescending stare. Historically, this style had been the domain of the judge. The original form of the adversarial judge was an overbearing, sarcastic overlord who loved to terrorize the vulnerable. Judges were known for being "witty upon prisoners of the bar," and one judge liked to refer to this sardonic exercise of judicial wit as his power of "lawful menace."[7] When the image of a judge changed to a neutral umpire, the lawyers took over the power of lawful menace. Cross-examination was conceived as a form of brutal probing, and thus was born the era of legal advocate as virtuoso:

> The 1780s and 1790s saw the rise of the trial advocate as virtuoso performers whose words and exploits were to be savoured. A stylistic change of great symbolic significance occurred in the late 1780s when the OBSP [a legal report] began regularly listing the names of counsel appearing in each case. The lawyers had become important in their own right rather than as adjuncts to the process. Their doings were reported in increasing detail, and it was their adversarial achievements as questioners and strategists that began to be the centre of attention in the OBSP.[8]

Today, some judges are still brutal, sarcastic and mean-spirited, but most avoid this spectacle because it no longer fits the idealized image of a judge. This is now the role of the lawyer. Verbal territorial pissing absorbs a lot of court time, as counsellors joust for forensic supremacy. We expect defence lawyers to be bold, brash and abrasive, because that is clearly their institutional role. Law Society rules speak of the duty of lawyers to "raise fearlessly any issue, advance every argument, and ask every question, however distasteful, which the lawyer thinks will help the client's case." But the prosecutor is supposed to be different. This is the idealized version from the Supreme Court of Canada:

> It cannot be overemphasized that the purpose of a criminal prosecution is not to obtain a conviction, it is to lay before a jury what the Crown considers to be credible evidence relevant to what is alleged to be a crime. Counsel have a duty to see that all available legal proof of the facts is presented; it should be done firmly and pressed to its legitimate strength, but it must also be done fairly. The role of prosecutor excludes any notion of winning or losing; his function is a matter of public duty than which in civil life there can be none charged with greater personal responsibility. It is to be effectively performed with an ingrained sense of the dignity, the seriousness of the justness of civil proceedings.[9]

The vision of a prosecutor dedicated to justice without any thought of winning or losing is undercut by contemporary practice. There are many cases in which appeal courts overturn convictions because the prosecutor got carried away by the competitive urge to win. The kick-ass culture of adversarial justice has infected the prosecutorial branch of government. This is serious. Here's an example of a fairly standard cross-examination of an accused charged with robbery:

> Q. All right. Tell me, if you believe in the teachings of the Bible, does it teach you to lie as you lied about Peter Michalakakos selling guns—that's what you told the police—does it teach you to do that?
> A. I don't know. I'm not aware of the findings of the Bible. I'm not a vivid reader.
> Q. Do you know the Ten Commandments?
> A. Not offhand, no.
> Q. You don't know the Ten Commandments? I beg your pardon.
> A. I don't see why—my relation has nothing to do with this, whether or not I know the Ten Commandments.
> Q. As far as you were concerned, your—
> THE COURT: Just a moment, Mr. Allan. I have very serious doubts about how far you should get into the question of whether this gentleman knows the Ten Commandments or whether he doesn't know the Ten Commandments.
> MR. ALLAN: All right, Your Honour, but in my humble submission to the court—

THE COURT: He has said that he feels bound in his oath by the Bible, and he has explained what he means by that.

MR. ALLAN: All right. Thank you.

Q. Now I take it, then, you are bound by it because the Bible tells you once you give your oath to God, your promise to God, you wouldn't lie, is that right?

A. Yes.

Q. It teaches you other things too, doesn't it, the Bible?

A. I don't know.

Q. You don't know anything more than that?

A. I'm not a vivid reader, as I stated before.

Q. Doesn't your moral teachings in the Bible tell you not to falsely accuse another person of a crime, as you did Peter Michalakakos?

A. Maybe it does. I don't know.

Q. You didn't know about that?

A. No, I don't.

Q. Nor do you care?

A. I care about my moral standards, yes.[10]

Notice that the prosecutor simply ignored the judge's direction to move on. Otherwise, this excerpt seems innocuous. Just a little sarcastic. Standard fare for lawyers. But gratuitous sarcasm is not acceptable to the courts. In this case, the robbery conviction was overturned by the Ontario Court of Appeal because of the prosecutor's conduct.

Prosecutors want to have fun bashing witnesses just like defence counsel. They want to win. They have ego-gratification needs just like everyone else. But they should resist. Appellate courts frequently overturn convictions on the basis of inflammatory jury addresses and prejudicial cross-examination by Crown prosecutors. The prosecutors know the rules of engagement; they know there are limits placed upon the vigour of their advocacy, but the adversarial justice game is just too alluring.

A man who was convicted of sexually assaulting his stepdaughter got a new trial in 1999 because the appeal court concluded that the Crown had injected too much of his "own credibility and belief into the case." The Crown knew the rules, but still had to tell the jury, "I hope that you will leave us with the impression that the Crown, that myself, as Crown prosecutor, that I am fair, that I am honest, that I am sincere, diligent but also vigorous in the pursuit of justice."[11] The personal integrity of the lawyer is irrelevant to any case, yet here the Crown jeopardized a serious conviction by promoting his moral integrity.

In 1998, a murder conviction was overturned by the British Columbia Court of Appeal because "The address by Crown counsel to the jury took about two and a half hours. Some of the comments regarding the defence included saying that the defence position was 'driven by desperation' and had 'no foundation at all in the evidence,' that certain defence theories were 'ridiculous,' 'fishy,' 'tricky' or 'laughable.' He referred to the upcoming defence submissions as 'bafflegab,' 'smoke,' 'fog,' 'bombast,' 'mudslinging' and 'so many balloons without enough helium to even make it off the floor.'"[12]

Prosecutors continue to adopt the "No More Mr. Nice Guy" approach to lawyering despite admonitions from appeal courts that they "find it most regrettable that Crown counsel would jeopardize the validity of the trial, especially one of historical sexual assault involving so many complainants"[13] or that "unless and until Crown counsel stop this kind of improper and prejudicial cross-examination, the court will regrettably have to remit difficult and sensitive cases of this nature back for a new trial at great expense to the emotional well-being of the parties, not to mention the added burden to the administration of justice."[14] But lawyers can't stop the bravado. Inundated with American television images of the lawyer as verbal bully and overwhelmed by the celebrity status afforded outspoken and abrasive lawyers, lawyers can't resist the temptation to insult and annoy. If you are tough, then you must be a good lawyer. But good for whom?

In 1993, a woman claimed to have been sexually assaulted. The first trial was a mistrial. The second trial resulted in a conviction. The accused spent two and a half years in prison before the Court of Appeal intervened in 1999. It overturned the conviction and stayed the proceeding. Six years after the allegation, the victim could not claim to have received justice, and the accused had spent time in prison for an offence he had never been properly convicted of. This is justice? And what was one of the reasons for staying the charges? Obnoxious conduct by all the lawyers:

> In this case, the performance of defence counsel (not counsel on appeal) was not a model of advocacy. On the contrary, he was at times provoking,

defiant and argumentative and his questioning of witnesses was difficult to follow and unnecessarily lengthy. Such conduct on the part of defence counsel should not be condoned and should be addressed by the trial judge. However, even when, as in this case, the trial judge fails to intervene, improper conduct by defence counsel does not justify improper conduct by Crown counsel.[15]

The lawyers should be invisible participants who recede into the background, but in most cases it is their performance, their oratory skills and their zany antics that become the focus. How many times has a jury convicted because they did not like the style of the defence lawyer? How many times has a jury acquitted because they found the Crown too overbearing and self-righteous? This should never happen, but I would wager that verdicts based upon the performance of counsel are a daily affair. The practice of law is a business, and lawyers seem to believe that putting on a good show leads to more business.

Don't get me wrong. I like a good show as much as the next person. But the determination of whether to punish someone as a rapist or a murderer should not depend on whether a lawyer asks the right questions or presses the right buttons in addressing the jury. A criminal trial should be about education, not entertainment. Although an entertaining presentation can be a good pedagogical approach to education, the justice system has to dampen the impact of entertainment. It is distracting. It erodes the solemnity of the occasion. Unfortunately, an adversarial conception of justice provides an ideal landscape for entertainment to flourish.

An adversarial jury trial is attractive primarily because of its entertainment value. It has all the elements of good theatre. Conflict, obviously. A willing suspension of disbelief, as reflected in the hallowed principle of the presumption of innocence. And intrigue and suspense, as the silent jury is sequestered in a small room to emerge with a verdict—a final score—but not an explanation. The explanation would be an anticlimax; it would be like a Q&A session with the director after you've seen a great film. The whole structure of the adversarial process is premised upon a formulaic plotline that resonates with every film- and theatregoer. Earlier this century, Thurman Arnold, in his classic work *The Symbols of Government*, wrote:

Much of [the system's] strength is due to the romance and color which is centered in the jury trial. More efficient methods of judicial investigation can easily be imagined, but none more picturesque. When a great government treats the lowliest of criminals as an equal antagonist, strips itself of the executive power which it possesses, and submits the case to twelve ordinary men, allowing the judge only the authority of an umpire, we have a gesture of recognition to the dignity of the individual which has an extraordinary dramatic appeal. Its claim is on our emotions, rather than our common sense.[16]

Although the dramatic appeal of the trial is good for capturing the public's attention, the bravado and fury of the messenger have the potential to overwhelm and obscure the message. Aspiring to put on a good show is fine for television courtroom drama, but should not be part of a legitimate system of criminal justice. Beyond the distorting effect, the infusion of wit and staging into a criminal trial creates a system in which justice can be achieved only for those who have the funds to hire the expensive entertainers. Not every lawyer can put on a good show, so we should neutralize the tendency of adversarial justice to foster entertainment values.

Rarely do lawyers learn what judges and juries think of their antics, but when we do get a glimpse into their thoughts, we often find the show was neither good nor persuasive. In 2001, the Court of Appeal ordered a new trial on a sexual assault charge because the trial judge had misdirected the jury on the meaning of reasonable doubt (as if the jury was even listening).[17] In her address to the jury, defence counsel had provided the jury with the proper instruction, but the appeal court concluded that this had not helped the jury understand the meaning of reasonable doubt. It was clear from the record that the jury found the defence lawyer's show a turnoff, and thus would not have accepted her instruction. The jury provided the judge with notes throughout the trial. The Court of Appeal made these comments about the notes:

in the circumstances of this case, there is reason to doubt that the defence closing submission on reasonable doubt impressed itself upon the jury. The two complainants were cross-examined over a period of five days and the trial lasted 12 days ... A review of the transcript indicates that defence counsel was prolix in the extreme ... This led the jury to deliver three notes of admonition to the trial judge, a level of response that is unprecedented in my experience.

The first note reads:

> *Your honour,*
>
> *With the greatest respect, we have been listening to one witness for 4 days up to now. Could you inform us when this case might wrap up. Could you tell us how many other witnesses will be called. My concern is that this case could be going on much too long. Will the defendant take the stand?*
>
> *Thank You*

The second note from the jury was more impatient:

> *Your honour,*
>
> *We are now at the end of the 3rd week!! The defence has been on every day (11 days), the prosecution has had less than 1 day. The defence is repeating herself with the same questions to every witness. Even though it's the 11th day she is still reviewing evidence covered on the 1st day. Your honour, how much do we need to know about this intersection, truck … windows, distances etc., etc., etc. We have the picture very, very clear. I believe it is unfair to be wasting unnecessary time. How did the defence calculate 1 1/2 wks for the duration of this trial?? Your honour, the jury is very tired and frustrated with this line of questioning. We would like the defence to introduce new evidence relevant to the charges in question. Let's wrap up this case before we fall asleep!! Let the jury do its job.*

The trial judge received a third note from the jury:

> *Sir,*
>
> *With respect to the court, the iteration and reiteration of questions from defence counsel to the video expert [i.e. Boris] is irritating and has little or no relevance to this trial. We seem to have taken an hour to confirm data which the jury can understand in a minute.*[18]

Because it's a human process, we do expect some verdicts to be overturned for legal errors, but this should not happen because the Crown was inflammatory, or because the defence was "prolix in the extreme." Justice should never be contingent upon the antics of lawyers. And why was the lawyer "prolix to the extreme"? Lawyers think that rattling witnesses with an endless barrage of questions is a sign of toughness and competence. Also, the longer the case goes on, the more money is made. As in any business, time is money, and lawyers know how to stretch a point to eternity. (Historically, lawyers were paid by the word in drafting contracts; that's why standard form leases still go on and on for pages.) The complainant may suffer, the jury may revolt and the verdict may be in jeopardy. But the lawyer gets paid handsomely, and the client is left with the impression that the lawyer was a real fighter.

There is another, more insidious, side-effect of adversarial posturing. Justice is not always compromised by ill manners. There are cases in which an aggressive, rude and brutal cross-examination does lead to hidden truth. But the institutional structure of this adversarial process leads to the exercise of very poor and callous judgement by many legal professionals. The institutional role adopted by lawyers fosters a myopic perspective in which the Crown is expected to say "white" whenever the defence lawyer says "black." Once in a while concessions are made, but the "No More Mr. Nice Guy" ethos demands that the lawyer take a contrary position to that advanced by their opponent. Lawyers naively believe that the clash of opposites will always produce a result consistent with the public interest. This cannot be true. Sometimes, maybe most of the time, justice requires a collaborative effort rather than a confrontational battle of wits.

The adversarial ethic allows lawyers to make thoughtless decisions that can be justified only within the narrow framework of their institutional roles. Most defence lawyers believe cops always lie, and most prosecutors believe cops always tell the truth. The truth obviously lies somewhere in between. But the institutional role of the defence lawyer requires that the police be approached with suspicion, and so the Crown adopts the contrary position. Lawyers hide behind their institutional roles, adopting positions without any exercise of independent judgement.

Many years ago, I went to a conference on impaired driving. On one panel were a defence lawyer and a Crown. The moderator asked the two whether they felt current sentencing practices for impaired drivers were too lenient or too harsh. Surprise, surprise, the Crown said too lenient and the defence lawyer said too harsh. Even when out of court, lawyers often cannot shed their institutional roles. These positions were not advanced because of some independent thought or study of the issue. Crowns are supposed to promote tough sentences, and defence counsellors are supposed to get their clients the lightest sentence possible. When lawyers think about the law, it is more reflexive than reflective.

A friend of mine, who is actually a very good lawyer, told me a story about one of his clients, who was being sought by American authorities for extradition on a securities offence. The American prosecutor's file had been destroyed when the World Trade Centre collapsed. He called my friend and requested that he provide a copy of the file. My friend refused. Just a reflexive, knee-jerk response. In terms of legal ethics, he didn't do anything wrong. The Crown wants help, and institutionally the defence is allowed to sit back and watch the Crown squirm. I just couldn't get my head around the fact that one of the most significant tragedies of modern times could not move the lawyer to abandon the characteristic adversarial response. Is the consideration of personal conscience and ordinary morality ever relevant in the adversarial ethic? Apparently not. The worship of the adversarial ethic led to a situation in which American police and prosecutors had to scramble to reconstruct a file while New York City was still reeling from the loss of thousands of lives and enormous social and economic chaos.

This entire book could be devoted to bad decisions made by public officials who worship adversarial justice, but I will just talk about three: one that is personal, one that is pathetic and one that is disturbing.

In 1992, I was asked by the Ontario Court of Appeal to act as *amicus curiae* (friend of the court) to assist a mentally disordered offender with his appeal. I was flattered that the court asked me to assist, but I had no idea of the convoluted and tortuous history of the case. Dwight Taylor suffered from schizophrenia. He was an intelligent man who had practised law in Toronto. As a result of client complaints of erratic behaviour, the Law Society was poised to take disciplinary action against him. Taylor went to the offices of the Law Society of Upper Canada to meet with their counsel. He confronted the Law Society lawyer in an agitated manner, and the lawyer pushed Taylor to the floor. An altercation ensued, and Taylor stabbed the lawyer a number of times. Fortunately, none of the wounds required even a stitch; after a week, the wounds had healed and the lawyer was back at work. Taylor was charged with aggravated assault and possession of a weapon for a dangerous purpose.

Everyone accepted that Taylor was ill. No one questioned the diagnosis. But legal professionals never know what to do with the mentally ill. Most people are scared when they encounter a dishevelled lunatic shouting obscenities and convulsing with anger. This is natural. I feel the same way when I pass obnoxious drunks. The unpredictability of these people is disconcerting. But the vast majority of people who suffer from serious mental disorders are not dangerous. Sure, there have been some pretty brutal murders committed by psychotics, but violence is more the domain of the sane. Legal professionals are not necessarily scared of the mentally ill, but these people need lots of attention, and their special needs get in the way of the ordinary processing of criminals.

Since the stabbing, Taylor had been detained in psychiatric hospitals while the criminal process ground to a halt. March 5, 1987—Taylor found unfit to stand trial. April 27, 1987—Taylor found fit to stand trial. November 9, 1987—Taylor found unfit to stand trial. September 26, 1988—Taylor found fit to stand trial. October 14, 1988—Taylor found not guilty by reason of insanity. August 26, 1991—Taylor received a new trial from the Court of Appeal. March 24, 1992—Taylor found unfit to stand trial. Taylor appealed this last ruling to the Court of Appeal, and that's when I got involved.

Taylor started calling me on a daily basis from the maximum security hospital. He was an engaging man, but clearly out of his mind. His entire universe was constructed on a grand paranoid delusion. He had gone through dozens of lawyers and spoke of starting malicious prosecution proceedings against almost everyone who had been involved with his case. Like many schizophrenics, he did not accept that he suffered from this illness. Because of his legal training, he was able to thwart any attempt by officials to seek orders allowing for involuntary treatment. He was sitting and rotting in the hospital, dreaming about the network of conspirators who had orchestrated his fall from grace. When I visited him, he was bruised, and sported a huge bump on his head. His teeth were rotting. He refused to receive conventional treatment even for non-psychiatric problems. He was a completely broken man. But he always had the energy to rant about the horrible injustice being perpetrated against him.

I managed to convince the Court of Appeal that the trial judge had erred in his approach to the fitness issue.[19] The case was remanded back for trial. By this time, Taylor had decided he trusted me, and he asked me to defend him at trial. I knew it would be an ordeal, but I was confident

I could convince the Crown to withdraw the charges against him. Taylor had been locked up for close to six years, much more than the amount of time he would have spent in jail had he been tried and convicted. And there was no real possibility he would be released in the near future, because he was on a continually renewing cycle of orders of involuntary commitment. Even if his illness did pose a threat to the community, the provincial mental health system was taking care of this. Finally, his doctors all agreed that his continued involvement with the criminal-justice system was anti-therapeutic—battling criminal-justice officials fuelled his paranoid delusions.

In January 1993, I approached the Crown to discuss my views on the continuation of this prosecution. The prosecutor agreed with most of what I said, but he was concerned about Taylor's potential threat if released. He told me he would exercise his discretion not to continue the prosecution if I secured a letter from Taylor's attending psychiatrist that would allay the prosecutor's fears. Within a few days, I received this letter from the doctor: "We continue to see Mr. Taylor as certifiable under the Mental Health Act. ... Without appropriate therapies this will be the case in the long term." That should have satisfied the Crown's fear for public safety. The doctor also wrote that the continuing prosecution "has been an ongoing factor and a perpetuant of the delusional ideas which characterize his mental state. At the very least, it poses an obstacle for successful treatment, and, at times, it can be seen as having aggravated his condition and brought him a great deal of stress." I called Taylor to tell him that his ordeal would soon be coming to an end.

For two months, I chased the prosecutor to confirm our arrangement. My phone calls were not returned. My letters were not answered. When I did manage to connect with the Crown, I explained to him that I did not intend to be a pest, but I had a very sick man calling me daily to inquire whether the Crown would be withdrawing the charge. With each passing day, Taylor became more agitated. With each passing day, he made increasingly bizarre demands upon me. He insisted that another lawyer had been wearing his clothes for the past six years and that if I did not call this lawyer to retrieve his clothing, I would be fired. I told the Crown I did not know how long I could continue to stickhandle through this mess. With each day with no word from the Crown, Taylor's suspicion of me was growing. I was being sucked into the "conspiracy." I pleaded with the Crown to make his final decision promptly.

The prosecutor didn't seem to care. He was waffling. I kept calling. My letters became increasingly aggressive. I tried to involve other senior Crowns in the problem. After three months I gave up. I told Taylor I could not get an answer from the prosecutor, and would prepare an abuse of process motion seeking a stay of proceedings to prevent the trial from being conducted. Taylor reluctantly agreed, despite his suspicion that I was working with the enemy.

Close to a year passed before a judge ruled on my motion. He concluded that the trial must proceed. Even though he agreed with me that there might not be a constructive purpose in continuing the prosecution, the absence of any purpose did not constitute an abuse of process in law. The judge took close to a year to also decide that the case should not be stayed because of unreasonable delay. A trial was eventually conducted, and Taylor was convicted and sentenced to time already served. No one seemed to care that this case kept a sick man frozen in his paranoid delusion.

This attitude is borne of indifference, not of malice. No one wanted to harm this poor man; it's just that being an advocate means not having to be a nice guy. If you are playing by the rules of your institutional role, you cannot be criticized for doing the wrong thing. The Crown had the authority to continue the prosecution. As long as prosecutors don't break any institutional rules, it does not matter if they exercise poor judgement. It does not matter if they act without compassion—acting compassionately is not part of the institutional role of the advocate. Compassion requires emotional engagement inconsistent with an adversarial ethic.

Why did the prosecutor fail to respond to Taylor's compelling claim for an exercise of compassion? I will never know. Maybe I pissed him off by harassing him for a decision. That's part of the adversarial ethic: screw people around who piss you off. Or maybe there was nothing personal about this. Maybe the Crown saw the stabbing as a more serious offence than I had judged it. There was blood on the plush carpets in the reception area of the Law Society of Upper Canada. Taylor's delusions led him to attack a member of the club. Everyone protects their own first and foremost.

Another manifestation of the "No More Mr. Nice Guy" syndrome is a stubborn and arrogant refusal to admit to being wrong. In 1997, a man named Oniel came to see me for advice on a malicious prosecution lawsuit he had been fighting against the police. He had been arrested for robbery in 1985. The case was a dog's breakfast. The victim/complainant was a shady character. The identification of Oniel was skewed. And the police failed to investigate obvious leads. Oniel's lawyer wrote to the Crown to have the case withdrawn, but without success. Oniel was acquitted at trial, and he sued the police. In the meantime, he lost his job, and his life spiralled downward. Eleven years after he commenced the suit, it had not yet been resolved. One trial, one appeal, endless motions and the drawing of battle lines. Oniel had represented himself throughout, and had done quite well, but government lawyers know how to dig trenches. When attacked, they defend by a strategy of attrition. They wear you down with motions and delay tactics until you are either bankrupt or lose your will to fight.

You see, the adversarial system fosters the attitude that it's okay to cover up your mistakes. Admitting wrong would be a sign of weakness. This case should have never gone to trial, but no one would admit they had fucked up. Once he was acquitted, no one in government apologized. They think you should just go home and thank god you were not wrongfully convicted. No one pays you for your pain and suffering. So you have to sue. And they will defend and defend in the face of obvious liability. They have in-house lawyers. They don't have to pay fees for a lawsuit that drags on for over a decade. The adversarial ethos tells these government lawyers to stand tall and fight the allegations of mistake and wrongdoing until the troublemaker goes away.

Oniel did not go away. I helped him with his second trial in 1998, and it was an uphill battle. He lost. But he did not give up. He couldn't. He had invested twelve years in the struggle to vindicate his name and receive some compensation. He appealed, and in 2001 the Court of Appeal found the police to be liable and ordered Oniel to be compensated in an amount exceeding $75,000.[20] It took sixteen years for a court to conclude that the police had proceeded recklessly, even though I suspect everyone must have known this from the start.

When you cast aspersions on the integrity of a legal professional, be prepared for retaliation. In 2002, the Supreme Court of Canada upheld a damage award in excess of a million dollars against the attorney general of Quebec for malicious prosecution.[21] In this case, prosecutors decided not to prosecute a man for murdering his ex-girlfriend because of a lack of evidence. However, after the man decided to sue numerous public officials for defamation of character, the Crown and police claimed to have discovered new evidence. They prosecuted and the man was convicted, only to have the Court of Appeal overturn the conviction because the case was a dog's breakfast. The new identification witness was of no value whatsoever. Any way you slice or dice it, it looks like this poor sap was wrongfully prosecuted and convicted as a pre-emptive strike to discredit him in his defamation suit against the government. The Crown's bad motives must have been transparent to the Supreme Court, because people rarely win when they sue police and prosecutors for an abuse of power.

The police are part of the "No More Mr. Nice Guy" problem. They are as infected as the legal professionals with the adversarial bug. In 1986, when Wesley Evans was twenty-one, he was convicted of first-degree murder for the stabbing death of two women. Here's a judge's description of this public enemy:

> As a child he suffered from attention deficit hyperactivity disorder. When he was 9 years old he was run down by a truck and suffered extensive brain damage. He also lost a significant amount of motor function in his left side. He has a measured IQ of 68 to 80. This range of scores is classified as borderline retardation. When he was 11 years old he was severely burned by an exploding lighter, resulting in prolonged periods of hospitalization over the following 9 years. His formal education does not extend past elementary school, although he did attend special classes in grades beyond that level.[22]

In 1991, the Supreme Court of Canada entered an acquittal on the basis that Evans's statements to the police were obtained in violation of the Charter of Rights.[23] Evans had served five years in prison before he returned to his parents' home. The police were pissed. They did not believe Evans was innocent. They believed he got a lucky break because some clever lawyer convinced the Supreme Court that rights were violated. So the police put Evans under surveillance. For this, I cannot fault them. If they truly believed he was guilty of these brutal murders, then a bit of surveillance was justified. But they did not stop there. Undercover officers were instructed to befriend Evans, gain his confidence and establish a dominant relationship with him.

The officers took Evans drinking. They "simulated" (who were they kidding?) smoking pot with him. They went to strip clubs and discussed "sexual exploits in the grossest possible language" with him. They started to recruit Evans for criminal activity. They boasted about their criminal activity, and told Evans he might be allowed to join their gang. This is criminal justice at its worst. Eventually, the police manipulated Evans into talking about wanting to kill two people. He was then charged with counselling murder. What a vicious set-up. Adversaries gone insane. How could the prosecutor go forward on these charges?

The trial judge saw through the masquerade. He stayed the proceedings as an abuse of process, noting:

> It was clear to the undercover operators that Mr. Evans was desperate to have friends. They referred to him as following them like a "puppy dog" and imitating them. He had barely enough money to survive at a subsistence level. The undercover operators bought him liquor, gave him money to buy drugs and shoes and bought him food. They held out to him the hope of becoming part of their organization and obtaining a secure friendship with them and their associates. They were confident, well dressed and financially comfortable. They were everything that he was not. He had no other friends.[24]

But the trial should not have happened in the first place. Judges should not have to clean up the messes created by crybaby adversaries who want to lash out at their opponents. It's a tragic waste of valuable judicial resources. More frightening is the fact that most judges sleepwalk through these travesties. Evans got lucky twice.

Defence adversarial posturing raises its own set of social problems. When Crowns lose perspective, we run the risk of wrongful conviction. When the defence pulls a fast one, we run the risk of the guilty escaping justice. After the Paul Bernardo case was finally laid to rest, a trial commenced to examine the conduct of his first lawyer, Ken Murray. Canadians have become all too familiar with this story. Soon after Bernardo's arrest, bumbling police officers searched his home for days without finding the horrific videotapes Bernardo had made of his victims. Murray went to the residence after the police left, found the tapes where Bernardo told him they would be, and held onto them for seventeen months before realizing that the tapes must be disclosed. The timing sucked. In the interim, the prosecutors signed off on their sweet deal with Homolka. They would have never given Bernardo's wife this deal if they had known of the existence and content of the videotapes. Murray was charged with obstructing justice and was ultimately acquitted on the basis that he did not truly understand that what he had done was wrong.[25]

Although there is some degree of ambiguity, it is generally understood that lawyers must take to the grave any communications or information provided by their clients. But it is also generally understood that this privilege does not extend to physical evidence. If a client admits guilt, the lawyer must respect this confidence, but the smoking gun provided by the client must be turned over to public officials. How could Mr. Murray not have realized he was skating on very thin ice?

Apparently, Mr. Murray believed he could use the videotapes for the legitimate forensic purpose of ambushing the Crown's star witness, Karla Homolka. The idea was that, at Bernardo's trial, Karla would try to sugarcoat her complicity in the crimes, believing that the tapes had not been found. Then in cross-examining her, the defence would dramatically confront her with the horrific tapes, destroying the credibility of her assertion that Bernardo was the murderer. It is irrelevant that Mr. Murray's strategy was designed to assist a notorious serial killer and rapist—the presumption of innocence demands no less from defence lawyers.

Defence lawyers must be prepared to champion unpopular causes and to engage in heated battle to secure acquittals. However, there are, and must be, limits to advocacy. These ethical limits are constantly under siege as the result of the operation of adversarial legal culture. Why didn't Murray realize his strategy violated these limits? He was probably just thinking about trying to win a difficult case. Defence lawyers often forget that they, too, are guardians of the public interest.

Winning at all costs is the measure of a lawyer's success. I gag when I meet lawyers who boast about not having lost a case in the last decade. I assume they must be pleading all their clients guilty. I talk about win–loss records only during hockey season. When trials become sporting contests, some lawyers will take ethical shortcuts, just as some Olympic runners will take performance-enhancing drugs. It's that simple.

Most lawyers are painfully aware of the horrors of working within an adversarial system of justice. As one lawyer has cautioned, "Law students cannot imagine the meat grinder that awaits them in an adversary system. Many young lawyers are shocked, offended and profoundly bruised by it. The deterioration of professional courtesy, professional integrity and professional competence generated by today's 'Rambo' adversarial process is causing wide-spread alarm."[26]

Studies have shown that lawyers are ambivalent about their work and that they agonize over the universal disdain shown to the profession. A

1998 American study showed that 49% of lawyers are dissatisfied with their lives.[27] Canadian studies reveal similar findings.[28] Lawyers are unhappy with their workloads and their inability to spend sufficient time with family and on personal pursuits. In 2000, a survey of first-year associates in Canada showed enormous malaise. These young lawyers were asked about survival skills for the profession and the responses ranged from the facetious ("Rolaids") to the pathetic ("Don't do it! It's not too late to start a new career").[29]

I have never seen as much misery and dissatisfaction within a profession as I have seen among my colleagues at the bar. A 1996 American survey, which applies with equal force to Canadian lawyers, concluded:

> The findings of the research ... suggest that the professional and personal well-being of lawyers is in serious jeopardy. Lawyers are working more, reducing vacation time, spending less time with family members, are prone to alcohol abuse, and face high levels of psychological distress ... A significant percentage of practicing lawyers are experiencing a wide variety of significant psychological distress symptoms well beyond that expected of the general population ... The dangers of psychological distress among members of the legal profession arise, at least in part, from two of the very elements that are traditionally associated with effective litigation strategy— directed anger and hostility. Both of these factors may often be counterproductive to one's overall well-being.[30]

The psychological distress enveloping this profession includes obsessive-compulsive behaviour, social alienation, anxiety and depression. A lot of unhappy advocates drink themselves into oblivion. Lawyering is not good for the spirit. The words of a thirteenth-century Buddhist monk, Nichiren, perfectly describe the spirit of one who engages in argumentative and adversarial posturing: "thunder that rolls but brings no rain."[31] The brash and overbearing aspects of legal culture can bring no rain. Legal culture cannot nourish. After all the hoopla of a thunderous performance in court, lawyers find their spirits to be barren and malnourished.

So it is no wonder lawyers are so rude and abrasive. This is the character armour that must be donned to live daily in a world of raging argument. Lawyers may know they have created a Boschian hell, but instead of working to restructure the system, they project their anger, frustration and dissatisfaction on other lawyers, clients and the public at large. Adversarial lawyering breeds an arrogant contempt for others. The lawyer's refrain is, "No one is a smart as me. No one even comes close. The clients are idiots and the judges are morons." Lawyers kiss ass in front of judges, but behind their backs they tear strips off the judiciary in vicious and insulting ways. The idea that lawyers view everyone else with contempt is not a new idea. In 1835, political theorist Alexis de Tocqueville published *Democracy in America*. This French jurist came to America to gain an understanding of the American perspective on justice, liberty and politics. He quickly realized that lawyers had become the most influential knowledge elite of the nineteenth century. They had become the new aristocracy. You cannot become a member of an aristocracy without acquiring the skills of condescension and an inflated sense of self-importance. Alexis de Tocqueville wrote:

> The special knowledge which lawyers derive from their studies ensures them a separate station in society; and they constitute a sort of privileged body in the scale of intelligence. This notion of their superiority perpetually recurs to them in the practice of their profession; they are the masters of a science which is necessary, but which is not very generally known; they serve as arbiters between the citizens; and the habit of directing their blind passions of the party in litigation to their purpose, inspires them with a certain contempt for the judgement of the multitude ... A portion of the tastes and the habits of the aristocracy may consequently be discovered in the characters of men in the profession of the law. They participate in the same instinctive love of order and formalities; and they entertain the same repugnance to the actions of the multitude, and the same secret contempt of the government of the people.[32]

De Tocqueville hit the nail on the head. Legal culture blends the aggressiveness of an adversarial ethic with the arrogance of an aristocratic worldview. And out of this deadly mixture you get Mr. Bastard.

In case you don't believe that lawyers entertain contempt and repugnance for the multitude, let's look at a few recent remarks made by lawyers concerning the rising wave of self-representation in courts. With legal services beyond the financial capacity of many, and with legal aid being scaled back throughout Canada, more and more people are choosing to represent themselves. Hallelujah! People are reclaiming lost territory. People are starting to once again take personal responsibility for their conflicts. But lawyers are not rejoicing. It's not just that they're unhappy about losing business, they truly believe that ordinary people have no ability to speak for themselves:

> Lawyers know that conducting a court case without a lawyer is like performing an appendectomy without a surgeon. The main difference is that the unassisted legal procedure is actually occurring at an alarming rate across the country ... Unrepresented litigants are already causing chronic delays and clogging an overburdened system ... They also pester an overworked court staff, including librarians, distracting staffers into spending unplanned time with them explaining unfamiliar and complex procedures. ...
>
> There is a proportion of know-it-alls who, out of sheer cussedness or a misplaced confidence in their ability to master everything, are going to take on the world because they know more about it than anyone else. These people will always be with us ... They claim to know what to do, but have no idea what is relevant. Instead of conducting a cross-examination, they end up arguing with a witness. ...
>
> The legal system was never set up to operate without lawyers. "Indeed it was established to work with them," [notes one lawyer]. "That is the structure. You can say theoretically anyone can access the legal system on his or her own. But that is not practical. It is not a simple system—not even for lawyers."
>
> And lawyers have a way of talking to each other [says another lawyer], "Together, we try to sift and sort through procedural or evidentiary issues. We talk to one another in a way that we are able to cut away at least some of the chaff. When the individual is representing himself or herself, it's not as easy to do that."[33]

These comments drip with contempt and derision. The next time you pay your lawyer $200 to $500 an hour, just remember that you are paying a professional who thinks you are an idiot. Don't come crying to me when your hired gun treats you like dirt, and don't tell me you want to kill all the lawyers. You bought into the "No More Mr. Nice Guy" crap. You want your lawyer to be rude and abrasive. You want to hire a pit bull, because you mistakenly believe this will enhance your chances at the gates of justice. So don't look so surprised and indignant when the dog turns on you.

16

The Training and Education of Mr. Bastard

IN THE LEGAL PROFESSION, psychiatric distress is carefully nurtured at an early stage in the breeding ground of neurosis we call law school. One study noted that the symptoms of distress "are directly traceable to law study and practice. They are not exhibited when the lawyers enter law school, but emerge shortly thereafter and remain, without significant abatement, well after graduation from law school."[1]

Studies clearly show that law students experience greater psychiatric distress than do medical students and the general population. Only 3% to 9% of the general population in industrial nations suffers from depression; however, 17% to 40% of American law students fall into clinical depression.[2] With respect to American law students, it has been observed that observed that: "First-year students are generally overwhelmed. The workload leaves many without time to sleep and relax adequately or to enjoy relationships with friends and relatives. Cramton states that 'the first year grades control the distribution of goodies: honors, law review and job placement, and because of the importance placed on these matters by the law student culture, even the students' sense of personal worth.'"[3] Things are no different in Canadian law schools.

Modern education is about marks. The acquisition of knowledge is secondary to the acquisition of grades. Sometimes there is a correlation between knowledge and grades, but often there is not. For reasons I will never understand, education has been built on the foundation of competition. The best rise to the top, and the worst drop out and smoke crack. In a competitive world, there is no time to help those with learning disabilities or unique cognitive needs. "Achieve or perish" is the motto of modern education. As Lenny Bruce wrote:

Our society is based on competition. If it isn't impressed upon you at home with the scramble for love between brothers and sisters, they really lay it down to you at school—in numbers any child can understand—that's what grading is. You bring home 100 percent, and your mother hugs you and your father pats you on the back. But not your schoolmates; they know they're in competition with you, and if you get a high percentage they must get a lower one. Everybody wants love and acceptance and he soon learns that one way to get it is by higher marks than the other fellow. In essence, you are gratified by your schoolmate's failures. We take this with us into adulthood.[4]

Competition may work in a free-market economy, but it should not be the carrot used to motivate students to learn. It can become a sickness in an educational context. We should be trying to motivate students with rewards other than a race for the highest grade. Let our students learn about competition on the football field. Let them learn about competition in the marketplace. Educational training should be a collaborative adventure shared by curious minds. It rarely is.

We often assume that education correlates to insight, intelligence and good judgement. For most people, going to university is not about acquiring knowledge and insight; it is just a rite of passage, something to do in between reckless adolescence and domesticated mid-life. I was naive about university. I thought everyone would be an Einstein. I was happy to escape from the world of weekend parties, Thai sticks and organized chaos. I thought that I could finally apply my mind to the pursuit of insight. I entered the University of Toronto to study physics. Unlocking some of the secrets of the universe, now that seemed like higher education. I lasted one month. The vast majority of my classmates were neurotic pre-med students who knew they had to achieve near-perfect grades. The classroom stunk with the stench of ambition, and my classmates viewed everyone around them with suspicion. It was a big turnoff. To hell with the universe. I switched to film school. Lacking the will to become the next Fellini, I found myself a few years later in law school.

In law school the level of competition is really cranked up. The markaholic is the ideal law school candidate. Type-A. Tenacious. Argumentative. Ambitious. Fastidious. Maybe intelligent—the jury is still out. Mr. Nice Guy will only get left behind in the hallowed halls of law school. You can still act like Mr. Nice Guy, but you'd best quietly develop your alter-ego Mr. Bastard.

For the most part, the faculty does not espouse an ethic of confrontation and aggression. At a symbolic and rhetorical level, law schools promote an ethic of caring and regard for others. But at a primordial level, the adversarial ethic of the profession infects the student body, fuelled by television and the competitive underpinnings of modern education. The stress of competition overshadows any efforts to instil a social conscience in the law student. So long as the law schools continue to evaluate students with brutal winner-take-all final examinations, any talk about distributive and restorative justice becomes purely theoretical. No one is listening unless it is on the exam.

In 2001, a grades scandal at the university of Toronto Law School made national headlines.[5] One-year suspensions were handed out to twenty-five students who misrepresented their grades in search of employment. This was news? All professional schools built on the ethic of competition will foster morally problematic behaviour. What *was* newsworthy was the response of the law school's administration to this breaking scandal. The law school apparently blamed some renegade law professor for counselling the deceit. What a shameless display of "No More Mr. Nice Guy" syndrome! Take no responsibility and try to shift the blame. So much for the professorial talk about compassion and natural justice. It's just talk.

Grades, grades and grades. When do the students stop to contemplate justice? Only when they will be graded on the fruits of their contemplation. It's all about the paper chase. It's all about flexing your muscles to intimidate the other students, who also aspire to become Mr. Bastard. When I entered law school, I was in my shy phase and reluctant to participate in class discussions. But there were always a few people, usually male, who expressed their opinions on everything under the sun. They spoke well. Intonation, modulation and gesticulation were all carefully controlled. Turns out the class talkers were usually the worst students. All form and no substance. They talked to mark their territory, not to contribute to the understanding of an issue. They talked to intimidate the quieter students. In a competitive world, posturing is a big part of the dynamic, and the law school experience promotes the development of adversarial posturing. In the competitive world of law school, speech is not a tool used to convey thought, speech is a weapon.

There are so many unsettling aspects of the law school experience, I'm not really sure where to start. As Professor Robert Stover says:

> At least five interrelated factors contribute to the high degree of stress felt by most beginning law students. First, the legal neophyte is confronted by the difficult task of mastering a new and confusing body of knowledge. Second, the law-school environment provides only minimal feedback regarding success; uncertainty concerning how to study and how much to study remains for much of the first year. Third, the student is faced with the challenge of the Socratic method of teaching and by the daily possibility of exposure to embarrassment that it presents. Fourth, almost all law students have known academic success throughout their prior careers; yet in law school, half of them must become accustomed to being "below average." This is especially problematic because of the importance of grades to success in the job market. Finally, the first-year students must integrate themselves into a new social environment and may attach added importance to academic performance in an attempt to win the respect of their classmates.[6]

In many ways, the law school experience is similar to indoctrination into a cult. Keep the prospective cult members tired, disoriented and stressed out, and eventually they will accept the thought-terminating clichés you have been teaching them. It has been suggested that "professional schools are highly invasive institutions that exert intense control by purposely influencing beliefs, values, and personality characteristics of students. In fact, law school appears to be the most invasive of all graduate education. Thus, it should not be surprising that law students 'learn the requirements of the system and turn themselves into the kind of people the situation demands.'"[7] The kind of person the situation demands is Mr. Bastard. Only Mr. Bastard can achieve the highest grades and win all the cases.

There are students who don't get caught up in the hypnotic spiral of ambition. I have taught and employed hundreds of law students, many of whom I was proud to call my friends. Many remain friends. There are also good lawyers—lawyers committed to public service. Not everyone in the profession is a bastard. But law schools breed a disproportionate number of bastards, who go on to become the inspiration behind lawyer-bashing jokes.

The stress of law school fucks people up in many different ways. The legacy of my law school experience was insomnia and gastrointestinal distress. I became neurotic. Others become psychotic. Few come out without any psychic scars. In my years as a professor, I encountered many bizarre and troubled students. Some of them are now lawyers. Every time I meet these troubled students, I wonder how they will ever be able to ethically and effectively provide legal assistance to others in trouble. Many troubled students achieve high grades in law school and then go on to embezzle, deceive and antagonize clients and colleagues. The only thing the law schools and the law firms care about is the grades. Lots of psychos out there graduated with honours.

Law schools are not just churning out arrogant and elitist lawyers by putting the malleable student into a competitive meat-grinder. They are also stunting the full development of the student's emotional intelligence—the ability to empathize and relate to others in a meaningful way. Law schools train students to see clients, plaintiffs and accused people as political categories, and not as real people.

The insidious effects of hyper-competition are largely ignored by the law schools because they are caught up in the throes of their own identity crisis: should the school be a trade school for lawyers or an academic institution dedicated to the study of theories of justice? This question has never been answered definitively. The majority of students want to enter a trade school. They want to learn how to become lawyers, as if such a thing can actually be taught like a skilled trade. But most law schools are run by faculty who have a disdain for lawyers and their practice, and who really just want to be critical thinkers. Most professors I know have little respect for the profession, and most lawyers I know think professors are smart but useless. The result is confused and unhappy students. These students then become easily duped into thinking that becoming Mr. Bastard is the right path to becoming a successful lawyer. The theories explored by professors just confound the student. So they end up believing that adversarial lawyering must be the right path, because this is the media and television image of the lawyer. This image is a lot easier to digest than a hermeneutic deconstruction of legal doctrine.

It's not a secret that law students are unhappy with the educational mission of law schools. Once considered the premier law school in Canada, recent surveys have consistently ranked Osgoode Hall Law School in Toronto at the bottom of the pile.[8] One consistent theme running through the survey is the students' discontent with a curriculum that focuses on theoretical and political constructs. In 1997, the survey noted:

> Osgoode has simply too many students and too much political ranting in its courses. It has been hearing this message every year this survey has been done and graduates consistently pull the school's rankings down because of these factors ... "More practical courses" is the chant of those who have been through Osgoode's doors. Though some students were quite willing to hear non-traditional views of the law and society, they also want these opinions placed in the perspective of the outside world. "I was literally booed in class for expressing pro-business thoughts," notes one respondent.[9]

Same thing in 2001:

> ... former students were begging for more black-letter law courses and less feminism and critical race theory. "Hire more practicing lawyers and focus less on irrelevant theory courses such as "Feminism and the Law" suggests one grad. Another says professors should not let "personal biases colour core classes."[10]

Here's where things get real screwy and confusing. The academic professor introduces theory, whether feminist or critical race theory or anything else, to open up the student to the political dimensions of law. Law is not neutral and objective. Law is about power, and students should be made to think about who has the power, how power is exercised and how the exercise of power is hidden in a maze of supposedly neutral legal rules. This theoretical perspective is supposed to give a human face to the law, by introducing considerations of moral imperatives and a social conscience. This should be a good thing. But with the exception of the social activists in the student body, students rebel against coercive introspection. Maybe the theorists are right—law is a tool of oppression. But for most students this knowledge will not help them make money and build prestige as a lawyer. In fact it is a handicap. It's easier to charge $400 an hour if you don't have to think about a neo-Marxist exegesis on law. Most students just want to know how to draft their pleadings and file their applications.

Law schools know their students are primarily interested in learning practical skills, but little is done to accommodate this. Professors chose to work in the academy primarily because they find the legal profession distasteful. It's hard to train students to be good plumbers when you never really wanted to be a plumber yourself. So the academic community invests its energy into scholarship and conferences, leaving little energy to deal with students and their needs. This is true in all universities and in every department. The teachers have little interest in teaching—and some actually hate it. No wonder there is growing discontent at most Canadian law schools.

A few years into my teaching career, I noticed a poster on a bulletin board at school, advertising a talk presented by the Osgoode Hall Women's Caucus. The talk was being given by four female law professors and was entitled "Stories of Survival: Four Feminists Who Lived Through Law School Tell Their Tales of Triumph, Trials and Tribulations." This bothered me, but I wasn't exactly sure why. Where had these four femi-nists been? Bosnia? Afghanistan? I didn't know it was an act of bravery to graduate from law school. I often felt nauseated and disgusted as a law student, but I never felt that a battle was being waged in the corners of the classroom. Women had to overcome barriers to enter many profes-sions, but when this advertisement was posted in the early nineties, the number of women enrolled in law school had finally overtaken the num-ber of men. What was I missing?

After looking at the poster for a while, I realized that I wasn't bothered by the title or the allusion to courage and bravery. I was bothered by a small notation at the bottom of the poster: "Women-Friendly Men Welcome." What the fuck did that mean? Did I qualify? What does it take to qualify? Don't get me wrong. I understand the reality of misogyny, of Marc Lepine. But I don't understand the concept of a "women-friendly" man. I suspected only those who agreed with the viewpoint presented at the talk would be considered "women-friendly." I was standing in a uni-versity building reading a poster that discouraged dissent. If there is any place in the world where controversial ideas and dissent should flourish it is a university. Something was not quite right.

Theoretical perspectives such as feminism and critical race theory have made monumental contributions to the development of an enlightened social policy. But ivory tower politics are the politics of exclusion—defin-ing what and who is right and relegating the dissenter to the category of a poor unfortunate operating under a false consciousness. Moral rela-tivity is still faintly recognized, but in the politically correct world of the university, relativism has to give way to dogmatic imperatives. Instead of being a forum for a free-thinking academic debate, law schools become an environment for developing a dogma fetish. Those who fail to play by the rules of this political fetish game will be branded racist, sexist or homophobic. Saying "he" instead of "he or she" becomes the barometer for assessing the moral and political integrity of the speaker. Everybody watches everybody to make sure the game is played in a politically correct manner. This is not an environment in which free thought can flourish.

When I started working as a professor in 1986, I sensed that something had changed at the law school. In the late seventies, when I was a law student, I remember that there was a smoking section in the classrooms and that bawdy jokes were a professorial mainstay. Eight years later, I was forced to smoke outside and complaints would arise if bawdy jokes were delivered. A few students complained in my first year of teaching about some of my hooker stories. I had spent a lot of time defending hookers, and some of the stories were hilarious. Most of the students were on the floor laughing, but a few approached the administration to complain about the disrespect I had shown to oppressed women forced to work as sex-trade pawns. I never knew who these students were, but I'm pretty sure they knew nothing about the sex trade. Their discomfort probably arose out of some theoretical construct suggesting that being paid for sex is demeaning, degrading and destructive. The concerned students never confronted me, so I never had the opportunity to discuss the issue with them.

I learned to moderate my profanity and my playful banter about sexuality. But no matter how sensitive I tried to be, I would always hit a raw nerve with some students. Everything became an issue. Everything had a political sub-plot. I showed a videotape about an impaired driver in a class on the law of admissions and confessions. This Halton Region police videotape was a comical interaction between a classic drunk and a cop asking some questions in preparation for a Breathalyzer test. The poor drunk was whining about a shoulder injury that prevented him from carrying a two-four of beer. Most of the class was in hysterics, but one or two students were plotting another dogma attack. That night I had a call from a student who claimed that a "bunch" of students were upset because I had shown a tape of an aboriginal man in a drunken state. I was perpetuating the stereotype of the alcoholic aboriginal. On the one hand, I thought this was really stupid: how can one judge when reality will be considered a description of things as they are, and when will it be characterized as having divisive political content? On the other hand, I felt bad. I wanted only to show students the police/suspect dynamic, and perhaps I had unwittingly reinforced a horrible stereotype about Native Canadians.

I went home that night and watched the tape ten times. The suspect was named McGee and was as white a man as I have ever seen. I'm not sure what would have led the student(s) to believe the suspect was aboriginal. I called the student to reassure her that after careful scrutiny of the tape I was convinced that the man was lily white. Of course, I never heard from the student again on the issue. There was no reason for her to apologize for making a mistake, because she had achieved her objective. The unreal projection of her fears made some white, male professor more careful about his choice of pedagogical material. As soon as someone throws out the spectre of racism or sexism at a law school, everyone adjusts themselves. I haven't shown the tape again in law school, though I have shown it to undergraduate classes without incident. Only in law school can every facet of daily life become a matter of debate. Everything is an issue, and you had better have an opinion and be prepared and able to vigorously promote your position, otherwise the institution will eat you for breakfast. This is what happens when petty politics enters an institution already geared for argument and debate. You end up with the politics of exclusion: a small minority are right and the rest of us are a bunch of fucking goofs. It's all so unhealthy.

In my third year of teaching, a personal memo from a student, outlining her views on the curriculum, was slipped under my office door. I have kept this for more than ten years as a constant reminder of the maxim "motivation affects perception." Political motivations can completely overwhelm one's perception of reality. I thought I was teaching criminal law, but the student's perception was entirely different:

> I decided I would write about something that I have been complaining about since first year. I feel like women's bodies are littered all over every law school book I pick up to read. I have been made to feel that you have to be a real misogynist to be a criminal defence lawyer or to study criminal law. I would have thought that in a capitalist economic system a lot of the crime would be against property. I assumed that I could learn about defending someone charged with shoplifting food to feed her children because she has no money and no job and no housing and no support. Instead I spend

a lot of my time reading about women (and children) who've been beaten, raped, shot at, sexually assaulted, murdered, mutilated and bruised by men. Maybe I am still reading about property crimes, in the sense of thefts of other men's property—women! ... We need to ask why women's butchered bodies are littered throughout the law school to "teach" us about legal reasoning and rule of law. We need to ask whether part of the pornography that Ted Bundy allegedly read before he raped and killed all those women were the readings he encountered as a law student. We need to know if there is something significant about the fact that he was a law student.

This is sad. Compelling and passionate, but sad. Rape is a crime, and rape cases will form the subject matter of criminal-law courses. I don't teach cases involving violence against women because men want to delight in images of women's "butchered bodies." If I chose not to teach any cases about sexual assault, I would be accused of ignoring a criminal-justice issue of grave importance to women. If I choose to teach a few sexual assault cases, I am accused of traumatizing women and glorifying the subjugation of women. Once reality is filtered through a political lens, your political opponent will always be wrong no matter what they do. You cannot win with the politics of exclusion; you either religiously follow the dictates of those included in the politically correct group, or run the risk of being excluded from the moral community on the basis of your latent racism or sexism. This fractious dynamic is already part of the adversarial legal culture, and it is aggravated by ivory tower politics.

For the most part, adversarial legal culture and ivory tower politics lead to the same personality type; aggressive, confrontational and argumentative qualities are valued in both worlds. But there is one divergence between adversarial legal culture and university politics. Legal culture worships the advocate's ability to argue both sides of a controversy. In this way, adversarial lawyering is amoral. The advocate merely advances a position, but does not need to embrace it. In university politics, there is an incontrovertible right and wrong.

I quickly learned that pornography was a fairly taboo subject in law school when a brouhaha erupted over a pornography mooting assignment:

> ... a young male law teacher asked students to prepare a legal factum [a memorandum of fact and law] challenging the constitutionality of a hypo-

thetical anti-pornography law. Some women in his class sought counselling because of their discomfort over having to argue against their own point of view. They were suffering identity crises. The teacher was then admonished by two of the university's sexual-harassment counsellors, who warned that "if a similar situation were to occur again, there would be a possibility of an investigation to determine whether sexual harassment was actually taking place."[11]

The young male teacher was not me. It sounds like something I would do, but luckily I was beaten to the punch. The young male teacher was a canary in a coal mine for me. I now knew that the traditional adversarial ethic of being able to argue both sides of a controversy was trumped by the politics of exclusion. It is better to be politically correct than a competent advocate. In many ways, I embrace this modified adversarial ethic because it appears to be infusing the process with considerations of personal conscience and morality. I encourage anything that allows a shedding of institutional roles and the infusion of humanity, with all its blemishes. But being politically correct is more about dogma than genuine introspection. The politically correct law student is simply rejecting one institutional role for another. There is no real humanity in paying lip-service to political dogma.

The student who slipped the memo under my door had participated in the pornography scandal, and she had this to say about it:

> Why in my first year did we have to deal with the stress of pornography, violence against women, and "censorship" all in the course of an already stressful LRW [Legal Writing & Research] factum and mooting situation? Why were we forced to argue about not wanting to see "9 1/2 Weeks" in the classroom! Why was the "pornographer" in the example a woman? Why were some women forced to defend the pornographer against their wishes? Why were some women assigned male mooting partners? Why was it assumed that a first-year class was a "community" which could discuss these issues and come to a consensus?

Note the tone and underlying subtext. This is not a reasoned argument; it is a series of rhetorical questions designed to silence the listener. The speaker talks of being "forced" to do things, thus invoking the entitlements of those who have been subjected to coercive violence. The speaker even questions the decision to have men and women work together. Nowhere is there a reasoned explanation as to why it is problematic for a woman to argue the pornographer's point of view; it is simply assumed, even though most of the female law students had no problem with this rudimentary role reversal.

Although the concerns expressed by this student were not shared by the majority of female students, the law school responded to these concerns as if they represented the views of the entire student body. Of course, there are some people who truly believe that pornography is degrading and dangerous for women, but this is only one point of view. Yet it appears to be the point of view adopted by the law school administration. The professor who initiated the pornography assignment was not praised for constructing a novel and challenging assignment—he was admonished. All he was trying to do was encourage students to re-evaluate their personal views and see if they could possibly mount an argument supporting a personally distasteful position. Perhaps the expectations of the professor were unrealistic, but that should not occasion admonishment.

Why do the law schools, and most university departments, give unquestioning support to politically correct viewpoints? Simple. White male guilt. The law schools are still basically dominated by white middle-class males, and historically, white middle-class males were oppressors. White males enslaved blacks and subjugated women. White males practised genocide and torture. Today, white males have to pay for their centuries of dominance by feigning agreement with the political aspirations of those they previously oppressed. White male guilt leads to dogmatic thinking. The enlightened white male lives in dread of being accused of racist or sexist thought or action. It is safer to admonish the male professor for exposing students to pornography than to address the question of whether there is something morally wrong with requiring female law students to argue the case for the pornographer. If you protect the male professor, you might be accused of operating within a misogynous mindset, so it is better to buy into the dogma.

In recent years, law schools have offered sweet financial packages to recruit feminist scholars and aboriginal professors. The law schools became obsessed with the optics of their faculties' racial and gender profiles. Even if the candidate has little to offer, law schools will do whatever it takes to land a token appointment to create an impression of racial and gender diversity within a white male–dominated institution. The same thing happens in the private sector, but without the same zeal as is found in academic institutions. White male guilt is more pronounced in an insular and isolated institution supposedly devoted to higher values. Many of the problems of the "real world" do not exist in the ivory tower, so the ivory tower has the tendency to make mountains out of molehills.

White male guilt works well in law schools because there are so many white males running the show. This has to change. But in the meantime, intellectual resignation in the face of theoretical constructs that see oppression in every facet of civilized life is not required. Some of the ideas generated within the context of political correctness are fatuous. They should be ridiculed. But many law professors lack the courage to challenge modern orthodoxy. They capitulate in the face of thought control. Law professors no longer relish the role of being champions of controversy:

> Professors are the high priests of the academy, enjoying enviable prestige, power and financial remuneration. It is apparent, however, that so many of us are fallen priests, going through the motions of performing sacraments in which we no longer believe. As Roberto Unger illustrates, professors can resemble a "priesthood that has lost their faith and kept their jobs" while standing "in tedious embarrassment before cold altars."[12]

Despite being jaded, law professors still try to indoctrinate their students. For most law schools, it's indoctrination with "left-wing" politics, and for some schools it is indoctrination into a pro-business, market perspective. But it is still all about indoctrination. I've been told I should be a role model for law students, that students look up to me and therefore I should be instilling the right values. Whose values? This is where political correctness supplies the answers. Simply follow the path of those who have mastered the cultivation of a politically sensitive personality.

I'm no fucking role model. I'm the guy who dreams of televising public orgies from the SkyDome in Toronto. I'm the guy who believes that dropping acid is more illuminating than studying the Bible. You don't want me as a role model for your children. And, anyway, despite sometimes being whiny, law students are not children. If they still need a role model, they are too lost for me to save.

I refused to modify and reconfigure my lectures to fit within the emerging orthodoxy. For the most part, the students embraced my politically neutral approach. I was neither left-wing nor right-wing. I'm a member of a species that has no wings. I just have a couple of feet that inconveniently find their way into my mouth every once in a while. I taught law students in a way that was true to my character and beliefs; most students had a good time, a few launched complaints.

The pursuit of petty politics within an academic institution leads to disharmony and divisiveness. Accusations of racism and sexism are substituted for a reasoned disagreement with a point of view. A giant shadow is cast over debate and discussion. At times, this world of accusation and guilt became so unbearable I've resorted to the "Thank God I'm a Jew" syndrome. I can lay claim to the greatest story of persecution and genocide ever told. The syndrome allows me to say, if absolutely necessary: "Don't tell *me* about oppression and bigotry. My ancestors have suffered more oppression and hardship than most disadvantaged minorities, so I know all about racism and sexism." I feel sorry for WASP professors, who cannot draw upon the misery of the past to shield them from accusations of prejudice in the present.

But Jewish suffering does not work as a shield when it comes to gender issues. Like all religions, the Jewish faith did not promote equality for women. Gender issues at a law school are potentially explosive. Just ask anyone who has had the misfortune of having to teach rape or sexual assault law, and you will quickly understand how divisive and destructive the law-school environment can be. Professors have even written articles chronicling their trials and tribulations in teaching rape law.[13] Why has it become so difficult in recent years to teach law students the legal realities of sexual violence? On one level, it is clear that teaching the law of rape is troubling because some students have been the victims of sexual violence. It's hard to listen to an abstract and academic rendering of a reality that has been a living nightmare for you. So it is important for the professor to adopt a sensitive approach to the topic.

This brings me back to the designation of a "women-friendly" man. You can be a women-friendly man only if you agree with the women's perspective. I thought I was being a women-friendly man when I delivered my lectures on sexual assault. I talked about misogyny; I talked about men taking responsibility for securing genuine consent before fucking; I talked about rape as a crime of power, dominance and violence, and not a crime of an overactive libido; I talked about the history of criminal-justice indifference to violence against women. What more

could I say? Every year I refined the presentation, and every year someone was unhappy for a different reason. Some women will never accept
anything I have to say about the law of rape because I have a dick. My
dick prevents me from laying any claim to understanding the plight of
women in a sexually aggressive world. So I should just shut up and
teach the law of theft.

This is what I mean by a divisive and destructive environment: I am
evaluated on the basis of political motivation. I am judged as an abstract
category, not as a real person. I am not a man, I am a representation of
patriarchy. Law school pits men against women and posits an unbridge-
able gap between them. This is not healthy.

I hate being treated as an abstraction. I can have a valid opinion
about sexual violence against women, just as a non-Jewish person can
have a valid opinion on the State of Israel or the reasons behind the
Holocaust. I may never fully understand the experience of having a
menstrual cycle or of giving birth, but this should not disentitle me
from having insightful thoughts on matters uniquely related to women.
The law schools prefer for people like me not to question the new world
order, but just to take on the role model image of the sensitive social
activist. I can play that role, and have done so, but any role is an abstraction. I prefer the idea of a mentor over a role model. As a mentor, I have
to be emotionally engaged with students. But the law school prefers the
abstract, because emotional engagement is too messy. It leads to having
feelings, not necessarily a good thing for evolving Mr. Bastards. It does
not matter that acting like a role model only infantilizes students.
Students have to learn to like being treated like children before they
appear in front of judges.

The legal construction of reality is already so far removed from the
reality of ordinary people that law schools should be trying to figure
out ways to bring budding legal professionals back into a world inhabited by real, non-political actors. Infusing all social conflict with political content is not a good first step. Law students should be trained to
deal with people as real people with real problems, instead of being
trained to analyze and explore the political underpinnings of the problem. The sanitization of discourse within the university invariably leads
to thought control and censorship. This is not a good recipe for intellectual and emotional growth.

In Chapter 5, I mentioned two controversial studies: A 1988
survey at Texas A&M University that revealed that 39% of woman

indicated they sometimes said no even though "they had every intention to and were willing to engage in sexual intercourse," and a 1994 survey of American university students that showed that 38% of women sometimes said no when they meant yes.[14] I have really wanted to discuss these studies in my criminal-law class, but have been afraid to. One of the pillars of political correctness is the slogan "No Means No," and the thought police at the law school would not tolerate my taking a shot at a defining political slogan. I always like to shake people up, but the net result would be the summary dismissal of the studies as methodologically flawed because they were probably done by men. In the end, no one would have learned anything, and I would have once again become the whipping boy for patriarchy.

The quest to achieve true sexual equality is a laudable objective, but the quest has at times perverted the pursuit of justice within the halls of the academy. In 1989, the law student legal clinic at Osgoode developed a policy barring representation of men charged with beating their girlfriends or wives. Other law schools followed suit, stripping half the population of the presumption of innocence. At Memorial University, a medical student was expelled for sexual harassment without even a hearing, because the politics of exclusion trumps the presumption of innocence.[15]

I saw this utter disregard for due process first-hand in 1993. I was asked to sit as the president of a disciplinary tribunal on a case of sexual harassment between a male student and two female students. Holding a hearing on this issue was a rarity, as harassment is rarely reported, and when it is reported the university manages to quietly resolve the complaints. I did not look forward to adjudicating the case, as I felt the whole university was watching to make sure I said and did the right things.

The case was a pretty standard sexual fiasco for students. Man meets woman (two women, in fact, on two separate occasions). Helps her out with some problem. Manages to get invited back to her residence at university. They start to fool around. The woman wishes to stop and the man keeps groping. The woman expresses some objection to the touching, but the objection is ambiguous and irresolute. Other than wondering why the women didn't just tell the guy to fuck off and leave their rooms, I had little difficulty concluding that the male student violated university standards for student conduct.

Ultimately, I think I said the right things. Here's an excerpt:

Until recent years, the burden of avoiding unwanted sexual activity has fallen on women. If they did not actively resist sexual advances, their silence was construed as consent. This anachronistic perspective on sexual relations must change, and the University has a legitimate role in ensuring that members of its community respect this change in perspective. Men must assume some responsibility in ensuring that sexual activity is mutually desired. Mr. A. was wrong in assuming that a lack of express objection combined with an absence of resistance was an invitation to sexual activity. First, he was clearly told at the outset what the limits would be, and if he sensed any change of heart it was his responsibility to clarify the situation. He should have been aware of the fact that the complainants did not want to offend him by explicitly rejecting his advances. He should have realized that he put them in a difficult position of first lending assistance and support, and then acting as if they owed him for his good deeds.

No man should expect a woman to go along with his sexual advances simply because he has initially acted as a good Samaritan. His initial acts of assistance are of no moral value if he performed them solely with an expectation of sexual payment. In addition, no man should construe an invitation to sleep in the same room as an invitation to having sex. Mr. A. has reduced male/female interaction to a zero-sum game—he was working on the insidious assumption that if a man and a woman are friendly to one another, this is an invitation to have sex, but if no initial offer of friendship is made then he would not expect sexual activity.

The normative standard that I believe emerges from this case can be simply stated. If there is any confusion or ambiguity as to the intentions of a man and woman with respect to sexual activity, then the man has a responsibility to clarify the situation. No longer should we accept the heedless and wilfully blind activities of men who will construe any equivocation as an invitation to impose their sexual desires on a woman. Considering that the man's sole interest in these situations is in sexual gratification and that a woman's interest is in protecting her sexual autonomy and the integrity of her body, it stands to reason men must assume the responsibility for ensuring that sexual activity is mutually desired. The potential violation of a woman's fundamental interest in liberty and security is of far greater weight than the man's interest in gaining sexual gratification. Accordingly, this Tribunal wishes to express in no uncertain terms that the University will not tolerate the actions of men who are so determined to gain sexual gratification that they will disregard all the signals that suggest they should inquire into the willingness of their partners.[16]

I think my judgement is a model of political correctness. I believed in everything I wrote, but the words had to be carefully crafted to resonate with those who wish to politicize male/female relationships. Mr. A. is no longer just an asshole who should be condemned. He is an abstraction for all men who impose their sexual drives on unwilling partners.

I carefully drafted the judgement knowing that my words, my thoughts and my actions would be closely scrutinized by an audience waiting to pounce on any political mistakes. Nobody pounced, because no one really knew about the judgement. It was like the university buried the decision. I may have said the right things, but I probably did the wrong thing from the university's perspective. The university wanted the student to be rusticated (great word for being kicked out on your ass). I did basically nothing. Why? To reflect the fact that the university's disciplinary process was more like a witch hunt than a fair proceeding. York University had done a better job than Memorial University—at least they held a hearing—but the hearing failed to respect the principles of fundamental justice.

What bothered me most was that the two female complainants had laid criminal charges of sexual assault against the male student a few weeks earlier, and the university failed to disclose this fact to the disciplinary panel. I discovered only this accidentally a few days into the hearing, when the male student could not attend the next date for hearing because he had to appear in court. I was pissed off. I felt that the university had set up the hearing to serve as an investigative tool for the state. Now I understood why such feeble efforts had been made at the outset for effective mediation of this conflict. I was prepared to walk away from the hearing, but I realized the university would continue the prosecution. It would be best for me to stay on, so I could make sure the university process did not simply become a tool of discovery for the police and prosecutor. The hearing went on for days and days. The women were assisted by the lawyer for the university. The accused man bumbled until I adjourned, suggesting he secure counsel. He showed up with his mother. In the end, I condemned the student, but would not rusticate him, even though it was tempting to do so just to be able to say that I have "rusticated" someone.

One of the reasons I chose not to strongly punish this kid was that I felt the university had not provided him with due process in many regards. I also felt that if the complainants wished to pursue the matter in criminal court, it should be the criminal court that did the punishing. The accused asked to stay the proceeding as a procedural abuse of process, but I thought it was important for the university that I discuss in a public document the standard of conduct expected of students in relation to sexual matters. My comments never made it into a public document. I guess the university did not like some of what I had to say:

> I do not find any ill-will or malice on behalf of Counsel for the University or on behalf of any other University official. However, that is not to say that this process was not tainted by other procedural problems. I can fully understand how Mr. A. would believe that an apprehension of bias existed considering that he was often left alone to face the complainants and their counsel and the numerous individuals who showed up in support of the complainants. Even the physical structure of the hearing room contributed to this impression that the "deck was stacked against him."
>
> ... Nonetheless, I believe that Mr. A. misconceived the procedural problems when he characterized them as leading to bias and a presumption of guilt. In my opinion, the procedural defects in this case are of a much more complex nature, and they largely arise as a result of a failure on behalf of the University to structure a procedural regime that is even-handed and that reflects a coherently stated objective.
>
> ...It is highly improper, and perhaps unconstitutional, for the University to become an investigative arm of the state. By not being promptly informed of the pending criminal case, the Tribunal did not have the opportunity to consider the implications of these concurrent proceedings. Perhaps this may have been one of the exceptional cases in which the civil/administrative proceedings should be suspended or, more likely, disclosure of the fact of the criminal prosecution may have led the Tribunal to take preventive measures (i.e., sealing of evidence or not transcribing the evidence) to ensure that the University would not be acting as an adjunct to the police. The disclosure of

the fact that criminal charges were being pursued took the Tribunal by surprise and prevented any real consideration of whether or not to suspend a hearing that had already commenced.

... In closing, the University should be commended for having established a forum in which complaints of sexual harassment can be heard. In the past these types of complaints have remained underground and invisible. However, the best intentions are not substitute for a fair, even-handed and coherent set of procedures to effect the laudable objective. The University must rethink its approach and ensure that mediation services and counselling services are available for cases of this nature. Further, the University must address the issue of proper legal representation for both sides to a dispute. In the absence of such reforms, the disciplinary process will remain ineffective and will constantly be exposed to challenge on procedural and jurisdictional grounds.[17]

This is the climate in which law students are being trained. It's bad enough that law students buy into the Mr. Bastard adversarial shtick, but in the foggy haze of academia, they also learn how to reduce people to abstract categories to fit within a politically motivated agenda. Historically, Mr. Bastard was a morally neutral player; now the bastard has lost even the dignity of objectivity.

The profession is reaching a point of crisis. Students graduate without learning the technical skills required, because professors aren't technicians. Instead of training students to respond to people as real people, and to care about these people and their problems, we are training students to see the larger political implications behind these people's problems. The students generally don't give a shit about this. Students want to enter the world of the professional knowledge elite. They want to be part of a world in which membership in the elite permits the member to harbour "contempt for the multitude." We should be doing something to counter these pretentious aspirations; instead, the law schools keep breeding politically correct little bastards.

17

The Illusion
of Wisdom

ON APRIL 17, 1982, the political landscape changed. Our judges were given a greater role to play in the development of this landscape by virtue of the proclamation of the Charter of Rights and Freedoms. They could strike down laws. They could stand in the way of the executive branch of government. They could shape public policy. Judges really didn't want this expanded role—they are great believers in the beauty of inertia—so I was pretty sure nothing dramatic would happen to the criminal-justice industrial complex.

Nineteen years later, I was quoted in *The Globe and Mail* in an article on judicial activism in the Charter era as saying, in my characteristic cynical fashion, that the Supreme Court of Canada acted "cowardly" in deciding a certain case. I vaguely remember calling the decision "cowardly," and in many ways I did believe this to be so. But this was just a dramatic way of expressing disappointment. The decision was weak. The court took the easy way out instead of boldly confronting the morally distasteful ways in which the state manipulates accused people. The court did not champion the rights of accused people. "Cowardly" was just a good media sound-bite.

I guess it's because I used the "c" word, but, for whatever reason, the editorial department of the *Globe* decided to write a column criticizing my remarks. I was flattered. It started: "The accusation could hardly be more serious. Alan Young, a professor at Osgoode Hall Law School in Toronto, has charged the Supreme Court of Canada with cowardice ... If true, Prof. Young's charge is tantamount to a capital offence ... the accusation should not go unchallenged."[1]

I was a bit confused by the statement about "capital offence." Were the editors saying that judicial cowardice is a crime, or that I should be executed for my statements? I'm pretty sure it's the former, even though the rest of the column is devoted to defending judges, who are "ferociously bright and capable and no one's order-taker" and who possess "great confidence and farsightedness when it comes to the criminal law."[2] After writing the column, the editorial department of the *Globe* must have had to apply lip balm to soothe the chafing that comes from too much ass-kissing.

Why would the *Globe* run to the rescue of the Supreme Court of Canada? Who are these robed men and women who are above reproach? I have called many politicians and public officials "cowards" with no backlash from the press, but when I point the finger at judges a national newspaper thinks it needs to run to the rescue. I have characterized lawyers and law students as bastards. No one will really care. But take a shot at a judge, and people start to squirm. This is silly. Where do you think judges come from? Some school of universal wisdom? Get real. They are just law students who have practiced as lawyers for a minimum of ten years. They bring to the bench all the ugly baggage collected while cultivating the "No More Mr. Nice Guy" persona over this time. Do you really think that judges shed their skin in some mystical metamorphosis when they are elevated to the bench?

The key phrase here is "elevated to the bench." Only judges can communicate with and speak on behalf of the great god of law. When entering the court, lawyers are supposed to bow to the judge. I just jerk my neck. No way am I bowing to another human being. When judges enter the courtroom, people stand. When they walk down the halls of the courthouse, people stand. In the high court they are referred to as "My Lord" or "My Lady." If I were a judge, I would have some fun with the sycophants. Might as well go all the way, making the lawyers refer to me as "Mr. Supreme King of Universal Justice." You can look high and low, but you will not find a greater degree of pomposity and privilege in any other social institution.

You are not permitted to criticize the character of our judges, because that is like blaspheming Allah. We are permitted to debate the merits of a particular decision made by a judge, but keep your hands off the actual judge. We recognize that judges will make wrong decisions, but we refuse to look behind those decisions. Generally this is a good thing. Judgements should speak for themselves. We should not have to probe into the background of the decision-maker to assess the merits of the judgement. But who are these men and women who have a dramatic impact on our liberty and security? Just a bunch of lawyers who have made the right political connection. We don't even have a school for judges, as is found within European legal education. We don't probe because we won't find anything that has prepared this individual for a life of judging others. We would not be able to maintain the facade of deification if we knew how ordinary our judges were.

In the late 1980s, renegade lawyer Harry Kopyto was frustrated by a judge's decision to dismiss a lawsuit against the RCMP. Kopyto was convicted for contempt for scandalizing the court with the following quote in the press:

> This decision is a mockery of justice. It stinks to high hell. It says it is okay to break the law and you are immune so long as someone above you said to do it. Mr. Dowson [the man who sued the police] and I have lost faith in the judicial system to render justice. We're wondering what is the point of appealing and continuing this charade of the courts in this country which are warped in favour of protecting the police. The courts and the RCMP are sticking so close together you'd think they were put together with Krazy Glue.[3]

Stuck together with Krazy Glue? Hardly. Glue leaves open the possibility that the bonding of cop and court is just an accident or the product of a prank. It's not. It's more likely that these public officials are stuck together with the jism of self-love from a lifetime of jerking each other off. Not a pretty image, but metaphorically sound. And as lewd as the metaphor might be, I should be entitled to say whatever I like about the men and women who sit in judgement of our lives. I was really upset when I heard that someone could be convicted of contempt of court for making harsh, critical comments about our judiciary outside the courtroom. I didn't know Mr. Kopyto, but his conviction made me wonder about the true health of free speech in Canada. Do judges believe that free speech applies only when they are doing the talking or when someone is singing their praises? I worried about intemperate remarks I had made in the press. The convicting judge noted that Kopyto's comments were "a vitriolic unmitigated attack on the trial judge" and "a blatant attack on all judges of all courts." So what? I thought that public criticism of public officials was a defining feature of democracy. Get off your high horse, my lord and my lady. You are public officials. You are fair game for critical attack. With all due respect, if you can't take the elevation, get off the fucking bench.

There is a happy ending to the Kopyto fiasco. In 1987, the Ontario Court of Appeal ruled that it was unconstitutional to convict someone of the offence of scandalizing the court.[4] How could the appeal court rule otherwise without the entire bench looking self-serving? But up to 1987 a person could be convicted of a crime for criticizing a judge.

The integrity and legitimacy of our entire criminal-justice enterprise is dependent upon unfailing confidence in the wisdom of judges. We have grown accustomed to the antics of lawyers. We don't worry about the excesses of adversarial posturing by lawyers because we believe there is a neutral and objective umpire who is capable of separating wheat from chaff. If attacks upon the integrity and neutrality of our judges are permitted, we run the risk that the weak link in the chain of justice will be exposed. We may come to realize that judges are just ordinary lawyers with all the warts and blemishes that come with the territory. So we dress them in robes, bow to them and address them as members of a privileged aristocracy, all in an attempt to maintain the illusion of wisdom.

There are some very bright judges who approach their jobs with sensitivity and integrity. Few are bold, but too many bold judges would be a recipe for chaos. But a few more fighters on the bench would be nice. Too many of the more progressive new judges become quickly co-opted into the conservative mindset of the institution.

In fairness, I cannot criticize judges for lacking wisdom. Many of us walk around with an encyclopedia of knowledge in our heads, but how many can truly claim to have acquired wisdom? There are some very smart judges. Articulate, with a keen mind for working out the logical implications of accepted principles and precedent. But is this wisdom? Hardly. This is just proficiency with language and the manipulation of rules. It may be unfair to condemn judges for not attaining an unattainable standard. But they are still fair game for criticism because they make a pretence of having wisdom. They project the illusion of wisdom. They like the trappings of prestige and power. They want people to think they are wise.

Lately, some high courts have finally abandoned the practice of calling judges "My Lord" or "My Lady." The courts decided this was not gender-neutral language. This affectation was not about gender. It was about pomposity and arrogance. Calling fellow human beings "My Lord" or "My Lady" does not violate some fuzzy norm of political correctness. It is offensive because it deifies judges and makes them the overlords of a feudal kingdom of justice. It also helps maintain the illusion of infallible judicial wisdom. Once the judiciary admits this, I will leave them alone.

It's time to admit that we do not appoint judges in Western liberal democracies to be wise men or women. Wisdom actually gets in the way, in the same way that compassion undercuts adversarial lawyering. Before institutionalized and professionalized justice reared its head in the latter half of the past millennium, conflicts were resolved by kings, priests, elders, shamans and oracles. All decision makers were supposedly blessed with divine justice and were therefore infallible. The biblical King Solomon story is a classic example. The Book of Kings tells the famous story of two women, both claiming to be the mother of the same child. The conflict was brought before Solomon, who was considered the wisest man in Israel. He ordered that the baby be split in two by sword, and each mother be awarded her fair portion. Of course, the true mother found the proposal abhorrent, and Solomon was able to discern that she was the real mother.

There are two possibilities. Either Solomon was just the Jewish precursor of the Marquis de Sade, or he had infinite wisdom. The conventional perspective is that he was one of the wisest men to ever live. Dividing a baby in half is wisdom? It was effective, but nothing more than clever trickery. But in its own ingenious way, it is wisdom. Wisdom requires flexibility and creativity. Wisdom does not need rules; in fact, rules get in the way of wisdom because they foreclose infinite flexibility and creativity. Rules are followed, whereas wisdom leads by example.

Solomon's unique insight into the human condition allowed him to approach problems and conflicts without having to rely upon intellectual shortcuts such as preordained rules. Modern justice is predicated on the rule of law—the principle of legality. Judges can convict and punish only if there is a clear rule in place governing the criminal accusation. A cornerstone of modern justice is the maxim *nullem crimen sine lege, nulla poena sine lege*—no crime without law, and no punishment without law. A crowning achievement in the evolution of modern justice has been the stripping of power from judges. They are now constrained by rules. Why? Because there is a tacit recognition that judges are not necessarily wise men and women, and therefore should be considered only messengers of the law and not creators of the message. For better or worse, the message is created by our elected officials; the judges are there just to administer and enforce the message.

Modern law is constructed on a distrust of public officials. This is often forgotten or denied. The premise behind the American Constitution and the Canadian Charter of Rights is that power corrupts, and absolute power corrupts absolutely. Cops need constitutional norms to constrain the exercise of their raw power, and judges need clear rules to prevent them from doing some really weird shit. If judges were truly engaged in the pursuit of wisdom, they would not need a Criminal Code to lead them in the right direction. Their job is mechanical and constrained. All they have to do is decipher the sacred text and apply the text, so interpreted, to the facts of the case before them.

The ability to weigh facts and interpret rules is the bare minimum needed for competence. But we don't seem to care whether our judges have this basic skill. In recent years, we have moved away from a patronage system of judicial appointment to merit appointments. It's still more important "who you know" than "what you know," but major strides have been made to minimize the extent to which judicial appointments are just gifts to lawyers who have befriended the government. Appointments now tend to be made after advisory committees review the merits of an application. But do these committees look for applicants who have a demonstrated aptitude for interpreting rules and weighing facts?

In 1990, I found an advertisement for a judicial appointment to the provincial court in Toronto that listed the professional and personal characteristics the advisory committee was searching for. I had never seen an advertisement like this before, and I never have again. Under personal characteristics, the ad listed "an absence of pomposity and authoritarian tendencies" and "an ability to make decisions." At least we know that indecisive Hitlers need not apply. But in terms of real qualifications, the ad fell short. It spoke of "an interest and some aptitude for the administrative aspects of a judge's role" and a requirement of a "10-year membership at the Bar." But the ad never said that the applicant should have mastered the basic skills of deciphering the sacred text of the Criminal Code and weighing competing facts. In fact, the ad suggested that people with no experience whatsoever in the world of criminal justice would be considered: "experience in the field of law relevant to the division of the Provincial Court on which the applicant wishes to serve is *desirable but not essential*" (emphasis added).[5]

Take a minute to let this sink in. Consider some of the things that a provincial court judge does: issues search warrants to invade your home; orders suspects detained prior to trial; orders psychiatric assessments and hospitalization; sends people to jail, even for life. But experience in the field of criminal law is only desirable and not essential? The sad reality is that lawyers who spent their careers closing real-estate deals or reviewing corporate mergers are suddenly masquerading as criminal court judges. At the time they were appointed to the bench, these lawyers had probably never met an accused person, they had probably never spent a minute in a prison, and they probably believed all cops tell the truth. How the hell do we expect corporate lackeys to administer criminal justice when they have gone directly from the boardroom to the bench?

A few years ago, a weird transcript was faxed to me that had been circulating around the legal community. It was purported to be an excerpt from a trial in Grande Prairie, Alberta. Mochan is the defence lawyer, and Stilwell is the Crown:

> The Court:... Having regard for all the above and notwithstanding the unexplained comment of one witness, "No, Roger, no," I am satisfied beyond a reasonable doubt that Russell Noskey caused the death of Arlene Thunder through an unlawful act ... Do counsel have anything further to say?
>
> Mr. Mochan: You didn't find him guilty.
>
> The Court: Uh, yes I—
>
> Mr. Mochan: Oh, fuck. That's ridiculous.
>
> The Court: I beg your pardon?
>
> Mr. Mochan: That's the worst decision I've ever heard in my entire fucking life. How can you convict someone named R-U-S-S-E-L-L of killing a woman who, whilst being beaten to death is yelling out, "No, R-O-G-E-R, no." Can you tell me that, My Lord?
>
> The Court: Well, I'm very sorry if I've upset you, but really, I'm new at this. The Chief Justice really shouldn't give these nasty criminal matters to guys with my background. I'm a commercial guy, you know, but I think your fellow must have done it—
>
> Mr. Mochan: Oh, fuck you. You should be in the Court of Appeal with an attitude like that—

Mr. Stilwell: I might just beg the forgiveness of My Lord for just a moment
to interject on your behalf, may I just say that, from my own point of view
rarely have I seen so insightful and, if I may without being too obsequious,
so well reasoned a decision—
Mr. Mochan: Shut the fuck up, windbag.
Mr. Stilwell: My Lord, he can't call me that.[6]

The transcript turned out to be apocryphal. The trial was real, but
the dialogue was cooked up. Mochan, the defence lawyer, was pissed
off, and he created this transcript to reflect his feelings and thoughts at
the time of verdict. I sensed all along that it was a fake transcript, and
not because of the defence lawyer's profanity. That has happened on
occasion. Not because of the over-the-top ass kissing by the prosecutor.
I've witnessed this type of sycophantic behaviour. I sensed it was fake
because a judge would never admit he was in over his head, that he was
ill-equipped to judge a murder case. The illusion of wisdom would go
down the toilet if judges ever let on that they were merely climbing the
corporate ladder en route to becoming King Solomon. The poetic
licence of this defence lawyer perfectly captures the frustration many
lawyers feel when appearing in front of obtuse judges.

In my journey through the legal universe, I have met some very good
judges who are dedicated to public service. But more characteristically I
have met judges who reek from indifference, who strut around with
pomposity, who engage in petty power games and who are remarkably
lazy. Early on in my career, it became clear to me that many judges were
averse to both thinking and working. They wanted to sleepwalk through
their appointments. In 1984, I conducted a preliminary hearing for a
man charged with counselling to commit murder. It was a sensitive case,
as it arose out of a increasingly violent rivalry between two factions in
the Sikh community. There were armed guards in the courtroom. The
late Judge Dnieper was assigned to the case. I speak of this judge by name
not because he has passed on but because he had a file of complaints a
mile high. He was famous in the county of York, but it was not the type
of fame you would wish even on an enemy. If he liked you, you would
receive special treatment. I saw him mete out a very lenient sentence to
a burglar, saying to defence counsel, "I owed you one." If he disliked you,
you had to prepare for constant abuse and sarcasm. I saw him make
many young lawyers cry. To me, he represented the antithesis of justice.

We had made it halfway through the hearing, and Dnieper had said nothing. He didn't interrupt me, nor did he make fun of my rather awkward lawyering skills (I was just a few months into practice). I started to get nervous. Why was he doing nothing? He should have been insulting me by now. I looked carefully at him and realized he had been doing the crossword puzzle from the newspaper. All along, I had thought he was taking notes, and he was not even listening to the evidence. I was mad, but I was too meek and junior to do anything. I wish this would have happened to me later in my career, when fear was replaced by audacity. I would have looked this judge in the eye, paused for that eternal second, and then said: "Your Honour, if I may be of some assistance, 5-down is 'miscarriage of justice.'"

One would think that laziness and indifference would make maintaining the illusion of wisdom difficult, but it doesn't. We assume that when a judge drifts off in court to dream of golf and cocktails, he must be pondering the case—deep in thought and not just sleeping. Judges are the master somnambulists—it is really difficult to discern whether they are awake or asleep. Let me give two examples of how laziness and the illusion of wisdom are not mutually exclusive.

In the early 1990s, I launched a constitutional challenge to our obscenity laws during the prosecution of an offensive rap tape by 2 Live Crew (see Chapter 4). Beyond the standard free-speech argument, I tried to introduce something unique, and hopefully refreshing. I argued that even if Parliament had the constitutional authority to abridge free speech in relation to obscene depictions, the manner in which the law was administered and enforced operated as an unconstitutional prior restraint. Prior restraint is an American doctrine that asserts that low-level public officials (such as cops, customs agents and censor board members) do not have the authority to ban speech without judicial intervention. In other words, to respect the fundamental freedom of expression, expressive materials cannot be removed from the market-place of ideas without a court order. The police are entitled to seize one copy of an impugned tape for purposes of trial, but they cannot seize the entire inventory until a trial is held and a judge rules the tape to be obscene. Only then can it be entirely removed from the marketplace. It all makes good sense, and I decided to introduce the doctrine of prior restraint to Canada.

I collected evidence to show how obscenity law was enforced in the manner of a prior restraint. This was easy because the case started with the police ordering bookstore owner Marc Emery to remove copies of the nasty tape from his store. Bingo! That in itself is a prior restraint. Who appointed the police as censors for civilized society? But things got better. I discovered that the police had used the same threats with the large chain HMV Records, and the president of the company was eager to tell his story. Some officers from the pornography squad of the Ontario Provincial Police were going to act as reluctant witnesses and would admit that they had no idea what was obscene, as the Criminal Code did not provide sufficient guidance. I thought I would finally destroy our archaic obscenity law because in this case there was compelling evidence of the constitutional shortcomings of the law, not just the usual abstract rhetoric about one person's lyric being another person's vulgarity.

I showed up armed with six or seven witnesses. The Crown objected to the admissibility of the evidence, and the judge, without even thinking, agreed. He said he did not need to hear this evidence. It would not be of any assistance to him. I reminded him that the Supreme Court of Canada has given strong exhortations that constitutional challenges should not be brought in an evidentiary vacuum, and that facts relating to the operation and impact of the law must be introduced. The Supreme Court wanted to ensure that constitutional decisions are made on an informed basis. The judge did not care. He did not want to hear evidence about how shitty the law was, because then he might feel compelled to do something about it. So I lost all my evidence and ended up losing the constitutional challenge.

Of course, we appealed. The appeal court judge upheld the constitutionality of the law.[7] However, I had argued that it was a breach of natural justice to prevent me from calling witnesses and evidence during my constitutional challenge. With precedent fully supporting my position, I argued that my client was entitled to a new trial so that the constitutional challenge could be properly reassessed in light of the wrongfully excluded evidence. This was a no-brainer. The trial judge missed the boat by avoiding the issue and ruling my evidence inadmissible. What did the appeal court judge do? Nothing. I mean literally nothing. In both my written material and my oral submissions, I raised six issues, with the sixth being the denial of natural justice. The judge addressed the first five issues, and did not even mention the sixth. When I received a copy of the judgement, I thought some pages must be missing. I couldn't believe it. The judge simply recreated reality to his liking; he did not have a response to my natural justice argument, so he wished it away.

This was my first introduction to the "pearls before swine" phenomenon of advocacy. I spent months developing and polishing the foundation for a novel claim in law, only to have the judge nod off and shoo me out of court as soon as the last word had left my mouth. This is not about being rude. I was usually shooed out in a polite, Ms. Manners way. This is about not giving a shit. The swine will never appreciate the gift of pearls, and many judges don't want to hear controversial and provocative arguments in their court—they might have to do some critical thinking. If a judge is faced with no easy way out, there's always the option of ignoring it. It happens every day. If the argument cannot be ignored because too many people will notice, then judges change the argument in a way that allows for an easy response.

In the early 1990s, I became involved with the gambling community. I had a bunch of clients who operated cafés on the Danforth in Toronto. Greek and Italian men would pass hours in the cafés playing cards. Low-level gambling of a social nature. A friendly game of poker or gin. Some of the locations had VLTs (video lottery terminals). All of the café owners ended up being charged with keeping common gaming houses. The early 1990s was the era of a gambling explosion. Provincial governments were running casinos and placing VLTs in any location where people might wish to waste a few bucks. Gambling became a major revenue source for provincial governments. Billions of dollars in government revenue are now generated every year from licensed gambling activities. If the government can make money off gambling, how can we call the Greek and Italian card players "criminals"? Surely it can no longer be considered an activity contrary to the public interest. The worst that should be said of these men is that they failed to secure the necessary licences needed to gamble. They should be charged with some non-criminal provincial offence, similar to fishing without a licence.

I decided to challenge the constitutionality of the law on the basis that gambling was no longer within federal criminal jurisdiction and was now a matter of provincial control, and on the basis that it violated the Charter of Rights to criminalize harmless conduct, especially when elected officials have made the decision to engage in the very same conduct. I spent a year preparing this argument. I had strong doctrinal support, and I compiled an eight-volume record documenting the exponential growth in state-sponsored gaming over the century. I knew that striking down the Criminal Code gaming provisions would be a bold step for a court, but the record was compelling. Also, it made perfect sense to reclassify private gambling as a licensing issue. I arranged to have two days set aside for the hearing. I was excited, but my excitement was short-lived. First off, the judge was very late. Typical. If I were late, I could be found in contempt; if a judge is late, it must be due to important business. Second, the judge was scowling. Things were not looking good. The judge told me he would like me to complete my argument in two hours. I reminded him that I had gone to the trouble of setting aside two days, which would have given me closer to five or six hours. He told me to pare down my argument in the hall.

I knew already this was going to be a waste of time. I was attending court to challenge the constitutionality of a law; this should be important. Yet I was told to rush through the argument, and no reason was given. When I came back after recess, I advised the judge that I could not make the argument in two hours. I suggested that perhaps the matter should be adjourned so that we could reconvene when the court had sufficient time to hear the argument. This was my way of getting away from this judge and before another one. The judge interrupted me and yelled, "Just get started!" I was a bit rattled by his booming voice, but when I gained composure, I wasn't sure what to do. I thought of walking out of court in protest. I thought of telling the judge exactly what I thought of him. Instead, I argued the case in two hours. The whole time I knew this was a complete charade. The judge was not listening and I was droning on with no passion or commitment. But I kept the judge there for the full two hours, and took some pleasure in his impatient squirming and occasional outbursts of anger.

Of course, I ended up losing the challenge.[8] The judge delivered a dozen pages of drivel. Despite the chilly reception in court, I remained determined to forge ahead. I believed I was right in advancing my position, and I had spent a year working on the details. I wasn't going to let some crabby judge deter me from going forward. We appealed to the Court of Appeal. This time, I was given two full days. I was allowed to say everything I needed to say. The three judges were polite and civil.

Maybe I was getting through to them. Fat chance. One can still be indifferent while appearing kind.

When I finished my argument, the court retired for ten minutes. When they returned, they had their judgement. This is decision-making on amphetamines! I spent a year preparing eight volumes of compelling evidence, and they disposed of it in ten minutes with a handwritten endorsement. When they read out the endorsement, I laughed to myself. The court moved so rashly that its half-baked reasons actually supported my argument. The court stated that laws are needed to protect the consumer from deceit and fraud within underground gambling. Consumer protection is a provincial matter, and the court was agreeing with me without realizing it. I explained this to my clients, and they were interested in taking the matter to the Supreme Court of Canada. I ordered a copy of the written endorsement to begin the process, but nothing was forthcoming from the Court of Appeal. I was advised that the endorsement could not be found. Months and months later, an endorsement was delivered to me.[9] It was not as I remembered. The reference to the interests of consumer protection had been deleted. The court was too lazy to struggle with my argument and the compelling evidence, but it wasn't too lazy to cover its ass.

Maintaining the illusion of wisdom necessitates foreclosing public criticism of our judges. That is why *The Globe and Mail* criticized me for calling judges "cowardly." Of course, there are times when a judge has to be condemned by the media, but for the most part public criticism of public officials is reserved for cops, defence lawyers, prosecutors and politicians. The judges come out relatively unscathed, as part of the larger enterprise of preserving the legitimacy of the criminal process.

Some people will still take brutal shots at our judiciary, as I'm doing right now. So, the law constructs some deep structural components of criminal justice that serve to minimize the occasions for challenging the finality of verdicts in criminal trials. This often goes unnoticed, but there are some strange aspects of criminal justice that can be justified only as serving the function of maintaining legitimacy. We worship the finality of the verdict. It may be wrong, but it is final. Finality is valued over accuracy, and the system is designed to reach a determinate result, even if it is the wrong result. Judges do not have a constitutional obligation to give reasons when they sit without a jury.[10] And juries never provide reasons. It is easier to hide folly if reasons need not be given. Further, it is a criminal offence to disclose jury deliberations. The jury may have used a Ouija board, but as long as no one knows, the verdict will stand. And no one will know, because people stand to be convicted of a criminal offence if they expose the process of a jury deliberation. The goal is to reach a decision, regardless of whether the decision-making process is sound, informed and thoughtful.

The finality of the verdict is protected by the doctrine of *functus officio*—once the verdict is rendered, the judge is without further power to act in the case. I've always liked this phrase. It seems kind of dirty—"I'd like to *functus* your *officio*"—but look at the implications. In one case, the jury acquitted an accused on attempted murder charges, but did not know at the time of delivering verdict that they could convict on some lesser included offences.[11] The accused was discharged before the jurors realized they had not notified the judge that they would convict on other charges. Too late. The judge was *functus*. The accused got a lucky break.

Even before a judge becomes *functus officio*, there is little that a judge or jury can do to satisfy their cognitive needs. Juries do not ask questions, nor do they take notes. Judges can ask questions, but it is rare for them to do so and rarer for them to call their own witnesses. In one case, during their deliberation process the jury asked whether the judge would call a witness they would like to hear, one whom counsel had not called at trial.[12] Despite the fact that the jury believed they needed the information this witness could provide in order to make an informed decision, the Court of Appeal ruled that a judge did not have the power to accommodate the jury. The important thing is to reach the verdict; it does not matter if you don't have the information needed to make an informed decision.

In an adversarial system, the judge is supposed to be a neutral umpire; that is why judges usually do not call witnesses. The judge is there to soak up the presentations made by the lawyers. They are not supposed to be proactive in seeking out information needed for an informed decision. In a particular drug case, the judge was puzzled by the accused's assertion that he had not travelled to a certain place because of inclement weather. On a hunch, the judge contacted a meteorological office to obtain information on the weather that day. There was no inclement weather, and the judge entered a conviction. The conviction was overturned because the judge had overstepped his role.[13] He should not have sought out information, even though the information was needed for an informed judgement. This judicial paralysis is another clever way to maintain legitimacy. If a judge makes a decision based upon incomplete information, we can blame the lawyers for not doing their jobs. We can live with lawyers being responsible for skewed decisions, but we cannot tolerate the idea that the judge may be to blame.

We only want a decision. We don't necessarily need to have the right decision. That is why the job advertisement for a judge spoke only of the "ability to make a decision" and not the "ability to make good decisions." The system values an insensitive and ignorant judge over an indecisive or irresolute one. Law has never been about reflecting reality; it is about filtering reality to make it manageable. This unconscious desire resides deep in the structure of institutionalized justice. Trial by ordeal, trial by battle and trial by oath-swearing were acceptable ways of trying criminals in ancient times because the process always led to a resolute result. It could not be challenged. It reflected the will of God. When these ancient forms of trial were abandoned in the thirteenth century, they were replaced with human decision makers—judges and juries. The introduction of human players raised the spectre of human fallibility, and the law constructed components to strengthen the finality of the human decision. Judges and juries may not be infallible, but if we act like they are, we achieve almost the same authoritative finality as trial by ordeal. So we treat the judge and jury like oracles. They issue decrees and pronouncements. They may be idiots, but as long as we promote them as geniuses and shield their decision-making process from intense scrutiny and challenge, the legitimacy of the process remains unimpaired.

There is nothing more dangerous than giving raw power to people who think they are smarter than they are. Strange things are bound to happen. Look at the Dudley Laws trial of 1993. Laws was a black activist who was facing charges relating to an alleged conspiracy to smuggle illegal aliens into Canada. In his eminent wisdom, the trial judge excluded from the courtroom certain people who were wearing headdresses for religious purposes. Lots of Somali and Muslim men wished to attend the trial. They were sent packing. The trial judge tried to explain:

> In order to avoid any misunderstanding, it is appropriate to set out the dress protocol which is required in a court over which I preside. It cannot be doubted that a presiding judge not only has the authority but also the duty to oversee the demeanor, solemnity and dignity which must prevail in a superior court of law. This is not simply a power to please a judge, but an obligation to all other persons in the court who do not need to be reminded of the importance of the matters being dealt with. It is an essential ingredient to the conduct of a trial. Appearance is an important aspect of the respect and dignity.[14]

Methinks My Lord has missed his calling. Maybe he really wanted to be a cross-dressing fashion designer, living in Milan. He should have stuck to judging and left trivial questions of fashion to people's individual judgement. I hope he put as much energy into judging the case as he put into judging the audience.

When I started lawyering, there was a judge who would not let counsel address the court if the lawyer was wearing brown shoes. Black is the only colour that shows respect for the judiciary. As long as everyone wears the right clothes, bows when the judge enters and addresses the judge with the requisite subservient tone, the illusion of wisdom is maintained, even if the judge does something really wacky. At least everyone looks good and the ritual remains intact.

The fact that judges care so much about attire suggests that they are engaged in an exercise of raw power, and not an exercise of wise judgement. I'm sure that King Solomon was not at all concerned with the clothes worn by gallery observers. He would have been too focused on the task at hand to waste his time and energy on bullshit trivialities. But modern judges likes to flex their judicial muscles. It's fun. It's a powerful ego boost. The judge in the Laws case went to the trouble of developing a code of dress for his court. He laid down five principles of court fashion:

1. The court welcomes the attendance of students, because the conduct of judicial business ought to be well known and part of their education. Attire normally acceptable in school should be the standard. However, male

heads must be bare and if females wear head cover, it must not interfere with other members of the public, or be flamboyant.

2. The mature general public have no such guide, and taste varies considerably. Obviously, slovenly, dirty or offensive clothes will not do. Nor will clothes which uncover any objectionable area of the body. Clean, obtrusive and widely common styles ought to suffice. It is a question of judgement.

3. It is a consideration that a particular type of case or subject-matter is before the court. Highly visible, but silent, groups in support of some outcome of the case will be requested to reduce their visibility by the removal of signs, pennants, other intrusive indicia, or to leave. A court is not a cheering section, even a silent one.

4. Sometimes, bizarre and intrusive attire appears in court; something that immediately draws attention from the proceedings. This must not be permitted.

5. Occasionally, bizarre, intrusive or simply impolite attire appears and some claim of religious obligation is made. The Charter of Rights protects against religious discrimination, but equally protects the principle of a public trial, among other matters. Some criteria is relevant.[15]

Does this show wisdom? I should be allowed to wear pink leotards to court if I feel like it. The judge made a fundamental mistake. He assumed that the court was his court. "These are the rules of fashion you will follow when you appear in *my* court." Hey judge, you're just renting space from the people. This is not your court, it is my court. And my court welcomes people wearing codpieces or leotards, and most importantly, people wearing cultural or religious headwear. It's arrogant to believe that your mandate to judge criminal accusations includes telling people how to behave when coming to court to watch you exercise wisdom.

All lawyers have their share of judicial horror stories. Some of them are really funny. But, then, they aren't funny at all. Keeping in mind the power and authority we have given to these ordinary people, the stories are actually quite scary. Lawyers understand that the #1 rule of advocacy is "know thy judge," and when you ask lawyers to assess your chances of success they will often answer with "it depends on the judge we get." Justice should never be contingent upon the vagaries of human competence and frailty. I say we disrobe the judges and parade them around the courthouse in the raw. Once we see all their blemishes and imperfections, we can send them back to the bench to do their jobs. Once the illusion of wisdom is lifted, judges can stop wasting so much energy maintaining the illusion and start spending a little more time searching for insight, cultivating empathy and polishing their spirits. Only the disrobed judge stands a chance of filling King Solomon's shoes.

18

Let's Make a Deal

I ONCE REPRESENTED a sultry stripper in Brampton, Ontario. Because Brenda was scared, I spent a lot of time with her. Here's why she was scared. One day her boyfriend took her on a drive. He was going to take out a guy on a contract killing; $5000 was the price of the contract. Quite a deal. Not much value put on life in Brampton, I guess. Brenda the stripper seemed to have no sense that it was wrong to drive with her boyfriend, knowing that he was going to end someone's life. She may not have been a murderer, but in the eyes of the law she was a party to the murder. Both the perpetrator and the party are sentenced as murderers, so she was looking at a life sentence.

At times like this, people bow down and pray to the great god of justice, Monty Hall. It's time to make a deal. Brenda got a pretty good deal. Her boyfriend was to plead guilty to first-degree murder, and she would plead guilty to conspiracy to commit murder and receive a five-year sentence. One catch: her boyfriend had to testify at the trial of the two men who had paid for the hit. The case could not be proved without the boyfriend as a Crown witness. Brenda was scared because her boyfriend was getting cold feet. He was going to be spending at least the next twenty-five years in prison, and felt it would be better not to enter the joint with the reputation of being a snitch. Brenda couldn't handle the pressure, and she ran.

Of course, the deal was off. Brenda called me every once in a while to check in. I never asked where she was. I feebly tried to convince her to come back. I told her I would try to get the deal set up again, but she knew her boyfriend would never live up to his end of the bargain. The police were also calling me. They assumed I must know her whereabouts. I always wondered if my phone was tapped. I have no idea if the police ever caught up with Brenda. All I learned from this brief encounter was that, in the marketplace of contract killing, the price of life is pretty cheap, and in the marketplace of justice, the cost of murder can be negotiated.

Modern criminal justice is all about horse-trading. "If you plead guilty today, I will ask for probation, but it's a one-time deal. Take it today or face jail if we have to go to trial." That is the standard prosecutorial approach to justice. But it is justice only in name. This process is more like selling used cars than meting out justice. Yet everyone is doing it. Close to 90% of cases are resolved by guilty pleas, and most of these are negotiated ahead of time by the defence lawyer and the prosecutor.[1] Criminal-justice policy is being set by lawyers engaged in an adversarial dance. I don't even know why we have judges. All we need are some trained monkeys who can point to the courtroom door leading to the holding cells.

There are many abuses associated with plea-bargaining. Innocent people get railroaded, victims are ignored, police overcharge, prosecutors mislead, defence lawyers bully their clients and judges sit back and enjoy the show. It's a tragic comedy, and it's the longest-running show in contemporary criminal justice. For decades, Crowns have been substituting lesser charges in exchange for guilty pleas. For decades, Crowns have been agreeing to lenient sentencing dispositions in exchange for guilty pleas. For decades, Crowns have been changing the facts behind the allegation to ensure that judges don't balk when presented with the negotiated plea. Sometimes the bargain does amount to an approximation of justice, but most of the time it is a distortion. The legal professionals just want to clear the docket. They just want to process the criminals quickly, with as little involvement as possible. It's all about moving inventory.

The adversarial jury trial is becoming an historical relic. Criminal law is evolving into a form of punitive civil law. Like all civil lawsuits, the lawyers banter, babble and posture until the eve of trial, when a settlement is invariably reached. This is fine when you are involved in a private civil claim. It's up to you whether you wish to proceed, fold or settle. But in criminal law, we have to look to the public interest and not just the private interests of the accused and victim (if there is one). Who in their right mind would put the lawyers in charge of the public interest? They're negotiating the cases for their own reasons, which may bear no relationship to what is in the public interest. Lawyers have completely appropriated the criminal-justice system. They decide when there will be a trial. They decide what type of sentence will be appropriate. They decide what to tell the judge. They decide everything and accomplish very little.

The notion of lawyer as champion of the underdog is a part of "kick ass" cultural representation. But in plea bargaining, legal culture devolves into a "kiss ass" practice. Kicking ass is an asset for trial work, but it gets in the way of plea negotiation. Negotiation is all about cultivating relationships. If you are well liked, you will get sweet deals. If you are despised, you may not even get a deal. The Crown calls the shots, and the defence lawyer learns how to embrace the enemy. When you get a bunch of schmucks oozing, you get schmoozing. The process becomes an exercise in networking. The "rule of law" is replaced by the "rule of human relations."

In March 2001, the *Toronto Star* ran a series on plea-bargaining. One small passage tells all: "The *Star* informally polled 50 lawyers—both crown and defence—and asked them to make a subjective rating on the men and women on the bench on a scale ranging from lenient to harsh. The lawyers who agreed—only a few refused—didn't want their names used; they have to face these same judges on a daily basis."[2]

It should trouble you that we rank our judges from lenient to harsh. Who cares about the judges' predilections? The question should be whether the law is lenient or harsh; the personality of the judge should be erased from the equation. Our entire sentencing process is contingent upon the personality of the judge. Lawyers spend a great deal of time checking into the character of the presiding judge. Plea-bargaining requires skilful judge shopping to make sure your bargain is put before a judge who is likely to uphold it. Defence lawyers have to cultivate good relations with both prosecutors and judges to become masterful plea negotiators, so they will never publicly reveal the disdain they have for some of the people they praise and flatter. I have trouble seeing where justice fits into this picture. I see good public relations, but justice has gone into hiding.

Putting aside the abuses triggered by negotiated justice, the concept of negotiated criminal justice is just wrong. Public opinion polls show that most Canadians feel this way.[3] Let me put it this way. As a teacher, I loathe marking final examinations. Deciphering chicken-scratch from panic-stricken law students is not my idea of a good time. I could propose a solution for both professor and student. If my students will waive their right to a fair and thorough evaluation of their examination, I will award all the students a grade of B across the board. Surprisingly, most of my students like the proposal. Only those who aspire to excellence find it disturbing. This little expedient would make everyone's life easier, but it completely strips the grades of any meaning. A negotiated grade bears no relationship to the student's achievement. Similarly, sentencing becomes devoid of meaning when the sentence is negotiated. In exchange for the accused waiving their right to have a trial, the accused receives a sentencing gift. The value of the gift depends upon the lawyers doing the shopping and the store/courthouse you find yourself in. Disparity in sentencing becomes so pronounced that the entire sentencing process loses rhyme and reason.

How did the historically celebrated jury trial end up being replaced by bargain-basement shopping? The historical record is not clear, but there are some plausible theories:

> The main historical explanation for the want of plea bargaining in former centuries is, I believe, simple and incontrovertible. When we turn back to the period before the middle of the eighteenth century, we find that common law trial procedure exhibited a degree of efficiency that we now expect only of our nontrial procedure. *Jury trial was a summary proceeding.* Over the intervening two centuries the rise of the adversary system and the related development of the law of evidence has caused common law jury trial to undergo a profound transformation, robbing it of the wondrous efficiency that had characterized it for so many centuries.[4]

This conventional perspective plays right into the hands of the legal professionals. Most legal professionals take a dim view of plea-bargaining, but justify it as a necessary evil. They say the courts are bursting at the seams, and chaos would ensue if most cases were not resolved by out-of-court negotiation. The "case-pressure hypothesis" has been the primary explanation for the proliferation of plea-bargaining. Plea-bargaining is the only way to smooth over the problems created by millions of charges being processed by a slow and inefficient system. This is all self-serving bullshit. If you really care about the clogging of court dockets, the solution is not in compromised justice for the multitude of accused persons; the solution is in reducing the multitude. Decriminalizing consensual crime and creating alternatives to criminal courts for minor interpersonal disputes would go a long way towards easing the congestion.

The few empirical studies show that the abolition of plea-bargaining in some American jurisdictions has not triggered a disaster in court administration.[5] But the studies also show that in jurisdictions that have attempted to abolish plea-bargaining legal professionals still find some way of reinstating the marketplace of justice.[6] It is not only court inefficiency that gave rise to plea-bargaining; the "rise of the adversary system and the related development of the law of evidence" played a significant role. The adversary system and the law of evidence were both nurtured and cultivated by lawyers seeking greater power in the late nineteenth century. Lawyers like the plea-bargaining process. It brings them practical benefits, and it resonates with the only theoretical perspective they can truly understand.

The list of practical benefits is endless. The practice of law is stressful and demanding. Lawyers are often miserable. Preparing for a hotly contested trial can suck the lifeblood out of a lawyer, and the good lawyers rarely get paid for all the time they put into a case. Not many accused people are millionaires (lots of criminals may be millionaires, especially corporate criminals, but not many of the rich and powerful end up being accused). So, in some cases it is a welcome relief for the lawyer to throw in the towel and negotiate a plea bargain. It is economically efficient and less stressful than a contested trial. Ass-kissing is not as draining as ass-kicking. So, despite the demeaning aspects of ass-kissing, lawyers are more than happy to replace the kick with the kiss to reduce their workload. Of course, there is also an economic incentive. Each plea takes ten to thirty minutes. The lawyer may get paid up to $2000 for the guilty plea (if it is simple, as most of them are), and five pleas can be fit into a day. You do the math. High-volume guilty pleas keep the lawyer in business.

Through clever manipulation of legal-aid tariffs, "dumptruck" lawyers in the early 1990s were able to make tons of money pleading virtually all of their clients guilty in rapid succession. Although most lawyers earn less than $100,000,

> ... there are criminal lawyers making an awful lot of money serving poor people, and they are the "dumptrucks." The last time the law society [of Upper Canada] looked, 14 lawyers were earning between $300,000 and $399,000 a year solely from legal aid fees; three lawyers were earning between $400,000 and $499,000 and two others topped $500,000. This is gross income, but there is not much overhead in doing guilty pleas.[7]

Obviously, lawyers cannot use crass commercialism as a justification for the practice of plea-bargaining, so they rely upon an easily digested theoretical construct to supply the justification. The legal professional views the process through the lens of the law of property. Feminists are right: in a patriarchal society everything is reduced to property rights, to rules of ownership. Lawyers understand property rights. They see plea-bargaining as a reflection of the capitalistic perspective that informs our culture. The accused has a constitutional right to a jury trial. Lawyers believe the defining feature of a right is that it be alienable—you can dispose of your property as you see fit. If you want to give it away, that is your business. If you want to sell it, go ahead. In criminal justice, we do not talk of giving away, or selling, rights. This is too crass. We talk about waiving rights, but it is the same thing. Lawyers see constitutional rights and property rights as one and the same. They are more than happy to negotiate on your behalf the selling price for your right to a trial.

In my early days as an academic, I was deeply troubled when I discovered that virtually every constitutional right has a purchase price. All rights can be waived. You can waive your right to counsel, you can waive your right against unreasonable search and seizure, you can waive your right against arbitrary detention and you can waive your right to trial. Criminal process is tilted to favour the waiver of rights, rather than the assertion of rights. The glory of the Charter of Rights becomes cheap and tawdry.

The notion of waiving rights has its roots in an economic conception of the world. Self-interested and rational persons structure their lives by entering a marketplace of goods to bargain and negotiate in their own interests. One need not know anything about Pareto optimality and transaction costs to know that an economic analysis has no application in a marketplace for incorporeal goods such as justice, truth, equality and freedom. Waiver allows one person to set the price for the purchase of constitutional rights, and eventually this devaluates the rights for everyone else.[8]

Constitutional rights are not like personal possessions. Legal professionals should be embarrassed by the stunted perspective they operate within. When a state decides to entrench rights, it is conceding that these are the minimum standards needed to ensure a fair and just process. Constitutional rights are designed to erect permanent boundaries to prevent the state from straying into oppression and persecution. Constitutional rights structure the relationship between state and individual. You can't bargain away these rights, or the entire structure will collapse. If you bargain away the right to minimum wage, then in effect there is no minimum wage.

It is also clear that "the fact that we permit a portion of defendants to waive trial rights by pleading guilty ... undoubtedly renders it more difficult for any particular defendant to assert his right to trial."[9] When justice becomes horse-trading, there is a settled expectation that all traders are going to want to strike a deal. Enormous pressure and coercion is put on those who do not wish to play the game.

It's kind of strange to go to the trouble to entrench rights in a constitution, call this the "supreme law of the land," and then let people go about selling these rights for their own personal benefit. The stock response is that people have a right to self-determination, and they can decide for themselves whether they want to waive their right to trial by pleading guilty. Even if this is true, it does not explain why accused people are rewarded with lighter sentences for waiving their rights. The next stock response is that people who plead guilty receive lighter sentences to reflect the mitigating factors of showing remorse and of sparing the state from wasting resources on a trial. Most guilty pleas have nothing to do with remorse, and most accused people don't give a rat's ass about sparing the state from wasting resources. The sentencing reward is there to induce guilty pleas. It is the carrot used to make people play the game.

Is the basic premise that a guilty plea is consistent with the right to self-determination even true? In Europe, trials never start by asking an accused for their plea. Many accused people in Europe confess, and this shortens the European trial, but no one wants to know how the accused feel about their guilt. The trial is not about the accused's feelings—it is about an accusation brought by the state. The state has accused a person of a crime, and it is has the moral and legal obligation to prove the case beyond a reasonable doubt. So the question is not whether the accused think they are guilty—that is irrelevant. The question is whether the state's accusation is true or unfounded. The whole notion of entering a plea may just be an irrelevant ritual we have set up to facilitate, induce and sponsor plea-bargaining. It is not surprising that the absence of a guilty plea ritual in most European countries means an absence of plea-bargaining. Plea bargaining is neither natural, nor inevitable.

I could overlook the absence of a principled justification for plea-bargaining if the practice did not taint the entire criminal process. The system is geared to the processing of guilty pleas, and the zeal to clear dockets through plea-bargaining has led to a criminal-justice system tainted by deceit and coercion. Accused people have to be persuaded that pleading guilty is in their best interests. I have attended numerous pretrial conferences with both prosecutors and judges, and invariably I am told that, if my client does not plead guilty at the earliest available opportunity, the Crown and court may consider incarcerating my client. So prison is not just a place of punishment for convicted offenders; prison is also a place where punishment is meted out for failing to play the game properly.

A great deal of time and effort is spent trying to secure or extort guilty pleas. The United States Supreme Court has ruled that accused people are entitled to plead guilty even if they are not guilty.[10] Canadian courts have not actually endorsed this idiocy, but they seem to operate on the same premise. We want our guilty pleas, and it's really of no moment whether you are actually guilty.

In 1995, a man named Rajaeefard showed up in court on a charge of domestic assault. He attended with a student from the University of Toronto Legal Clinic. The student arrived in court solely to seek an adjournment. The judge said there would be no adjournment, but that if the accused pleaded guilty that day, he would receive probation. However, if a trial were held, the accused would be given a ten- to fifteen-day jail sentence upon conviction. The judge asked the prosecutor and student lawyer to discuss the matter in the hallway outside the courtroom. The student was flabbergasted. He was there only to seek an adjournment, as the clinic had just been retained. He advised the client of the judge's decree, and the accused decided he would plead guilty. When the court resumed, the following exchange took place:

> The Court: Let's call that Rajaeefard case again. Do you know what he is going to do with himself?
> The Student: Yes, Your Honour. I have discussed the matter with my client. I put to him what we can expect on a guilty plea and what he could be expecting if he had that trial and I said, he cannot expect an adjournment

and he thought it over and he has decided to enter a plea of guilty at this time.

The Court: Okay. That's good counselling.[11]

Good counselling? I think the judge meant "good coercion." The Court of Appeal allowed the accused to withdraw his guilty plea because it was coerced, so the travesty of justice was set right.[12] But the actions of this judge reflect the attitude of many legal professionals. It doesn't matter if you are innocent. It doesn't matter if you want to clear your name. If a good deal is offered, and the prosecutor's case has a prospect of conviction, legal professionals will twist the arms of accused people to accept the deal.

A young offender, Stephen K., was facing ten counts of sexual assault involving five young women. Halfway through the trial, the defence lawyer approached the Crown suggesting a deal for a non-custodial term. The lawyer advised the kid to take the deal, as it might be the only way to stay out of custody. The kid insisted that he was innocent, but his parents and his lawyer convinced him that a guilty plea was the way to go. The mother was concerned about her son admitting in court that he was guilty of assaulting five women, and the lawyer assured the mother that he would do that on behalf of her son; her son need not himself admit guilt. The plea bargain was completed, and both defence and Crown sought a non-custodial term. The judge flipped out and meted out sixty days in jail and twenty-two months' probation. Why? Because the kid showed no remorse. Of course he wouldn't show remorse—he did not think of himself as guilty. Then the kid was threatened with breach of probation because one of the terms of probation was to seek treatment, and one cannot be treated if one does not admit there is a problem. The kid had finished serving his sentence before the Court of Appeal allowed him to withdraw his plea of guilty. The court noted that "the system was tilted askew by the simple fact that a person protesting his innocence became engaged in plea bargaining."[13]

Accused people often have no idea what is happening in court, and their lawyers are too important or too busy to explain things to them. I saw this phenomenon every day in practice—clients walking around the courthouse, dazed and confused, looking for their lawyers, who would only brush them off once found. A fascinating 1982 study of accused people and their lawyers, *The Ordering of Justice: A Study of Accused Persons as Dependants in the Criminal Process*,[14] presents first-hand evidence of the lawyer as bully and the accused as dependant. This interview from the study is characteristic of the confusion borne by most accused people:

> Q. Was it the assault or the obstruct charge that she read?
> A. The ... both.
> Q. She read out both?
> A. Yes, I think so.
> Q. Did you plead guilty to both of them in court or just to one of them?
> A. Well, I think both. Both.
> Q. Now, in fact, you were only convicted of "obstruct police" and the Crown withdrew the assault charge.
> A. Is that what happened?[15]

Confused and trembling at the gate of justice, most accused people just want to get things over with. They are rarely put in a position to make an informed and independent assessment of the situation. Here's another accused caught bumbling through his case:

> A. I didn't know what they were talking about 'cause they named all these— do you to want to go to judge and jury, da, da, da, da, I didn't know what was happening. So ... after I went and says [to the duty counsel] "What have you been talking about?" And he says, "Well, I just want you to know [your options]." And I says, "I just wanted to get it over with today, okay, tell him [judge] that." So that's what I did.
> Q. When they read out the mischief charge, did you understand that?
> A. Not really.
> Q. Okay.
> A. I didn't understand anything. I just wanted to get it over with, and get out of there.[16]

Laypeople are misled into believing law is a science that can be deciphered only by learned judges and experienced lawyers. Accused people who enter the gates of justice in confusion and fear resign themselves to letting the expert make the decision. Accused people are truly dependent, and lawyers are always ready to exploit this vulnerability. Being in a knowledge elite, lawyers acquire "contempt for the multitude," and this means that "good counselling" entails barking orders instead of providing explanations and advice. Here's a fairly representative comment from a lawyer, taken from the same study:

> [At the bail hearing, I told the accused] to keep his mouth shut and let me do the talking ... Any lawyer who's worth his salt tells his client how to dress, how to have his hair cut, how to have it combed, how to behave, how to answer questions ... I don't allow my clients to have reservations [about me], they either follow my advice or find another lawyer.[17]

What a pompous ass! People come to lawyers for advice, counsel and defence. Instead they receive domination and manipulation: "I command you to plead guilty or else find yourself another saviour." Arrogant lawyers feel no need to explain the situation to their clients. The elitist always assumes that the client is too dumb to understand. Here's one last excerpt:

> A. I basically made the decision for him.
> Q. And he didn't put up any—
> A. No, I really have a tendency to decide myself which is better for my client and I don't say, well, these are the avenues, because I don't think they understand enough of what I am talking about. I don't think they're capable of me explaining everything to them because it took me a long time to learn what the different avenues meant too.[18]

Beyond the coercive elements of plea-bargaining, the entire structure of this resolution process is built on a foundation of deceit. Police often overcharge the accused to extort a plea. Prosecutors take insensitive, hard-line positions to extort pleas, and defence lawyers misrepresent the value of the deal to secure agreement from the client. Then the lawyers will mislead the court if necessary. Although "fact-bargaining" is considered unethical, it is a daily occurrence.

Let's say my client is charged with assault with a weapon. He did not use the knife, but he threatened to do so. The Crown and I agree that the client will enter a guilty plea to common assault for a twelve-month term of probation. If the Crown reads in the fact that my client was brandishing a knife at the time of the assault, there is a good chance the judge will "jump the joint submission." So an agreement is also reached that when the Crown reads the facts of the offence in court, reference to brandishing a knife will be omitted. Reality is distorted, and the judge sentences the accused based upon the distorted reality. There is no truth in sentencing.

A plea bargain is a faulty contract, but accused people are never told about the faults. The contract may bind the defence and the prosecutor, but the judge is not bound by it. Most judges simply sleepwalk through negotiated pleas, but some reject the bargain and the accused gets shafted. Also, the attorney general can still appeal the negotiated sentence; this is rare, but it does happen. However, the accused cannot automatically appeal the sentence just because the judge decides to jump the joint submission and whack the accused real good. Most of the time, plea bargains turn out as expected, but sometimes all hell breaks loose. This should not happen when one has entered into a valid and binding contract, but the plea bargain is a bastardized version of a valid contract.

Sentencing is a solemn and difficult task even for the wisest judge. We avoid this mess by turning sentencing into an exercise in administrative processing. No one really knows what it means to mete out a "fit" sentence that is "proportionate to moral blameworthiness."[19] Plea-bargaining just muddies the water, and moral blameworthiness is no longer the benchmark for a fit sentence.

Look at this difficult case. In 1992, a mother was charged with murder in the death of her young son. The accused was an alcoholic who had suffered physical, mental and sexual abuse throughout childhood. She also suffered from significant intellectual deficits. Her child was hyperactive, and she often covered his mouth to mute the screaming from his frequent tamper tantrums. She was afraid of being evicted. Beyond this restraint, the mother started to beat her child. One time, covering the child's mouth led to his suffocation.

I find this to be a troubling and difficult case. So you know what happens. Time to make a deal. It was agreed that the mother would plead guilty to the lesser offence of manslaughter, and the Crown and defence would recommend upon a joint submission a sentence of eighteen months' incarceration, followed by three years' probation. The trial judge was not impressed, and jumped the joint submission to impose a ten-year prison sentence, followed by three years' probation. From eighteen months to ten years—that is probably the Guinness record for jumping a joint submission. The sentence was appealed, and the Court of Appeal vacated the sentence and awarded a four-year prison sentence with no probation.[20]

So what is the fit and appropriate sentence? Eighteen months, four years or ten years? A group of legal professionals all looked at the same facts, but arrived at very different conclusions. We have no idea what is a fit sentence. We just pull numbers out of the air like pulling rabbits out of a hat. And that is why we have rampant plea-bargaining. Because there is no truth in sentencing. A fit sentence is whatever sentence the legal professionals fix upon as final. And to avoid the distressing uncertainty of sentencing, accused people are compelled to plea-bargain. The numbers arrived at may be arbitrary, but at least by bargaining all the players know which ballpark they are playing in.

Plea-bargaining may exist in a world of deceit, but for legal professionals, it is a sacred world. All lawyers have stories of plea-bargaining horrors. All lawyers know of the abuses inherent in a system geared to inducing guilty pleas. But I am one of the only practising lawyers who has called for the abolition of plea-bargaining. Lawyers admit that plea-bargaining is morally problematic, but they delude themselves into believing that this process is a "necessary evil" to combat court overload. This begrudging acceptance of bargaining as a necessary evil is completely disingenuous. Lawyers love plea-bargaining. They will defend the practice if it looks like there is a serious chance that lawmakers will try to abolish or regulate it.

Once again, and for a final time, we return to the Homolka/ Bernardo fiasco as proof that legal professionals have no interest in reforming or abolishing this "necessary evil." In 1995, Bernardo was sentenced to life imprisonment. Two years earlier, Homolka had inked a great deal. Her lawyer must have known how to press the right buttons. For drugging, raping and killing her sister, and kidnapping, raping and killing two teenage girls, she received a twelve-year sentence. People were outraged. Sure, the Crown was desperate. They knew in their guts that Bernardo was the villain they had been pursuing for years, but without Homolka's testimony they were scared that Bernardo might escape justice. Remember, the police had bungled the search and had not discovered the hidden videotapes. So Homolka was in a good bargaining position.

In the wake of Bernardo's 1995 trial, many laypeople clamoured for re-opening Homolka's plea bargain. Both defence lawyers and prosecutors agreed that this could not be done. The conventional perspective espoused by the legal professionals was that "a deal is a deal," and the whole future of the plea-negotiation process would be jeopardized if a deal could be unravelled just because it seems distasteful in retrospect.

I had a different perspective. I thought the Homolka debacle could be used to trigger a backlash against plea-bargaining. I had spent the previous five years doing victims' rights work, and one recurring theme in their contempt for criminal justice was the way in which serious offenders negotiate plea bargains. Plea-bargaining has been the bane of the victims' rights movement. Attacking the Homolka deal might be the first step in a return to a system of contested trials for serious breaches of the social order. I refused to concede that Homolka's deal was carved in stone, like the Ten Commandments. Not one legal professional agreed with me.

Bernardo's trial itself was fairly boring, and I spent a lot of my time in court reading transcripts, studying Homolka's plea resolution agreement and reviewing precedent dealing with plea-bargains. Everything became clear when Homolka took the stand. At the beginning, she was stoic and righteous. She was actually impressive. But as the days wore on, I could see Homolka's duplicity as if she wore it like a halo. She had a sinister intelligence that undercut her claims of being the abused wife of a serial killer. During her performance on the stand, it became apparent that she had not been forthright with investigators when she inked her sweet deal. This was the ammunition I needed to bring Homolka and the whole plea-bargaining process under attack.

During the trial, I wrote to the attorney general of Ontario to advise him that I was of the legal opinion that there was a valid and lawful way to revisit her sentence. I asked to meet with the relevant officials to discuss my proposal. Since the Bernardo trial was underway, the state took the position that they could not discuss the issue until the trial was complete. I was being given the bureaucratic shuffle. Meantime, the revelations at the Bernardo trial were fuelling public discontent. A petition of 300,000 signatures was sent to the attorney general requesting that something be done about the lenient sentence awarded to Homolka. I waited until the day Bernardo was convicted and then took the opportunity as CTV's commentator to announce on the national news that there was a lawful mechanism for reviewing Homolka's plea bargain. A few months later, the government announced that they had appointed a retired Court of Appeal judge to review the Homolka plea-negotiation process. So far so good.

I prepared a legal memorandum outlining my position and fowarded it to the reviewing judge. I contended that "the Attorney General would be legally entitled to have the Court of Appeal review the fitness of Ms. Homolka's sentence. In my opinion, Ms. Homolka perpetrated a fraud on both the Crown and the sentencing court. This fraud is manifested by significant nondisclosure of criminal wrongdoing at the time Ms. Homolka negotiated her plea agreement." I outlined nine potential crimes she could have been charged with had she been forthcoming at the time of negotiating her deal. I also provided extensive case law demonstrating how a plea-negotiation agreement would be considered voidable if there had been significant and material nondisclosure by the accused.

The memorandum was lengthy and detailed, and although controversial it did provide basis for legal action. I fully realized that it would take an innovative approach and an exercise of will for the reviewing judge to recommend that the government take action against Homolka. Regrettably, the retired Court of Appeal judge upheld the status quo. He did a thorough and thoughtful review, but it lacked vision. He considered the deal struck appropriate in the circumstances:

> It is my firm conclusion that, distasteful as it always is to negotiate with an accomplice, the Crown had no alternative but to do so in this case ... The conduct by counsel on both sides was professional and responsible, having regard to the duties which they owed to the respective parties.[21]

As for my proposal to seek leave to appeal her sentence,

> In my view, the evidence does not support a conclusion that Karla Homolka committed fraud upon either the Crown or the Court which sentenced her. In the absence of fraud there is no basis to institute further proceedings against Karla Homolka arising out of the homicides ... The law in Ontario is that resolution agreements, as a general rule, must be honoured and the exceptions to that rule must be rare.[22]

When the dust settled, the government threw up its hands and said "nothing to be done." The reviewing judge never called into question the larger systemic concerns raised by plea-bargaining. He was an apologist for the criminal-justice industrial complex. Maybe he was right, and nothing could be done about Homolka, but why was there not even a suggestion that we should examine the plea-bargaining process to determine if it can be regulated in the public interest? In light of the public outrage shouldn't the legal professionals have taken a second look at the unregulated world of plea-bargaining?

In a plea-bargaining world, we will always have to make deals with accomplices to get at the murderer. So we should set administrative or legislative limits on the sweetness of the deals available. The rule could be that a party to murder who becomes a Crown witness can never receive a sentence of less than fifteen years. Homolka would still deal, because this is better than a life sentence. Or how about a rule that requires consecutive sentences for each death caused? Under this regime, Homolka would have received a thirty-six-year sentence (twelve years for each of three deaths) instead of twelve years running concurrently for all three murders. These are simple solutions to curb the worst excesses of plea-bargaining in murder cases, but the Homolka review and the government's response show that legal professionals like the world just the way it is.

Plea-bargaining is the profession's sacred cow. The profession would be spiritually nourished if they just ate this fat cow, but they are afraid to operate without the sacred cow wandering the hallways of the court. Perhaps the reviewing judge was not moved to attack the Homolka deal because he was worried about the overall implications for the future health of plea-bargaining. It is interesting that he makes occasional reference to some greater principle at stake:

> The rectitude and honour which the Crown must always have and must always demonstrate that it has, demand that it stand by the considered decisions which it takes in the course of criminal litigation ... when the Crown makes a tactical decision, it is stuck with it. It seems to me that the obligation of the Crown to stand by its decisions applies to all of its decisions, even ones as distasteful as this.[23]

It's kind of noble to speak of the "rectitude and honour" of the Crown, but let's put this in proper perspective. Homolka helped her husband secure victims. She sadistically participated in three homicides. Assuming she serves her full sentence, she will be released from prison at the age of thirty-five. She will not even be on parole. She'll dye her hair and snag a boyfriend, probably get married and, if she moves quickly enough, have her very own family. She gets this wonderful opportunity for a second life because the legal profession is obsessed with protecting and promoting the "rectitude and honour" of the Crown. Somewhere along the line our criminal-justice priorities got all fucked up.

The "let's make a deal" approach to criminal justice infects the entire process. Haggling over sentencing deals strips justice of its majesty and dignity. Rational calculation of self-interest is the lifeblood of business, but in the pursuit of justice the calculation of self-interest is nothing more than a corrupting influence.

Picture this. You are a fifteen-year-old young offender charged with sexual assault. The night of your arrest, your mother retains a lawyer. She doesn't know he has a reputation as a dumptruck. The lawyer does not show up at your bail hearing the next day. Another lawyer is sent. (This is not unusual as many lawyers are not free on one day's notice.) Bail is denied. Four more court appearances follow. Your lawyer never shows up. Someone always conveys a message on his behalf. The lawyer has given you his home phone number, and you manage to speak with him on two occasions. He remembers having spoken to you more like four or five times. He never comes to visit you in jail. He never conducts a formal interview. Two months after you are arrested, you finally meet your lawyer on the morning of your trial. At the mid-morning break, the lawyer interviews you and is informed there is a friend available to provide supporting evidence. You take the stand and tell your story. The judge doesn't like the way you tell your story. Your friend testifies. It doesn't matter. The judge convicts you.

No matter what the outcome of your trial, you would feel like you had been sold down the river by your lawyer. How is it possible for a trial to be conducted when the first face-to-face meeting with your lawyer is on the morning of the trial? In the world of "let's make a deal," this is a reality. Lawyers often go into cases unprepared in the hope and expectation that a last-minute deal can be struck. In the real version of the scenario I just described, the young offender appealed his conviction. The appeal was largely based upon "ineffective assistance of counsel." Here's the Court of Appeal's description of the lawyer's explanation for never attending jail to interview his client:

> He said, in reference to all client detention centre visits, "I don't do jails." … It is clear from a review of defence counsel's evidence that his decision not to "do jails" had an economic, not a philosophic, basis. That is to say, Mr. S. does not appear to have a basic aversion to visiting custodial

314 V LEGAL PROFESSIONALS AS FALLEN PRIESTS

institutions. Rather, he had a high-volume "resolution-oriented" legal-aid practice ... It seems to me that because of his schedule, defence counsel did not have the time, or make the time, to meet with his clients other than in court. In addition, it seems to me that the fact that defence counsel was working on a block-fee legal aid case, where his profit margin would have been adversely affected by extra transactions such as detention centre visits, may have had more to do with his decision not to "do jails" than he cares to admit.[24]

I hate going to jail. No lawyer likes the stuffy interview room in the smelly and dank detention centres. Yet I can't imagine how one could practice criminal law without occasionally being required to sign in at a detention centre. But for this lawyer, as for many, business considerations interfered with the pursuit of justice. Plea-bargaining fuels this economic perspective. In fairness to this lawyer, the Court of Appeal did not believe the lawyer's cavalier approach affected the validity of the verdict:

> In summary, I am not satisfied that there is a probability sufficient to undermine confidence in the verdict (a reasonable probability) that but for defence counsel's alleged errors, the result of this proceeding would have been different. Thus, I do not think that the appellant's constitutional right to have the effective assistance of counsel was breached.
>
> In reaching this conclusion, I do not mean to endorse defence counsel's block-fee approach to his professional duties. I do not, however, think the somewhat casual approach defence counsel took to his obligation to prepare for trial, and prepare the appellant for trial, was consequential. I would, therefore, dismiss the appeal.[25]

This is really not the point. Perhaps the young offender was rightfully convicted, but the troubling aspect of the case is the appearance of justice. This case is a public-relations nightmare for lawyers. Even if this kid had been acquitted, he would harbour resentment towards lawyers. Are lawyers so indifferent and cold-hearted that they won't even visit a fifteen-year-old boy waiting in jail to face a serious criminal charge? I'm sure that's what the boy and his mother think. Actually, most people think this way.

With all the wheeling and dealing going on in the "let's make a deal" world of criminal justice, we are never left with a tangible feeling of justice. Everything is happening in a subterranean way. It's too fleeting to leave an impression. Victims are shut out, and accused people are processed like cattle. There is no emotional engagement. There is no universal struggle between good and evil. Criminal justice is often nothing more than a bunch of legal professionals sipping coffee and squabbling behind the scenes over the fair resolution of a horrible crime, and all of this has to fit within the concept of the "billable hour."

Justice may not always be denied in this foul system of justice we have invented, but it is almost always defiled. The long arm of the law has atrophied, only to be replaced by the stench of marketplace justice.

Afterword

I INTENDED THIS BOOK to shed light on some of the nasty side effects of delegating responsibility for the administration of criminal justice to a professional knowledge elite. You can draw your own conclusions. But there is something in the way of a conclusion I should get off my chest: there are too many lawyers in North America. Their numbers keep growing, and there's not a lemming among them. Too much of anything is bad for the soul. *Meden Agan*. Too many soldiers and not enough peace. Too many cops and not enough liberty. Too many lawyers and not enough justice. That's the conclusion, plain and simple.

But I care more about beginnings. Fresh starts. Enough of all this talk about lawyers being a cancer on society. Don't forget that we invited this virus to stay, so we really should stop moaning about the disease. I must have satisfied your appetite for lawyer-bashing, and now the question is what to do with your full belly. You might just purge yourself and go back to watching reruns of *Ally McBeal* in syndication. That would be a mistake. I hope I haven't written this professional suicide note for nothing.

It's easy to poke fun, but a lot harder to fill the holes once you're done with the poking. I have not really tried to fill the holes; but I guess that is what I want you to do. I have provided plenty of reasons for advocating lawyercide, and now you have to figure out what type of justice system you want once the lawyers are run out of town. The reconstruction of contemporary criminal justice is a daunting task, and I ask your forgiveness for not providing you with a complete vision for the future. But this book is animated by the Japanese philosophy of *kaizen*; that is, taking small steps towards the achievement of a goal instead of trying to achieve change through dramatic upheaval. As Lao Tze said, "a journey of a thousand miles must begin with the first step." The first step has been the advocating of lawyercide, and now the real work begins of constructing a justice system that is responsive to the needs of ordinary people.

Despite the gloomy tone of this book, I wrote it in the hope of leading people to discover how important it is to take personal responsibility for the conflicts in their lives instead of delegating responsibility to legal professionals. I feel the same way about delegating responsibility to doctors. The ordinary person has to regain control over two vital facets of everyday life: health and interpersonal relations. Medical and legal professionals do not have a monopoly on truth. Doctors and lawyers are good at dealing with a problem when it has reached an interminable impasse. Cut out the tumour. Replace heart valves. Send a criminal to jail. These are all desperate measures taken when the problem has not been attended to at early stages. Most doctors know shit about measures that can be taken to allow health and vitality to flourish. And most lawyers are pathetically inept when it comes to restoring harmony. In fact, both doctors and lawyers are in a conflict of interest when it comes to harmony, whether it be in health or interpersonal relations. If doctors focused their energies on preventive medicine, they would lose a lot of business in cutting people open and maintaining them on pharmaceutical cocktails. If lawyers focused their energies on mediating social conflict as it arose, they would lose a lot of business conducting show trials for their clients.

Life can be hard. Life can be depressing. At times, the weight of responsibility can become so overbearing that we welcome the opportunity to have Mr. Bastard clean up our conflicts. It makes sense to hire someone to clean your home, walk your dog or prepare your income tax return. You lose nothing by delegating some of the boring necessities of life, but you lose a great deal when you hide behind a lawyer instead of directly confronting a source of serious conflict in your life. It's kind of like selling your soul to the devil. The devil may be able to solve your problem, but you are left with a hole where your heart used to be. As hokey as it may sound, adversity builds character, and you can acquire great moral strength by getting your hands dirty taking care of your interpersonal conflicts.

Ted Kaczynski hit the nail on the head. He was a mathematics professor. Now he's better known as the Unabomber. From 1978 to 1995 he conducted an increasingly deadly campaign of violence that included thirteen bombings and three deaths. His reign of terror was prompted by fear that technology was stripping us of our humanity by taking away all sense of personal responsibility. The Unabomber expressed a theme that dominates modern thought: we fear we are losing control over our lives. Many people are not affected by the alienation from self and society. But others either lash out like the Unabomber or become withdrawn shells of humanity, passing their time with television and the Internet.

Both the Unabomber and I feel strongly about the importance of instilling a sense of personal responsibility into our alienated lives; the Unabomber planted a few bombs, and I wrote this book. Time to shake the foundation. As we move deeply into the Internet age, the alienation that defines the modern era is bound to grow by leaps and bounds. Soon we will all be fucking in virtual reality, with no fear of STDs and no chance of authentic emotional engagement. We are headed towards a digital world of instant gratification. Conflict is analog. It's messy. So we're more than happy to call in the lawyers to tell us what to do. This is a bad habit that must be broken.

There is so little justice in this world, and it is easy to blame the legal professionals. They have not delivered on their promise of justice for all. But the first step in taking personal responsibility is to mute the impulse to blame others for the screw-up. The lawyers we hate are a product of human design. We want our lawyers to be arrogant and aggressive pit bulls, but we condemn the very metaphor of advocacy we have spun. The lawyers are not really the villains in this sordid tale of justice defiled. They are just "moral menials"—a profession that bears the burden of having to engage in morally suspect behaviour on our behalf. I came across the term "moral menials" when reading a book called *The Anatomy of Disgust*, and the following passage convinced me that it is unfair and disingenuous to condemn legal professionals for corrupting the ideal of justice. Professor William Ian Miller wrote:

> Notice that a considerable number of the vices that prompt disgust—cruelty, hypocrisy, betrayal—tend to be institutionalized politically and socially. Take hangmen, lawyers, and politicians, for example. All are what might be called necessary evils. Without hangmen and lawyers, the judicial system cannot carry out its mission; without politicians public order seems largely unachievable and only imaginable as utopian fantasy. I call these people *moral menials;* they perform functions in the moral order similar to those played by garbagemen and butchers in the system of provisioning, by hod carriers in building, by scavengers and bottom feeders in various ecosystems. Moral menials deal with moral dirt, or they have to get morally dirty to do what the polity needs them to do. And despite the fact that we need to attract people to this kind of labor, we still hold them

accountable for being so attracted. They are seduced by its benefits; they choose to do these labors. Their having so chosen; however, is not what disgusts; their choosing is only cited as partial justification for blaming them for disgusting us on other grounds ... It is not just that their evils are necessary; it is that the notion of necessary evil so often involves vices that disgust: these are the ordinary vices of hypocrisy (lawyers and politicians), betrayal (politicians), fawning (politicians and lawyers), and cruelty (hangmen and politicians).[1]

If legal professionals are just doing what we want them to do, then it is time to put an end to all the lawyer-bashing. But if you really care about the pursuit of justice, it is time to break the addiction of having legal professionals do your dirty work. Real justice will emerge only with a high degree of emotional engagement and personal responsibility. Letting lawyers do your dirty work gives you only the illusion of justice. You're just being stroked when real criminal justice should be more like good sex: personal, intimate, messy and powerful.

Both community and personal involvement in criminal-justice issues are required. It was done in the past and can be recaptured today. Of course, community involvement works much better in tight-knit communities and pre-industrial societies. I don't even really know what community means in an urban mosaic, other than distinctions borne by ethnicity and race. But ethnicity, religion or race are categories of exclusion that cannot be fairly employed in defining community for the purpose of providing an essential public service. There is nothing preventing us from defining community in any manner we so choose.

Today we have no idea what it means to live in a community for the purposes of the administration of criminal justice. We put up those "Neighbourhood Watch" signs, with the peering eyes and the illusion of constant surveillance, but that is not what I mean by community. I'm talking about a community court that deals with all instances of minor criminality within a certain defined geographical area. Justice would be dispensed by community members who serve on a rotating volunteer basis. The breach of social or community order would be explored without the filters of evidentiary rules and procedural imperatives. Supervision of convicted offenders could be undertaken by ordinary residents who have a vested interest in making sure the morally indifferent offender does not evolve into the cruel bastard.

There is so much that can be done to reclaim control over inter-personal conflict. There are so many prototypes to draw upon, from the current aboriginal sentencing circles to the Kpelle moot of pre-industrial Liberia. But before we can even begin to reconfigure and privatize criminal justice, we have to get over our characteristic aversion to "getting involved." I am saddened every time I read about a pitched battle over the placement of a halfway house for paroled convicts in a residential neighbourhood. I understand the fears of parents, but I can't understand the short-sighted indifference to the importance of reintegrating offenders into society. We don't have the death penalty, so everyone will be released from prison at some point. Putting them in a halfway house on Baffin Island will not help. They have to move into our neighbourhoods, and we have to accept some responsibility for their re-entry into our world. "Take a felon out for lunch" would be a much better approach than our characteristic "Keep that son of a bitch out of my community." Unless we accept greater personal and community participation in the administration of our criminal law, justice will always be defiled. I know that the idea of community and community involvement can sound creepy and suffocating. I usually get all shaky when people start talking about community initiatives. Nonetheless, this is our only hope if we truly care about the importance of taking personal responsibility for the protection of our moral universe.

The legal universe we currently inhabit is destructive to the spirit. Did you know that you can stumble upon a drowning child and simply pull up a lounge chair and watch the show? Anglo–American–Canadian criminal law does not impose any obligations to rescue a stranger from peril. There are some obligations between defined family members, and some obligations placed upon people in a position of care, but our system of law generally shields people from personal involvement. Remember Kitty Genovese? In New York in 1964, dozens of people watched her being attacked outside of an apartment complex, and not one resident called the police. This is all legally proper. This is the type of world you buy into when you delegate responsibility to legal professionals. I'm not saying we all have to act like Superman and try to save anyone we see in peril, even if puts us at risk. But I'm sure lots of you don't want to live in a legal universe that fosters indifference, selfishness and *schadenfreude* (the malicious enjoyment of another's misfortunes).

I know in my heart that most people reading this book have the intelligence and wherewithal to take care of their personal conflicts. Sure, when the conflict escalates into a very serious crime we want the assistance of the state in prosecuting the offender. But don't be fooled into thinking that you don't have the acumen and the courage to stay personally involved in the morality play of the criminal trial. It is your morality play, and you are the leading character. Criminal justice should focus on the offender/victim dynamic instead of on the performance values of legally trained monkeys. The criminal trial should focus on real people with real problems instead of such knowledge-elite-constructed illusions as "urban survival psychosis," "black rage," "television intoxication" and "post-traumatic stress disorder." The experts want to put us into categories to avoid dealing with the chaos of engagement with the real person. The human spirit cannot thrive when it is being jammed into a Procrustean bed of abstract legal categories.

I leave you with this. In 1996, there was a case involving a woman in Alberta who had been beating her naked seven-year-old child with a spatula. The child also suffered brain injuries consistent with being thrown down or violently pushed against a wall. The mother had no memory of the assaults. Ultimately, she was convicted of aggravated assault, but her conviction was appealed to the Alberta Court of Appeal in 1996. Why? Because the lawyers claimed that the trial judge misapprehended the evidence they tendered relating to "intermittent explosive disorder (IED)." The appeal was ultimately dismissed, but one of the three judges would have ordered a new trial.[2] For what? To properly explore the operation of intermittent explosive disorder as a defence to assault. I don't care whether you call it IED, CIA, PCB or TIT, this woman simply had a bad temper. Bad temper cannot be a defence to assault even if you dress it up in the language of the knowledge elites. Intermittent explosive disorder. What a crock of shit, and what an avoidance of personal responsibility! It's insulting to the accused, and it's hurtful to the victim. Expect more of the same if we don't start to do something about the knowledge elites and their monopoly over criminal justice.

My parting advice, in the words of Voltaire, is "tend to your garden." Get your hands dirty with real-life problems. Justice is not a metaphysical exercise understood only by people with LL.B or Ph.D. after their names. It may not harm the human spirit to buy fruits and vegetables grown in other people's gardens, but it is spiritually unhealthy to hire professionals to pull the weeds from your interpersonal garden.

I thank you for reading my book, and I invite you to dream of a world in which time is not measured in billable hours, a world in which everybody recognizes that a handshake has more power than a contract, a world in which the right to silence is traded in for the right to scream on your own behalf. In 1620, Dick the Butcher set out the blueprint for the future: "the first thing we do, let's kill all the lawyers." I have tried to lay the foundation for Dick's master plan. The rest is up to you.

Namaste.

Endnotes

Chapter 1
Killing All the Lawyers

1. See, for example, Ekos Research Associates Inc., *Rethinking Government* (Ottawa: March/April 1997); C. Wilson, *Quo Vide: A Matter of Public Trust* (Ottawa: Centre on Governance, University of Ottawa, March/April 1998). Working paper subsequently published in the Canadian Bar Association's *National*, vol.7(2); see also the annual *Maclean's*/CTV poll, published in *Maclean's* magazine.
2. Mojo Nixon, "Destroy All Lawyers," *Otis*, Enigma Records, 1990.
3. L. Bruce, *How to Talk Dirty and Influence People: An Autobiography* (New York: Fireside, 1992) at 52.
4. D. Brazier, *The Feeling Buddha: A Buddhist Psychology of Character, Adversity and Passion* (New York: Fromm International, 2000).
5. As quoted in D.P. Goleman, *Emotional Intelligence* (New York: Bantam Books, 1995) at 114.
6. R.K.L. Collins and D.M. Skover, *The Trials of Lenny Bruce: The Fall and Rise of an American Icon* (Naperville, IL: Sourcebooks Inc., 2002) at 3.
7. *Supra* note 3.
8. S. Hansen, J. Jensen and W. Roberts, *The Little Red Schoolbook* (New York: Pocket Books, 1971).
9. A. Hoffman, "Revolution for the Hell of It" in *The Best of Abbie Hoffman* (New York: Four Walls, Eight Windows, 1989) at 141.

Chapter 2
When the Honourable Profession Meets the Oldest Profession

1. A. Kinsey, *Sexual Behavior in the Human Male* (Philadelphia: W.B. Sanders Co., 1948); A. Kinsey, *Sexual Behavior in the Human Female* (Philadelphia: W.B. Sanders Co., 1953).
2. *R. v. Tremblay* (1993), 84 C.C.C. (3d) 97 (S.C.C.).
3. Statistics Canada, *Juristat: Street Prostitution in Canada* (Ottawa: 1997).

Chapter 3
Is the Buddha in Paul Bernardo?

1. A. Einstein, *Why War?: The Correspondence Between Albert Einstein and Sigmund Freud*, trans. Dr. Fritz and Dr. Anna Moellenhoff (Chicago: Chicago Institute for Psychoanalysis, 1978).
2. *Ibid.* at 44–45.
3. A. Calaprice, ed., *The Quotable Einstein* (Princeton: Princeton University Press, 1996) at 224.
4. R. Graysmith, *Zodiac* (New York: Berkeley Books, 1976) at 54–55.

5. "Canadians Indifferent to Killings," *Halifax Chronicle-Herald* (19 May 2001) C1.
6. As quoted in C. Wilson, *A Criminal History of Mankind* (London: Grafton Books, 1985) at 214.
7. M. Wolfgang, "Pioneers in Criminology: Cesare Lombroso (1835–1909)" (1961) 32 J. Crim. L., Crim. & Pol. Sci. 361 at 369.
8. D. Thomas, *The Marquis de Sade: A New Biography* (New York: Citadel Press, 1992) at 253.

Chapter 4
As Nasty as I Wanna Be

1. *My Secret Life*, as quoted in C. Wilson, *A Criminal History of Mankind* (London: Grafton Books, 1985) at 499.
2. T.F. Berger, *Lie with Me* (Toronto: Gutter Press, 2001) at 71.
3. L. Bruce, *How to Talk Dirty and Influence People: An Autobiography* (New York: Fireside, 1992), cover.
4. *R.* v. *Stewart* (1980), 16 C.R. (3d) 87 (Ont. Prov. Ct.).
5. See A. Young, "News from the Front: The War on Obscenity and the Death of Doctrinal Purity" (1987) 25 Osgoode Hall L.J. 306 at 309.
6. *R.* v. *Brodie* (1962), 132 C.C.C. 161 (S.C.C.).
7. *R.* v. *Towne Cinema Theatres Ltd.* (1985), 45 C.R. (3d) 1 at 17.
8. M. Cronin, "X Rated," *Time* (7 March 1990) 62.
9. 2 Live Crew, *As Nasty as They Wanna Be*, Lil' Joe Records, 1990.
10. *Ibid.*
11. A.D. Clay, *"Woman Comics": The Day the Laughter Died*, Def American, 1990.
12. S. Kinison, *Leader of the Banned*, WEA/Warner Bros, 1990.
13. *R.* v. *Emery*, Transcript of Proceedings, May 13, 1991, at 80.
14. *R.* v. *Emery* (1991), 4 O.R. (3d) 344 (Ont. Prov. Ct.).
15. *Ibid.*
16. *Supra* note 13 at 109.
17. *Reference Re: ss. 193 & 195.1(1)(c) of the Criminal Code* (1990), 56 C.C.C. (3d) 65 at 97.
18. *Switzman* v. *Elbling*, [1957] S.C.R. 285 at 306.
19. *R.* v. *Butler* (1992), 70 C.C.C. (3d) 129 (S.C.C.).
20. *Ibid.* at 164.
21. *R.* v. *Duthie Books Ltd.* [1967] 1 C.C.C. 254 (B.C.C.A.).
22. *R.* v. *Wagner* (1985), 43 C.R. (3d) 318 (Alta. Q.B.).
23. *R.* v. *Emery*, Transcript of Proceedings, May 13, 1991, at 80.
24. B. Kutchinsky, "Pornography and Obscenity" in R. Dharvan and C. Davies, eds., *Censorship and Obscenity* (Totowa, N.J.: Rowman & Littlefield, 1978) at 111.

Chapter 5
Getting Laid

1. R. Davenport-Hines, *Sex, Death and Punishment: Attitudes to Sex and Sexuality in Britain Since the Renaissance* (London: Fontana Press, 1991) at 95.
2. *Ibid.* at 64.
3. *Ibid.* at 65.
4. *Ibid.* at 82.
5. *R. v. Potts and McKeigan*, [1999] O.J. No. 4737 (Ont. Ct. Jus.) at para 4.
6. *Ibid.* at para 5.
7. S. Bell, *Whore Carnival* (New York: Autonomedia, 1995) at 15.
8. *R. v. St. Pierre* (1974), 17 C.C.C. (2d) 489 at 491 (Ont. C.A.).
9. *Ibid.* at 492.
10. As quoted in Parker, "The Legal Regulation of Sexual Activity and the Protection of Females" (1983) 21 Osgoode Hall L.J. 187 at 194.
11. *Ibid.* at 201.
12. *Ibid.* at 200.
13. *Ibid.* at 202.
14. United States Commission on Obscenity and Pornography, *The Report of the Commission on Obscenity and Pornography* (New York: Random House, 1970).
15. *R. v. Pappa John* (1980), 14 C.R. (3d) 243 (S.C.C.).
16. *R. v. C. (M.A.)* (1995), 98 C.C.C. (3d) 481 (Ont. C.A.).
17. *R. v. F. (R.P.)* (1996), 105 C.C.C. (3d) 435 (N.S.C.A.); *R. v. S. (M.)* (1996), 111 C.C.C. (3d) 467 (B.C.C.A.).
18. *R. v. Sloan* (1994), 89 C.C.C. (3d) 97 (Ont. C.A.).
19. "Ottawa Talking Tough on Prostitution Curves," *Toronto Star* (22 September 1994) A1.
20. *R. v. Chase* (1987), 37 C.C.C. (3d) 97 at 103 (S.C.C.).
21. *R. v. K.B.V.* (1993), 82 C.C.C. (3d) 97 (S.C.C.).
22. *R. v. Chau*, [1986] A.J. No. 1019 (Alta. Prov. Ct.) at para 9.
23. *R. v. Cuerrier* (1988), 127 C.C.C. (3d) 1 at 34 (S.C.C.).
24. *R. v. Ewanchuk* (1999), 131 C.C.C. (3d) 481 (S.C.C.).
25. *Ibid.* at 499.
26. D. Hatch, "Culpability and Capitulation: Sexual Assault and Consent in the Wake of *R. v. Ewanchuk*," (1999) 43 Can. L.Q. 51, at 62–63.
27. *Ibid.* at 58–59; S. Schulhoffer, "Unwanted Sex," *The Atlantic Monthly* (October 1998).
28. *Supra* note 24 at 513–16.
29. *Ibid.*
30. *Ibid.*
31. A. Dworkin, *Intercourse* (New York: The Free Press, 1987) at 63.
32. *Ibid.* at 122.

Chapter 6
Approaching the Fringe

1. "Frankly the Public Doesn't Give a Damn," *Toronto Sun* (25 August 1999); "Swingers Aren't So Tacky After All," *X-TRA* (9 September 1999).
2. "Convicted Owner of Montreal Swingers Club Ordered to Pay $2500 Fine," Canadian Press (20 September 2000).
3. See *Little Sisters Book and Art Emporium* v. *Canada* (2000), 150 C.C.C. (3d) 1 (S.C.C.)
4. "Police Make Secret Deal with Gay Bars," *Now* (10 August 1999).
5. "Pussy Bites Back," *Now* (28 September 2000); "The Paw That Scratches," *Eye* (14 June 2001); "Barging In," *The Globe and Mail* (25 September 2000).
6. *R.* v. *Tremblay* (1993), 84 C.C.C. (3d) 97 (S.C.C.).
7. *R.* v. *Mara* (1997), 115 C.C.C. (3d) 539 at 551–52 (S.C.C.).
8. *R.* v. *Blais-Pelletier* (1999), 142 C.C.C. (3d) 288 (S.C.C.).
9. *R.* v. *Bedford*, Ruling, August 21, 1998, at 1380.
10. *R.* v. *Bedford*, Transcript of Evidence, August 20, 1998, at 1261.
11. *Ibid.* at 1262–63.
12. *Ibid.* at 1333.
13. *Ibid.* at 1226–27.
14. As quoted in R.F. Baumeister, *Masochism and the Self* (Hillsdale, NJ: Lawrence Erlbaum Associates, 1989) at 102.
15. *R.* v. *Bedford*, Transcript of Evidence, July 27, 1998, at 970.
16. *Ibid.* at 974–75.
17. *Ibid.* at 1003–4.
18. *R.* v. *Bedford*, Ruling, August 21, 1998, at 1355.
19. *R.* v. *Bedford*, [1998] O.J. No. 4033 at para 11.
20. *R.* v. *Bedford* (2000), 143 C.C.C. (3d) 311 at 321 (Ont. C.A.).
21. See Baumeister, *Masochism and the Self*, at 102.

Chapter 7
Getting Stoned

1. J.E. Harrison, *Prolegomena to the Study of Greek Religion* (Cambridge: Cambridge University Press, 1903); T. Szasz, *Ceremonial Chemistry: The Ritual Persecution of Drugs, Addicts, and Pushers* (New York: Anchor Press/Doubleday, 1974).
2. Szasz, *Ceremonial Chemistry*, at 19.
3. Statistics Canada, *Juristat: Canadian Crime Statistics, 2000* (Ottawa: 2001).
4. Addiction Research Foundation, *Cannabis, Health and Public Policy* (Toronto: 1996).
5. R. Siegel, *Intoxication: Life in Pursuit of Artificial Paradise* (New York: E.P. Dutton, 1989).
6. J. Shedler and J. Block, "Adolescent Drug Use and Psychological Health" (1990) 45 Am. Psych. 612.

7. C. Baudelaire, *Artificial Paradises*, trans. S. Diamond (New York: Citadel Press, 1996).

8. Ram Dass, *Be Here Now* (New York: Crown Publishing, 1978).

9. Statistics Canada, *Juristat: Drug Use and Crime* (Ottawa: 1994); Statistics Canada, *Juristat: Homicide in Canada, 1999* (Ottawa: 2000).

10. *R.* v. *Rowbotham* (1988), 41 C.C.C. (3d) 1 (Ont. C.A.).

11. E. Murphy, *The Black Candle* (Toronto: Coles, 1922/1973) at 332.

12. "Marijuana Smokers Seized with Sudden Craze to Kill," *Toronto Star* (2 February 1938).

13. S. Grof, "The Effects of LSD on Chromosomes, Genetic Mutation, Fetal Development and Malignancy" in S. Grof, *LSD Psychotherapy* (Alameda, CA: Hunter House, 1994); L.A. Henderson, "Adverse Reactions to LSD" in W.J. Glass, ed., *LSD: Still with Us After All These Years* (New York: Maxwell Macmillan, 1994).

14. A. Hoffman with J. Silvers, *Steal this Urine Test: Fighting Drug Hysteria in America* (New York: Penguin Books, 1987) at 123.

15. B.K. Alexander, *Peaceful Measures: Canada's Way Out of the "War on Drugs"* (Toronto: University of Toronto Press, 1990) at 160.

16. *Iorfida* v. *MacIntyre* (1994), 93 C.C.C. (3d) 395 (Ont. Gen. Div.).

17. *R.* v. *Clay* (1997), 9 C.R. (5th) 349 (Ont. Gen. Div.); *R.* v. *Clay* (2000), 146 C.C.C. (3d) 276 (Ont. C.A.).

18. "Life's a Risky Business: Health and Accident Statistics," *Ottawa Citizen* (8 August 1997).

19. D. Lenson, *On Drugs* (Minneapolis, MN: University of Minnesota Press, 1995) at 108.

Chapter 8
The Wages of Hypocrisy

1. K. Pemberton, "Police Shot Dog in Front of Mothers, Babies, Hearing Told: Officers Busted in on a Children's Birthday Party Looking for a Drug Suspect," *Vancouver Sun* (1 December 1999) A3.

2. *R.* v. *Clay*, Transcript of Evidence, Testimony of Patricia Erickson, senior research scientist, Addiction Research Foundation, vol. 2, at 473, 531–33; vol. 4 at 906.

3. Statistics Canada, *Juristat: Homicide in Canada, 1999* (Ottawa: 2001).

4. *R.* v. *Garcia-Guiterrez* (1991), 65 C.C.C. (3d) 15 at 19 (B.C.C.A.).

5. *R.* v. *Monney* (1999), 133 C.C.C. (3d) 129 at 151 (S.C.C.).

6. *United States* v. *Montoya de Hernandez*, 105 S. Ct. 3304 (1985).

7. *Ibid.* at 3312.

8. Profile obtained from a law student who had been working with Canada Customs.

9. *United States* v. *Montoya de Hernandez*, 105 S. Ct. 3304 (1985) at 3319; see also "Strip Search Statistics Analysis to Continue," *The Globe and Mail* (15 December 2000) A22, which discusses how strip searches conducted

by Metropolitan Toronto Police fail to yield evidence 47% of the time. A recent American study shows some improvement in the success rate of intrusive body searches at American airports: 23% of strip searches led to the finding of drugs, see S. Barr, "U.S. Study Finds Wide Disparity in Customs' Intrusive Searches," *Washington Post* (10 April 2000).

10. J. Duncanson and J. Quinn, "Five Officers Seek Stay of 193 Charges," *Toronto Star* (9 October 2001) B7.

11. See R.C. Way, "The Law of Police Authority: The McDonald Commission and the McLeod Report" (1985) 9 Dalhousie L.J. 683.

12. *R. v. Brezack* (1949), 9 C.R. 73 at 78 (B.C.C.A.).

13. *R. v. Shirose* (1999), 133 C.C.C. (3d) 257 at 301 (S.C.C.).

14. *R. v. Barnes* (1991), 63 C.C.C. (3d) 1 at 5 (S.C.C.).

15. *Ibid.*

16. *R. v. Molis* (1980), 55 C.C.C. (2d) 558 (S.C.C.).

17. A. Young, "Privacy as an Endangered Species: The False Promise of the Charter" in *Annual Lectures of the Law Society of Upper Canada—2000* (Toronto: 2001); A. Young, "Adversarial Justice and the Charter of Rights: Stunting the Growth of the 'Living Tree'—Part I," (1997) 39 Can. L.Q. 406.

18. Solicitor General, Canada, *Annual Report on Electronic Surveillance, 1999* (Ottawa: 2000).

19. *Ibid.*

20. T. Tyler, "2 Jailed for Dealing $20 in Crack," *Toronto Star* (14 September 1996) A2.

21. N. Prion, "Metro Officers Must Serve 60 Days for Role in Planting Coke on Suspect," *Toronto Star* (29 June 1994) A22.

Chapter 9
Why We Punish

1. F.W. Nietzsche, *On the Genealogy of Morals*, trans. W. Kaufmann (New York: Vintage Books, 1969) at 69.

2. J. Roberts and A. Doob, "Sentencing and Public Opinion: Taking False Shadows for True Substances" (1989) 27 Osgoode Hall L.J. 491.

3. As taken from G. Watson, "Responsibility and the Limits of Evil: Variations on a Strawsonian Theme" in F. Schoeman, ed., *Responsibility, Character and the Emotions: New Essays in Moral Psychology* (Cambridge, England: Cambridge University Press, 1987) 268–71.

4. The primary study is reviewed in *McCleskey v. Kemp*, 107 S. Ct. 1756 (1987).

5. G. Thomas III and D. Edelman, "An Evaluation of Conservative Crime Control Theology" (1988) 63 Notre Dame L.R. 123.

6. Statistics Canada, *Juristat: Trends in Criminal Victimization: 1988–1993* (Ottawa: 1994).

7. *Supra* note 3 at 272–73.

8. Statistics Canada, *Juristat: Public Attitudes Toward the Criminal Justice System* (Ottawa: 2000).

Chapter 10
Our Criminal Code
1. Government of Canada, *The Criminal Law in Canadian Society* (Ottawa: 1982); Law Reform Commission of Canada, *Our Criminal Law* (Ottawa: 1976).
2. *R. v. Sedley*, [1663] as described in Curll, *Cobbett's Complete Collection of State Trials*, Vol. 17 (1727) at 155.
3. *Frey v. Fedoruk* (1950), 97 C.C.C. 1 (S.C.C.).
4. *R. v. Jobidon* (1991), 66 C.C.C. (3d) 457 (S.C.C.).
5. As taken from *Lawyers: Jokes, Quotes and Anecdotes—2001 Calendar* (Kansas City: Andrews McMeel Publishing, 2000).
6. *R. v. Lofthouse* (1988), 62 C.R. (3d) 157 (Ont. C.A.).
7. *R. v. Campbell* (1973), 21 C.R.N.S. 273 (Alta. Dist. Ct.).
8. *Ibid.* at 280.

Chapter 11
The True Nature of Crime in Canada
1. *R. v. Kuyan* (1988), 43 C.C.C. (3d) 339 (Ont. C.A.).
2. Statistics Canada, *Juristat: Crime Statistics in Canada, 2000* (Ottawa: 2001).
3. Statistics Canada, *Juristat: Homicide in Canada, 1999* (Ottawa: 2000).
4. See, for example Stone, "Interpersonal Violence in English Society" (1983) 101 Past & Present 22; Paul Brantingham and Patricia Brantingham, *Patterns in Crime* (London: Collier MacMillan Publishers, 1984); J.M. Beattie, *Crime and the Courts in England, 1660–1800* (Princeton: Princeton University Press, 1986); T. Gurr, "Historical Trends in Violent Crime: A Critical Review of the Evidence" in M. Tonry and N. Morris, eds., *Crime and Justice: Annual Review of Research* (Chicago: University of Chicago Press, 1981).
5. Statistics Canada, *Juristat: Break and Enter, 1999* (Ottawa: 2000).
6. F. Adler, *Nations Not Obsessed with Crime.* (Littleton, CO: F.B. Rothman, 1983).
7. *Supra* note 3.
8. Statistics Canada, *Juristat: Public Perceptions of Crime* (Ottawa: 1995).
9. "Crime Rates Down, Our Fears Are Up," *Toronto Star* (20 August 1995) A12.
10. *Ibid.*; L. Miljan, *Homicide in Canada: What Television News Does and Does Not Say* (Fraser Forum, September 1998).
11. Statistics Canada, *Juristat: Crime Trends in Canada, 1962–1990* (Ottawa: 1992); Statistics Canada, *Juristat: Crime Statistics in Canada, 2000* (Ottawa: 2001).
12. *Supra* note 2; Statistics Canada, *Juristat: Crime Statistics in Canada, 2001* (Ottawa: 2002).
13. Statistics Canada, *Juristat: Crime Statistics in Canada, 1999* (Ottawa: 2000); Statistics Canada, *Juristat: The Justice Factfinder, 1998* (Ottawa: 2000); Statistics Canada, *Juristat: Crime Statistics in Canada, 2001* (Ottawa: 2002).

14. *Supra* note 2.

15. *Ibid.*; Statistics Canada, *Juristat: Crime Statistics in Canada, 1999* (Ottawa: 2000); Statistics Canada, *Juristat: Crime Statistics in Canada, 1996* (Ottawa: 1997); Statistics Canada, *Juristat: Criminal Harassment* (Ottawa: 2000).

16. Statistics Canada, *Juristat: Criminal Victimization in Canada, 1999* (Ottawa: 2000); Statistics Canada, *Juristat: Victims' Use of Police and Social Services* (Ottawa: 1995).

17. Statistics Canada, *Juristat: Trends in Criminal Victimization: 1988–1993* (Ottawa: 1994); Statistics Canada, *Juristat: Criminal Victimization in Canada, 1999* (Ottawa: 2000).

18. Statistics Canada, *Juristat: Youth Violent Crime* (Ottawa: 1999); Statistics Canada, *Juristat: Youth Court Statistics, 2000/01* (Ottawa: 2002).

19. Statistics Canada, *Juristat: The Justice Factfinder, 1998* (Ottawa: 1999); Statistics Canada, *Juristat: Canadian Crime Statistics, 1996* (Ottawa: 1997); Statistics Canada, *Juristat: Violent Crime in Canada, 1996* (Ottawa: 1997); Statistics Canada, *Juristat: Crime Statistics in Canada, 2001* (Ottawa: 2002).

20. Statistics Canada, *Juristat: Sex Offenders* (Ottawa: 1999).

21. Statistics Canada, *Juristat: Trends in Criminal Victimization: 1988–1993* (Ottawa: 1994); Statistics Canada, *Juristat: Criminal Victimization in Canada, 1999* (Ottawa: 2000); Statistics Canada, *Juristat: Gender Differences Among Violent Crime Victims* (Ottawa: 1992); Statistics Canada, *Juristat: Violent Crime in Canada* (Ottawa: 1996).

22. Statistics Canada, *Juristat: Homicide in Canada, 1999* (Ottawa: 2000); Statistics Canada, *Juristat: Homicide in Canada, 2001* (Ottawa: 2002).

23. *Supra* note 3.

24. *Ibid.*

25. *Ibid.*; Statistics Canada, *Juristat: Homicide in Canada, 2001* (Ottawa: 2002).

26. Statistics Canada, *Juristat: Homicide in Canada, 2001* (Ottawa: 2002).

27. Statistics Canada, *Juristat: Sentencing in Adult Provincial Courts—A Study of Nine Canadian Jurisdictions, 1993/94* (Ottawa: 1997).

28. Statistics Canada, *Juristat: Adult Criminal Court Statistics, 2001/02* (Ottawa: 2003).

29. Statistics Canada, *Juristat: Adult Criminal Court Statistics, 2001/02* (Ottawa: 2003).

30. Statistics Canada, *Juristat: Justice Spending in Canada, 1998/99* (Ottawa: 1999); Statistics Canada, *Juristat: Justice Spending in Canada, 2000/01* (Ottawa: 2002).

31. Statistics Canada, *Juristat: Justice Spending in Canada, 1998/99* (Ottawa: 1999).

32. *Ibid.*; Statistics Canada, *Juristat: Justice Spending in Canada, 2000/01* (Ottawa: 2002).

33. Statistics Canada, *Juristat: Adult Correctional Services in Canada, 2000/01* (Ottawa: 2002).

34. *R. v. Gladue* (1999), 133 C.C.C. (3d) 385 at 407 (S.C.C.); Report for the Federal/Provincial/Territorial Ministers Responsible for Justice, Corrections Population Growth, (Ottawa, May 1996); Statistics Canada, *Juristat: Adult Correctional Services in Canada, 2000/01* (Ottawa: 2002).
35. Correctional Service of Canada, *Basic Facts about Federal Corrections* (Ottawa, August 2000).
36. Correctional Service of Canada, *The Safe Return of Offenders to the Community* (Ottawa, April 2000); Statistics Canada, *Juristat: Adult Correctional Services in Canada, 1995/96* (Ottawa: 1997); Statistics Canada, *Juristat: Adult Correctional Services in Canada, 2000/01* (Ottawa: 2002).
37. Statistics Canada, *Juristat: The Justice Factfinder, 1997* (Ottawa: 1999); Statistics Canada, *Juristat: Adult Correctional Services in Canada, 1998/99* (Ottawa: 2000); Statistics Canada, *Juristat: Adult Correctional Services in Canada, 2000/01* (Ottawa: 2002).
38. Statistics Canada, *Juristat: The Justice Factfinder, 1998* (Ottawa: 2000); Correctional Service of Canada, *The Safe Return of Offenders to the Community* (Ottawa, April 2000).
39. Correctional Service of Canada, *The Safe Return of Offenders to the Community* (Ottawa, April 2000).
40. Statistics Canada, *Juristat: The Justice Factfinder, 1997* (Ottawa: 1999).
41. Statistics Canada, *Juristat: Public Attitudes Toward the Criminal Justice System* (Ottawa: 2000).
42. *Ibid.*; Statistics Canada, *Juristat: Trends in Criminal Victimization, 1988–1993* (Ottawa: 1994); Statistics Canada, *Juristat: Public Perceptions of Crime* (Ottawa: 1995); Statistics Canada, *Juristat: The Justice Factfinder, 1998* (Ottawa: 2000); Statistics Canada, *Juristat: Criminal Victimization in Canada* (Ottawa, 2000.).

Chapter 12
A Taste of Cruelty

1. C. Wilson, *A Criminal History of Mankind* (London: Grafton Books, 1985) at 614.
2. T.E. Gaddis and J.O. Long, *Killer: A Journal of Murder* (New York: The Macmillan Company, 1970).
3. *Ibid.*
4. *Ibid.*
5. *Ibid.*
6. *Ibid.*
7. J.H. Abbott, *In the Belly of the Beast: Letters from Prison* (New York: Vintage Books, 1981).
8. *Ibid.* at 110.
9. P.E. Dietz, R. Hazelwood and J. Warren, "The Sexually Sadistic Criminal and His Offenses" (1990) 18 Bull. Am. Acad. Psychiatry L. 27.

Chapter 13
The Legal Construction of Crime

1. G. Walker, *Love and Anger* (Toronto: Coach House Press, 1990) at 13.
2. M. Kelman, "Interpretive Construction in the Substantive Criminal Law," (1981) 33 Stanf. L. Rev. 591.
3. *Ibid.* at 592.
4. R.J. Lifton, *Thought Reform and the Psychology of Totalism: A Study of "Brainwashing" in China* (New York: Norton, 1961).
5. *R. v. Smithers* (1977), 40 C.R.N.S. 79 (S.C.C.).
6. *R. v. Lavallee* (1990), 55 C.C.C. (3d) 97 (S.C.C.).
7. *Her Majesty v. Meli*, [1954] 1 W.L.R. 228 (Privy Council).
8. *R. v. Cooper* (1993), 78 C.C.C. (3d) 289 (S.C.C.).
9. *Ibid.* at 292.
10. *Ibid.* at 299.
11. *D.P.P. v. Morgan*, [1976] A.C. 182.
12. *U.S. v. Chadwick*, 433 U.S. 1, 9 (1971).
13. L. Mayers, *Shall We Amend the Fifth Amendment?* (Westport, CT: Greenwood Press, 1959); W. Schaefer, *The Suspect and Society* (Evanston, IL: Northwestern University Press, 1967); H. Kalven and H. Zeisel, *The American Jury* (Boston: Little, Brown, 1966); K. Greenawalt, "Silence as a Moral and Constitutional Right" (1981) 23 William and Mary L. Rev. 15.
14. *R. v. S. (R.J.)* (1995), 96 C.C.C. (3d) 1 (S.C.C.).
15. L. Levy, *Origins of the Fifth Amendment* (Oxford: Oxford University Press, 1968).
16. K. Greenawalt, "Silence."

Chapter 14
The Circle of Victimization

1. *Vanscoy and Even v. Her Majesty the Queen in Right of Ontario* (1999), O.J. No. 1661 (Ont. S.C.).
2. Victims' Bill of Rights, S.O. 1995, c. 6.
3. *Supra* note 1 at para 22.
4. *Ibid.* at para 38.
5. R. Elias, *Victims Still: The Political Manipulation of Crime Victims* (Newbury Park, CA: Sage Publications, 1993) at 45.
6. E. Erez, "Victim Participation in Sentencing: And the Debate Goes On ..." (1994) 3 Int'l Rev. Vict. 17 at 28; S. Garkawe, "The Role of the Victim During Criminal Court Proceedings" (1994) 17 U. New S. Wales L. Rev. 595 at 599; E. Erez and K. Laster, "Neutralizing Victim Reform: Legal Professional's Perspective on Victim and Victim Impact Statements" (1999) 45 Crime and Delinquency 530; H. Kury, M. Kaiser and R. Teske, "The Position of the Victim in Criminal Procedure: The Results of a German Study" (1994) 3 Victimology 111.

7. K. Kennard, "The Victims' Veto" (1989) 77 Calif. L. Rev. 417; E. A. Ziegenhagen, *Victims, Crime and Social Control* (New York: Praeger, 1977); Focus Consultants et al., *Victim Impact Statements in Canada* (Ottawa: Department of Justice, 1990).
8. J. Roberts and A. Doob, "Sentencing and Public Opinion: Taking False Shadows for True Substances" (1989) 27 Osgoode Hall L.J. 491.
9. *R. v. K. (M.)* (1992), 74 C.C.C. (3d) 108 (Man. C.A.).
10. A. Young, "We Must Make Parole Work," *Toronto Star* (5 April 1995).
11. As quoted in Elias, *Victims Still*, at 1.

Chapter 15
No More Mr. Nice Guy

1. "Bernardo Author Hires Top Legal Gun," *The Globe and Mail* (23 September 2000) A20.
2. R. Dooling, "When You Prick Us …," *The National Law Review* (11 October 1999) A19.
3. T. Tyler, "Civility in the Legal Profession," *Toronto Star* (17 October 2001) A1.
4. As quoted in the *Ontario Criminal Lawyers Association Newsletter*, vol. 12 (November 1991).
5. S. Landsman, "The Rise of the Contentious Spirit: Adversary Procedure in 18th Century England" (1990) 75 Cornell L. Rev. 497 at 502.
6. R. Pound, *The Causes of Dissatisfaction with the Administration of Justice*, 29 A.B.A. Rep. 395 (reprinted in 1971), 57 A.B.A.J. 348 at 404.
7. *Supra* note 5 at 515–16.
8. *Ibid.* at 562.
9. *R. v. Boucher* (1954), 110 C.C.C. 263 at 270 (S.C.C.).
10. *R. v. Logiacco* (1984), 11 C.C.C. (3d) 374 at 382 (Ont. C.A.).
11. *R. v. S. (F.)* (2000), 144 C.C.C. (3d) 466 (Ont. C.A.).
12. *R. v. Siu* (1998), 124 C.C.C. (3d) 301 at 319 (B.C.C.A.).
13. *R. v. B. (R.B.)* (2001), 152 C.C.C. (3d) 437 at 441 (B.C.C.A.).
14. *R. v. F. (A.)* (1996), 30 O.R. (3d) 470 at 472 (Ont. C.A.).
15. *R. v. Henderson* (1999), 134 C.C.C. (3d) 131 at 144 (Ont. C.A.).
16. T. Arnold, *The Symbols of Government* (New Haven: Yale University Press, 1935) at 145.
17. *R. v. LaBrecque*, [2001] O.J. No. 3993 (Ont. C.A.).
18. *Ibid.* at para 10.
19. *R. v. Taylor* (1992), 77 C.C.C. (3d) 551 (Ont. C.A.).
20. *Oniel v. Metropolitan Toronto Police Force* (2001), 195 D.L.R. (4th) 106 (Ont. C.A.).
21. *Proulx v. A.G. (Que.)*, [2001] S.C.J. No. 65 (S.C.C.).
22. *R. v. Evans*, [1996] B.C.J. No. 3141 (B.C.S.C.).
23. *R. v. Evans* (1991), 63 C.C.C. (3d) 289 (S.C.C.).

24. *Supra* note 22 at para 14.
25. *R. v. Murray* (2000), 144 C.C.C. (3d) 322 (Ont. S.C.).
26. As quoted in J.W. Teeter Jr., "The Daishonin's Path: Applying Nicherin's Buddhist Principles to American Legal Education" (1999) 30 McGeorge L. Rev. 271 at 287.
27. A. Campo-Flores, "An Ambivalent Profession" (1998) 20 American Lawyer 26.
28. See the Law Firm Associates surveys, published annually in *Canadian Lawyer*.
29. "The 2000 *Canadian Lawyer* Law Firm Associates Survey," *Canadian Lawyer* (November/December 2000).
30. C. Beck et al., "Lawyer Distress: Alcohol Related Problems and Other Psychological Concerns Among a Sample of Practicing Lawyers" (1996) 10 J.L. & Health 1 at 2.
31. As quoted in Teeter, "Daishonin's Path," at 274.
32. A. de Tocqueville, *Democracy in America*, vol. 1, trans. H. Reeve (New York: Schocken Books, 1961) at 322.
33. L. Cohen, "Unrepresentative Justice," *Canadian Lawyer* (August 2001) at 40.

Chapter 16
The Training and Education of Mr. Bastard

1. Beck et al., "Lawyer Distress: Alcohol Related Problems and Other Psychological Concerns Among a Sample of Practicing Lawyers" (1996) 10 J.L. & Health 1 at 2.
2. *Ibid.* at 4; S. Shanfield and G.A.H. Benjamin, "Psychiatric Distress in Law Students" (1985) 35 J. Legal Education 1.
3. G.A.H. Benjamin et al., "The Role of Legal Education in Producing Psychological Distress Among Law Students and Lawyers" (1986) 2 Am. Bar Foundation Research J. 225 at 247.
4. L. Bruce, *How to Talk Dirty and Influence People: An Autobiography* (New York: Fireside, 1992) at 20.
5. See, for example, D. Gambrill, "Law School Should Probe Hiring Practices," *Law Times* (25 June 2001).
6. R.T. Stover, "Making It and Breaking It: The Fate of Public Interest Commitment in Law School" in R.L. Abel, ed., *Lawyers: A Critical Reader* (New York: New Press, 1977) at 79.
7. Benjamin et al., "Role of Legal Education," at 252.
8. See "Judging Canadian Law Schools," *Maclean's* (6 October 1997); "Schools of Thought: The 1997 Law School Survey," *Canadian Lawyer* (January 1997); "The 2001 *Canadian Lawyer* Report Card on Canadian Law Schools," *Canadian Lawyer* (January 2001).
9. "Schools of Thought: The 1997 Law School Survey," *Canadian Lawyer* (January 1997) at 22.

10. "The 2001 *Canadian Lawyer* Report Card on Canadian Law Schools," *Canadian Lawyer* (January 2001) at 28.
11. J. Fekete, *Moral Panic: Biopolitics Rising* (Montreal: Robert Davies Publishing, 1994) at 211.
12. As quoted in J.W. Teeter, "The Daishonin's Path: Applying Nicherin's Buddhist Principles to American Legal Education" (1999) 30 McGeorge L. Rev. 271 at 274.
13. See, for example, J. Tomkovicz, "On Teaching Rape: Reasons, Risks and Rewards" (1992) 102 Yale L.J. 481.
14. S. Schulhofer, "Unwanted Sex," *The Atlantic Monthly* (October 1998).
15. *Healey* v. *Memorial University* (1992), 106 Nfld. & P.E.I.R. 304.
16. York University Discipline Tribunal, In the Matter of Mark Ashton, July 1993, at 20–22.
17. *Ibid.* at 25, 38–39.

Chapter 17
The Illusion of Wisdom

1. "The Court's Strong Voices," *The Globe and Mail* (3 February 2001) A14.
2. *Ibid.*
3. *R.* v. *Kopyto* (1987), 61 C.R. (3d) 209 at 265 (Ont. C.A.).
4. *Ibid.*
5. The advertisement was run in the *Ontario Reports* in 1990. I have kept a copy in my files since then. When the *Ontario Reports* are bound for placement in library stacks, the advertisements located in the beginning portions of the Reports are deleted. However, if one did not believe that such a fatuous advertisement ever existed, one could check with the original materials, possessed by the Law Society of Upper Canada.
6. This transcript was widely circulated among lawyers. I recently spoke with the prosecutor on the case, Mr. Stilwell, and he confirmed that the transcript was merely a fictionalized creation produced by the defence lawyer on the case.
7. *R.* v. *Emery*, [1992] O.J. No. 1371 (Ont. Gen. Div.).
8. *R.* v. *Andriopoulos*, [1993] O.J. No. 3427 (Ont. Gen. Div).
9. *R.* v. *Andriopoulos*, [1994] O.J. No. 3630 (Ont. C.A.).
10. *R.* v. *Burns* (1994), 89 C.C.C. (3d) 193 (S.C.C.). In 2002, the Supreme Court of Canada ruled that the failure to give reasons will constitute an error of law in some circumstances. See *R.* v. *Sheppard* (2002), 162 C.C.C. (3d) 298.
11. *R.* v. *Head* (1986), 55 C.R. (3d) 1 (S.C.C.).
12. *R.* v. *Brown*, [1967] 3 C.C.C. 21 (Que. C.A.).
13. *R.* v. *Pallett*, [1970] 2 O.R. 222 (Ont. C.A.).
14. *R.* v. *Laws*, unreported decision of the Ontario Court of Justice (Gen. Div.), Whealy J., November 22, 1993.

15. *Ibid.* at 3–4. It should be noted that the Ontario Court of Appeal found the trial judge to be in error in excluding the public for wearing headgear, see *R. v. Laws* (1998), 128 C.C.C. (3d) 516 (Ont. C.A.).

Chapter 18
Let's Make a Deal

1. The Canadian Sentencing Commission, *Sentencing Reform: A Canadian Approach* (Ottawa: 1996) at 406; "Closed Doors: Justice by Plea Bargain," *Toronto Star* (10 March 2001) A1, A26.
2. "A Close Look at Courts," *Toronto Star* (10 March 2001) B5.
3. S. Cohen and A. Doob, "Public Attitudes to Plea Bargaining" (1989) 32 Can. L.Q. 85.
4. J. Langbein, "Understanding the Short History of Plea Bargaining" (1979) 13 L. & Soc. Rev. 261.
5. M.M. Feeley, *The Process Is the Punishment: Handling Cases in a Lower Criminal Court* (New York: Russell Sage Foundation, 1979); M. Heumann, "A Note on Plea Bargaining and Case Pressure" (1975) 9 L. & Soc. Rev. 515; S. Schulhofer, "Is Plea Bargaining Inevitable?" (1984) 97 Harv. L. Rev. 1037; R. Weninger, "The Abolition of Plea Bargaining: A Case Study of El Paso" (1987) 35 U.C.L.A. L. Rev. 265.
6. J. Brown, "Politics and Plea Bargaining" (1994) 45 Hastings L.J. 697; C. McCoy, *Politics and Plea Bargaining: Victims' Rights in California* (Philadelphia: University of Pennsylvania Press, 1993); T. Cairns and J. Kruse, "Alaska's Ban on Plea Bargaining Reevaluated" (1992) 75 Judicature 310.
7. "Clayton Ruby Says Some Lawyers are Earning Big Bucks from Legal-Aid Guilty Pleas," *The Globe and Mail* (23 March 1999) A22.
8. See A. Young, "Not Waving but Drowning: A Look at Waiver and Collective Constitutional Rights in the Criminal Process" (1989) 53 Sask. L. Rev. 47.
9. G. Dix, "Waiver in Criminal Procedure: A Brief for a More Careful Analysis" (1977) 55 Texas L. Rev. 193 at 219.
10. *North Carolina v. Alford*, 400 U.S. 25 (1970).
11. *R. v. Rajaeefard* (1996), 104 C.C.C. (3d) 225 at 230.
12. *R. v. Rajaeefard* (1996), 46 C.R. (4th) 111 (Ont. C.A.).
13. *R. v. Stephen K.*, [1995] 24 O.R. (3d) 199 at 202.
14. R.V. Ericson, *The Ordering of Justice: A Study of Accused Persons as Dependants in the Criminal Process* (Toronto: University of Toronto Press, 1982).
15. *Ibid.* at 188.
16. *Ibid.* at 101.
17. *Ibid.* at 98.
18. *Ibid.* at 96.
19. *R. v. Martineau* (1991), 58 C.C.C. (3d) 353 (S.C.C.).

20. *R.* v. *Vaudreuil* (1995), 98 C.C.C. (3d) 316 (B.C.C.A.).
21. The Honourable Patrick T. Galligan, Q.C., *Report to the Attorney General of Ontario on Certain Matters Relating to Karla Homolka*, March 15, 1996, at 111.
22. *Ibid.* at 201.
23. *Ibid.* at 210–11.
24. *R.* v. *L.C.B.* (1996), 104 C.C.C. (3d) 353 at 370 (Ont. C.A.).
25. *Ibid.* at 374.

Afterword
1. William Ian Miller, *The Anatomy of Disgust.* (Cambridge, MA: Harvard University Press, 1997) at 184.
2. *R.* v. *Bergamin* (1996), 111 C.C.C. (3d) 550 (Alta. C.A.).

Index

Copyright Acknowledgements